The Three Levels of Sustainability

THE
THREE LEVELS OF
SUSTAINABILITY

Elena Cavagnaro and George Curiel

Greenleaf
PUBLISHING

Published by Greenleaf Publishing Limited
Aizlewood's Mill
Nursery Street
Sheffield S3 8GG
UK
www.greenleaf-publishing.com

Cover by LaliAbril.com
Photo of Dr Cavagnaro by Foto Dikken & Hulsinga, Leeuwarden (NL)

British Library Cataloguing in Publication Data:
  A catalogue record for this book is available from the British Library.

  ISBN-13: 978-1-906093-68-6 [hardback]

This book is dedicated to:
Laetitia, Matteo, Mick, Paul, Pietro, Reinier, Sander, Tommaso in Europe
and
Alec, Jayden, Collin, Chloe in the Caribbean.
May they all live their lives with compassion for all living creatures.

Contents

Figures, boxes, and tables

Figures

Boxes

Tables

Foreword

Robbin Derry

Associate Professor of Strategy, University of Lethbridge, Edmonton, Alberta, Canada

So often, when I am talking with students about environmental concerns and the impact of their choices, I realize that the answer to one question only succeeds in raising other questions. As we struggle with the dilemmas of sustainable development and sustainable living, we find we are retracing a long thread of questions and attempted answers that go back decades, even centuries. In the first chapter of this book, the authors unravel the knot of why, in today's market systems, short-term economic growth drives long-term planning, by returning to the meeting of the Allied leaders at Bretton Woods, New Hampshire, prior to the end of World War II. The question the leaders of the free world confronted at that moment in history was how to foster widespread economic well-being and stability, so as to avoid falling back into the social unrest that could lead to yet another world war. Their solution of free trade, currency stability, increasing growth in consumer markets did indeed lead to peace, prosperity, and increased consumption in the Western world. It also led to the economic dominance of multinational corporations, with assets greater than many sovereign countries; corporations that continue to grow and promote increased consumption (and disposal) of their products. As Elena Cavagnaro and George Curiel make so clear, we cannot successfully strive toward maximum sustainability of our communities and our planet without a holistic understanding of historic decisions and the deep roots of recent trends of social responsibility and caring leadership.

The beauty of this book is found in its comprehensive scope. The authors have boldly addressed themselves to the daunting task of explaining how we, as a global collective, arrived at this point, asking and answering the hard questions about sustaining life on Earth as we know it. We are faced with the urgent challenge of altering what we demand from our society, how we envision our organizations, and how we relate to each other, in order to save the life of our planet and to vouchsafe the lives of our children. It is an ambitious project and the authors do not shy away. An enormous range of research is presented with explanations and discussions that will be readily grasped by students as well as knowledgeable scholars, but there is no dumbing down here. Cavagnaro and Curiel are meticulous in their critical assessment of highly respected scholarship as well as less familiar theories. They are fearless in building bridges across disciplines to identify useful concepts.

As you read, take careful note that the ideas woven into the Three Levels of Sustainability framework come from practice as well as from academic research. This is not a book that should live only on library shelves. It is a volume to be carried around and applied to daily life. It is written to reach out to individuals at different levels of organizations, in different roles in the private and public institutions of our communities. The triangle of sustainability provides guidance for developing practical strategies.

I am eager to share this book with my graduate students, helping them to recognize the key roles played by researchers they may have already encountered in scattered articles and texts. The authors have created a remarkable map locating the contributions of such thinkers as: Donella and Dennis Meadows, Ernst Schumacher, Amartya Sen, Herman Daly, Sara Parkin, Robert Doppelt, Petra Kuenkel, Prakash Sethi, Archie Carroll, Carol Gilligan, Danah Zohar, and Ed Freeman, to name just a handful of the characters in this grand story. Most amazingly, they all fit onto Cavagnaro and Curiel's map. Few scholars would have the courage to map this broad collection of ideas onto one framework for sustainability. That these authors have dared to do so is to their credit and our benefit. Each of these researchers is acknowledged as offering key insights into the dynamic balance of people and organizations in society.

One further feature of the book that is worth mentioning and celebrating, is its not-restricted-to-North-American viewpoint. While there are vibrant American contributors, theirs are not the only, nor the loudest voices to be heard. Cavagnaro and Curiel bring the clear strengths of European and Caribbean education and work experience to their analysis of history and contemporary issues. Their understanding of the change processes in social institutions is informed by teaching, consulting, and working intimately with those affected by such change in many countries.

For those of us who have lived through a few decades cognizant of the emergence of sustainability thinking, this book is a deeply satisfying gift, as it makes meaningful connections between seemingly disparate and independent theories. For those just entering the field of organizational sustainability or perhaps looking at questions of social responsibility for new answers, this book offers reliable footholds on what can be a slippery slope of skepticism about positive social change. I remain awed and grateful that Elena Cavagnaro and George Curiel took on the challenge of explaining to the rest of us the vital tasks for each level of sustainability. With great patience and care, they have provided us with roles to play in the many aspects of our lives. Following their guidance we can actively contribute to the ongoing efforts to create sustainable communities and organizations, and to live in ways that protect vital natural systems.

Acknowledgments

The journey that finds its conclusion with this book started a decade ago. A simple thought, born in times of considerably less awareness about the meaning and relevance of sustainability in our scholarly and organizational environment, grew to become an ambitious endeavor. Finding our way through sometimes less traveled territory and some very bumpy roads, we managed to reach our destination. This effort would not have been possible without the continuous support, advice, and encouragement of many colleagues, students, friends, and relatives who were genuinely attached to our writing project. Many people have been our companions along the route, some for a shorter some for a longer period. While we are thankful to them all, we would like to specifically recognize some people without whom our efforts would have never produced the same fruits.

First of all we would like to thank Klaas Wybo van der Hoek, Vice President of the Executive Board of Stenden University of Applied Sciences. Klaas Wybo has believed in our project from its start, and has been supportive in assuring Stenden's commitment.

It is often said that if you cannot explain something to others, it is because you have not understood it yourself. We had the proof of the truth of this saying during the discussions with master's students enrolled in the Sustainable Value Creation classes at Stenden. Their questions and critical comments have been essential in helping us clarify our thoughts and choose our words. Among them we would like to thank in particular Xiaomin Wen, who proofread the first version of Part I.

We are also thankful to all colleagues who provided feedback on specific chapters of the book and in particular to the members of Stenden University's Research Group in Service Studies. We are grateful to Sarah Seidel for her careful reading of Part II and III and to Sonja Schuil for her support that has stretched far beyond her administrative role. We owe a special thanks to Mario Cavagnaro who, in proofreading Part I and II, was able to find inaccuracies that had escaped others' keen eyes.

A project of this span could not have been accomplished successfully without the constant support and encouragement of the people nearest to us. We hereby express our gratitude to our partners Mark Stuijt and Marnid Curiel-Jacobs.

The authors and publisher gratefully acknowledge the permission granted to reproduce the copyright material in this book.

Every effort has been made to trace copyright holders and to obtain their permission for the use of copyright material. The publisher apologizes for any omissions in this regard and would be grateful if notified of any corrections that should be incorporated in future reprints or editions of this book.

Abbreviations

3Ps	people, planet, profit
4C	Common Code for the Coffee Community
BoP	Base of the Pyramid
BSC	Balanced Scorecard
CBS	Dutch Central Bureau of Statistics
CEO	chief executive officer
Ceres	Coalition for Environmentally Responsible Economies
CFC	chlorofluorocarbon, a class of chemical compounds
CO_2	carbon dioxide
CSP	corporate social performance
CSR	corporate social responsibility
DDT	dichlorodiphenyltrichloroethane, a synthetic pesticide
ECMT	European Conference of Ministers of Transport
EEC	European Economic Community
EFQM	European Foundation for Quality Management
EPA	Environmental Protection Agency
EU	European Union
FAO	Food and Agriculture Organization
GDP	gross domestic product
GRI	Global Reporting Initiative
HDI	Human Development Index
HRM	human resource management
ICC	International Chamber of Commerce
ICIDI	Independent Commission on International Development Issues
ICT	information and communication technology
IETA	International Emissions Trading Association
ILO	International Labour Organization
IMF	International Monetary Fund
IPCC	Intergovernmental Panel on Climate Change
ISEW	Index of Social Economic Welfare
ISO	International Organization for Standardization
IUCN	International Union for Conservation of Nature and Natural Resources

LCA	life cycle assessment
MDG	UN Millennium Development Goal
MEA	multilateral environmental agreement
MIF	Measuring Impact Framework
MIT	Massachusetts Institute of Technology
MNC	multinational corporation
MNE	multinational enterprise
MSC	Marine Stewardship Council
NCDO	National Committee for International Cooperation and Sustainable Development
NGO	nongovernmental organization
OEC	Organization Effectiveness Cycle
OECD	Organization for Economic Co-operation and Development
SAM	Sustainable Asset Management
SDS	sustainable development strategy
SME	small and medium-sized enterprises
TBL	triple bottom line
TEEB	The Economics of Ecosystems and Biodiversity
Tk	taka (currency of Bangladesh)
TLS	three levels of sustainability
UNCTAD	United Nations Conference on Trade and Development
UNDP	United Nations Development Programme
UNEP	United Nations Environment Programme
UNFCCC	United Nations Framework Convention on Climate Change
UNFPA	United Nations Population Fund
UNGC	United Nations Global Compact
UNUDHR	United Nations Universal Declaration of Human Rights
UV	ultraviolet
VOC	Vereenigde Oost-Indische Compagnie (Dutch East India Company)
WBCSD	World Business Council for Sustainable Development
WCED	World Commission on Environment and Development
WWF	World Wildlife Fund/World Wide Fund for Nature
WWII	World War II

Introduction

The ultimate goal of sustainable development is securing a better quality of life for all, both now and for future generations, by pursuing responsible economic growth, equitable social progress, and effective environmental protection. These three dimensions refer to a sustainable society. Sustainable societies, however, cannot be achieved without organizations and individuals who are convinced of the need to be part of the sustainability project. National governments and multilateral institutions have started to include sustainable development as a fundamental principle in their constitutions and treaties. Nongovernmental organizations and business organizations are also more and more considering sustainable development as an important element of their vision, and as a strategic objective. To achieve this higher level of conscientiousness, governments, institutions, and organizations need individuals who can steer the process toward this superordinate goal: a higher quality of life for all. This process of change toward sustainability depends on the choices made by people. It is therefore essential that not only societies and organizations choose sustainability, but also individuals.

This book departs from the premise that the journey toward sustainability is by its very nature a process that has to involve all three levels mentioned above and each one with their respective dimensions. The process ends and starts with the human being.

By introducing the **three levels of sustainability** (TLS) framework (Fig. 1) the authors hope to address at least some of the weaknesses inherent in a fragmented approach in the debate on sustainability. To arrive at this multilevel and multidimensional framework, concepts were borrowed from the field of sustainable development, corporate social responsibility, and personal leadership. In the framework the interrelated nature of these concepts is visualized.

Figure 1 **Three levels of sustainability (TLS) framework**

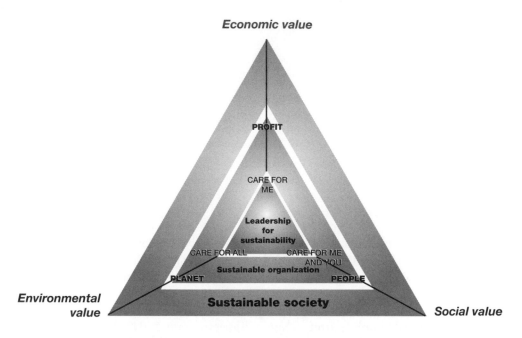

The outer triangle of the TLS framework illustrates the three dimensions of sustainable development on the societal level: responsible economic growth, equitable social progress, and effective environmental protection. These three dimensions refer to a sustainable society. As mentioned above, sustainable societies cannot be achieved without sustainable organizations and individuals. This insight is borrowed from the field of social sciences and is represented in the TLS framework by two other triangles drawn inside the triangle representing a sustainable society. The middle triangle corresponds to the organizational level of sustainability and the inner one to the individual level. Sustainable organizations are described by borrowing the concept of a triple bottom line from John Elkington's landmark book, *Cannibals with Forks* (1997). A sustainable organization strives to create value on three dimensions: profit, people, and planet. These three dimensions are in line with the three dimensions of sustainable development at the level of society: economic, social, and environmental value creation.

While the societal and the organizational levels are well-known concepts in the discourse on sustainability, the individual level is very seldom touched on in the debate and, as far as the authors know, its three dimensions were never described nor directly associated with the dimensions on the two other levels.

In the authors' view, the basic qualities of each individual on the personal level are considered to be the core of the matter. The cultivation of specific qualities forms the basis for the individual to be a leader of Self, a prerequisite for leadership for sustainability. Theories on human development reveal that individuals have the capability to accept values that go beyond the material values related to "me." It is a complex process where decreasing egocentrism is accompanied by increasing compassion, i.e. the ability to open up for values related to "others" and to the "universe." The three dimensions of the inner level of the TLS mirror this insight. "Care for me" relates to the value of the individual human life. "Care for me and you" relates to the value of relationships. "Care for all" relates to the value of all living creatures and the universe. Creating value on the three dimensions of care characterizes leadership for sustainability on the individual level. This makes each person a potential leader with a unique way to participate in the transition toward sustainability.

The three care dimensions correspond to the dimensions at the level of organization and society. The message is that individuals who are able to develop the three care dimensions will be in a better position to lead organizations with clear principles and values. These organizations will strive for values that are aligned with the principles of the leader and of a sustainable society.

For the last two centuries Western society promoted economic growth as the predominant way to achieve a better quality of life. This path was undoubtedly successful and there is no precedent in human history for the abundance of goods and services experienced by those who live in the so-called North, in regions such as North America and Western Europe and countries such as Japan, Australia, and New Zealand. Upcoming economies, such as Brazil, Russia, India, and China, have from the 1990s on embraced the Western model of economic growth. Their success is illustrated not only by the double digit figures of GDP growth in China, but also by offers such as the one made by Dilma Rousseff, President of Brazil, during her visit to Portugal in March 2011. An ex-colony (Brazil) offers to help its colonizer badly hit by the worst economic crisis since the 1930s.[1]

Notwithstanding the apparent success of economic growth as a path toward development, in the last five decades more and more people have become aware of the limitations of an approach that equates well-being with material prosperity. In the last two decennia the discourse on sustainability has come a long way and has seen a dramatic move forward. More people have started to realize not only that there are limits to growth, but also (and more importantly) that the promise of a better quality of life for all cannot possibly be met by a focus on economic growth alone. Meanwhile more and more people are starting to comprehend a reality that Albert Einstein eloquently described in 1950:

> A human being is a part of a whole, called by us "universe," a part limited in time and space. He experiences himself, his thoughts and feelings as something separated from the rest . . . a kind of optical delusion of his consciousness. This delusion is a kind of prison for us, restricting us to our personal desires and to affection for a few persons nearest to us. *Our task must be to free ourselves from this prison by widening our circle of*

---

1 From the Dutch newspaper *NRC Handelsblad*, "Ex-kolonie Brazilië wil Portugal wel wat helpen," March 30, 2011: 12.

> *compassion to embrace all living creatures and the whole of nature in its beauty.* Nobody is able to achieve this completely but the striving for such achievement is in itself a part of the liberation and a foundation for inner security [emphasis added].[2]

During the journey to develop the TLS framework it became clear that a wide range of concepts and interpretations had to be clarified. In search of these clarifications and interpretations we did not find the systemic and holistic approach to sustainability we were looking for. This book attempts to fill this gap by elaborating on the basic concepts and their relation to each other.

The book starts with the assumption that the reader is interested in the sustainability discussion and wants to familiarize him or herself with the basics of the discussion in a logical and integrated way. It aims to serve those who are already in management and leadership positions or aspire to be in such a position, either in the private sector, the public sector, or the nonprofit (voluntary) sector. The book will also be of assistance to students of management and leadership in colleges and universities.

The three levels of the TLS framework and its dimensions constitute the backbone for the layout of the book. The first part is dedicated to the level of society; the second to the level of organizations; the third to the individual level.

The first part, dedicated to the level of society, explores in four chapters how the concern for economic growth, environmental protection, and equitable social progress emerged over time. Thus Chapter 1 is dedicated to economic growth while Chapters 2 and 3 focus, respectively, on the concern for the natural environment and social development. Chapter 4 shows how these three concerns come together in the concept of sustainable development proposed by the World Commission on Environment and Development in 1987. It also reviews the steps set since 1987 at international, regional, and national level toward a more sustainable world.

Part II, dedicated to the level of organizations, is also composed of four chapters. On a similar line to Part I, it reconstructs first how the concern for the three specific dimensions of sustainable organizations developed over time. Chapter 5 discusses the concern for profit while Chapter 6 covers the concern for both planet and people. Finally, Chapters 7 and 8 highlight the most important instruments and tools at the disposal of organizations that wish to set sustainability principles at the core of their vision, mission, and strategy.

Part III is dedicated to the inner level of the TLS, the leadership level. It follows a different structure. Chapter 9 starts with a brief introduction on the leadership discussion and recognizes that many great books have dealt with leadership in the past decades and that the debate is still ongoing. The variability in definitions and terms used will be touched on to indicate the fluidity of the leadership discussion. Chapter 10 uses the TLS framework to introduce the three distinct dimensions of

---

2 Quote from a letter of condolence Einstein sent to Norman Salit on March 4, 1950 (AEA 61-226). Kind courtesy of Mrs Barbara Wolff, Einstein Information Officer, Albert Einstein Archives Hebrew University of Jerusalem, Jerusalem 91904 Israel.

the individual level, analogous with the three dimensions of the organizational and the societal level. Finally, Chapter 11 will zoom in on the importance of the leadership of self and the critical role of the third dimension ("Care for all"). This most critical dimension has the essential qualities to support the path toward leadership for sustainability.

A last note. A holistic approach to sustainability presents several challenges. One of the most daunting is the diversity of the disciplines involved. In preparing for this book the authors have studied or consulted works on economics, environmental studies, human ecology, chemistry, biology, sociology, psychology, philosophy, corporate social responsibility, stakeholder analysis, leadership, management, human development, ethics, and so on. It may indeed be said that the sustainability debate relates to many fields of study. There is, moreover, a growing number of publications from governments (supranational, national, and local), UN agencies, nongovernmental organizations, and practitioners.

It has been exciting for the authors to keep stretching the boundaries of their knowledge. Yet they will never pretend to have become experts in some let alone all of the fields of research involved in the sustainability debate. On a similar line they are familiar only with a fraction of the existing literature. In the end it will take a real interdisciplinary effort to move the sustainability project forward.

The authors' philosophy has been to enter territories that were unknown to them cautiously, and to take a respectful stance to other people's opinions and more so when these were different from their own. The reader may judge if they were successful in their attempt.

Part I
Sustainable society

Introduction to Part I

For generations human beings have searched for pathways to achieve better living conditions for themselves, their children, and their communities. For the last two centuries Western civilization promoted economic growth as the pre-eminent way to reach a better quality of life. This path undoubtedly brought positive results and there is no precedent in human history for the abundance of goods and services experienced by those who live in the so-called North, in regions such as North America and Western Europe and countries such as Japan, Australia, and New Zealand.

In the last five decennia, however, more and more people have become aware of the limitations of an approach whereby well-being is equated with material wealth. This awareness started to evolve in the early 1960s thanks to the discovery of the gravity of global pollution and gained strengths in the following decades. The first oil crisis at the beginning of the 1970s made the Western world suddenly realize that some of the natural resources needed to fuel their economy might not be available forever. On the basis of these new insights, many scholars, environmentalists, and even industrialists expressed the concern that the actual path of economic development could not be maintained indefinitely. In their opinion, limits in the Earth's capacity to absorb pollution or in the availability of natural resources will be met in the foreseeable future and halt economic expansion. This alarming conclusion was reinforced by data showing that, despite all efforts directed to the economic development of the so-called South, poverty was still growing and the gap between rich and poor countries (and between rich and poor in the same country) was still widening. The images of dying children during the Biafran famine in 1968 made this abstract concern very concrete and touched the hearts of millions of people.

Thus, more and more people started to realize not only that there are limits to growth, but also (and more importantly) that the promise of a better quality of life for all could not possibly be met by a focus on economic growth alone. Both these concerns became the driving force behind different global conferences and scientific studies leading to a new understanding of quality of life and the type of development needed to achieve it. In this new interpretation, quality of life is no longer equated with material wealth, but is acknowledged as the outcome of the interaction among the environmental, the social, and the economic dimensions of society. This outcome cannot be reached if the focus lies primarily on economic growth. This means that the concept of development has to be redefined to include along with the economic also the environmental and social dimensions. This redefinition was the main achievement of a study published in 1987 by the World Commission on Environment and Development (WCED). The WCED was not only successful in bringing together the three vital dimensions mentioned above in their concept of sustainable development, but also in pointing to the necessity of simultaneously considering the needs of both this and future generations in an equitable way when implementing development policies. This new development path will lead to sustainable societies. More precisely stated, sustainable societies create value on three distinct dimensions—the economic, the social, and the environmental—to achieve a better quality of life without jeopardizing the possibilities of other societies (now and in the future) to achieve the same. This new concept of development has meanwhile been adopted by multilateral organizations, nations, and by partnerships among countries, such as the European Union (EU). Two examples are presented in Box I.1.

Box I.1 The EU and Canada on sustainable development

The European Union (EU) is an economic and political partnership between 27 countries in Europe. The general political direction and priorities of the EU are defined by the European Council. In June 2006 the European Council adopted an ambitious and comprehensive renewed Sustainable Development Strategy (SDS) for the EU. It builds on the Gothenburg Strategy of 2001 and is the result of an extensive review process that started in 2004. The renewed EU SDS sets out a single, coherent strategy on how the EU will more effectively live up to its long-standing commitment to meet the challenges of sustainable development.

Sustainable Development stands for meeting the needs of present generations without jeopardizing the ability of future generations to meet their own needs—in other words, a better quality of life for everyone, now and for generations to come. It offers a vision of progress that integrates immediate and longer-term objectives, local and global action, and regards social, economic and environmental issues as inseparable and interdependent components of human progress.

Sustainable development will not be brought about by policies only: it must be taken up by society at large as a principle guiding the many choices each citizen makes every day, as well as the big political and economic decisions that have [ramifications for many]. This requires profound changes in thinking, in economic and social structures and in consumption and production patterns.

Source: ec.europa.eu/environment/eussd (accessed 12 July 2011)

In 1997 the Ministry of Environment expressed Canada's vision on sustainable development with these words:

> The economy, the environment, and society affect each other in profound ways. Sustainable development means taking all of these areas into account when decisions are being made. When sustainable development becomes a part of government planning, it affects planning at all levels of society. This eventually makes sustainable development part of the very fabric of our lives.
>
> *Source*: Canada Ministry of Environment 1997

The way the concept of sustainable development is translated by the countries quoted in Box I.1 confirms that the ultimate goal is to achieve a better quality of life now and in the future by creating value on all three dimensions. To achieve this ultimate goal, however, input is needed from all parts forming a society, based on choices to be made by organizations and citizens. This indicates that the role of both organizations and individuals should be taken into account when defining the path toward sustainable societies. Their role will be discussed in Parts II and III, respectively. This first part starts with sustainability at the societal level as the main objective of the process of sustainable development. To visualize the societal level the economic, social, and environmental dimensions are plotted in a triangle (Fig. I.1). The form of an equilateral triangle is used to indicate that the three dimensions are interrelated and that value has to be created on all three simultaneously.

Figure I.1 **Sustainable society**

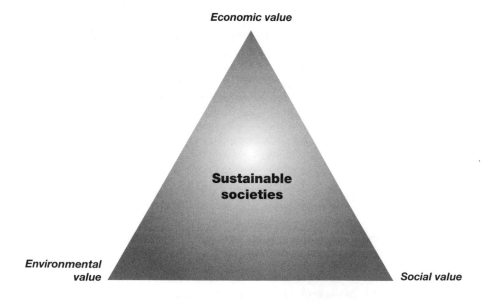

Part I will elaborate on how these three dimensions evolved separately as important spheres of concern for different groups at different times (Chapters 1 to 3). In Chapter 4 we will see how these three concerns came together in the concept of sustainable development proposed by the World Commission on Environment and Development in 1987. The same chapter will review the progress made since 1987 toward a more sustainable world.

1

The concern for economic growth

> The economic health of every country is a proper matter of concern to all its neighbors, near and far (Franklin D. Roosevelt at the opening of Bretton Woods 1944).

Addressing Congress on February 12, 1945, the U.S. President Franklin D. Roosevelt said that to achieve a lasting peace after the war the world needed "more goods produced, more jobs, more trade, and a higher standard of living for us all" (Roosevelt 1945). The hope of a world united in prosperity was not cherished by the U.S. president alone. Already in July 1944 representatives of all 44 allied nations met at Bretton Woods (New Hampshire) to envision the monetary and financial institutions that could help economies to regain momentum after the war (see Box 1.1). To appreciate the work of these visionary men it should be remembered that, when they met, the end of World War II was not yet in sight. Even though Mussolini had already been overthrown, it would take another ten months before Nazi Germany capitulated and thirteen before Japan surrendered. The threat that after the war economic life would come to a halt was severe. Politicians and economists knew all too well that economic and monetary instability can feed dictatorship and in the end cause war. That was exactly what happened after World War I. So the challenge at Bretton Woods was to avoid a recurrence of that scenario.

Avoiding instability, social unrest, and a new war constitute the most powerful reasons why growth in produced goods, jobs, and trade (i.e., economic growth) became the major concern of national governments and international institutions after World War II. In the words of Ernst von Weizsäcker (1994: 7), "Economic thinking, so gloriously represented by the U.S.A., the liberator of the devastated Old Continent, meant peace, freedom and the prospect of material welfare."

This chapter explores in four sections different themes connected with our concern for economic growth. The aim of the first two sections is to do justice to our fascination with economic growth and concentrate, therefore, on its merits and worth. The third explores different answers to the question of how economic growth begins and can be maintained. The fourth focuses on what exactly is supposed to grow when economic expansion takes place and paves the way for the last section. Here a more critical approach to the idea of never-ending growth is introduced. The last section forms, thus, a bridge to the next two chapters, on the concerns for social development and environmental protection.

Box 1.1 **The centrality of economic growth in post-WWII policy:**
         Bretton Woods and the Treaty of Rome

The main concern for the delegates at Bretton Woods was to design a new monetary system that could support and regulate free trade among nations. Free trade was considered to be the best vehicle to achieve long-run economic growth and a better standard of living for all people all over the world. A key feature of the system was free convertibility of currencies. To make this possible, currencies were allowed to fluctuate only marginally in respect to the "reserve currency," the U.S. dollar. The International Monetary Fund (IMF) was created to be the rule keeper and the supervisor of global financial issues. A second institution (the International Bank for Reconstruction and Development, now the World Bank) was charged with the task of financially feeding recovering economies and stimulate growth. The key role that the U.S. dollar got in the system mirrored and at the same time consolidated the economic and political power of the U.S.A.

The centrality of economic growth in post-WWII policy is also evident in the Treaty of Rome, the document signed in 1957 that marked the birth of the European Economic Community (the nucleus of what will become the European Union). Article 2 of the treaty states:

> The Community shall have as its task, by establishing a common market and progressively approximating the economic policies of Member States, to promote throughout the Community a harmonious development of economic activities, a continuous and balanced expansion, an increase in stability, an accelerated raising of the standard of living and closer relations between the States belonging to it (EEC 1957).

1.1 **No growth: a Malthusian society**

In human history economic growth is the exception rather than the rule. This may sound incredible to us, used as we are to the idea that an economy should grow. For as long as two thousand years our ancestors lived in societies where the quantity of goods and services produced hardly grew at all. Italy was the first country to experience a sensible increase in the size of its economy in the period known as the Renaissance (literally, rebirth) in the fourteenth and fifteenth centuries. The raw materials flowing to Europe from the colonies in the sixteenth and seventeenth centuries helped sustain the growth in Europe while Asian and African countries experienced a weakening of their economic activities. In the late eighteenth and early nineteenth centuries the application of non-animal power to drive machines fueled the industrial revolution and caused a third growth spurt. And even then the growth realized was rather insignificant from a modern point of view. The leading nation in the years 1580–1820, The Netherlands, experienced an average annual growth of 0.2% of gross domestic product (GDP; see Fig. 1.1).[1] The United Kingdom, where the industrial revolution first took off, took the lead in the period 1820–1890 with a mere 1.2% (Ray 1998: 48).

Figure 1.1 **Growth in GDP**

Source: drawn by the authors on the basis of Ray 1998; Maddison 2001; and Ventura 2005

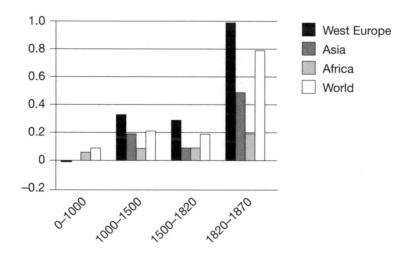

Throughout most of human history, thus, GDP grew very little. This means that the quantity of goods and services at the disposal of a certain country stayed almost the same and could be considered as fixed. The challenges inherent in this situation are skillfully depicted by the Anglican clergyman Thomas Robert Malthus. In

---

1   The GDP is the total market value of the final goods and services produced by a country in a certain period, usually one year.

his *Essay on the Principle of Population* (1798) Malthus observes that man's ability to increase the supply of food, our most important resource, is constrained in three particular ways: through land scarcity, the limited production capacity of cultivated land, and the law of diminishing returns (see Box 1.2). He also argued that in a given period population doubles (or in other words expands exponentially), while (owing to the above-mentioned constraints) food production only increases at an arithmetic (or linear) rate. As a consequence, population growth will exceed the growth in the means needed to support human life (what Malthus calls "subsistence"), causing widespread poverty and famine. Many will die and the survivors will have enough subsistence means at their disposal to start reproducing again, causing a new cycle to occur. A Malthusian society is trapped in a never-ending contest between a growing population and the limited resources at its disposal.

Box 1.2 **Diminishing returns**

The economic law of diminishing returns states that in a production system with fixed and variable inputs, beyond some point, each additional unit of variable input yields less and less additional output.

Let us take chocolate, a sweet most people like, as an example. Eating the first Belgian bon-bon is a delicious experience. Eating a second bon-bon, maybe with a different flavor, is also nice. We could enjoy a third one; a fourth one maybe, but for sure with less enthusiasm than the first bon-bon as our stomach (that happens to have a fixed capacity) starts to complain.

Let us consider now someone who has to cover by car a distance of, say, 30 kilometers from work to home. If he drives at a speed of 30 kilometers per hour it will take him a whole hour to reach home; doubling the speed to 60 will take the driver home in half of the time. The gain is thus 30 minutes. Doubling the speed again, to 120, will signify a gain of only 15 minutes, and so on.

The same applies to land. A farm usually has a fixed size. Suppose also that all other factors needed to produce crops (such as seeds and rain and manure) are fixed and that one farmer obtains one ton of crop from the farm. The law of diminishing returns tells us that a second farmer on the same land (doubling labor) will not push the growth up to two tons, doubling the output, but rather to less than that. The return of adding a third farmer will be even less, and at the end the costs involved with adding a new farmer will outstrip the gain in crop yield.

A society where the GDP does not grow lives under the threat individuated by Malthus unless it is able to gain access to more means of subsistence, in Malthus' days mostly land, not (yet) owned by others. The European urge to explore and colonize new continents from the sixteenth century onwards can be thus explained as an effort to escape the Malthusian trap and find new resources to support a growing population (Goldsmith 2001: 19-22; see also Chapter 3 Section 1 on the historic context).

A second possibility to sidestep the Malthusian trap is to reduce population growth. Already in Malthus's time, William Godwin (1756–1836) pointed to education as a mean to teach to the masses the benefits of late marriages and of having to raise fewer children. Education would, in the view of other thinkers of that age, also provide means of enjoyment other than sexual pleasure, contributing in this way to lessen population growth (Dresner 2002: 11-13). In the Europe of the late Middle Age and early Modernity the idea of being able to escape the Malthusian trap some-day sounded quite unrealistic. The contemporaries of Malthus and Godwin could easily interpret their recent and less recent history as a never-ending chain of wars leading to famine and plagues, leading to new wars. They would have agreed with Roosevelt that only a growth in goods and services and a higher standard of living for all could guarantee stability and peace. Yet they would consider widespread prosperity impossible because their world was constrained by a limited and fixed amount of resources.

1.2 Escaping the Malthusian trap: economic growth

From 1820 on, various regions of the world departed from the Malthusian trap and experienced a considerable rise in the growth rates of their economies. A graph drawn by the economist Oded Galor (2011: 2) offers a striking illustration of this point. In Figure 1.2 he uses per capita income, the total gross domestic product (or GDP) divided by the number of inhabitants.

Galor's graph teaches us that from 1820 on in some countries economic growth outstripped population growth and led to the highest standard of living ever experienced in human history. This while world population continued to grow at a faster and faster pace (see Box 1.5). The same message can be conveyed in several other ways: by pointing to the skyrocketing expenditures on goods and services in these regions, as shown in Box 1.3, or by remembering that nowadays most people in the world can be cured of diseases that 150 years ago killed the wealthy and mighty. To quote only one, striking, example: in 1836 Baron Nathan Mayer Rothschild, at that time probably the richest man in the world, died of an infected abscess. Nowadays such an infection could be easily prevented and cured thanks to penicillin (Landes 1999: xvii).

Figure 1.2 **Evolution of regional income per capita over the years 1–2001**

Source: GALOR, ODED; *UNIFIED GROWTH THEORY*. Princeton University Press. Reprinted by permission of Princeton University Press.

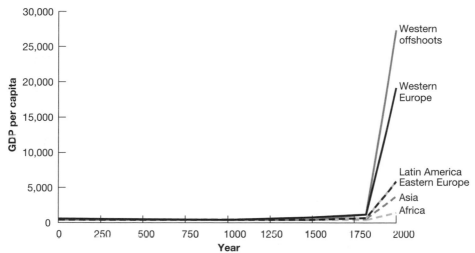

To compose the graph Galor used data from Angus Maddison (2001). According to Maddison's classification, "Western offshoots" consists of United States, Canada, Australia and New Zealand. See also Maddison 2003.

Box 1.3 **The rise and spread of the consumer class**

"By virtually any measure—household expenditures, number of consumers, extraction of raw materials—consumption of goods and services has risen steadily in industrial nations for decades, and it is growing rapidly in many developing countries.

By one calculation, there are now more than 1.7 billion members of 'the consumer class'—nearly half of them in the developing world.

A lifestyle and culture that became common in Europe, North America, Japan, and a few other pockets of the world in the twentieth century is going global in the twenty-first. Worldwide, private consumption expenditures—the amount spent on goods and services at the household level—topped $20 trillion in 2000, a four-fold increase over 1960 (in 1995 U.S. dollars).

As incomes rise, people are gaining access to a multitude of consumer items associated with greater prosperity:

- In 2002, 1.12 billion households—about three-quarters of humanity—owned at least one television set.
- There were 1.1 billion fixed phone lines in 2002, and another 1.1 billion mobile lines.
- The internet now connects about 600 million users" (World Watch Institute 2004).

How this could happen is a fascinating question that will be discussed briefly in the next section. For the moment it is important to notice one thing: as these examples above already show, GDP has a broader meaning than a mere measure of the economic activities in a country. Governments and the broad public see their own future reflected in the GDP. A growing GDP indicates a growth in employment opportunities and fiscal revenues; a drop in GDP, a decrease in both. To have a job means for the majority of people to be able to satisfy their needs and wants—in short, to be able to pay their bills. Fiscal revenues, in their turn, are needed by governments to support social legislation and healthcare schemes; to invest in education and research; to sustain the arts; to alleviate poverty and even to pursue an environmental friendly policy (as skillfully noted by von Weizsäcker *et al.* 1998: 273).

A quote by Jack McConnell, First Minister of Scotland (2001–2007), may illustrate that this is actually the way political leaders perceive economic growth:

> It is easier to close gaps in opportunity if we have a growing cake—rather than trying to do more and more with an existing set of resources. That is why creating growth in our country is so important for me . . . (McConnell 2002).

On the same line the economist William Easterly (2001: 4) states:

> We experts don't care about rising GDP for its own sake. We care because it betters the lot of the poor and reduces the proportion of people who are poor. We care because richer people can eat more and buy more medicines for their babies.

For Benjamin Friedman, professor of Political Economy and former Chairman of Economics at Harvard University, the blessings of economic growth go far beyond a higher material standard of living. In his opinion economic growth has a direct, positive influence on non-material values, such as "tolerance of diversity, social mobility, commitment to fairness, and dedication to democracy" (Friedman 2005: 4). By reviewing several examples from history, Friedman concludes that communities' values are strengthened by economic growth and weakened in periods of economic stagnation. In opposition to a long tradition in economic and moral thinking (see e.g. Keynes 1930; Daly and Cobb 1989: 49-51) Friedman then concludes that it is the economy that feeds communities' moral values and not the reverse.

Notwithstanding this last point, looking back to the past and to the challenges faced by a Malthusian society it is impossible not to recognize the worth of economic growth. Considering that economic growth means an increase in material opportunities (and maybe even moral values) and facing the fact that there are still millions of people living in poverty, it is then easy to understand why the question of how to achieve and maintain growth is considered vital by economists, politicians, and the public at large.

1.3 **Drivers of growth**

Economists have no clear-cut answer to the question: what is the source of economic growth and how can it be maintained? Here only the most frequently recurring answers are touched on: savings, cultural heritage, geographical and climatic conditions, and technology.

One widely accepted theory is that savings are the main driver of economic growth. Economic historians, for example, remind us that, during the reign of Queen Elizabeth I, England was able to accumulate the capital later needed to fuel the industrial revolution mostly thanks to the capture of Spanish ships loaded with silver and gold from the newly discovered world (Scott 1912: 81-82). Also in the post-WWII economic thinking, capital accumulation is considered key to growth. In its simplest terms, economic growth is seen as the result of abstention from current consumption. This generates savings that can be invested in capital goods. Economic growth is positive when investments exceed the amount necessary to replace depreciated capital, thereby allowing the following economic cycle to recur on a larger scale (Ray 1998: 54). The policy implication of this view on drivers of economic growth is that to stimulate growth in poor countries capital should be provided in the form of financial aid. And this is exactly what happened from the 1960s on: the rich countries (the so-called North) lend through the World Bank huge sums of money to countries in Latin America and Africa (the so-called South). Their expectation was that the money lent would be invested in productive activities thus helping these countries' economies to take off and lift them out of poverty. As is widely known, unfortunately, the result was quite different from that expected (see also Chapter 3 Section 1 on this point).

A second set of explanations refer to particular cultural characteristics of one region above others. A widely quoted exponent of this view is the German political economist and sociologist Max Weber (1864–1920). In his essay *The Protestant Ethic and the Spirit of Capitalism*, Weber argued that the stress posed by some forms of Protestantism on thrift, self-denial, and work as a calling by God prepared the terrain for capitalism and the pursuit of economic gain. In Weber's view it is not the mere possession of capital that sustains economic growth and welfare, but the moral values leading to the preference for future consumption above present needs' satisfaction. Without this set of values, for example, if people happen to get some extra money they will immediately spend it for their own or their friends' enjoyment and not invest it in the hope of future returns.

On a similar but distinct line, some scholars argued that modern, sustained economic expansion is the result of a process guided by natural selection that began centuries ago, even since the emergence of the human species. In an article published in 2002 entitled *Natural Selection and the Origin of Economic Growth*, Oded Galor and Omer Moav argue that all along history hereditary human traits that raised earning capacity, generated an evolutionary advantage. These traits could be physical characteristics (e.g. immunity and resistance to diseases; longevity), but also mental ones (e.g. ability and preference for quality). This selection process ultimately triggered a reinforcing interaction between investments in human capital and technological progress that brought about the take-off from stagnation to growth.[2]

Evolutionary explanations of growth are captivating, also because of the continuity that they postulate between the different ages in human history. On the other hand, evolution alone does not explain why economic growth was triggered in one country and not in another. Theories that point to cultural differences (as Max Weber did) offer this explanation but are unable to account for the presence of economic growth also in societies with different cultural and religious backgrounds, for example, Renaissance Italy and contemporary China. Moreover, they do not seem to offer any recipe to stimulate growth in countries with a different cultural heritage than Protestantism.

A recent view, proposed by Jared Diamond (1997, 2005), is that "societies developed differently on different continents because of differences in continental environments, not in human biology," nor in cultural and moral values (2005: 426). His major point is that only in some regions of the world can agriculture easily produce the surplus needed to sustain further economic development and that most valuable wild species that can be domesticated are concentrated in only nine small areas in the European and Asian region. This made it possible for the original inhabitants of these areas to gain a head start in developing complex societies, new technologies and even stronger resistance to diseases. In the end this led to the supremacy in modern times of Europe and its offspring, as well as North America (Diamond 2005). As fascinating as Diamond's account is, it offers only a limited number of keys to stimulate growth in communities that experience economic stagnation. One of his lessons, though, should be remembered: it is the basic role of agriculture for all societies. This sounds like a vindication of those who opposed the heavy investment in industry and infrastructure in the South supported by the IMF and the World Bank and insisted on self-reliance and the need to invest first in agriculture (see e.g. the Arusha Declaration by the Tanzanian President Julius Nyerere on February 5, 1967).

Most economic historians endorse the view that it is technology that pushed and still pushes economic growth beyond the limits experienced in history (for some examples see Box 1.4). A wide range of improvements are grouped under the label "technology," from the invention of the plug to the development of navigation; from bureaucracy, an essential tool for the administration of complex societies, to military technology; from improvements in the quality of intellectual life with the development and spread of universities to the introduction of the printing press; from banking to chemical fertilizer and pesticides. Common to all these

---

2 See also Galor 2011: Chapter 7. In this book Galor argues that "the transition from stagnation to growth has been an inevitable by-product of the process of development" (2011: 5). Development in its turn is driven by several forces, of which natural selection is only one.

improvements is that they resulted from new knowledge about how to do things, in particular how to produce valued goods and services for the satisfaction of human needs: put simply, they are the result of technology (Szirmai 2005: 117).

Box 1.4 **Technology and economic growth**

The renowned economist and Nobel Prize laureate Simon Kuznets (1962) identified the age of "modern economic growth" as one where growth came to be driven by scientific and technological advance. Angus Maddison, the economic historian quoted above, also explains Europe's long-run economic performance by its superior technological progress. And, indeed, the experience of the first industrial revolution itself has been viewed as the triumph of "ingenuity rather than abstention" (McCloskey 1981: 108).

Technology can be seen as the human capacity to generate new ideas. As Paul Romer of Stanford University states:

> Economic growth occurs whenever people take resources and rearrange them in ways that are more valuable. A useful metaphor for production in an economy comes from the kitchen. To create valuable final products, we mix inexpensive ingredients together according to a recipe. The cooking one can do is limited by the supply of ingredients, and most cooking in the economy produces undesirable side effects. If economic growth could be achieved only by doing more and more of the same kind of cooking, we would eventually run out of raw materials and suffer from unacceptable levels of pollution and nuisance. Human history teaches us, however, that economic growth springs from better recipes, not just from more cooking. New recipes generally produce fewer unpleasant side effects and generate more economic value per unit of raw material (Romer 2007: 2).

Technology, however, has its drawbacks or, as some scholars put it, the technology invented to solve a problem causes new problems that call for non-technological solutions (Meadows *et. al.* 1972: 119ff.; 1992: 161ff.). From the 1950s onwards, for example, the application of chemical fertilizer and pesticides to agriculture made possible an increase of yields per hectare of land that was previously inconceivable. The surplus in food obtained sustained the unprecedented population growth that the world experienced after WWII (see Box 1.5). Yet pesticides accumulate in the soil to levels that can threaten human and animal life, as Rachel Carson proved in her influential book *Silent Spring* published in 1962 (for more on Carson's work, see Chapter 2 Section 2).

Box 1.5 **Unprecedented population growth**

From the dawn of our species some 2 million years ago until roughly 12,000 years ago, there were never more than some tens of millions of our brethren walking the planet at any one time. With the advent of agri-culture and surplus food production, however, our species embarked on a path of population expansion that continues to this day. By the time of the American Revolution, the human family had grown to approximately one billion. Propelled further by the expansion to the New World and the industrial revolution, the population continued to grow so that by the close of World War II, there were two billion people on the planet.

As a baby boomer born in 1952, I entered the world of about two billion people. In less than half a century, that population ballooned to more than six billion. If I live to ripe old age, I could easily see eight billion or more people on the planet. Thus in *a single lifetime*, the human population will have grown from two billion to more than eight billion . . . It seems self-evident, therefore, that the policies we adopt, the decisions we make, and the strategies we pursue over the next decade or two will determine the future of our species and the trajectory of the planet for the foresee-able future (Hart 2007: xxxv-vi, italic in original).

Marten (2001: Chapter 3) gives a brief and clear overview of human pop-ulation history, the forces driving population growth and its consequence for the ecosystem.

Concluding, the quest for the origin of economic growth reflects the complexity of the world we live in and has not yet brought the discovery of one single source. All explanations are true to a certain extent: economic expansion is probably the result of different causes and, as Ricardo Hausmann (2006) proposes, can be best stimulated and maintained by removing the constraints that at a certain moment impede it, be these constraints of technological, financial, political, or cultural nature.

1.4 **Quantity and quality of growth**

Economic growth, as measured by GDP, is a measure of the quantity of goods and services sold and bought in one country over a certain period. In other words, eco-nomic growth is the expansion of a country's productive capacity which in its turn leads to an increase in total national output. The result is, on average, a greater material welfare and a rise in the standard of living. This is, as we have seen above, the reason why economic growth is considered vital to our society and forms the top priority on the agenda of governments worldwide. However, economic growth as measured by the GDP fails to account for different important social and economic factors such as the size of the black market, domestic or other unpaid work, and the distribution of income and thus the possible inequality between different groups in society. In their report to the French President Nicolas Sarkozy, economists Joseph E. Stiglitz, Amartya Sen, and Jean-Paul Fitoussi (2009: 8) refer to the last issue and write:

> When there are large changes in inequality (more generally a change in income distribution) gross domestic product (GDP) or any other aggregate computed *per capita* may not provide an accurate assessment of the situation in which most people find themselves. If inequality increases enough relative to the increase in average [per capita] GDP, most people can be worse off even though average income is increasing.

Moreover, even supposing that *all* individuals in a community enjoy a better standard of living, it might still be questionable whether an increase in the quantity of goods and services (welfare) equals an increase in the well-being of individuals or as some say their quality of life.[3]

Ernst von Weizsäcker (1994: 197) illustrates the difference between welfare and well-being in a disquieting way:

> Two cars pass each other quietly on a country lane. Nothing happens and they contribute little to GDP. But then one of the drivers, not paying attention, wanders over to the other side of the road and causes a serious accident involving a third approaching car. "Terrific" says the GDP: air ambulances, doctors, nurses, breakdown services, car repair or a new car, legal battles . . . all these are regarded as formal, professional activities which have to be paid for.

All the activities that have to take place because of the accident lead to expenditures that positively affect GDP, but it is questionable if they better the quality of life of individuals involved in the car accident. At best, all these activities do is to help recover the quality that was lost.[4] This can easily be seen if we ask ourselves if we will approve of a policy that enhances the probability of accidents to stimulate economic growth. It seems absurd; it is, however, what we do when we stimulate growth without considering if people's quality of life is increased by it. To the same effect, others ask for attention to the consequences of economic growth on the environment. Pollution, for example, could represent a cost for people's well-being that outstrips the gain in material welfare obtained through economic growth. Quality of life and well-being, though, are difficult to value in monetary terms and it is

---

3 For a critical reflection on the GDP as an indicator of the *economic* progress of a country see Morse 2004: 39ff. and Stiglitz *et al.* 2009. Stiglitz's conclusion is that "time has come to adapt our system of measurement of economic activity to better reflect the structural changes which have characterized the evolution of modern economies" (2009: 11). See also Cobb *et al.* 2005 for a brief history and critique of common measures of national income and prosperity, including GDP.

4 On these so-called "defensive expenditures" see Stiglitz *et al.* 2009: 28-29.

therefore difficult to weigh them against an index, such as the GDP, that is designed to take into account the *measurable* staple of goods and services produced.[5]

How the quality of growth became a more and more general concern is the theme of the next two chapters. Here, we will briefly focus on the debate on growth and its limits because the answer to this question has direct implications for the possibility to sidestep the Malthusian trap through economic growth (as discussed above, Sections 1.1 and 1.2). If the economy, our source of subsistence means, cannot grow forever and human population keeps increasing (Box 1.5), then Malthus is right: there will come a moment when population growth will outstrip subsistence means.

1.5 **Limits to growth**

On December 17, 2007 Jacques Diouf, Director-General of the Food and Agriculture Organization (FAO) delivered a press conference that was labeled by different commentators as alarming and even shocking. He warned of a possible global food shortage in the long term and the consequences that soaring food prices already have on poor countries. To quote his words:

> **The FAO food price index rose by nearly 40% over a one-year period in 2007**, while the increase in 2006 over the previous year was only 9% . . . High food prices are leading to social tensions in many parts of the world. Political unrest directly linked to food markets recently occurred in Morocco, Uzbekistan, Yemen, Guinea, Mauritania and Senegal (Diouf 2007: 1, 3; bold in original).

In his speech Jacques Diouf pointed to different causes of this sharp increase: historically low levels of global stocks; unusual weather conditions negatively affecting the harvest; demand for certain types of crop to produce biofuels; rising demand for food in developing countries due to population growth (he reminded the press that global population is increasing by 78.5 million per year) and increasing wealth.

The situation depicted by Diouf resembles in a troubling manner a Malthusian scenario. The needs of a growing population for food and other subsistence means (biofuels) outstrip the land's production capacity. The only possibility to avoid social unrest and famine is immediate help to the most affected people and, more substantially, the expansion of food production. In the eyes of Jacques Diouf both are feasible.

This is the point where the vision of Diouf departs from the vision of Malthus. In Malthus' vision there is a point when an extra increase in production capacity will be impossible owing to the law of diminishing returns. In other words: if food production is an activity taking place in a finite environment (land) then there is an

---

5 In Chapter 4 Section 2 we will come back to alternative measures of progress.

upper limit to its growth. For people reasoning as Jacques Diouf does in the quote above there are no limits, as if the law of diminishing returns does not apply to the economy as a whole (see Box 1.6).

In our time, the debate on limits to growth has been resumed by scholars and activists who were worried about the consequences of unbridled economic growth on the environment. Voiced in different ways, their point is that the economy is part of a bigger, limited whole—the ecological system called Earth—and cannot therefore grow forever. In the words of one of the first critics of never-ending economic growth, Ernst F. Schumacher (1973, 1999: 16-17):

> An attitude to life which seeks fulfillment in the single-minded pursuit of wealth—in short, materialism—does not fit into this world, because it contains within itself no limiting principle, while the environment in which it is placed is strictly limited.

If the whole is limited, then one of its parts cannot grow forever. Further, a part cannot grow beyond a certain size without causing irremediable damage to other parts of the whole. A figure may help grasp this point. Figure 1.3 represents the size of the economy as a balloon inside a second balloon, bigger but of limited size. It seems obvious that the smaller balloon cannot grow beyond the size of the bigger one, and that, if left growing, it will squeeze other balloons which happen to be also hosted by the bigger one. One of these other balloons could represent, for example, the habitat of wild animals; another one the still intact rainforests. As Ray C. Anderson, the founder of Interface, a multi-million business in carpet tiles, puts it:

> . . . all wealth ultimately comes from the earth: the forests, the fields, the mines, the oil wells, and the oceans. If so, it must follow that wealth creation at the cumulative expense of a finite earth is, by definition, not infinitely sustainable. Humanity cannot keep trying to live off a bank account we did not open and cannot add a penny to. Though it might take a while . . . there will come a day when our checks come back stamped "Insufficient Funds" (Anderson 2009: 247).

In short: in a closed system of finite capacity infinite growth of a subsystem is impossible without causing a collapse of the entire system (see e.g. Meadows *et al.* 1972: 74, 1992: 45; Daly 1999).

This world view represents a complete shift from the way the champions of never-ending economic growth consider the environment. In their eyes it is not the economy that is a part of the natural environment, but the other way round: the ecosystem Earth can be considered as a subsystem of the economy, to be more precise that part that provides natural materials and allows for the disposal of waste (see Fig. 1.4). From this point of view the goods and services provided by the Earth will abide by the law governing the economy. For example, even if some natural materials become scarce or disposal of waste difficult, the economic system will find a solution to sidestep these problems through investing resources in the development of substitutes. Nature is, in this view, disposable and all support it offers to

Figure 1.3 **The economy as a subsystem of a finite system**

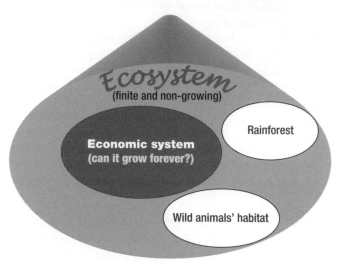

life in general and economic activity in particular can be (in proper time) substituted by goods and services made by humans. In this sense there are no ecological limits to growth and a Malthusian scenario can be avoided (in Chapter 2 Section 6 we will come back to this point).

Figure 1.4 **The economic system as the whole**

Source: adapted from Daly 1999: 8

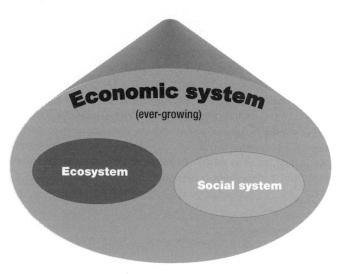

The same answer could be given to those who point to social limits to economic growth. With social limits we refer here to a range of very different issues: from unfair distribution of resources causing malnutrition and chronic poverty in an affluent world to the erosion of moral values caused by the dissolution of traditional bonds in a globalizing world. If social matters are part of the wider economic system, and not its support, then an expansion of the economy will offer all we need to solve any possible social concern. "A rising tide will lift all boats," as the old adage goes.

This last view on the relationship between the economy, the ecological system, and the social system became dominant after World War II. As we have seen above, economic growth became the overarching policy objective and as such shaped not only the activities of the modern world but even the criteria we use to understand it. As Ernst F. Schumacher (1973, 1999: 27) said:

> In the current vocabulary of condemnation there are few words as final and conclusive as the world "uneconomic" . . . Anything that is found to be an impediment to economic growth is a shameful thing, and if people cling to it, they are thought of as either saboteurs or fools.

If Schumacher (and others with him) is right in describing the economic view as the prevalent world view,[6] then it is clear why it required so much time and effort to realize that the effects of a rising economic tide on the social and environmental "boats" are not by definition positive, and that these "boats" are not to be considered as part of the economy and do not abide by its law.

The next two chapters explain how the prevalent world view was challenged from an environmental (Chapter 2) and a social (Chapter 3) perspective. In Chapter 4 we will see how the idea developed that the concern for economic growth, for social development and environmental protection are interlinked and interdependent. In short: how the concept of sustainable development shaped a new view of the world where the economy, the environment, and the social system are seen as an integrated whole.

---

6 Different voices have risen to remind us that economics should concern itself with more than measurable goods and services and include social and environmental consideration. See, for example, the distinction made by Daly and Cobb (1989: 138-39) between *chrematistics* (focus on short-term monetary gain, *chrema* is the ancient Greek word for money and possessions) and *oikonomia* (where the focus is on the long-term health of the common house we all live in, the Earth; in ancient Greek *oikos* means home). See, more recently, Heertje 2006.

Box 1.6 **The law of diminishing returns and the ever-growing economy**

The view of nature as a subsystem of the economy helps clarify why one of the most fundamental economic laws, the law of diminishing returns, seems to apply to all economic activities but not to the economy as a whole. The law of diminishing returns (see Box 1.2) tells us that there is a moment when the costs of adding an extra unit of capital or labor to a certain pursuit will equal the extra benefit obtained. Beyond this point growth will be uneconomic as the costs will be higher than the benefits. Costs here are opportunity costs: that is, the loss or gain that could have been made if the extra input were applied to another part of the economic system. Opportunity costs do not apply to the whole because there is no other part at the expense of which the growth of the whole takes place (see e.g. Daly 1999: 8).

The moment we shift our perspective and see the economy as part of the larger ecosystem of nature, it becomes evident that there are costs to economic growth. Let us think, for example, of the loss of open spaces to build factories, or to the costs connected to a loss of free time to spend with our children or friends. In other words: the law of diminishing returns applies to economic growth, too. This, finally, implies that more growth is not the answer to the problem caused by growth. As Paul Hawken puts it: "you cannot grow out of a problem if it is embedded in the thing that is growing" (Hawken 1993: 208).

2
The concern for the environment

Only One Earth (Barbara Ward and René Dubos 1972)

The first man to look to the Earth from space, a Soviet astronaut, is reported to have exclaimed, "how beautiful it is, our Earth" (Ward 1966: 146). The image of our colored planet on the background of infinite darkness was instrumental in conveying the message that the Earth is unique in her capacity to sustain life, but at the same time finite and fragile. The concern for our planet, championed by the environmental movement, became the first driver of the debate on sustainability and the most important power behind it for decades (Elkington 1997: 43). The influence of this concern was and still is so strong that several authors, politicians, and the general public still equate sustainable development with environmental protection and a proper use of natural resources.

This chapter reviews some of the different ways in which the concern for the environment was voiced. Even though the history of this concern might be traced back at least to the nineteenth century,[1] we focus here on the years 1950–1987: from the economic boom after WWII till the publication of the report *Our Common Future* by the World Commission on Environment and Development (WCED 1987). The first section links back to the chapter on economic growth and the two different paradigms discussed there on the relationship between the economy and nature. Three different concerns are then presented: pollution (Section 2.2), resource depletion (Section 2.3), and the disruption of the self-regulating systems that keep the Earth a place fit for life (Section 2.4). Sections 2.5 and 2.6 review the

---

1 See Sutton 2007: 74ff. for a review of early environmental concern and pp. 91ff. for a brief history of the origin of the environmental movement in the nineteenth century and its differences from the modern, mass movement of the second half of the twentieth century.

debate on responsibilities for the damage inflicted on the environment and the actions taken before 1987, the date of the publication of the WCED report.

2.1 **Nature and economy**

The notion that the natural environment is endangered by human activity and that humanity has to take responsibility for the damage inflicted on nature, developed slowly and amid great resistance. Chapter 1 on the concern for economic growth has already provided some keys to understanding why the process was so difficult. Economic thinking does not see the natural environment as the context in which human activities take place but as one of the factors, alongside labor and capital goods, that have to be managed to make economic growth possible. From this point of view, the ecosystem is not considered to be a limiting factor to growth, as we have seen above (see Chapter 1 Section 5). Yet there is more to be said on the relationship between nature and the economy when this last is seen as the context, or the whole, from which to consider all other activities (as in Fig. 1.4). The delicate point here is that the natural environment enters economic calculations only as land and other natural resources that are needed for the production of goods and services (see e.g. Daly and Cobb 1989: Part 3, Chapter 13). The function these natural resources can have in other respects is not taken into consideration. A forest is, from an economic point of view, timber. The fact that it keeps soil from eroding, absorbs carbon dioxide, and offers a place to live for different species is insignificant at least as long as these so-called natural services are not traded on the marketplace and receive a price.[2] Moreover, from an economic perspective, only scarce resources can command a price on the market. Land, water, and air have long been seen as plentiful and, therefore, free to use for all. "The definition of 'costs' in the early industrial system took on a minimum content which they have to some extent retained. Costs were what the entrepreneur could not avoid paying. Anything else was left to others or left undone" (Ward and Dubos 1972: 57). This means, for example, that for a long time there was (and in certain regions still is) no cost involved in the use of land, water, or air as sinks to discharge wastes.

The modern economic view on nature as a mere factor of production, alongside labor and capital, has deep roots in the Western philosophical and religious tradition. To quote once again the economist Ernst F. Schumacher (1973: 14), "modern man does not experience himself as a part of nature but as an outside force destined to dominate and conquer it." Biblical texts such as Genesis 1:26 were called upon to support the idea that God has given to men full dominion over nature and that therefore men are entitled to use all natural resources to better their own

---

2   Environmental economics follows this path and tries to set a price on nature. On environmental economics see e.g. Tacconi 2000: 47-48 and on its difficulties pp. 63-64.

position. While opposing the church, the Enlightenment, a philosophical stream that reached its apex in the second half of the eighteenth century in France, voiced the same thought on the relationship between men and nature: it is men's right and duty to master nature.[3] Humans' ingenuity was seen as the most important asset to achieve this goal. The nineteenth century saw the beginning and the expansion of industrialization and a spurt in discoveries and technological innovations. Even though, as we have seen in Chapter 1, the majority of people saw their living conditions only slightly improved, or even not at all. After the end of WWII it seemed as if (at least in the so-called North) the time had finally come when all the promises enfolded in the vision of man as a master of nature could become true. Prolonged economic growth, sustained by continuous technological progress, brought increasing prosperity. Thanks to technological innovations, such as pesticides and fertilizers, a growing population could be fed. Mechanization of agriculture and the following rationalization resulted in lower prices of food. The loss of jobs in agriculture (and manufacturing) was compensated by the growth of other sectors of the economy, such as services. More and more people had money to spend on luxury goods, lived in urban surroundings and had jobs seemingly independent from the natural environment (see also Chapter 3 Section 1).

In this context, it is understandable why nature happened to be regarded as a commodity, valued only by its price on the market, and why bending this view toward the appreciation of nature as valuable in itself, was and is far from easy. Different warnings were needed before we started to realize that nature sustains all life forms (as in Fig. 1.3), including human life and that in this capacity nature cannot and should not be considered as a good among other goods on the market (as in Fig. 1.4).

The next three sections follow the slow development of the acknowledgment that nature has a value beyond her market price, that man is not the master of nature but (at best) her steward, and that human life ultimately depends on the services provided by the natural environment.

2.2 **A poisoned planet: pollution**

In presenting Dr Paul Müller, the discoverer of the insecticide DDT, with the Nobel Prize for Medicine in 1948, Professor George Fischer reminded the audience that illnesses brought by parasites are a scourge of past and present times. They could decimate an army, as typhus did when Napoleon was retreating from Russia and threatened to do when the U.S. army was stationed in Naples (Italy) in October

---

3 Lynn White (1967) traced the idea back to the Middle Ages. For a vindication of the Christian faith in respect to nature see Ward 1973. See also Pepper 1996: 151ff. and Sutton 2007: 19ff. on the role of religion, the Enlightenment and the scientific revolution in changing our perception of the environment.

1943. They could wipe out entire villages, as malaria annually did in the past and unfortunately still does in our own time. Professor Fischer then saluted DDT as a *deus ex machina*, a godly intervention, and an example of what science could achieve for the improvement of human life (Fischer 1948).

The role of DDT as a lifesaver was not limited to the fight against parasites that endanger human life. Being a cheap, easily manufactured, and very stable insecticide, DDT was also amply used in agriculture. Alongside two other major technological innovations (chemical fertilizers on the one hand and quick growing and highly productive hybrid strains of maize, rice, and wheat on the other), it laid the foundation for the "green revolution," a spurt in agricultural production from the 1950s on that helped feed a growing population without a sensible increase in the surface of crop land.

Chemical fertilizers and pesticides, including DDT, were considered absolutely safe. It was only in the second half of the 1950s that, using newly developed instruments, scientists discovered that what were considered small and not lethal quantities of chemicals accumulate in the soil, air, and (ground) water to levels threatening life. These discoveries were done in fields as diverse as toxicology, ecology, and epidemiology by institutions such as the Food and Drugs Administration in the U.S.A. and companies such as Shell in the UK. The wider public would have had little chance to hear about these troubling findings, were it not for Rachel Carson, a biologist by formal training, who in her book *Silent Spring* (1962) uncovered in a simple and engaging style the havoc humans were heading for.

Human-synthesized chemicals have never before existed on the planet and, therefore, no organisms have evolved in nature to break them down and render them harmless. As a consequence they build up in, for example, water. All creatures living in the contaminated water, such as fishes, are directly threatened. Yet also all other living species that feed on fish from those contaminated areas, such as some species of birds, are at risk. Human beings, who are at the top of the food chain, are also threatened (see Fig. 2.1). Carson contended that if we continue to indiscriminately spray chemical insecticides on the land, one day we could wake up in a world where no flowers blossom and no birds sing: the "silent spring" of the title. Human life is threatened, too: indirectly by the destruction of the natural environment, the "web of life" (p. 69) in Carson's words, and directly because "for the first time in the history of the world, every human being is now subjected to contact with dangerous chemicals, from the moment of conception until death" (p. 31). Carson compared the indiscriminate use of pesticides with the fallout from nuclear testing, a danger that people began to recognize and protest against in the 1960s. In contrast to nuclear weapons, however, pesticides were considered, as we have seen, as lifesavers not destroyers. *Silent Spring* pointed to the unintended and unpredicted consequences of technology developed to improve human life, inflicting thus a sensible blow to all naïve belief in the blessings of technological innovation.

Figure 2.1 **Where do all the chemicals go?**

Source: www.sustainablecotton.org/downloads/Toolkit_2007.pdf, p.11, accessed August 20, 2011.
Reproduced by the kind courtesy of the Sustainable Cotton Project

A warning sign at San Francisco Bay. It warns children, pregnant and breastfeeding women not to eat
fish from this lake more than once in a month. Others may enjoy the fish twice in a month.

The importance of *Silent Spring* as a trigger of worldwide environmental concern
is generally recognized (Elkington 1997: 8; Lovelock 2000: 144; Dresner 2002: 21;
Kroonenberg 2006: 301) and can hardly be overstated. On the basis of Rachel Carson's conclusions, for example, the newly born environmental movement called on
a ban on the use of DDT. The chemical industry reacted fiercely, accusing Rachel
Carson and her supporters of willingly throwing humanity back into the grasp of
famine and illness. Notwithstanding this opposition, a ban on the domestic use
of DDT was issued in the U.S.A. by the Environmental Protection Agency (EPA) in
June 1972. Different European countries quickly followed the EPA. The ban on DDT
was saluted by the environmental movement as a victory over the business world
and surely contributed to its affirmation as a force to be reckoned with.

The polluting effects of pesticides, fertilizers, and other human activities were
considered to be locally confined: a limited, although sometimes quite large area,
was poisoned by their use, not the entire planet. Symbolic of this way of looking
at pollution is the metaphor used by people landing in the 1970s at Los Angeles

airport to describe the smog that surrounded the city. They spoke of a shield (or cap), covering the city area.[4] It was only in the late 1960s and early 1970s that proof of the worldwide consequences of pollution was provided by the independent scientist James Lovelock. Using the same device that brought others to demonstrate the accumulation of pesticides in the natural environment, Lovelock proved that the haze that, during English and Irish summers, even in the countryside, limited vision to half a mile was actually pollution and that it originated in cities in the south of France and in the north of Italy. The most important chemical components in the haze were CFCs (chlorofluorocarbons)—then used in aerosol cans and refrigerators under the trade name "Freon." Subsequent measurements on the Atlantic Ocean in 1971–1972 showed that high concentrations of CFCs could also be found there (Lovelock 2000: 205). Pollution was thus proved to be a global issue.

It is interesting to note that the introduction of CFCs in refrigerators as a substitute for ammonia was at the time considered a major step forward, as ammonia is highly toxic and CFCs are not (Proops and Wilkinson 2000: 21). As in the case of DDT, a technological innovation introduced to improve human life could prove on application to actually make it worse. How worse was discovered few years after Lovelock's findings by Mario Molina and Sherry Rowland, two scientists working on the stratosphere, the upper layer of the atmosphere. In 1974 Molina and Rowland published a paper where they argued that CFC gases could deplete stratospheric ozone. The ozone filters out ultraviolet light (UV) before it reaches the Earth, and UV light is commonly seen as very toxic for organic life (carcinogen). The scientific community was impressed by this masterpiece of deductive work. One American state (Oregon) reacted almost immediately to the publication, enacting a ban on CFCs in 1975. The United States and several European countries banned the use of CFCs in aerosol spray cans in 1978, but continued to use them in refrigeration, foam blowing, and as solvents for cleaning electronic equipment. The wider public heard of the study in the early 1980s only when a deep reduction in the ozone layer over Antarctica (the "ozone hole"; Fig. 2.2) was discovered and people could, thanks to Lovelock's work, without great difficulty point to the villain: CFCs.

The wider public was deeply affected by these findings, and more so when in 1986 the discovery followed of ozone decrease in the Northern hemisphere, at least during certain seasons, and images of the ozone hole started to be used as an emblem of the environmental movement. The pressure on governments for a total ban on CFCs increased, and as a result a call for a dramatic reduction in the production of CFCs was signed by 35 countries during an international meeting in Montreal in 1987. The Montreal Protocol on Substances that Deplete the Ozone Layer was reviewed in 1990 in London: this time the call was for a complete elimination of CFCs by the year 2000 in developed and by the year 2010 in developing countries.

---

4 It was with these words that Elena Cavagnaro's father relayed his experience in the 1970s; years later, in 2000, she saw the same when landing at Cracow (Poland).

Figure 2.2 **The ozone hole**

Source: NASA/Goddard Space Flight Center, Scientific Visualization Studio, svs.gsfc.nasa.gov/vis/a000000/a002500/a002580/index.html, accessed August 20, 2010

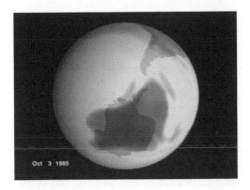

Oct 3 1985

In this photograph by NASA the dark area indicates the hole in the ozone layer above the South Pole.

In 1997 the ozone layer started to recover but it is not expected to close earlier than 2068.[5]

The discovery of the ozone hole is generally considered as an ultimate proof of the global consequences of pollution. Moreover, it brought with it the definitive recognition that the natural environment, even on a global scale, is not always resilient to stress provoked by human activity and has therefore to be protected. With the intensification of economic growth on a global scale that took place from the 1990s, the danger that global growth would ultimately lead to global collapse is even more acute (Marten 2001). That humankind was and is poisoning the Earth is a sad discovery, indeed. However, the rather quick reaction that led to the ban on DDT and CFCs contains a message of hope: humans can become the Earth's stewards.

Box 2.1 **Fighting pollution**

Fighting pollution was, in the beginning and sometimes still today, tied with its presumed local effects. Building higher chimneys, for example, was deemed an effective measure because it brought the smog "further away." Most measures applied were in most cases end-of-the-pipe techniques intended to remove already-formed contaminants from the air, from a water stream, from waste and from products at the end of the production process. Alongside smokestacks, catalytic converters on automobile tailpipes are an example of this type of measure.

A more effective measure is prevention, i.e., designing the production process to prevent pollution from occurring. Energy-saving measures and designing for the environment (which strives to include environmental

5 The ozone story is nicely told in *Limits to Growth: The 30-Year Update* (Meadows *et al.* 2005: Chapter 5). See, for the last piece of news, Newman *et al.* 2006.

consideration from the drawing table) are examples of this new trend. Cradle-to-cradle design goes a step further: it requires that products' components are designed to be used indefinitely or to be returned to nature without harm. For more information on Design for the Environment, a program by the U.S. Environmental Protection Agency, see www.epa.gov/dfe (accessed March 31, 2008); for cradle-to-cradle see McDonough and Braungart 2002. See also Part II.

2.3 A limited planet: resource availability

As we have seen above both Rachel Carson and James Lovelock came across unintended and unpredicted consequences of technologies developed to improve human life and, at the same time, showed that there is a limit to the capacity of the environment to cope with the stress that human activities impose on it. The notion that a finite Earth cannot accommodate ever-expanding human activities is the central theme of *Limits to Growth*, a study commissioned by the Club of Rome to the influential Massachusetts Institute for Technology and published in 1972.[6] In their 1992 review of *Limits to Growth* the authors say,[7] "The earth is finite. Growth of anything physical, including the human population and its cars and buildings and smokestacks, cannot continue forever" (1992: 7). Nevertheless, our world was and is characterized by accelerating industrialization and rapid population growth. In their study the MIT team showed that accelerating industrialization and rapid population growth are interlinked with three other factors: availability of food, depletion of nonrenewable natural resources, and degradation of the environment (pollution). A change in one factor has a direct influence on all others. For example, if population grows, food production also has to grow to avoid famine (see the discussion in Chapter 1 on Malthus). Growth in food production, in turn, can be the

6 The Club of Rome was founded in 1968 by 36 European scientists, economists and industrialists who shared a deeply felt concern for the growing number and complexity of the problems that confronted humanity.
7 *The Limits to Growth* was not the first study to warn of the consequences of an ever-expanding population and increasing demands of society on a finite resource base. It was preceded and accompanied by works such as *The Economics of the Coming Spaceship Earth* (Boulding 1966); *Spaceship Earth* (Ward 1966); *The Population Bomb* (Ehrlich 1968); *The Entropy Law and the Economic Process* (Georgescu-Roegen 1971); and *Blueprint for Survival* (Goldsmith *et al.* 1972). It was not the first, but surely the most influential work also because in 1992 its authors, D.H. Meadows, D.L. Meadows, and J. Randers, published a second book (*Beyond the Limits: Confronting Global Collapse, Envisioning a Sustainable Future*) that they positioned clearly as a sequel to the first one. In 2005 a third book was published, *Limits to Growth: The 30-Year Update*, again defending the same conclusions. All three books will be used in the summary given in the text.

cause of further degradation of the environment through, for example, deforestation to expand farmland.[8] All five factors have, moreover, different traits in common: their growth is exponential (see Box 2.2); possible negative consequences of their exponential growth are not easily or directly detected (see Box 2.3); corrective actions are not always possible owing to irreversible degradation and, when they are possible, often difficult to implement and resource consuming (see Box 2.2).

Box 2.2 **Exponential growth in a finite system**

One of the most simple and impressive examples of the consequences of exponential growth in a finite system is that of the lake where a white water lily is left growing freely. Imagine that this plant has the capacity to double its size every day and to cover the lake in 30 days, suffocating in this way all other forms of life. At day 29 the white water lily will have covered half of the lake, leaving only one day for action to the person who notices its growth and wishes to cut it to preserve other forms of life in the lake (Meadows *et al.* 1972: 34; Marten 2001: 15-16). The conclusion is simple: untamed, exponential growth in a limited, complex system (as both the lake and the world are) will bring life (including human life) to the edge of a catastrophe.

Box 2.3 **Detecting and acting on trends**

The difficulty of detecting trends when their consequences are not immediately visible was already signaled by Rachel Carson. Sutton (2007: 28) argues that an environmental issue (like other types of problem) has to be recognized first, then evidence has to be collected and properly communicated and at least a certain level of consensus reached before action can be taken.

That corrective action is not always possible and, when it is possible, difficult to take, can be proven by the discussion in Europe on the quotas for fisheries. Although it is widely recognized that the levels and quality of stocks of some fish species in the North Sea (e.g., cod) and the Mediterranean Sea (e.g., tuna fish) are rapidly deteriorating, the EU faces serious difficulties in reaching a consensus on a ban on fishing these species. The proposed measures are year by year fiercely opposed by the fishing industry, and declared far from sufficient by environmental organizations.

See Marten 2001: 83-88 for a discussion of a fishery as a system that could collapse as a result of overexploitation in terms very similar to those used by the MIT team.

8 This is called a positive feedback loop. For a basic explanation of feedback loops see Marten 2001: Chapter 2.

Using computer modeling, the MIT team constructed and tested different scenarios of humanity's future. The conclusion was disturbing: if the growth trends of the five factors mentioned above continued unchanged, human civilization will collapse before 2100. In two out of the five tested scenarios collapse is reached owing to an environmental crisis where pollution plays the most important role; in one case the collapse results from a combination of pollution and a crisis in the availability of food. In two cases the crisis will be primarily due to food scarcity.

That pollution is seen as the most likely cause of collapse is in line with the discovery of the global effects of pollution some years before the publication of *Limits to Growth* and reinforced by subsequent discoveries such as the role of CFCs in causing the ozone hole (Reid 1995: 35). To quote the 1992 study:

> . . . the important limits to growth are not limits to population, cars, buildings, or smokestacks, at least not directly. They are limits . . . to the ability of the planetary *sources* to provide those streams of material and energy [on which economic growth depends], and limits to the ability of the planetary *sinks* to absorb the pollution and waste (pp. 7-8, italic in original).

Pollution can thus be interpreted as a warning that we have surpassed the Earth's capacity to absorb the output of our activities: it is a result of the fact that the Earth's sinks are limited. What nature cannot break down, as Rachel Carson teaches us, accumulates in the soil, in the water or in the air and will in the end show up as pollution (see Section 2.4).

The concern for limits to the Earth's resources became a common worry, at least in the form of a concern for the availability of nonrenewable natural resources, after the oil crises in 1972–1973 and 1978–1980. As the National Geographic Special Report on Energy (February 1981: 4) observed: oil "seemed endlessly abundant . . . [and] cheap . . . And so we became addicted to oil"; however:

> Once a barrel of oil is burned, it is gone forever.
>   Over the long sweep of history, human beings will look back and note with awe (and chagrin) that their ancestors stripped the planet of most of this exhaustible endowment within the span of a few hundred years (p. 17).

Also thanks to this historic momentum, *Limits to Growth* was a very influential book. The dramatic scenarios that it presents about the future of the world fueled an intense public debate. Supporters pointed to the need to change life-patterns that revealed themselves as self-defeating. Critics accused the MIT team of pessimism and of drawing a doomsday scenario with a careful choice of (wrong) indicators. Still today, when even oil companies such as Shell are trying to envisage a future without fossil oil, skeptics point to the fact that past predictions on the date when certain nonrenewable resources would have been used up, proved wrong; suggesting in this way that recent anxieties on this point are futile.[9]

---

9 See e.g. the much-discussed book by Lomborg (2001).

Box 2.4 **Are resources limited?**

The debate on this point is not yet settled. As noted above, many predictions on when a certain resource will become scarce have proved wrong. Another criticism to the same effect is that the MIT team has not considered human inventiveness, technological development, and people's capacity to adapt. In the 1975 report by the Dag Hammarskjöld Foundation, *What Now? Another Development*, for example, we read that determining factors are not only the quantity of resources present and the law of nature, but also "the action of society on nature, in particular its technological options" (p. 35). Here an observation by Daly and Cobb (1989: 198) might serve as a warning. After noticing that the idea that there are limits is often attacked by pointing to a new resource that is limitless, they continued:

> This unlimited ultimate resource is variously referred to as technology, information, knowledge, or the human mind. Anyone who asserts the existence of limits is then accused of wanting to place limits on knowledge and is presented with a whole litany of things that someone once said could never be done but which subsequently were done. Certainly it is a dangerous business to specify limits to knowledge. But it is even more dangerous to presuppose that new knowledge will contain not the discovery of new limits, but only the discovery that old limits are not really binding. It is one thing to say that knowledge will grow (no one rejects that), but it is something else to presuppose that the content of new knowledge will abolish old limits faster than it discovers new ones.

Indeed, if one thinks of the fate of CFCs and DDT one is prone to side with Daly and Cobb.

A profound echo was also left by the rejection of technology as the possible solution of the world's problems by a team from a well-known technological institute. Rachel Carson and James Lovelock had already shed doubts on technology as a positive force of progress. Now, the MIT team warns that technology may be able to solve the problems originated by the growth of one factor, but in so doing this may aggravate the consequence of the growth of other factors.

Finally, *Limits to Growth* commanded public attention with the attack it launched on economic thinking. The ultimate causes of the world collapse were discovered to be two pillars of economic thinking: its faith in unlimited growth and its underestimation of nature (Meadows *et al.* 1972).

If economic thinking in general, and the free-market economy in particular, are the causes of world collapse, they cannot be the cure. Other ways should be found to reach a condition of ecological and economic stability where, as the MIT team states, the basic needs of each person are met and each human being has an equal opportunity to realize his or her individual potential (Meadows *et al.* 1972: 137-40). Notwithstanding this attention to the basic material needs of the world population, the call for abandoning economic growth explicitly present in the MIT study enraged many representatives of the South. Poverty, and not pollution, was their most pressing problem, and poverty, as commonly believed, can be alleviated only through economic growth.[10]

Despite these criticisms, it is undeniable that the MIT work roused the awareness that unbridled growth in a limited system is, in the long run, self-defeating and that humans have to reconsider their relationship with the natural environment. In all probability, the most impressive achievement of *Limits to Growth* lies in its insistence that to devise a new path of development humans should first understand the links among social, environmental, and economic factors and the consequences of these links in our limited world. *Limits to Growth* foreshadowed the definition of sustainable development that was to be given in 1987 by the UN World Commission on Environment and Development discussed below.

2.4 **A self-regulating planet: nature services and pollution**

People have always been fascinated by the mystery surrounding the origin of life. Religious, poetic, and scientific works were inspired by it and still there is no clear cut answer to the question how life began on Earth. Equally intriguing and evading is the question how life, once started, could keep developing against all odds. Take for example Earth's temperature: it remained in the "life bearing" range between 10 and 20 degrees Celsius although the sun at the start of life on Earth, 3.5 billion years ago, was 25% less warm than it is now.

> If the Earth's climate were determined solely by the output from the sun, our planet would have been in a frozen state during the first one and a half aeons of life's existence. We know from the record of the rocks and from the persistence of life itself that no such adverse conditions existed (Lovelock 2000: 18).

How is this possible? Earth's atmosphere is puzzling, too: it is an unstable mixture of combustible gases and at the same time its composition remains constant. Gases, if left alone, tend toward a chemical equilibrium: in the atmosphere they do not. What keeps the gas mix that we call air unstable and yet constant in composition?

In *Gaia: A New Look at Life on Earth*, first published in 1979, James Lovelock gave a startling answer: "the whole evolving system of life, air, ocean, and rocks" regulates itself at a state fit for life (2000: 144). Lovelock refers to this self-regulating entity as "Gaia," using the Greek name for the Earth seen as a life-bearing goddess.

---

10 At the Stockholm UN Conference of the Human Environment (1972) Indira Gandhi said that poverty was the biggest pollution (von Weizsäcker 1994: 3). At the end of this chapter and in the next we will come back to the contrast between North and South. On economic growth as a force to escape poverty see Chapter 1 Section 2.

The mechanisms through which Gaia keeps itself a place fit for life are not immediately evident and are difficult to understand. They constitute a complex system of checks and balances where both living creatures and nonliving matter have an essential role. To this complex system we are indebted for a long list of so-called "natural services." For example: the moderation of Earth's climate by, *inter alia*, greenhouse gases and forests; the filtering of dangerous radiation from the sun by the ozone layer; the constant level in ocean salinity and soil fertility.[11]

These services are essential to human survival and are provided for free by the ecosystem. In a recent attempt to calculate what it would cost to reproduce two of the many services offered by the tropical forests (climate moderation and irrigation), Lovelock comes to a staggering amount: £300 trillion a year (1994: 113). This means that in monetary terms these services are more valuable than the use of the same forest land for farming. If this is true, stripping forests for crop land is an uneconomic activity: yet this process still goes on in many countries such as Indonesia and Brazil.[12]

Some authors have criticized the term "nature's service." William McDonough and Michael Braungart, for example, state (2002: 80):

> We don't like to focus on *services*, since nature does not do any of these things just to serve people. But it is useful to think of these processes as part of a dynamic interdependence, in which many different organisms and systems support one another in multiple ways. The consequence of growth—increases in insects, microorganisms, birds, water cycling, and nutrient flows—tend toward the positive kind that enrich the vitality of the whole ecosystem.

Notwithstanding, Lovelock's point is that human beings are "part of the community of living things that unconsciously keep the Earth a comfortable home, and that we humans have no special rights only obligations to the community of Gaia" (2000: ix).[13] Yet, Lovelock continues, it seems that we are no more aware of

11 See Marten 2001: 63-66 for a brief explanation of these mechanisms as "global ecosystem homeostasis" and Marten 2001: 68-69 and 145-146 on the limits of increasing inputs in capital or labor (human inputs as he calls them) to compensate for diminishing natural resources and services.

12 See for more recent calculations of the monetary value of natural services the UNEP report GEO-4 (2007: 161) (www.unep.org/geo/GEO4/report/GEO-4_Report_Full_en.pdf, accessed September 4, 2011). On a similar line The Economics of Ecosystems and Biodiversity (TEEB) study draws attention to the global economic benefits of biodiversity and highlights the growing costs of biodiversity loss and ecosystem degradation. Based on the services they provide to humanity, TEEB for example calculated that coral reefs represent a value of $1.2 million a year per hectare (TEEB 2010).

13 Despite this obligation, humans should not overestimate their influence: in her capacity as a self-regulating system, Gaia is able to respond to threats of a much bigger magnitude than any threats men can pose to her. In Lovelock's words: "The very concept of pollution is anthropocentric and it may even be irrelevant in the Gaian context" (2000: 103). As can be already inferred from this quote, the way Lovelock related to and judged the

our position in the Gaia community. The point here is that the system of checks and balances in Gaia is as complex as it is delicate and that human activity has grown to a level where it can negatively influence its functioning. Every form of activity, including human activity, generates waste. The growth in human activity that we have experienced in the past decades has created an amount of waste that greatly exceeds the capacity of nature to dispose of it. Waste accumulates and creates sinks. Sinks, the places where the output of human activities interact with the natural system, may interfere with natural services and deregulate them. That this is not a remote possibility but a reality is proved by the depletion of the ozone layer by CFCs. The consequence could be the end of life as we know it.

Lovelock and other authors after him[14] put pollution back on the agenda as the most global, dangerous, and therefore urgent problem. The concern for the availability of natural resources was pushed back by the awareness that we are poisoning Earth to death.

Box 2.5 **Limits to knowledge**

That there are limits to human knowledge is a recurring theme in the literature connected with concern for the environment. R. Carson, the MIT team, J. Lovelock and also H. Daly and J. Cobb all agree that human knowledge is limited and that an increase in knowledge very often has resulted in the understanding of limits that were beforehand unsuspected (see Box 2.4). The complexity of Earth's ecosystem confronts us, too, with the limits of our understanding. It is on the basis of these reflections that a precautionary approach toward nature started to be recognized as the best possible option. See also Chapter 4 Section 3 and Box 4.8.

2.5 **Economic growth versus environment**

The impact of studies such as *Limits to Growth* and *Gaia* was, as we have seen, significant. It became lasting, thanks to the capacity of the environmental movement to convey the core message of these studies to a large number of people: the

---

environmental movement cannot be considered to be that of a friend. In spite of this, some authors have considered the notion of Gaia as a boost for the environmental movement (Elkington 1997) or even as an expression of extreme environmentalism (Proops and Wilkinson 2000: 23).

14 That the capacity of the biosphere to absorb pollution is limited was argued also by authors such as Kenneth Boulding (1966), Nicholas Georgescu-Roegen (1971) and his disciple Herman Daly (1977, 1992, 1999, 2005). Al Gore (in his film, *An Inconvenient Truth*, 2006) can be considered as one of the last voices in this line.

price that has to be paid for unbridled economic growth is too high, as it brings our planet and the forms of life on it, including human life, into danger.[15]

Even though not all souls of the environmental movement are anti-growth, it was this form of deep-ecologism that for a long time influenced the debate (Pepper 1996: 35). With each and every event proving that modern, growth-oriented industry and nations were, if not purposefully, surely without much regret, endangering natural and human life, environmentalism got more and more support. Above we have highlighted the ban on DDT and CFCs as two victories that helped strengthen the environmental movement. The discovery of forest and lake acidification in the 1970s and some particularly disturbing environmental disasters (see Box 2.6) reinforced the message: economic growth endangers nature and ultimately human life, and should, therefore, no longer be considered as something worth pursuing without any regard for its consequences.

Box 2.6 **Symbolic environmental catastrophes (1976–1986)**

Some environmental disasters in the decade 1976–1986 have achieved a symbolic status. They caused deep changes in the institutional environment, e.g., in law and regulations, and in social norms and expectations. In this sense they were true catastrophic, disruptive events (Hannigan 1995; Hoffman 1999).

First in time among these is the accidental release of the toxic dioxin from the ICMESA chemical plant at Seveso (Italy) in 1976. The most contaminated area of over 110 hectares had to be evacuated and is now a park.

Worse beyond imagination was the Bhopal disaster eight years later (December 3, 1984) in India: chemical releases from the Union Carbide pesticide plant killed more than 15,000 people and injured at least ten times as many. Notwithstanding the shock it caused and the media coverage it got, the international community proved powerless in forcing Union Carbide to take full responsibility for the tragedy. The consequences of this disaster, for many the worst industrial disaster in history, are still visible: the site is still contaminated; local wells polluted; the health of thousands of people still endangered.

Seveso and Bhopal were not the only environmental catastrophes to capture public attention in these years. Two other well-known events are the *Amoco Cadiz* oil spill on the coast of Brittany, France (March 16, 1978), and Three Mile Island nuclear reactor leak in Pennsylvania, U.S. (March 28, 1979). The explosion at the nuclear plant in Chernobyl (Russia) in 1986 showed again how dangerous and destructive to life nuclear power is, even in its peaceful use.

---

15 It has been observed that what distinguishes the modern environmental movement from its predecessors is its capacity to reach the masses (Pepper 1984: 16; Sutton 2007: 91ff.).

As we have already noticed in discussing the influence of *The Limits to Growth*, developing countries could not agree with this message. Subordinating growth to the environment meant for them closing the only way open to their countries to fight poverty. Very revealing in this respect is Lovelock's discussion with Mother Theresa at the Global Forum held in 1988. Mother Theresa voiced the concern of many people from the South when she stated in her speech that the first priority of humanity was "to take care of the poor, the sick and the hungry." God could take care of the Earth. Lovelock (2001: 376-77) contested that if "people do not respect and take care of the Earth, we can be sure that the Earth, in the role of Gaia, will take care of us and, if necessary, eliminate us."

The divide between North and South was made more deep and the debate sour when environmentalists and other parties started pointing to the explosive population growth in developing countries. In the years 1950–1980 population grew in the South almost three times as fast as in the North.[16] The North feared a recurrence of the Malthusian trap: every gain in economic prosperity would be wiped out by rocketing population expansion. Paul R. Ehrlich coined the term "population bomb" (1968) and went so far as to state that both private and government-sponsored food aid to nations that were not taking action to reduce population growth, had to be stopped. Notwithstanding that few could follow him on this road, the need for slowing down the pace of population growth was widely recognized (see also Box 1.3).

Reducing population growth, however, would never offer a solution to the problems connected with the limits of our planet, if the issue of consumption is not addressed. The lifestyle of people in developed countries requires a huge amount of resources. As Ernst von Weizsäcker reminded us, a 0.6% population growth in the North creates more environmental pressure than the 2.2% population growth of the South (1994: 92-93; see also the discussion on the ecological footprint in Chapter 4 Section 5 and Fig. 4.3).

The interaction between population and consumption is clearly illustrated in a formula proposed by Paul Ehrlich and John Holdren: Impact = Population × Affluence × Technology. The formula states that human impact on the environment varies with changes in population, technology, and affluence. Affluence is a measure of material throughput or per capita consumption while technology refers to the processes used to obtain resources and transform them into useful goods and wastes. Growing population and affluence means higher impact on the environment. Technologies can worsen the scenario if they are not designed to reduce the environmental impact of the process of production and disposal of goods. Sadly most existing technologies are for the most part extractive, "linear (take–make–waste),

---

16 Calculated on the basis of data in: Population Division of the Department of Economic and Social Affairs of the United Nations Secretariat, *World Population Prospects: The 2006 Revision* (www.un.org/esa/population/publications/wpp2006/wpp2006.htm) and *World Urbanization Prospects: The 2005 Revision* (www.un.org/esa/population/publications/WUP2005/2005WUPHighlights_Final_Report.pdf) (accessed March 5, 2008).

fossil fuel driven, focused on labor productivity (more production per worker), abusive, and wasteful—destructive, voracious, consuming technologies of the first industrial revolution" (Anderson 1998: 19). This type of technology augments the environmental impact of population and consumption growth. Yet technology can be geared toward resource productivity, can be cyclical (cradle-to-cradle), and sun-powered and therefore reduce the total impact. Then and only then the formula may be corrected: $I = P*A/T$ (see Box 2.7).

When first developed, though, the formula was intended to underlie how population growth, consumption, and technology contribute to environmental degradation. Even though in the formula a warning against the wasteful lifestyle of the North could be read, its message seemed directed mostly to the South. The interests of the natural environment were stated again to be in conflict with the interests of the poor for better living conditions. The conflict between protection of the natural environment and poverty alleviation made in those years (and still makes) the institutional response to the environmental challenge very difficult, as we will see in the next section.[17]

Box 2.7 **Coping with limited resources**

The oil crisis and books like *Limits to Growth* called for a more efficient use of limited natural resources. If the Earth is a closed system with finite limits, then humanity cannot organize its economic activities as if our planet were an infinite reservoir of materials and offered unlimited possibilities for the deposit of pollutants. In essence, this means that humans have to reduce their use of natural resources to the rate that these can regenerate themselves and of natural sinks to the rate these can break up waste. The triad "reduce–reuse–recycle" offers a venue.

In this context technology was again called on as a positive force that would help in "doubling wealth" while "halving resource use." *Doubling Wealth, Halving Resource Use* is the subtitle of the influential book *Factor Four* by Ernst von Weizsäcker, Amory Lovins, and Hunter Lovins (1998). Their major point was that technology can improve resource productivity so that economic growth can be achieved with less and less environmental impact. The same authors (and many others with them) argued moreover that it was mandatory to harness market forces to stimulate a less resource-intensive economy. When properly informed, was their conviction, the market would take care of a proper distribution of resources. All that is needed is to remove from the market wrong information such as perverse incentives (e.g., taxing labor but not the inefficient use of natural resources) and give it the right information (e.g., on the costs of pollution). Already Daly and Cobb (1989) insisted on the need to put a price on polluting activities or, in other words, to force companies to internalize environmental costs. That prices

17 A clear summary of the population vs. environment and poverty vs. environment issues can be found in Tacconi 2000: 8-10.

should include environmental costs and thus, as the saying goes, tell the environmental truth is one of the points on which environmental economists, ecological economists, extreme and moderate environmentalists agree. See also Chapter 4 Section 3.

2.6 **The institutional response**

Rachel Carson, the MIT team and James Lovelock all called for action to prevent further environmental damage. The environmental movement joined and reinforced this call protesting against the idea that no special action was needed because the market will take care of any difficulty. The reasoning backing up this idea, as we have already seen in Chapter 1 Section 5, is that if a resource becomes scarce, its price will increase giving an incentive to look for alternatives. If the oil price rises above a certain level, for example, then investing in alternative energy sources such as sun and wind will become profitable and attract investments. The delicate point here is that, as most economists recognize, markets are not perfect: even without considering the role of subsidies and other forms of perverse incentives, vested interest could prevent a signal from being felt and action could be delayed by the inertia of the system itself (on this point see also Box 2.3). Oil refineries cannot be converted into wind farms instantly and even admitting that a price rise can bring a better solution in the long run, in the short run "price rises are usually unavoidable and this fact leads not simply to economic but to political problems. If costs and prices rise, something has to give, either private standards or public spending—or the planets' integrity" (Ward and Dubos 1972: 62). Moreover, a price rise will hit poor people more strongly than rich people, increasing inequality.

The difficulties inherent in detecting and acting on complex environmental trends bring most authors to call for action at an institutional and possibly global level. In the years that we are considering, three different but connected lines can be distinguished in the institutional response to the signaled environmental problems: the origin and growth of environmental groups; the organization of international conferences dedicated to the environment; and the creation of (inter)national agencies whether or not as a result of international conferences.

In the paragraph above we have already pointed to the growing force of the environmental movement. WWF, Friends of the Earth, and Greenpeace were all born between 1961 and 1971 and offer a good illustration of the different souls of the environmental movement. WWF was created as a wildlife conservation organization open to dialogue with business while Friends of the Earth positioned itself as an anti-business, anti-growth, and anti-profit group. Greenpeace took a similar stance and, thanks to its activism, spectacular actions and good use of modern media, grew to became the most respected and feared environmental group both in Europe and in the U.S.A.

The growth of environmental organizations was not the only proof of the extent to which people started worrying about the state of our world. Another, powerful demonstration of this concern, was the first Earth Day held in 1970 when an estimated twenty million people participated in peaceful demonstrations all across the U.S.[18]

An institutional response could not wait any longer. At national level, the first to act was the U.S.A. with the creation of the first national agency for environmental protection in 1969: the EPA, Environmental Protection Agency.[19] One of the first acts of the EPA was the ban on DDT of 1972, remembered above as a spin-off effect of Rachel Carson's *Silent Spring*. In 1971 Britain established the International Institute for Environment and Development (IIED) with the mandate to seek ways to enhance economic growth without destroying the environment or exhausting resources. Two years later the European Economic Community (EEC) launched the European Environmental Action Program in 1973. This was the first attempt to synthesize a single environmental policy for what later would be the European Union.

This activity at the international level in the late 1960s and early 1970s culminated in the United Nations Conference on Human Environment held in Stockholm in 1972. The focus of this conference, which had as a motto "Only One Earth," was on exploring solutions for the quickly accelerating deterioration of the environment (Linnér and Selin 2003). It will by now be no surprise that this agenda encountered the opposition of the representatives of different developing countries. They subscribed to the view proposed in 1971 (during one of the preparatory meetings for the conference held in Founex, Switzerland) that, while concern about pollution springs from the production and consumption patterns of the industrialized world, many of the environmental problems in the world are a result of underdevelopment and poverty. Economic growth is needed to solve these problems and cannot be restricted by a concern for ecological degradation. The divide between North and South follow along the same lines that have been individuated in the debate following *Limits to Growth* and Lovelock's *Gaia* (see Chapter 2 Section 5). The conference tried to solve this impasse recognizing in its final document, the *Stockholm Declaration on Human Environment* (which become part of the UN constitution alongside the *Declaration of Human Rights*, as Reid [1995] reminds us), the importance of social issues (see Box 2.8). Notwithstanding, most of the 26 principles in the Stockholm Declaration focus on environmental concerns. Even its second major result, the establishment of the United Nations Environment Program (UNEP), confirms its focus on the environment.

---

18 www.earthday.org (accessed September 26, 2011).
19 Until the Reagan administration took over from the democratic Carter administration, the U.S.A. took the lead in environmental policy.

This sprouting of national and international activity was ironically brought to an end by the same oil crisis that fueled the discussion on exhaustion of natural resources. The economic crisis that followed the increase in oil prices pushed concern for the environment down the political agenda. The initiative passed to the church: in 1974 the World Council of Churches organized a conference with the title "Science and Technology for Human Development." The conference was centered on social justice as a reaction to the environmental focus of the Stockholm conference and because of the churches' experience with and concern for the South (Dresner 2002: 30; see also Chapter 3 Section 3).

The attempt made by the churches to reconcile social development and environmental protection (also known as the eco-justice movement; see Bakken 2000) is not well-known. It remained unmatched till 1987 when the WCED commission, chaired by Gro Harlem Brundtland, published *Our Common Future*. In the meantime, the focus was again on the environment through the publication in 1980 by the International Union for Conservation of Nature (IUCN) of the *World Conservation Strategy* (a study co-financed by WWF and UNEP) and the first issue of *The State of the World* by the Worldwatch Institute in 1984.

The Worldwatch Institute was established in 1975 in the U.S.A. to raise public awareness of global environmental threats to the point where it will support effective policy responses. In 1984 the Institute published its first *State of the World Report* and has done this ever since on an annual basis. All reports are devoted to monitoring changes in natural resources on a global scale, focusing particularly on how these changes affect the economy. The conclusion of the first report reinforced the conclusion already reached by *Limits to Growth* that we are living beyond our means, largely by borrowing against the future.

Similarly to the Worldwatch Institute, the IUCN has had a clear focus on protection and conservation of the natural environment since its inception in 1948. Although the IUCN affirmed in the *World Conservation Strategy* that its approach does not deny the importance of social needs, this document remains heavily oriented toward the environment (see Box 2.8) and was seen by many countries in the South as a renewed attack from the North to their right to cope with poverty through economic growth. To counteract this interpretation, the IUCN organized a conference in 1986 in Ottawa on Conservation and Development. Here the IUCN stressed the need for an alternative type of development where economic, social (meeting basic human needs; equity and social justice; self-determination and cultural diversity), and ecological (conservation and restoration of ecological integrity) issues are all taken into account. All these elements come back in the WCED report *Our Common Future* and offer the backbone for this definition of sustainable development.

Box 2.8 **Toward sustainable development**

In this box some quotes are collected that foreshadow the path taken by the WCED or Brundtland Commission to reconcile the concern for environment with the need for economic growth.

Stockholm Declaration on Human Environment (1972)
Proclamation 6 states:

> To defend and improve the human environment for present and future generations has become an imperative goal for mankind—a goal to be pursued together with, and in harmony with, the established and fundamental goals of peace and worldwide economic and social development.

Principle 1 recognizes that a safe environment is a human right:

> Man has the fundamental right to freedom, equality and adequate conditions of life, in an environment of a quality that permits a life of dignity and well-being, and he bears a solemn responsibility to protect and improve the environment for present and future generations.

On the Declaration see further Linnér and Selin 2003: 7ff.

Conference on Science and Technology for Human Development organized by the World Council of Churches (1974)
It was at this Conference that the term "sustainable society" was coined to describe a society where the scarce resources are equitably distributed and where there is common opportunity to participate in social decision-making (democratic participation); where food supply is higher than the need for food; and the emission of pollutants is below the capacity of the ecosystem to absorb them; where the use of nonrenewable resources does not out-run the increase in resources made available through technological innovation; where the level of human activity is not negatively influenced by (natural) variations of global climate. The conclusions of the Conference were very visionary, far ahead of their time. The concept of "equitable distribution," for example, would form a cornerstone of the Brundtland approach to sustainable development almost fifteen years later, while democratic participation gained a central place in the debate on sustainability only twenty years later at the Earth Summit in Rio de Janeiro (1992). Maybe because of this, the results of the conference did not become widely known.

World Conservation Strategy (1984)
Development is "the modification of the biosphere and the application of human, financial, living and non-living resources to satisfy human needs and improve the quality of human life" (1984: section 1.1.3.).

Conservation is "the management of human use of the biosphere so that it may yield the greatest sustainable benefit to present generations while maintaining the potential to meet the needs and aspirations of future generations" (1984: section 1.1.4.).

2.7 **Concluding remarks**

As we have seen the environmental movement has a long history and the themes it brought to public attention are numerous and complex. Yet the major legacy of this movement can be summarized in three major themes.

The first main theme is that our planet is limited and that, thus, nothing on it can be kept growing indefinitely: neither population nor the economy. Earth's limits are particularly evident if we look at natural resources and sinks. Pollution is a warning that we have exceeded the capacity of the planet to break down the output of our activities. Similarly "peaks" in resource exploitation (i.e., the tipping point from which the curve measuring the quantity of a certain material extracted from Earth starts descending) are a warning that we are depleting them. To avoid major havoc, we should reduce the use of natural resources to the rate that these can regenerate themselves and of natural sinks to the rate these can break up waste. To achieve these goals, environmental economists, ecological economists, extreme and moderate environmentalists alike have proposed to put a price on polluting activities and on the unwise use of natural resources. Only if prices tell the environmental truth shall the market respond and adopt a more environmentally friendly course.

A second main theme is that the Earth is not a rock wandering in the universe, but actually a very complex system where all parts function together to sustain life. Even though the ecosystem is rather resilient, it may be disrupted by (for example) a rapidly increasing level of pollutants to a point where fragile and essential subsystems such as the ozone layer break down. We need to acknowledge our lack of knowledge of the intertwining ecosystem and, thus, behave respectfully and carefully toward it: more as stewards than as conquerors of nature.

Connected to this second main theme is the insistence on the value and worth of nature services. Keeping the Earth a place fit for life is a huge task that humankind will never be able to accomplish on its own. We have neither the financial resources nor the technical capacity needed for the task. Thus before "developing" a still virgin area (such as a primeval forest) we should consider the services that this area already offers to all living creatures including us. Then it may appear that leaving it "undeveloped" is the best economic choice. Thus, again, calculating this service and letting the person or company disrupting it pay what it cost is seen as the only way to steer the economic system away from a path of doom and toward a better future.

The third and last theme dear to the environmental movement is the need to change humankind's attitude toward nature. Nature has an intrinsic worth and therefore people need to respect it even without reference to any type of service it can offer to them. In this sense many early environmentalists fought for the conservation and restoration of natural areas, such as the Yosemite National Park in California, and still fight for the right of wild animals to a place where they can live freely. There is Only One Earth, for us and for them.

3

The concern for social development

The human person is the central subject of development and should be the active participant and beneficiary of the right to development (UNHCHR 1986 Declaration on the Right to Development, art. 2, 1).

The Canadian Commissioner of the Environment and Sustainable Development, Johanne Gélinas, wrote in her 2001 report to the House of Commons that "while the social sciences have a long history and are well documented through a large body of literature, the meaning of the social dimension within the context of sustainable development is less understood" (Gélinas 2001: Chapter 5: 3). This might appear astounding if one considers that the ultimate goal of sustainable development is improved quality of life and standard of living for all people. Yet the issues connected with the social dimension of sustainable development are so many and so complex that one may even wonder whether it is possible to grasp this dimension properly. These issues extend far beyond poverty reduction and include, alongside the satisfaction of material and non-material needs, a just distribution of wealth inside a nation and among nations; equal access to health care and education; equal opportunities to participate in civil and political life; social cohesion and strengthening of community ties; respect for cultural heritage; and the like.

Much of the sustainable development discourse, especially when it appears in the economics literature, focuses on environmentally sustainable development. Since the Brundtland Report, however, there has been considerable effort to broaden the concept of sustainability beyond environmental concerns by recognizing the myriad social dimensions of sustainability. The report itself highlighted the ways in which poverty is both a cause and an effect of environmental degradation. But the social dimensions of sustainability extend beyond poverty and its connection

> to the environment to include a range of issues often ignored in environ-
> mental circles (Wise 2001: 47).

A first clarification of what social development entails may be found in a recent
paper by the World Bank, where it is stated that this term can refer to "improvement
in the welfare and quality of life of individuals; or changes in societies—in their
norms and institutions—that make development more equitable and inclusive for
all members of a society" (Davis 2004: iv).

This description makes clear that the social dimension is the key to achieve sustainable development. Development—as distinct from growth—has to be understood as a multidimensional process involving major changes in social structures,
popular attitudes, and national institutions, as economist Michael P. Todaro already
pointed out (1977). If this is true, economic growth and even environmental protection are necessary but not sufficient conditions of development. Deep changes
in social structures, attitudes, and institutions are vital to support a holistic and
therefore sustainable approach toward development. To clarify, let us consider the
role of GDP. As noted in Chapter 4 Section 4, the focus on GDP as the only measure of national success is considered to be one of the major causes of the present
unsustainable state of world affairs and at the same time one of the obstacles to
achieve sustainability. One has only to think of the huge social and institutional
changes needed to substitute the GDP with a more sustainable index to comprehend the importance and pervasiveness of the social dimension of sustainable
development.

A last consideration concerns the historic context in which the social *problématique* evolved. In reconstructing this context scholars are confronted with a variety
of complex and still sensitive phenomena, ranging from the slave trade to colonization and from the industrial revolution to the rise and fall of communism—to
mention only some examples. Taking all this into account, it would not come as a
surprise that draconian choices have to be made when discussing the social dimension of sustainable development. This chapter will explore the most important historic roots of the concern for social development (Section 3.1) and touch on the
institutions that championed major social issues (Sections 3.2–3.4). The aim here
is to offer a first understanding of this complex dimension. The conclusion of this
chapter (Section 3.5) sums up the information offered so far and offers a bridge to
the discussion of sustainable development.

3.1 **Historic roots**

This section briefly touches on the historic context in which the social *problématique* evolved: the Industrial Revolution; colonialism with the post-WWII decolonization process; and globalization.

The Industrial Revolution

Most people associate the Industrial Revolution with smoky chimneys, heavy industry, and blue-collar workers. This is, however, only a partial truth. The Industrial Revolution was made possible by the application of non-animal power to production, both in agriculture and manufacturing. Coal first and then oil fueled newly invented machines and their use on a large scale accelerated an already existing yet till then rather slow process of social change that modified profoundly the way people worked, lived, and traveled.

To better understand the major social changes that the Industrial Revolution brought about, consider that, at the end of the eighteenth and the beginning of the nineteenth centuries, most people lived and worked primarily on farms in extended families. This was the foundation of their economic security. This way of living changed dramatically when the introduction of non-animal powered machines made food production much more efficient. The hands that were no longer needed on the countryside looked for employment in the cities where new industries developed at a rapid pace. As more and more people became wage-earners, working for others, the extended family and the family farm as sources of economic security became less common. Some numbers may illustrate how rapid the process was: in 1800 in the U.S.A. 90% of all workers were employed in agriculture; today this is less than 5%. A similar process is visible in upcoming economies: in the last 20 years the percentage of people employed in agriculture in China fell from nearly 90% to 50%.

The main assets and drivers for economic prosperity in the industrial age became financial capital and machines. Labor was necessary but replaceable and people became like things, as supply exceeded demand owing to the huge immigration from the countryside. Wages were more often than not set at or under subsistence levels, forcing women and children to work to support their family. Collective health insurances and retirement funds did not exist. Factories were grimy, noisy places; working days were long; days-off scarce. According to management scholar Peter Drucker, in 1913 industrial workers worked a minimum of 3,000 hours a year (almost 58 hours a week, all year round) and their unions were still officially prohibited or, at best, hardly tolerated (Drucker 2001: 301-303).

Industrialization is often seen as a recipe for the creation of wealth, yet the transition from an agricultural to an industrial society was (and still is) a painful process. Consider, for example, that the first half of the nineteenth century was one of the darkest times in the economic history of England, the country where the Industrial Revolution took off (Rauschenbush 2007: 181-82). Men learned to make wealth much faster than they learned to distribute it justly. The social dimension of development evolved from the growing concern for the sub-human living conditions of children, men, and women employed in factories: they owned nothing, except their own strength and, for men and women, their children.[1]

---

1   The word "proletarian" comes from the Latin "*prole*," which means children.

Several forces pressed for the improvement of workers' condition in the nineteenth and early twentieth centuries and, as we will see later on (Chapter 3 Section 2), halfway through the nineteenth century governments started responding to this pressure with legislation on child labor, working times, and later on employees' and civil rights.

As observed above, before the Industrial Revolution economic production (for example, weaving) was spread over the country. The new mode of production, however, concentrated around machines and factories in the cities. Emigration to cities is a common feature of industrial revolutions, both in the past and in the present: booming cities in nineteenth-century England, at the forefront of the Industrial Revolution, and in China, Brazil, and India today are testimony to this. Thus, the Industrial Revolution is a direct cause of a second social issue, urbanization, with its new way of life, insecurity, and poverty.

Colonialism

The Industrial Revolution is seen by scholars as one of the drivers toward the new wave of colonialism in the late nineteenth century, sometimes referred to as (new) imperialism. Industrialized nations needed raw materials to fuel their economy; they sought new, sheltered markets to sell their products and longed for physical space and employment for their growing population (see on this last point Chapter 1 Section 1). During this period industrialized European countries such as England, France, Belgium, Germany, and later on Italy conquered one-fifth of the Earth's surface, mostly in Africa, Asia, and the Pacific.

Colonialism in its nineteenth century form did not only mean the political control by a great power over a less powerful country or trade in commodities to serve the Western market. It usually also meant the redesign of the economy in the colonized country to serve the need of the colonizing power. This can be briefly illustrated by the ban imposed by the British Empire on spinning wheels in India. Cotton—one of the major resources in India—had to be shipped to Britain, spun and woven there to be re-imported as garments and sold for a profit. The spinning wheel became a symbol of the Indian opposition to the British Empire, and it was set at the center of the Indian national flag. Old colonial powers, such as the Netherlands in Indonesia, followed the same path and reoriented the agriculture of their colonies toward export. One of the consequences of this policy is that countries such as Angola, Ethiopia, and Indonesia become producers of coffee while the most coffee per capita is consumed in Europe and, another, that several African countries (e.g., Ivory Coast and Ghana) became top producers of cocoa while the leading cocoa processing countries are the Netherlands and the U.S.A.

The process of decolonization after WWII often left intact this pattern of economic relationship: the former colony kept producing raw materials and food for the former colonial power and still offered a market for its products. Of course, this relationship is an uneven one: prices of raw materials are usually lower than for finished products; food crops grown for export often exhaust the soil more quickly than local crops that are not appreciated in the Western market. This has led economists to speak of a dependency relationship of former colonized countries (the periphery) toward the so-called center of economic power (the Western countries, most of whom were former colonizers; see on this point also Chapter 4 Section 5).

The imbalance in the relationship became apparent to a large public during the so-called debt crisis in the early 1980s. The causes of this crisis are very complex. Yet scholars agree that it was a combination of falling commodity prices (see Fig. 3.1), huge interest rates, mismanaged lending and poor investments partly dictated by the Western financial institutions (see Chapter 1 Section 3) and partly devised by ineffective and corrupt governments in search of prestige and legitimacy. As a consequence of the interplay of these causes, developing countries found themselves in 1982 unable to bear the costs of the annual interest payment on their debts, an amount that in several cases was higher than their GDP (Brown 1990).

Figure 3.1 **Falling commodities prices and rising debt**

Source: World Bank, World Resources 1988–89; L.R. Brown (ed.), Worldwatch Institute, *State of the World 1990: A Worldwatch Institute Report on Progress Toward a Sustainable Society,* www.worldwatch.org

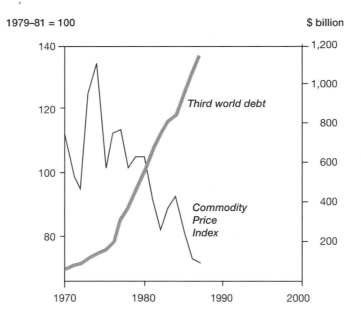

To better understand the linkages between the debt crisis and colonialism it may be remembered that in the 1960s a sum of $59 billion was considered as the share of the former colonies in the debt of the colonizing powers (Guissé 2004; Mandel 2006: 21-22). The interest rate was unilaterally set at 14% and thus caused the debt to increase rapidly. Thus, the newly independent countries were saddled with a heavy debt even before they could start organizing their economy.

It is true that different countries reacted differently, and that some were able to successfully cope with the 1980s debt crisis (Sachs and Collins 1989). Yet few scholars deny that here lies one of the most important sources of continuing, dehumanizing poverty in many former colonies, especially in Africa. The debt crisis and the recurring famines in Africa brought this sour effect of colonialism to the attention of a wider public. A new aspect of the social *problématique* thus came to the foreground: poverty connected with fragile economies; huge debts; weak international organizations; and weak local governments.

Globalization

Globalization of trade is considered by several scholars and activists as cause and at the same time effect of economic and social inequalities among countries. Although fully globalized trade was devised as a means to ensure worldwide peace and economic prosperity during the Bretton Woods conference after WWII (see also Chapter 1 Section 1), barriers to the free movement of goods, services, and capital had to be removed to assure free international competition. This in turn (so went the reasoning) would lead each and every country or region to focus on those economic activities that could give it an edge in the global arena assuring prosperity to all. Without wishing to enter into the sensitive debate between detractors and supporters of globalization, it has yet to be noticed that at the dawn of the modern globalization process different regions of the world hold a very different position in term of institutional capacity, economic development, social cohesion, and the like. We only have to refer to the situation of the newly independent countries briefly illustrated above, to see that a so-called "level playing field" was missing and that this imbalance carried in itself the risk that more powerful countries would once again take advantage of the economies of less powerful ones.

Concluding, industrialization, colonization, and the subsequent process of decolonization have left a difficult heritage of inequality in the distribution of and access to world resources. Loosened community and family ties, weak institutions, unsafe and even exploitative working conditions, poverty in city slums and in the countryside, illiteracy, limited or no access to health care resulting in infant mortality, and a short life expectancy are parts of this sad heritage. Notwithstanding some successes, globalization of trade relations has not been able to essentially change this situation for the better. From this perspective it is understandable that many countries from the so-called South opposed in the 1970s and 1980s the call by environmentalist to spare the planet in the name of a more urgent issue: the fight against poverty and, more broadly, a more equitable distribution of world resources (see also Chapter 2 Sections 5 and 6).

3.2 **Fighting for a better world in the 19th and early 20th centuries**

Forces of a very different nature backed up the fight against unfair social structures in the nineteenth and early twentieth centuries. Here the focus is on the major forces that acted at the broader level of society: Marxism, the Catholic Church, and one multilateral institution, the International Labour Organization (ILO). As a conclusion, this section touches also on the reaction of governments.[2]

Marxism

It has been noted above that industrialization is a painful process that, at least in the beginning, brings alongside prosperity for the few poverty for many. Karl Marx, a German philosopher, happened to live in London in the high days of the Industrial Revolution and witnessed the inhumane conditions in which the so-called working class lived and worked. Marx stated that the cause of workers' exploitation was the underlying economic structure of the industrial society where the means of production (in the form of financial capital, land or machines) are separated from labor. Those who possess no means of production (the proletarians) can survive only by selling their and their children's capacity to work to those possessing such means (the capitalists). In a situation where there is a larger workforce than needed, following the law of supply and demand, capitalists will set the price of labor as low as possible to gain as high a profit as possible. The resulting economic and social stress would, in Marx's opinion, fuel the class struggle between proletarians and capitalists. In the transition to a more equitable society, violent class struggle is in the eyes of Marx unavoidable.[3] Due to its sheer numerical power, the working class will overthrow the political, liberal system based on the capitalist economic structure and give birth to a stateless, classless society: communism. In the transition toward this ideal society, private property should be abolished; workers should become owners of the means of production and production itself geared to satisfy primary needs instead of fancy wants.

Marx's influence was limited during his life (1818–1883). Yet it became stronger and stronger after his death when political parties and the then emerging labor unions became inspired by his ideas. When the Bolshevik party got the upper hand

---

2   Later in this chapter we consider the work of other international organizations. In Part II we discuss the role of the unions (of different political affiliation) and enlightened capitalists.

3   This will become a thorny point in the development of political parties inspired by Marx, together with the issue of whether a true communist society could be achieved by a nation (such as Russia at the beginning of the nineteenth century) that had not yet undergone the Industrial Revolution. Several political movements—usually referred to as socialist— gradually abandoned the idea of class struggle and embraced reforms as a more suitable way to better workers' conditions.

in the Russian Revolution of 1917 and declared the dawn of the Communist State, Western societies were seriously alarmed. Reactions from the church, national governments, and international organizations to prevent the virus of communism from spreading further are a testimony to this alarm.

The Catholic Church

The opening of the encyclical letter *Rerum Novarum* issued in 1891 by the Catholic Pope Leo XIII makes an open reference to the state of social turmoil in Europe at the end of the nineteenth century and the role of the political movements inspired by Marx's theories (see Box 3.1).

Box 3.1 **The *Rerum Novarum***

"That the spirit of revolutionary change, which has long been disturbing the nations of the world, should have passed beyond the sphere of politics and made its influence felt in the cognate sphere of practical economics is not surprising. The elements of the conflict now raging are unmistakable, in the vast expansion of industrial pursuits and the marvelous discoveries of science; in the changed relations between masters and workmen; in the enormous fortunes of some few individuals, and the utter poverty of the masses; the increased self reliance and closer mutual combination of the working classes; as also, finally, in the prevailing moral degeneracy. The momentous gravity of the state of things now obtaining fills every mind with painful apprehension; wise men are discussing it; practical men are proposing schemes; popular meetings, legislatures, and rulers of nations are all busied with it—actually there is no question which has taken deeper hold on the public mind" (Leo XIII 1891: p. 1, par. 1).

"To remedy these wrongs the socialists, working on the poor man's envy of the rich, are striving to do away with private property, and contend that individual possessions should become the common property of all, to be administered by the State or by municipal bodies. They hold that by thus transferring property from private individuals to the community, the present mischievous state of things will be set to rights, inasmuch as each citizen will then get his fair share of whatever there is to enjoy. But their contentions are so clearly powerless to end the controversy that were they carried into effect the working man himself would be among the first to suffer. They are, moreover, emphatically unjust, for they would rob the lawful possessor, distort the functions of the State, and create utter confusion in the community" (Leo XIII 1891: p. 1, par.4).

In his encyclical, Pope Leo XIII clearly expresses the concern of the Catholic Church with regard to the social developments caused by the dramatic changes during the Industrial Revolution and denounces in forceful terms the poor living conditions of workers in the emerging industrial societies. In the same document, however, the Catholic Church criticizes the solution proposed by the new socialist (and communist) movement, emphasizes the rights and duties of both capital and labor and insists on the rights for people to own private property. The *Rerum Novarum* states then clearly what the Catholic Church sees as the central aim of any social policy: to foster respect for each and every human being as a heavenly creature and to develop a society that respects and promotes all the dimensions of the human person (O'Brien and Shannon 2006: 395). On this fundament, violent struggle was condemned and gradual reform by governments and private capitalists alike promoted as the right means to achieve a fairer society. In the process, charity could be sent in to relieve the poor.

Successive encyclical publications continued to be used by the Catholic Church as special means of intervention on broad social issues (Pontifical Council for Justice and Peace 2000: Article 1). In 1931, celebrating the fortieth anniversary of the *Rerum Novarum*, Pope Pius XI published the encyclical message *Quadragesimo Anno*. It reflected the thinking of several European economists and theologians, projecting new structures for economic self-government to overcome the injustices of capitalism and socialism. According to O'Brien and Shannon (2006: 40-41), "a new phrase—social justice—appeared in *Quadragesimo Anno* to describe the type of justice that demanded due recognition of the common good, a good which included, and did not contradict the authentic good of each and every person."

Sixty years afterwards, in the new geopolitical context characterized by the end of communism in the Soviet Union, Pope Ioannes Paulus II issued the *Centesimus Annus* to celebrate the hundredth anniversary of the *Rerum Novarum*. Box 3.2 contains a passage on how some of the concerns of *Rerum Novarum* have evolved. Chapter 4 will come back to this encyclical letter.

Box 3.2 **The *Centesimus Annus***

"At the beginning of industrialized society, it was 'a yoke little better than that of slavery itself' which led my predecessor to speak out in *defence of man*. Over the past hundred years the Church has remained faithful to this duty. Indeed, she intervened in the turbulent period of class struggle after the First World War in order to defend man from economic exploitation and from the tyranny of the totalitarian systems. After the Second World War, she put the dignity of the person at the center of her social messages, insisting that material goods were meant for all, and that the social order ought to be free of oppression and based on a spirit of cooperation and solidarity. The Church has constantly repeated that the person and society need not only material goods but spiritual and religious values as well. Furthermore, as she has become more aware of the fact that too many people live, not in the prosperity of the Western World, but in the poverty of the developing countries amid conditions which are still 'a yoke little better than that of slavery itself' she has felt and continues to feel obliged to denounce this fact with absolute clarity and frankness, although she knows that her call will not always win favor with everyone.

> One hundred years after the publication of *Rerum Novarum*, the Church
> finds herself still facing 'new things' and new challenges" (Ioannes Paulus
> II 1991: par. 61; see also O'Brien and Shannon 2006: 484).

Multilateral organizations: the ILO

One of the multilateral organizations that from its inception has been involved
with the concern for the social side of development is the International Labour
Organization (ILO).[4]

The ILO was created in 1919, as part of the Treaty of Versailles that ended World
War I, based on the belief that universal and lasting peace can be accomplished
only if it is based on social justice. Parties involved in the creation of the ILO were
aware of the exploitation of workers in the industrializing nations at that time and
set as a goal for the ILO to improve workers' conditions through the development of
international labor standards. The ILO got thus the mandate to consider all issues
connected with labor, varying from the length of working days and weeks to health
care and safety; from fighting child labor to provisions for aged workers; from freedom of association to equal remuneration for equal work. For example, the first
ILO convention limited working hours in the industry to eight in one day and forty-
eight in a week (issued in 1919, it came into force in 1921). The same year saw the
first attempt by the ILO to ban the heaviest forms of child work in industry.

A tripartite organization, the ILO brings together representatives of governments, employers, and workers in its executive bodies and influences social legislation mainly through its conventions and recommendations. Conventions that
are (voluntarily) ratified by a specified number of governments become treaties in
international law. Governments have to report to the ILO on implementation of
ratified conventions and even though the ILO cannot directly enforce application,
it has influenced a great part of social legislation in many parts of the world.

Box 3.3 **Fundamental ILO principles**

In 1944 the Declaration of Philadelphia explicating the aims and purposes of
the ILO, defined the following fundamental principles on which the organization is based:

- "Labor is not a commodity
- Freedom of expression and of association are essential to sustain
  progress

4 It is interesting to note that at the origin of the idea of an international organization dealing with labor issues were two enlightened industrialists, Robert Owen (1771–1853) of
Wales and Daniel Legrand (1783–1859) of France.

- Poverty anywhere constitutes a danger to prosperity everywhere
- The war against want requires to be carried on with unrelenting vigor within each nation, and by continuous and concerted international effort which the representatives of workers and employers, enjoying equal status with those of governments, join with them in free discussion and democratic decision with a view to the promotion of the common welfare."

For the full text of the declaration, see ILO 1944.

Governments

Pressed by these and other forces—including the unions and enlightened capitalists—several governments started addressing social and labor issues through legislation. Yet progress was slow and from a contemporary point of view the laws passed by several governments in the eighteenth and early nineteenth centuries seem very weak and sometimes utterly incomprehensible. For example, the first landmark of modern labor law, the British Health and Morals of Apprentices Act of 1802, limited an apprentice working day to twelve hours while apprentices could be as young as children of six!

Governmental efforts to prevent and alleviate social misery became more and more incisive as the years passed by. Yet, to use child labor as an example again, notwithstanding many laws protecting children, child labor was widespread in Europe till halfway through the nineteenth century. Existing and new social legislation was ineffective in the eighteenth and early nineteenth centuries because departments or ministries responsible for its enforcement were weak or did not exist at all. Ministries for social affairs were instituted or duly strengthened only after World War I and with them a new stream of social legislation and enforcement policy ensued in the industrialized countries. The timing was not casual. Governments realized that the soldiers on which they had relied during the Great War could not be sent back to work in unsafe environments, for low wages, devoid of any retirement and health provision without risking a violent revolt. The Bolshevik Revolution in Russia offered a frightening reminder. Something similar may be said for the period immediately after WWII, when the wish not to repeat the political mistakes after WWI (see Chapter 1 Section 1) and the fear of the spread of communism brought most governments in industrialized countries to enforce more incisive social and labor legislation and develop programs for poverty alleviation.

In short, notwithstanding several efforts, enforcement of social and labor laws took off only after the two World Wars (Deane 1980; Ashton 1966). In most Western countries government legislation and, after WWII, sustained economic growth were able to take the edge off (Marxist) class struggle and transform unskilled, penniless workers into skilled workforce and property owners. As was briefly seen above, this process has still to be carried on in many developing countries for complex and sensitive historical reasons.

3.3 **Fighting for a better world after WWII: poverty and discrimination**

Of all the social issues mentioned above, poverty reduction—with a focus on the newly independent countries—received wide attention after WWII. This is easy to understand if we consider the dramatic situation in most ex-colonies and the fact that even in the richer North poverty was far from being over.

Poverty is a complex issue. The first difficulty in discussing poverty arises from defining what exactly "poverty" is and entails. Poverty might be looked at from an exclusively economic viewpoint. In this sense, it is about the line below which disposable income is insufficient to guarantee survival of the individual and the people dependent on him or her. From this perspective it is not surprising that major (international) policy efforts after WWII were directed toward enhancing economic growth in all regions where poverty had to be fought. The idea was that, thanks to a growing economy, prosperity will trickle down to the poor: "a rising tide lifts all boats," was the adage. Yet, for a complex set of reasons (some of which have been delineated above and in Chapter 1), it did not happen. As civil rights activist Jesse Jackson put it, speaking in 1984 to the U.S. Democratic National Convention, "Rising tides don't lift all boats, particularly those stuck at the bottom" (Jackson 1984). The message here is that poverty is more than only income, and the fight against poverty entails more than pushing economic growth.

The same concern was expressed more than ten years before Jesse Jackson's speech by a group of experts, mostly from developing countries, who met in 1971 in the Swiss Founex to prepare the upcoming UN Conference on the Human Environment. To quote their words:

> In the past, there has been a tendency to equate the development goal with the more narrowly conceived objective of economic growth as measured by the rise in gross national product. It is usually recognized today that high rates of economic growth, necessary and essential as they are, do not by themselves guarantee the easing of urgent social and human problems. Indeed in many countries high growth rates have been accompanied by increasing unemployment, rising disparities in incomes both between groups and between regions, and the deterioration of social and cultural conditions. A new emphasis is thus being placed on the attainment of social and cultural goals as part of the development process. The recognition of environmental issues in developing countries is an aspect of this widening of the development concept. It is part of a more integrated or unified approach to the development objective (Founex Declaration, UN 1971, 1.6).

Box 3.4 **Infant mortality versus national income**

A vivid illustration of the consequences of unequal access to resources for people living in different countries is given in a Gapminder World Map by Hans Rosling, Professor in International Health at the Karolinska Institutet and Director of Gapminder Foundation (Stockholm, Sweden) (see overleaf).[a] The map was produced in May 2010, with the latest available data (2008). It compares all countries and territories by income (measured by GDP) and health (measured by life expectancy at birth). Life expectancy at birth is a very strong indicator of social development because it depends on several other indicators of development, such as access to food, healthy dwellings, hygiene, health care, and education.

Many conclusions can be drawn considering this graph. First, that life expectancy at birth varies hugely in the world: from around 45 years in Afghanistan and Zimbabwe, to above 80 years in Japan and several European countries such as Italy and France. Second, the map shows that there is a relation between economic prosperity (GDP) and life expectancy: the higher the GDP the higher people might expect to live. This seems to support the view (referred to above) that a "rising tide lifts all boats."

However, the story told by the map is more complex. Consider the position of Vietnam and China on the life expectancy axis: it is almost the same (respectively, 75 and 73 years). Yet China has a much higher GDP per person (around $7,300) than Vietnam (slightly above $2,600). Something similar can be said for Cuba (less than $10,000 GDP per capita) and the U.S. (above $40,000 GDP per capita). Without wishing to discuss the intrinsic merit of these very different societies, it seems clear that high life expectancy does not depend exclusively on the GDP but also on choices that governments and individuals make on how to spend their money.[b]

This conclusion is reinforced by considering the impressive example of the state of Kerala in southwestern India. It has a population of above 30 million people and a gross domestic income of $1,000 per person. Yet mortality rate are one of the lowest in the developing world; life expectancy is 72 years;[c] women have 1.7 children (less than in the U.S.); and 90% of the population is literate (comparable to Spain). This is the result of a policy investing in health standards and education, supporting active participation, and an equitable distribution of resources (Edwards 2005: 131-32).

See also Chapter 4, Figure 4.2 on income distribution.

a Our thanks go to Professor Hans Rosling for the informative discussion on this map and its implications we had via email. The map is reproduced by kind courtesy of Gapminder. Please visit www.gapminder.org for more information on Professor Rosling's project.

b All data is from the Gapminder Map. As Professor Rosling remarked in our discussion, Vietnam is indeed an outlier in health in relation to income but this could be due to either exceptionally good health policy or exceptionally bad economic policy. In his opinion both mechanisms are involved.

c In 2005 (the year of Edwards publication from which the data from Kerala are quoted) life expectancy in India was 62 years (see Gapminder Map).

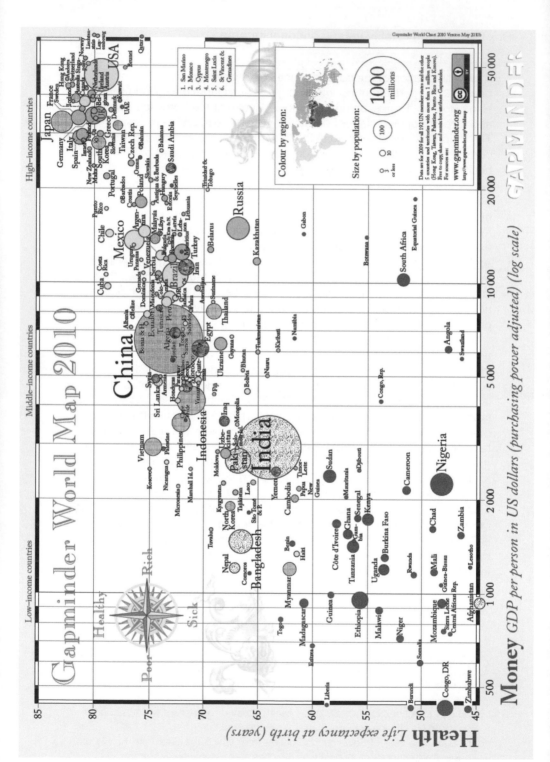

The Founex Declaration and the words by Jesse Jackson quoted above call for a more broad understanding of poverty. Poverty might be the result of a lack of financial resources but can also be caused by difficult or no access to education and health care; by difficult or no access to markets in order to sell products; by being denied civil rights or a decent job. Access to these resources was and still is very unequal and a strict economic approach is not satisfactory because it does not consider that—even when financial resources are available—these can be spent differently on the basis of different political choices (see Box 3.4). Development is, as was stated in the introduction, more than growth alone. On the same line, in its broader sense poverty outgrows its economic dimension and embraces everything that hinders the full development of a human being.

Our understanding of poverty as an impediment to the full development of a human being has been enhanced by several studies. Here the focus is on two very influential approaches that were proposed in the 1970s and 1980s, partially as a response to the failure of the fight against poverty through stimulating economic growth in developing countries. The first is the basic needs approach; the second the so-called capability approach.

Basic needs

Economic thinking considers human needs as infinite, ever changing over time and different in different cultures. Moreover, their satisfaction is considered to be the motor of growth. However, the moment we recognize the finitude of the Earth's ecosystem (including resources and sinks) and the gap in standards of living among different countries, it becomes unavoidable that we ask ourselves which needs should be satisfied first. This is the origin of the distinction between "basic" needs that should be addressed by society and "non-basic" needs that should be disregarded.

The basic needs approach was voiced in the 1970s in a wide range of studies and policy documents.[5] In the words of the Dag Hammarskjöld Institute, both developed and developing countries faced by then a crisis in development: in the North due to a sense of dissatisfaction notwithstanding material wealth; in the South due to the failure to meet the basic needs of the population for food, water, shelter, education, health care, and a decent job. These two crises are, for the basic needs approach advocates, related and caused by an economic system that focuses on things and their production and not on people and their development. Yet the goal of development should always be to develop people and not things. On the basis of this general principle, a new form of development is called for where the basic

---

5 Among the most influential were the already mentioned UN Founex Declaration (1971); the *Limits to Poverty* report published by the Bariloche foundation in 1974; the UNEP/UNCTAD Cocoyoc Declaration of 1974 and in 1975 the publication by the Dag Hammarskjöld Foundation *What Now? Another Development*; Schumacher's *Small is Beautiful* (1973); Galtung 1980; Max-Neef *et al.* 1989. See also Chapter 4 Section 1.

needs of the poorest people are met and fulfillment is assured of the human needs for expression, creativity, and conviviality. To achieve this, development should be self-reliant and in harmony with the environment.

The moral appeal of the basic needs approach was duly underlined by the already mentioned Conference on Science and Technology for Human Development organized by the World Council of Churches in 1974 (see Box 2.8): in a world of limited resources equity and justice require that the basic needs of the world's population are satisfied first.

Yet the distinction between basic and non-basic needs is problematic. First of all, because it is not that easy to draw a line between what should be considered a "basic" need in different societies and what should not. For example, is a computer a "basic" need in the knowledge society? Second, because it is unclear to whom or which institution the authority could be given to make this distinction without creating a form of "ecological dictatorship." A third difficulty is connected with the wish (that will become central, as we will see, to the concept of sustainable development) to consider also the needs of future generations. If needs are changing over time how can the present generation foresee the needs of future generations?

Manfred Max-Neef, a Chilean economist and ecologist, made an important contribution to the understanding of needs with the distinction between needs and satisfiers (Max-Neef *et al.* 1989). He states that "fundamental human needs are finite, few and classifiable" and "are the same in all cultures and in all historical periods. What changes, both over time and through cultures, is the way or the means by which the needs are satisfied" (Max-Neef *et al.* 1989: 20). Max-Neef identifies nine fundamental human needs: subsistence, protection, affection, understanding, participation, idleness (later re-named as recreation in the sense of leisure and time to reflect), creation, identity, and freedom. He also recognizes four dimensions of human life (in his terminology "existential needs"): being, having, doing, and interacting. Different dimensions ask for different satisfiers. For example: in the dimension "having," the need of subsistence calls for a shelter or food; in the dimension "doing," for work and rest; in the dimension "being," for health; in the dimension "interacting," for a social setting. Thus different satisfiers (shelter, food, work, rest, health, social setting) are connected with the same need (subsistence). From this one example it is already clear that satisfiers are not necessarily goods (artifacts). Max-Neef firmly opposes the idea that satisfaction of human needs can occur only through the consumption of goods. Goods are means to meet certain human needs and are not ends in themselves (Max-Neef *et al.* 1989: 27) in the same sense that "the purpose of the economy is to serve the people, and not the people to serve the economy" (1989: 23). As satisfiers vary among different communities, each and every community should have the right to decide through a process of participative consultation how they wish to satisfy their needs. No central institution should therefore be appointed with this task.

Max-Neef's approach thus helps to solve several difficulties connected to the concept of basic needs.

Capability approach

The capability approach proposed by the Indian economist and Nobel Prize laureate Amartya Sen (and almost contemporarily with and independently from him by the philosopher Martha Nussbaum) goes a step further than the basic needs approach. Satisfaction of basic needs is an essential but, in Sen's approach, insufficient condition to relieve people from poverty. A meaningful human life can be lived only if a person is free from wants (and thus his or her basic needs are met) *and* has the freedom of choice. Both forms of freedom (also referred to as "freedom from" and "freedom of") are essential for people to develop their capabilities as unique human beings. Freedom of choice includes classic civil rights such as the possibility to join a union, freedom of speech, participation in the political debate, and so on.[6] Governments should take care not only that these freedoms are guaranteed to all (e.g., by law), but also that citizens are in a position to actually exercise them. For example, to have the right to vote is not the same as being in the position to actually exercise this right. This depends on things such as education, transportation to the polling place, absence of intimidation, and so on. Governments have the duty to assure that their citizens can exercise their rights, their freedom: in short that they can fully develop their capability as human beings. In this sense, capabilities can serve as a way to assess the efficiency and equity of social policies.

Sen's capability approach had a profound influence also thanks to the work he has conducted with Mahbub ul Haq for the United Nations Development Programme (UNDP) on an alternative index of human welfare (see Chapter 4 Section 2). Sen's influence on the UNDP view on human development is evidenced in Box 3.5.

Civil rights and the fight against discrimination

As noted above and as is also clear from Box 3.5, in Sen's capability approach fighting poverty is not reduced to satisfying the basic needs but includes the right to actually exercise the freedom to choose the life we value. Essential to achieving this goal is respect and enforcement of what we are used to calling civil rights. The civil rights movement can be considered a very influential force in increasing attention to social injustice after WWII. It therefore merits brief consideration here.

In its most specific sense, the civil rights movement started in the U.S. was active in the period 1955–1968, and fought overt and covert racial discrimination. Yet discrimination can be intended more broadly than a race issue. It is then defined as treating some groups of people differently than other groups in a way that is detrimental to them and, to use Sen's terminology, reduces their freedom to choose on the basis of a characteristic they possess, such as language, skin color, or gender, that is in fact unrelated to the issue at hand. In this broader sense, the fight for civil rights includes the fight for the right to vote and be elected notwithstanding

---

6 It should be noted that, unlike Martha Nussbaum, Amartya Sen has never drafted a list of capabilities or freedoms.

Box 3.5 **UN Development Programme: human development defined**

Source: Box 1.1 in hdr.undp.org/en/media/hdr_1990_en_chap1.pdf (accessed September 26, 2011)

In its 1990 report the United Nation Development Programme defines human development with these words (1990: 10, Box 1.1):

> Human development is a process of enlarging people's choices. In prin-
> ciple, these choices can be infinite and change over time. But at all levels
> of development, the three essential ones are for people to lead a long
> and healthy life, to acquire knowledge and to have access to resources
> needed for a decent standard of living. If these essential choices are not
> available, many other opportunities remain inaccessible.
>
> But human development does not end there. Additional choices, highly
> valued by many people, range from political, economic and social free-
> dom to opportunities for being creative and productive, and enjoying per-
> sonal self-respect and guaranteed human rights.
>
> Human development has two sides: the formation of human capabili-
> ties—such as improved health, knowledge and skills–and the use people
> make of their acquired capabilities—for leisure, productive purposes or
> being active in cultural, social and political affairs. If the scales of human
> development do not finely balance the two sides, considerable human
> frustration may result.
>
> According to the concept of human development, income is clearly
> only one option that people would like to have, albeit an important one.
> But it is not the sum total of their lives. Development must, therefore, be
> more than just the expansion of income and wealth. Its focus must be
> people.

income or gender; the fight for universal education; the right of equal income for equal work and so on. Just to quote a few examples, Norway was one of the first countries to grant women the right to vote (1913) while American women had to wait until 1920 to obtain the same right, which is still denied to women in some countries today. The right to basic education for the lower classes emerged as an issue earlier in the British Health and Morals of Apprentices Act of 1802, quoted in Section 3.2. Yet it was only after 1850 that the call for universal education intensi-fied. One of the first countries to develop a system of universal primary education for both men and women was Prussia (Germany): here in 1871 90% of men and 85% of women could be defined as literate. As a comparison, around the same time in Italy almost 80% of the population was illiterate and this figure did not change much at the beginning of the twentieth century, at least in the south of Italy and among women (Clark 2008: 160-65). In nineteenth-century England tables were compiled with the different wages of children, women, and men doing the same job.[7] In short, the fight against discrimination has a long history and the broad

---

7   Today women are still paid less than men for the same type and level of work in many
    countries where discrimination is forbidden by law, including the Netherlands where

spectrum of social issues it covers can be considered a constitutive element of the social dimension of sustainability.

3.4 **Fighting for a better world after WWII: universal human rights**

The message of the preceding section is that fighting poverty is broader than fighting for the fulfillment of basic needs and that eliminating discrimination means more than enforcing civil rights by law. Both include and refer to fundamental issues such as freedom, human dignity, and economic and social equality, in short, to universal human rights. Human rights are "what makes the second half of the twentieth century such an important moment of world history," as Stéphane Hessel, one of the contributors to the United Nations Universal Declaration on Human Rights (UNUDHR; UN 1948), is reported to have said (quoted in Emmerij *et al.* 2004: 7).

The idea that individuals have inalienable rights by the simple fact that they are human beings is one of those concepts that developed slowly over centuries. It might be compared to a river that runs underneath and is fed by several religious, scholarly, and political streams. Some of these have been briefly touched on above: the call by the church to respect human dignity; the fight for universal voting rights; for the right to universal education; for freedom of association; for equal pay for equal work and against racial discrimination. Sometimes the river surfaces and spreads on land with particular force. So it did in the late eighteenth century when the call for freedom, equality, and brotherhood was loudly shouted during the French Revolution (1789). As early as 1776 the same sentiment found its way into the U.S. Declaration of Independence where it is forcefully attested that "all men are created equal." The United Nations Universal Declaration on Human Rights might be seen as the lake where all the streams converge and re-emerge from it strengthened and with a better view of the reciprocal connections.

Notwithstanding the long history that fed the UNUDHR, it is only with this declaration that the idea of universal human rights took a firm hold in international and national policy. Paradoxically, the cruelty of WWII, the suffering of the civil population during and immediately after the war and above all the unspeakable, inhumane conditions under which innocent people were held in the Nazi concentrations camps paved the way for the recognition of the need to attribute inalienable rights to individuals by the simple fact that they are human beings.

---

women earn 6% less than men of the same age doing the same job with similar social security packages (Eurofound 2007). Possible explanations for this phenomenon that do not point in the direction of direct discrimination may be found in Anger and Schmidt 2008.

Adopted by the UN General Assembly on December 10, 1948, the UNUDHR has not the legal force of a treaty, yet it is a fundamental constitutive document of the United Nations and therefore is considered by many as part of customary international law. Moreover, even though not formally legally binding, the Declaration has been adopted in or influenced most national constitutions since 1948. It is, therefore, not surprising that more and more governments, NGOs, and individuals appeal to its principles for the protection of their human rights.

The first article of the UNUDHR affirms that "all human beings are born free and equal in dignity and rights," and article two specifies that rights and freedom apply to all humans "without distinction of any kind, such as race, color, sex, language, religion, political or other opinion, national or social origin, property, birth or other status." The main body of the declaration is formed by four main parts. The first one (articles 3–11) states the rights of the individual, such as the right to life and the prohibition of slavery. The second (articles 12–17) constitutes the rights of the individual in civil and political society. The third (articles 18–21) is concerned with spiritual, public, and political freedoms such as freedom of religion and freedom of association. The fourth (articles 22–27) sets out social, economic, and cultural rights. It is not difficult to recognize in these four parts the influences of the traditions remembered above: freedom rights (such as the freedom of thought, conscience and religion; the freedom of movement; the freedom of association); civil rights (such as the right to vote; the right to be treated equally before the law); and broader social rights (such as the right to work, to decent pay, to equal pay for equal work, to health care, and to education). The main achievement of the Declaration is, as stated above, to have assured the breakthrough of the idea that individuals are entitled to these rights for the sole reason that they are human beings (Glendon 2002).

3.5 Concluding remarks: growth versus development, again

This chapter and the previous one have offered a quick review of the rich tradition that supports the view that development cannot be equated with economic growth because, to quote again the Dag Hammarskjöld Foundation's report (1975: 7): "development is a whole; it is an integral, value-loaded, cultural process; it encompasses the natural environment, social relations, education, production, consumption and well-being."[8]

---

8   That the relation between the concept of development and the concept of growth was widely debated in the 1960s, 1970s, and 1980s should by now be clear. Alongside the already quoted literature, see also UN 1962; the Arusha Declaration written by the Tanzanian President Julius Nyerere (1967); the UN Stockholm Declaration (1972); and the UNEP/UNCTAD Cocoyoc Declaration (1974). See also Dresner 2002: 70 and Szirmai 2005: 6-8.

The need to distinguish growth and development is thus not new and, even though many prefer to think so, it is not a prerogative of alternative or leftish think-tanks. It was identified by Simon Kuznets, one of the designers of the national account system. To quote his words (1962):

> As a general formula, the desirability of as high and sustained growth rate as is compatible with the costs that society is willing to bear is valid; but in using it to judge economic problems and policies, distinctions must be kept in mind between quantity and quality of growth, between its cost and return and between the short and the long run.

To stress the need to consider the quality of growth alongside its quantity, the expression "quality of life" started to be used in the 1960s (see also Chapter 1 Section 4). Quality of life is surely a catchy phrase. An easy way to grasp its meaning is to contrast it with standard of living. The standard of living of a certain country represents the per capita rate of consumption of purchased goods and services. It is thus quantifiable and its increase or decrease can be measured by changes in the gross domestic product (GDP). Quality of life on the other hand is a qualitative term that relates broadly to human well-being. Most of its components are not quantifiable and cannot be directly related to an increase in income or GDP (see Box 3.6).

Box 3.6 **Indicators of quality of life**

Source: Douthwaite 1999: 12

The following list compiled by R. Douthwaite gives an indication of factors that play a role in determining the quality of life.

1. The quantity of goods and services produced and consumed (standard of living)
2. The quality of the environment people enjoy, including space, energy, natural resources, and plant and animal species
3. The fraction of their time available for leisure
4. How fairly—or unfairly—the available income is distributed
5. How good or bad working conditions are
6. How easy it is to get a job
7. The safety of our future
8. How healthy we are
9. The level of cultural activity, standard of education, and then ease of access to it
10. The quality of the housing available
11. The chance to develop a satisfactory religious or spiritual life
12. The strength of one's family and community ties

One may argue that economic growth leads to a higher standard of living (the first point in the list in Box 3.6) but not necessarily for the majority of citizens in the society considered (point four on the list). A better quality of life on the other hand implies that the economic and social structures that impede the full mobilization and participation of all citizens are changed (see e.g., points 5, 6, 7, 8, and 9 in the list in Box 3.6), in line with Sen's discussion of human capabilities summarized in Chapter 3 Section 3 and the definition of development given in the introduction. Very recently the Commission on the Measurement of Economic Performance and Social Progress, chaired by economist Joseph Stiglitz, also pointed clearly to this distinction by stating: "quality of life is a broader concept than economic production and living standards. It includes the full range of factors that influences what we value in living, reaching beyond its material side" (Stiglitz *et al*. 2009: 41) and "quality of life includes the full range of factors that make life worth living, including those that are not traded in markets and not captured by monetary measures" (2009: 58).

Notwithstanding this strong tradition, today political leaders and captains of industry regularly confuse quantity and quality of growth. Rising GDPs and higher standards of living are often the end in mind for political intervention and business strategies, scarcely considering issues such as those discussed in this chapter. Or, when these issues are considered, far too often the credo is that they will be solved by and thanks to economic growth (for a notable exception see Box 3.7). Yet, to paraphrase again the words of Jesse Jackson, a rising tide may not lift the boats that are stuck at the bottom.

True, as was mentioned in the introduction, the amount and complexity of the social issues is astounding, and if they are considered together with environmental challenges even more so. This is because creating a better, more equitable world seems impossible without posing further stress on the environment. To remember an example referred to above, eradication of poverty is considered to be at odds with conservation of natural resources and abatement of pollution. If this is so, then humanity is caught in a perfect "Catch-22" situation: we are living beyond our means, and yet we will need to consume more so that people living in developing countries can enjoy the same freedoms (in Sen's understanding of the word) as people living in developed countries. This conclusion seems unavoidable. And yet it was questioned by the UN in 1984 when the World Commission on Environment and Development was set up and given the task of looking at ways to escape the Catch-22 situation and reconcile the concern for economic growth with the concern for the natural environment and for social development. To this effort the next chapter is dedicated.

Box 3.7 **Report by the Commission on the Measurement of Economic Performance and Social Progress**

In 2008 Nicolas Sarkozy, President of the French Republic, asked renown professors in economics and sociology:

> to identify the limits of GDP as an indicator of economic performance and social progress, including the problems with its measurement; to consider what additional information might be required for the production of more relevant indicators of social progress; to assess the feasibility of alternative measurement tools, and to discuss how to present the statistical information in an appropriate way (Stiglitz *et al.* 2009: 8).

The Commission on the Measurement of Economic Performance and Social Progress was then formed. The Commission's report, published in 2009, states that there is a need to understand the appropriate use of each measure. It also insists that the GDP is not wrong as such, but is wrongly used when it is considered the only measure of a country's long-term prosperity and well-being. It should therefore be integrated with instruments measuring other aspects of the economic life (such as real household incomes) and the social and environmental dimensions of societal well-being. In one word: sustainability (2009: 8).

Referring to the major economic and social crisis that hit the world in 2008 some members of the Commission observed:

> one of the reasons why the crisis took many by surprise is that our measurement system failed us and/or market participants and government officials were not focusing on the right set of statistical indicators . . . perhaps had there been more awareness of the limitations of standard metrics, like GDP, there would have been less euphoria over economic performance in the years prior to the crisis; metrics which incorporated assessments of sustainability (e.g., increasing indebtedness) would have provided a more cautious view of economic performance (2009: 8-9).

4

Toward sustainable development

> The optimist proclaims that we live in the best of all possible worlds; and
> the pessimist fears this is true (James Branch Cabell, *The Silver Stallion*,
> 1926).

In 1980, 35 years after the end of WWII, the world was far from having reached that level of prosperity that was envisioned at Bretton Woods. To mention some numbers: an estimated 800 million people were so poor that they were not able to secure for themselves the basic necessities for life. Average life expectancy in sub-Saharan Africa was about 45 years while in most fortunate countries in Southeast Asia it was 10 to 15 years longer; 25 million children below the age of five died every year from easily cured diseases such as diarrhea (ICIDI or Brandt report, 1980: 50 and 55). The natural environment was under major stress, as we have seen in Chapter 2, while financial resources that could have been used to alleviate poverty or restore the environment were thrown into the bottomless pit of the cold war (ICIDI 1980: 14 and 117). The North–South divide was deepening: the interests of the South seemed irreconcilable with those of the North.

As already noted, one of the most evident conflicts of interest between developing and developed countries ran along the divide between the concern for economic growth and the concern for environmental protection. To solve this conflict, the challenge was to integrate environmental considerations into policies directed toward economic development. This was the seemingly impossible task that the United Nations presented to the World Commission on Environment and Development (WCED) in 1984.[1]

---

1 Although in the mandate by the UN the focus was still on the environment, the commission was also asked to consider in its analysis the relation between environmental

This chapter examines first the concept of sustainable development as exposed by the WCED (Section 4.1) and then the efforts carried on to reconcile growth and environment (Sections 4.2–4.4) and growth, environment, and social justice (Sections 4.5–4.6). In these sections we will also refer to the institutional activities that stemmed from the call by the WCED for a more equitable and environmentally friendly form of development. Then (Section 4.7), the key question is raised: "What is needed to speed up the change toward a more sustainable world?" Concluding remarks on the interplay of the societal, organizational, and individual level in the process of change toward sustainability close this section.

4.1　**The WCED and sustainable development**

The WCED was the last of three commissions created by the United Nations to study the reasons behind the debt crisis and to offer solutions to improve the living conditions of the populations in developing countries.[2] The WCED, chaired by the former Prime Minister of Norway, Gro Harlem Brundtland, published its report in 1987 under the title *Our Common Future*. Central to the report is the concept of sustainable development presented as a "framework for the integration of environment policies and development strategies" (WCED 1987: 40), where development strategies are seen as focusing primarily on economic growth. The association of development with economic growth is not surprising considering the mandate received by the WCED from the UN and its background: the wish of the South to see recognized its right to consider poverty as the worst form of pollution and its responsibility to eradicate it first (see also Chapter 2).

A few lines after the sentence quoted above, sustainable development is defined by the WCED as a development that "seeks to meet the needs and aspirations of the present without compromising the ability to meet those of the future" (1987: 40).[3]

Sustainable development is here presented as a matter of equity: equity among people living now (meeting "the needs and aspirations of the present") and equity between the present and future generations ("without compromising the ability to

---

concerns and resources on one side and people and (economic) development on the other side (WCED 1987: ix). For the historic background and the political significance of the WCED or Brundtland report, see Dresner 2002: 64-65.

2　The WCED was created after a suggestion by the Norwegian Government to the UN (von Weizsäcker 1994: 99). Of the other two commissions, the already quoted Independent Commission on International Development Issues (the Brandt Commission) started its work in 1977 and the Independent Commission on Disarmament and Security Issues (the Palme Commission) in 1980.

3　The reference to *aspirations* is not present in the first definition of sustainable development given in the report itself (see, e.g., p. 8) and is usually omitted by authors using the Brundtland definition. We prefer this definition as it seems to point beyond basic, material needs.

meet those of the future"). The WCED definition, mostly referred to as the Brundt-land definition, became a classic, and the term sustainable development of wide-spread use (Elliott 2001: 25). This success rests to some extent on the use of rhetorical elements in the WCED definition, on its appeal to our responsibility to leave our common home no worse than we found it and the sentiment of guilt it inspires for the actual state of affairs. This strong emotional accent, however, also had a negative spin-off: it seems to prevent a clear understanding of the term sustainable development, of the definition itself and its implications (Reid 1995; Roberts and Cohen 2002; Sutton 2007). To avoid misinterpretations, it is therefore important to analyze the WCED definition of sustainable development and its evolution. Two main questions have then to be answered: what is the meaning of "needs" in the definition? And: how is the appeal to future generations to be understood?

The Brundtland definition of sustainable development is intended, as stated above, to constitute a framework for the integration of environmental consider-ations in strategies directed to the eradication of poverty through economic growth. In this context, the use of the term "needs" in the definition can be interpreted as a reference to our responsibility to combat poverty now and to prevent poverty in the future. Although the concept of (human) needs is not discussed at length in the report, there is a clear reference to enough food, water supply, shelter, energy, jobs (livelihood), and health care (WCED 1987: 55). All those are "basic needs," a well-known concept from the development agenda of the 1970s (see Chapter 3 Sec-tion 3). The first appeal of the definition is therefore for using the world's resources to meet the basic needs of the world's population. It is a plea for the eradication of poverty and moderation in the use of limited resources (see also Boxes 4.1 and 4.2).

Box 4.1 **Needs**

The definition of sustainability proposed by the Brundtland commission refers to the needs and aspirations of the present and future generations alike. One of the difficulties connected with implementing sustainability is directly related to the complexity of the concept "needs," in general, and in particular the (supposed) infinity of needs and their changing content in time and in different cultures.

The Brundtland report refers to "basic needs" such as water and shelter, even though it does not exclude the pursuit of human expectations. In Chapter 3 Section 3 we have already discussed some difficulties connected with the notion of basic needs and presented the interesting approach taken by Max-Neef. Box 4.2 discusses the theme of how to foresee future genera-tions' needs.

The second half of the WCED definition prescribes the conditions under which this task has to take place: without compromising the ability of future genera-tions to meet their own needs. Although the appeal to future generations will be

Box 4.2 **Looking forward: how far is far enough?**

In discussing the definition given by the WCED we observed that it asks us to consider the needs of future generations without posing any limit to the time span. This unlimited time dimension constitutes, however, one of the difficulties in implementing sustainability. In considering the consequences of a specific decision uncertainty increases with the length of the time considered (on uncertainty see Tacconi 2000: 62-63).

If we pose a limit, though, it is not easy to agree on exactly how far we should look forward before calling a decision sustainable. How far is far enough? The lifetime of our children, say seventy years from now? Some consider this a long period of time indeed and agree with John Maynard Keynes in saying that the whole exercise is useless, because "on the long run we are all dead." Others consider seventy years quite a short time span, pointing to the persistence of pollution on one side and geological time on the other side (Kroonenberg 2006: 13ff.).

In Box 4.1 and Chapter 3 Section 3 we have seen a similar difficulty in coping with the concept of needs. There we quoted Max-Neef's view that while basic needs stay the same, satisfiers of these needs among communities and generations will change over time. Max-Neef insists in his work that a consequence of his perspective on needs is that each community should define for itself which satisfiers cope with its needs. This brings us back to the problem of foreseeing, if not directly the needs, at least the satisfiers of future generations' needs, to be able to assess if a society is sustainable, i.e., not violating the right of future generations to satisfy their own needs.

Arnold Heertje, a Dutch economist, offers a first step in resolving this issue. He proposes to assume that the present generation is able to "relate" or "identify" with their children and grandchildren. This opens the possibility to identify (supposed) preferences of future generations for needs' satisfaction and take these into account when decisions are taken on, for example, giving up nature for a new road. As Heertje appropriately notes, we will know if we got it right or not only when the next generation makes their assessment of the world as we have left it (Heertje 2006).

A second step is taken by industrialist Stephen Schmidheiny (1992) when he notices that:

> some argue that we have no responsibility for the future, as we cannot know its needs. This is partly true. But it takes no great leap of reason to assume that our offspring will require breathable air, drinkable water, productive soils and oceans, a predictable climate, and abundant plant and animal species on the planet they will share (1992: 11).

popularized as an appeal to the generation of our (grand)children, in the definition there is no indication of any limit to the time span to be considered. The focus is on preserving chances for future generations to meet their own needs in the very long term. In the eyes of the WCED this implies taking care of the natural environment through conservation and improvement of the resource base. In other words, the generation living now has to be aware that there are limits to the exploitation of natural resources and, in using these resources to meet the needs of the present, has the duty to renew them or to create alternatives for the generation to come (WCED 1987: 49).

At this point, it is important to notice that the Brundtland commission, differently than authors such as Rachel Carson, Donella and Dennis Meadows, James Lovelock, Herman Daly, and John Cobb, does not see the limits to our resource base as absolute ones. The WCED does not see the future of the world as one of "ever increasing environmental decay, poverty, and hardship in an ever more polluted world among ever decreasing resources" (1987: 1). The reason for this optimism is that the limitations we are confronted with are "imposed by the present state of technology and social organization on environmental resources and by the ability of the biosphere to absorb the effects of human activities" (1987: 8). Technology can be improved and organizations can be changed "to make way for a new era of economic growth" (1987: 8).

Even though the Brundtland Commission does not recognize absolute limits to resource use,[4] it does recognize relative ones due to the "present state of technology and social organization" (1987: 8). The existence of limits (absolute or not) makes sharing among different communities living now and among the present generation and future ones necessary. Different scholars have observed that if we accept the notion of limits then we have to confront choices with a moral dimension at every point of the economic process.[5] In the words of one of them, Nicholas Georgescu-Roegen: "What do we need to make? What are the real long-term costs of production, and who is required to pay them? What is truly in the interest of man, not in the present only, but as a continuing species?" (quoted in Reid 1995: 27).

Our Common Future answers these questions calling for an equitable and just distribution of resources between poor and rich in the present generation (inter-generational equity) and between the present and future generations (intra-generational equity). Only when equity and social justice are taken into account, will the results of the process of sharing be fair and therefore sustainable. It is a call for social justice that is reminiscent of the eco-justice literature and of the appeal by the World Council of Churches in 1974 and in 1975 by the Dag Hammarskjöld

---

4 On this point see Chapter 2 and in particular Box 2.2.
5 See, e.g., *Limits to Growth* (Meadows *et al.* 1972: 140 in the Italian edition and 2005: 255); *What Now? Another Development* (Dag Hammarskjöld Foundation 1975: 6-7 and 25-26); Galtung 1980: 24; Daly 1992: 21.

Foundation's report *What Now? Another Development* for redistribution of wealth and opportunities through sharing.[6]

The point that has to be emphasized here is that the reference to equity and social justice in *Our Common Future* broadens the scope of sustainable development in a very significant way. The concept of sustainable development that, as noted above, was introduced as a framework to integrate environmental concerns and economic development includes a third concern: the concern for a just and equitable society. Sustainable development integrates economic growth, environmental protection, and social justice. In reviewing the progress toward sustainable development in 1997, the UN summarizes this point as follows: "the achievement of sustainable development requires the integration of its economic, environmental and social components" (Earth Summit II, 1997: chs. 1, 3). As far as the authors know, this is the first time that sustainable development was seen as involving three interrelated dimensions: an economic, a social, and an environmental one. In other words, in the context of sustainable development, the pursuit of a better standard of living through economic growth has to be qualified twice. On one side growth should be directed to the satisfaction of the most immediate needs of humanity and the support of their full development (aspirations). On the other side it should prevent in the process any irremediable damage to Earth's resources so that future generation will also be able to meet their needs and aspirations. In short, sustainable development aims at a better quality of life for all now and in the future (see Box 4.3 and Chapter 3 Section 5).

Box 4.3 **The three levels of sustainability: the level of society**

In the three levels of sustainability (TLS) framework, a sustainable society is defined by its aim to improve quality of life and positively impact on all three dimensions of sustainable development: economic value, social value, and environmental value. In Chapters 1, 2 and 3 we have discussed several issues connected with specific dimensions. Sustainable development asks us to look not only at the issues in isolation but also at the links among them. For example deforestation (an environmental issue) is in some regions linked with poverty (need for fuel and for marginal land to grow food crops) and excessive consumption in rich countries, both social issues.

The drawing below visualizes this interconnectedness of the three dimensions of sustainable societies:

---

6   If we believe in the existence of absolute limits to economic growth and are less sanguine on the role of technology (see Box 2.4), Brundtland's call for equity and social justice is indeed not weakened but strengthened. See also the literature quoted in note 5 and the report of the World Council of Churches' Conference on Science and Technology for Human Development (1974: 5).

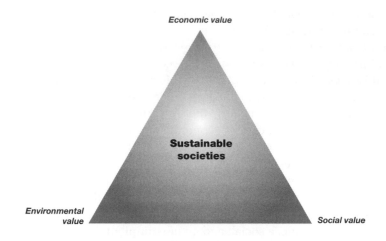

4.2 **Measuring sustainable development**

In *Limits to Growth* (1972) the MIT team observes that if we do not know where the world is heading, at which velocity, and which forces are at play, we will neither develop the ability nor find the motivation to steer away from the current, unsustainable path. They insisted that we need scientific knowledge to inform our choices and that new indicators should be developed to measure not only the standard of living—as the GDP does—but also the quality of life of a certain community.

With this statement the MIT team follows the same track as Simon Kuznets who warned that "the welfare of a nation can scarcely be inferred from a measurement of national income" (1934) and that "goals for more growth should specify more growth of what and for what" (1962).[7] On the same line Kenneth Boulding (1966) stressed the necessity to develop a new form of economy, where the indicator of success is not ever growing production and consumption, "but the nature, extent, quality and complexity of the total capital stock, both including in this the state of the human bodies and minds." All these insights may be summarized by the words of Robert Kennedy (1968): the GDP "measures everything in short, except that which makes life worthwhile."

After the WCED report, *Our Common Future*, was published, scholars focused on the design of sustainability indicators and sustainability indexes in which social and environmental concerns would be included alongside a measure of economic growth.

---

7 Both quotes by Kuznets are from Cobb *et al.* 1995.

In a recent report, *Measuring Sustainable Development*, OECD Senior Economist Candice Stevens writes:

> Progressing towards sustainable development implies that the objectives of increasing economic efficiency and material wealth must take into account social and environmental objectives. Explicit in the concept is a focus on inter-generational equity, implying that future generations should have opportunities similar to those now available. Sustainable development also puts emphasis on equity that applies both across and within countries . . .
>
> Indicators are needed to illustrate to policy makers and the public the linkages and trade-offs between economic, environmental and social values; to evaluate the longer-term implications of current decisions and behaviours, and to monitor progress towards sustainable develop ment goals by establishing baseline conditions and trends. But simple and easily-understood measures that do not compromise the underlying complexity of sustainable development have been difficult to formulate (Stevens 2005: 2).

The task to devise proper indicators is never an easy one. One of the challenges is that some indicators may seem adequate even though they are actually counterproductive. Former World Bank economist Herman Daly and theologian John Cobb quote the example of the U.S. military that for a while assessed its dentists by the number of teeth pulled out. This is, of course, not a good output indicator if the end in mind is to help soldiers maintain healthy teeth (Daly and Cobb 1989: 148-49). On the same line, if the end in mind is to achieve a better quality of life, a measure of the increase in produced goods and services (such as the GDP) cannot aspire to the role of indicator. New ones have to be devised. In this process there are other issues that have to be taken into account such as the quality of available data, the expenses involved in collecting new data, their relative weight, and level of aggregation (see Morse 2004). Subjectivity cannot be ruled out in dealing with most of these issues (Morse 2004).

A major difficulty in designing a *sustainability* index is that while sustainability is an aggregated concept, indicators measure only individual aspects of its dimensions. If in a community air pollution is going up, water pollution down and literacy rates up, is this community moving toward sustainability? Champions of strong sustainability would answer in the negative, because in their eyes compensation between different dimensions (natural, social, economic) is not possible (see Section 4.3 and Table 4.1). If compensation is allowed, then the next step is to agree—at least inside a certain community—on how to weight different dimensions of sustainability against each other. Until now there is no consensus on this point and there is therefore no, universally, accepted standard for sustainability against which we can pronounce a society as definitely unsustainable or on its way to a more sustainable state.[8] Some authors do not see this as an acute problem because:

8 For more unresolved issues see Pearce and Barbier 2000: 85; Bell and Morse 2003: 13-18.

Box 4.4 **Index of Sustainable Economic Welfare**
Source: Jackson 2007: 1-2

"The basis for the index is consumer expenditure. Positive and negative adjustments are made to this basis to account for a series of social, economic and environmental factors. For example, the values of household labor and volunteering are added to the index, together with public expenditure on health and education. On the negative side, the ISEW subtracts environmental costs associated with habitat loss, localized pollution, depletion of nonrenewable resources and climate change; social costs associated with crime, divorce, commuting and unequal income distribution; and the health costs of accidents on the road and in the workplace. Some additional adjustments are made to account for net capital growth and net international position. These may be positive or negative depending on the particular economic situation in each year.

In summary:

ISEW = Personal consumer expenditure
– adjustment for income inequality
+ public expenditures (deemed non-defensive)
+ value of domestic labor and volunteering
+ economic adjustments
– defensive private expenditures
– costs of environmental degradation
– depreciation of natural capital"

---

the dispute over the relative importance of competing values lies at the heart of politics. If an indicator inspires citizens to move from knowledge to action, it is sure to be value-laden and thus political. Avoiding controversy in the name of consensus does not transcend politics; it means siding with the status quo (Cobb 2000: 2).

Notwithstanding these difficulties, from the end of the 1980s on, different candidates for a sustainability index were proposed.[9] Here the focus is on three promising ones, the Index of Sustainable Economic Welfare; the Human Development Index; and the Well-being Index.

---

9 For a critical analysis of up to ten different possibilities see Pearce and Barbier 2000; even more candidates are discussed in Stiglitz *et al.* 2009: 62-71. See also Daly and Cobb 1989: 69-84. Recently, the need to cooperate and to achieve more synergy between all initiatives working on new systems of wealth measurement was expressed during the 2nd OECD World Forum on "Statistics, Knowledge and Policy" held in Istanbul in June 2007. See www.oecd.org/site/0,3407,en_21571361_31938349_1_1_1_1_1,00.html and www.oecd.org/progress (accessed September 10, 2011).

In 1989 Herman Daly and John Cobb suggested complementing the GDP with twenty other indicators to take into account social and environmental liabilities, costs, and revenues, alongside economic and financial ones. Even though specific indicators were devised to measure different aspects of each dimension individually, Daly and Cobb insisted on the point that the social, environmental, and financial dimensions of sustainability are intertwined. They named the result the Index of Sustainable Economic Welfare (or ISEW; see Box 4.4).

Herman Daly and John Cobb calculated the ISEW index for the U.S.A. in the years 1950–1986 and plotted it against the GDP for the same years. The results were striking: the ISEW shows a very different pattern of growth than the GDP. After the mid-1970s, the ISEW no longer rises with rising GDP but actually falls "largely as a result of growing income inequality, the exhaustion of resources, and the failure to invest adequately to sustain the economy in the future" (Daly and Cobb 1989: 455; see also von Weizsäcker *et al.* 1998: 273). Similar results were found for different countries both at national and local level (see Fig. 4.1 which plots the GDP against the ISEW for the Netherlands; see also for example Pulselli *et al.* 2005 and Stockhammer *et al.* 1997). The conclusion is unavoidable that, after a certain standard of living is reached, the total quality of life of a community decreases even though the GDP increases.

Figure 4.1 **GDP vs. ISEW for the Netherlands**

Source: community.foe.co.uk/tools/isew/international.html (accessed March 12, 2008); reproduced by courtesy of Friends of the Earth (England, Wales & N. Ireland), August 2011

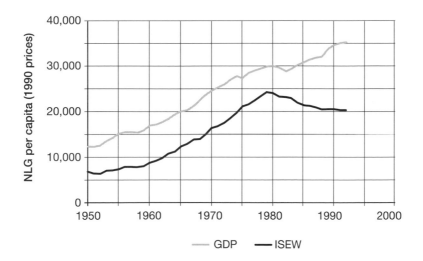

One year after Herman Daly and John Cobb, the Pakistani economist Mahbub ul Haq proposed the Human Development Index (HDI) as a measure of the development of a country in economic and social terms. The focus on people or "human development" originated with Amartya Sen, the Indian economist and Nobel laureate introduced in Chapter 3 Section 3. Sen stresses in his work that a society's welfare should not only be judged by its level of income but also according to people's capability to lead the life they value and act meaningfully in their community. Human capability to act is impaired by poverty, but also by lack of knowledge, infirmity, unsafe communities, and undemocratic social patterns. The HDI represents the first attempt to measure how well a society is able to support the development of its citizens' capabilities. It aims to put people, not things, at the center of development policies. In this respect it differs widely from measures such as the ISEW that are intended more as adjustments of the GDP to take into account some costs and revenues not considered by it.[10]

Alongside the GDP as a measure of the standard of living in a society, the HDI includes two components to measure citizens' capacity to conduct a good life: an indicator of a long and healthy life (life expectancy at birth) and an indicator of the level of education attainment (literacy of the adult population and enrollment in primary, secondary, and tertiary education). As Stephen Morse (2004: 156) noted, "the three components of the HDI resonate loudly with the major concerns of many: education, health and income." The three components of the HDI could be considered basic human needs, even though Amartya Sen insists that a distinction should be kept between capabilities and basic needs (as we have seen in Chapter 3 Section 3). An important feature of the HDI is that it is endorsed by the United Nations Development Programme (UNDP) and that it has been used since 1993 for the UNDP annual Human Development Report.

The HDI was designed as a measure of human development and, therefore, as a measure of sustainable development it is incomplete because it does not contain indicators for the environmental dimension.[11] From an environmentalist perspective the HDI was also criticized for its anthropocentrism: it sets human development as the end and everything else as a means (Ravaillon 1997). Moreover, it includes the GDP as one of only three factors in its calculations with the result that there is no dramatic difference between GDP and HDI. The ISEW and indexes constructed in a similar way—such as the Genuine Progress Indicator developed by Cobb *et al.* (1995)—are therefore seen as the most suitable complements to the GDP to assess a society's stance toward sustainability.[12]

The third and last effort to measure sustainability considered here is the Well-being Index proposed by the Commission on the Measurement of Economic Performance and Social Progress (also called the Stiglitz Commission) by its chairperson,

10 See Cobb 2000 and Morse 2004: ch. 4. See on growth vs. development Section 4.1 and Chapter 3 Section 5.
11 For a critical discussion of the HDI and the few efforts made to "green" it, see Morse 2004: ch. 4.
12 Daly and Cobb (1989: 76ff.) level a similar criticism to the alternative measure of welfare proposed by Nordhaus and Tobin in 1972 and Zolotas in 1981. See also Cobb 2000 and Venetoulis and Talberth 2007.

Professor Joseph E. Stiglitz. Interestingly the Stiglitz Commission warns that a distinction should be made between indexes measuring the well-being and quality of life of people and indexes measuring sustainability. Sustainability needs measures that do not only focus on the *present condition* of people, such as existing indexes on standard of living, well-being, and quality of life. Sustainability indicators assess whether the current level of well-being can be maintained *in the future*. In this sense a sustainability index tries to predict that future (Stiglitz *et al.* 2009: 16 and 61). It is indeed important to distinguish measures directed toward the recent past and present from measures directed toward the future. The main focus of measures directed toward the future should be on the possibility to maintain or increase the current quality of life on the long term. Indexes that adjust the GDP for social and environmental expenditures—such as the ISEW—fall short of this target, as the Commission notes (Stiglitz *et al.* 2009: 67). Though this is true, a holistic approach is essential to achieve the aim of sustainability that is, as repeatedly said, a better quality of life for the people living *now* and in the *future*.

Along the lines taken by the authors discussed above, the Commission also states that well-being and quality of life are multidimensional concepts. Though the Commission recognizes that there is still debate on what exactly these dimensions are, it also recognizes that (Stiglitz *et al.* 2009: 15):

> there is a consensus that quality of life depends on people's health and education, their everyday activities (which include the right to a decent job and housing), their participation in the political process, the social and natural environment in which they live, and the factors shaping their personal and economic security.[13]

An interesting addition to the debate is that, for the Commission, measurement of quality of life should include both objective and subjective (such as happiness and satisfaction with one's own life) data; should assess inequality among people, socioeconomic groups, generations and gender; and should consider linkages among the different dimensions (Stiglitz *et al.* 2009: 15-16 and 54-57).

In the eyes of the Commission, sustainability measures should focus on maintaining and increasing the quality and quantity of critical capital, whether natural, social, physical, or human, because "the capacity of future generations to have standards of well-being at least equal to ours depends upon our passing them sufficient amounts of all the assets that matter for well-being" (Stiglitz *et al.* 2009: 72). Quite surprisingly, the Commission seems to defend a weak approach to the issue of which natural capital should be maintained (see Table 4.1 on page 89), though they admit that in devising appropriate measures for sustainability much work is still to be done.

In conclusion, it is fair to state that progress has been made in the search for indicators to measure how sustainable our societies are. It can also be said that

13 Further discussion of these features of quality of life can be found in Stiglitz *et al.* 2009: 44-54. See also Chapter 3 Section 5 and Box 3.7.

influential institutions are gradually moving away from the traditional economic measurements such as GDP per capita toward a more comprehensive system of indicators that reflect the well-being and quality of life in societies. Paradoxically, the recent, severe economic crisis has been considered a new wake-up call. As the Stiglitz Commission wrote (2009: 9):

> The economic crisis is teaching us a very important lesson: those attempting to guide the economy and our societies are like pilots trying to steering [*sic*] a course without a reliable compass. The decisions they (and we as individual citizens) make depend on what we measure, how good our measurements are and how well our measures are understood. We are almost blind when the metrics on which action is based are ill-designed or when they are not well understood.

Change is thus necessary and the direction of change by now is known. Considering the complexity of the challenge, it may, however, still take quite some time and combined effort before political leadership, captains of industry, and some influential multilateral institutions start to change the simple rhetoric about economic growth as a cure for all societal problems.

4.3 **Reconciling growth and environment**

In Chapter 2 we saw that for decades the major critics of unbridled economic growth were people concerned with the environment. The concept of sustainable development proposed by the WCED paved the way for reconciliation between economic growth and environmental protection. In the debate that ensued on the means needed to achieve this goal all possible positions were taken: from a firm belief in the capacity of the free market economy to bring about a more sustainable world if helped by a mild form of state intervention; to an even firmer call to abandon the fixation on growth and create a new economic system in which material growth is substituted by immaterial development, via redirecting market forces to bring about sustainability through a better use of resources.[14]

At the core of the tension between concern for the environment and concern for economic growth lies the issue of the use of natural resources and sinks. Modern economies are focused on growth in throughput and consumption and this poses a strain on environmental resources and services (see Chapter 2). The expanding

---

14 Champion of the first view, that the free market economy is the only way to prosperity, is Friedman (2005); of the second, although with different nuances, are Meadows *et al.* (1972: ch. 6 and 2005: 254ff.); WCED (1987: 53); Schumacher (1973: ch.1 and 2); and of the last one, harnessing market forces for sustainability, von Weizsäcker *et al.* (1998) and McDonough and Braungart (2002). See, for a similar categorization of different perspectives, Bell and Morse 2003: 8.

scale of human activities, boosted in recent years to a new all-time record by the growth of the Brazilian, Russian, Indian, and Chinese economies, has exacerbated the problem and has given new force to the call for a more sustainable use of the limited resources of our planet.[15]

What is implied by a sustainable use of natural resources? Most scholars agree that sustainability requires that we should leave the world no worse off than we found it and that we should leave to future generations the natural basis they will need to cope with their own needs. Disagreement starts when we have to detail what these broad principles mean for daily life on one side and what exactly future generations will consider a good material basis to satisfy their needs on the other (see also Chapter 3 Section 3 and Box 4.1). Here, too, answers cover the whole spectrum, from the need to completely refrain from the use of natural resources because of the damage that humans have already inflicted on the complex texture of nature, to unrestricted use referring to the uncertainty about future generations' needs and our capacity to find new, innovative solutions. A capacity, some say, that will be enhanced by a small stock of natural resources (see also Box 2.4).

A more balanced position was proposed by Herman Daly and John Cobb (1989: 72ff.) who argued that destroying resources is a waste; not using them is a waste, too; thus a wise use is what is needed.[16]

For Daly and Cobb a wise use means first of all realizing that we have to treat different types of natural resource differently. They propose to distinguish among renewable resources, nonrenewable resources, and natural capacities or services (such as absorbing pollution). With regard to the last one, the assimilative capacity of the environment should be regarded as a maximum ceiling for the emission of pollutants while the rate of use of renewable resources (such as fish stocks and timber) should not exceed their rate of regeneration. If we consider these two types of natural resource as a form of capital, then it would be wise to use only the interest on this capital as an input for our economic activities and not the capital stock itself (Daly and Cobb 1989: 72; Box 4.5). Nonrenewable resources (such as oil) should be consumed at the same pace as sustainable and renewable substitutes are developed. To make this possible, part of the revenues generated by the use of nonrenewable resources should be invested in the development of renewable resources that could replace the nonrenewable ones after their depletion. In the last few years, to quote just one example, major oil companies such as BP and energy companies such as Dutch Eneco have taken the hint and started investing in the development of renewable sources of energy such as the sun (solar PV), wind (wind turbines), and biofuels.

---

15 The focus of this paragraph is on the environmental dimension of sustainability. The issue of a just distribution of resources is not considered here.

16 Daly and Cobb recognize here their debt to Gifford Pinchot (the first director of the U.S. Forest Service).

Box 4.5 **Living on the interest or eating up our capital?**

Referring back to the limitations of the GNP to measure adequately a nation's prosperity, Stephen Schmidheiny (1992: 30-31) notes that:

> when a forest is felled for timber, GNP includes the income earned, but no loss of future productive capacity is recorded. If countries were run like businesses, there would be an accounting for depletion of valuable assets such as forests, oil, topsoil, and water.

His message is clear: if businesses were run as countries they would be bankrupt in no time.

Climate change offers a frightening example of the consequences of eating up our capital, in this case the natural capacity of the atmosphere to absorb CO_2 and other greenhouse gases while keeping the Earth's temperature at a range that makes it fit for life. The increased use of fossil fuels and the consequent release of CO_2 are disrupting this capacity.

On the assumption that we need to limit temperature rise to 2°C worldwide to avoid major disasters connected with climate change, the UNDP 2007 report estimates that the world carbon budget for the twenty-first century is:

> around 14.5 Gt CO_2 on a simple annual average basis. Current emissions are running at twice this level. Put in financial budget terms, expenditure is outstripping income by a factor of two (UNDP 2007: 47).

Reducing expenditure to the level of our income, so that we do not eat up our capital, is made more difficult by increasing population and further growth of a fossil fuel-based economy. "Using IPCC scenarios, the 21st Century budget consistent with avoiding dangerous climate change could expire as early as 2032, or in 2042 under more benign assumptions" (UNDP 2007: 47).

By now, Herman Daly's and John Cobb's proposal has been accepted as a standard for the sustainable use of environmental resources. The debate concentrates on two issues: on one side how large exactly is the stock we have to maintain considering the different rates of regeneration of specific renewable resources, and on the other side whether human-made capital (such as sewage treatment facilities) can be seen as a substitute for natural resources and services (such as the natural capacity by air and water to absorb pollution). From what we have said above and in discussing James Lovelock's view on Gaia (Chapter 2 Section 4), it might be fairly clear that there is no agreement on this point. Table 4.1 is an attempt at summarizing the positions taken in the debate. In this matrix the idea of natural capital is used to refer to everything nature has to offer: renewable resources; nonrenewable resources; and services. With total capital we refer to both natural and human-made capital, where the second is seen as a possible substitute for the first (e.g., filters to purify polluted water).

Table 4.1 **Stances in the debate on sustainable use of natural resources**

	No decline of natural capital	**No decline of total capital**
No substitutability of natural capital	Very strong environmental sustainability	Moderate weak environmental sustainability
Substitutability of natural capital	Moderate strong environmental sustainability	Very weak environmental sustainability

Defenders of a very strong environmental sustainability, such as the pioneer of wildlife conservation John Muir, do not accept any decline in natural capital. Resources should not be depleted and this claim, in the case of nonrenewable resources such as oil, implies no use. That natural capital should stay constant is also the view of moderate strong sustainability; however, here the possibility is opened to compensate for a loss. For example, if trees are cut in one place, then somewhere else trees of the same type should be planted, and if oil is used, then part of the revenues should be invested in technology for renewable energy. The basis of this idea is that between human-made capital (including labor and financial means) on one side and natural capital on the other side there is an essential difference; they complement each other and therefore the first cannot and should not be used as a substitute for the second. "To put it crudely, what good is the capital represented by a refinery if there is no petroleum?" (Daly and Cobb 1989: 198).

In moderate weak environmental sustainability human-made capital is allowed to substitute for natural capital as long as the total capital (the sum of the two) does not decline. This means that an investment in education may compensate for the use of oil. The idea is that enhanced knowledge and skills are essential in looking for alternatives for nonrenewable resources. However, also in this view critical natural capital should be conserved as long as there is no technology available for a human-made substitute. David Pearce, the pioneer of environmental economics, and World Bank economist Andrew Steer are two champions of this view.

The last stance is that of infinite substitutability of all forms of capital. This ultimately means that human ingenuity can solve any problem connected with the scarcity of resources. This is a difficult point to maintain, as, among others, Herman Daly and John Cobb noted (1989: 199):

> Surely knowledge can help us define limits and adjust to them in the most reasonable way. We can even learn to squeeze more welfare from the same resource flow, perhaps without limit. But that does not remove limits on the physical scale of the economy resulting from finitude, entropy, and ecological dependence [see also Box 2.4].

A similar, cautious approach to human knowledge resonates in the so-called precautionary principle. The Rio Declaration on Environment and Development formulates it as follows (Earth Summit 1992): "In order to protect the environment ... where there are threats of serious or irreversible damage, lack of full scientific certainty shall not be used as a reason for postponing cost-effective measures to prevent environmental degradation" (Principle 15).[17] This principle is usually interpreted as saying that, on one side, in case of doubt of possible environmental damage, we should avoid any risk, choose the safest alternative for the environment or in the end completely refrain from action and, on the other side, that, even on the basis of incomplete scientific proof, we have to act to restore nature's integrity when it seems compromised.[18] In practice, the principle means that someone who is willing to act and take risks has to prove that his or her action does not bring (irreversible) damage to nature (see Box 4.6).

Box 4.6 **Precautionary principle in practice**

On September 7, 2007 the European Court of Justice ruled on a case that two Dutch environmental organizations brought against the Dutch Ministry of Fishery, Agriculture and Nature concerning the interpretation of Directive 92/43/EEC, Conservation of Natural Habitats and of Wild Flora and Fauna, in the case of mechanical cockle fishing in the Wadden Sea area, a protected area.

The Court rule is a clear application of the precautionary principle. It states that an annual license for this type of fishery, even though it has been conducted on the site for many years, can be granted only if the authorities "have made certain that it will not adversely affect the integrity of that site. That is the case where no reasonable scientific doubt remains as to the absence of such effects" (see Judgment c-127/02 published in the *Official Journal of the European Union* 2004).

As a consequence the mechanical cockle fishery in the area has been abandoned and in 2008 the licenses for muscle seed fishing were not renewed pending the results of a scientific study commissioned by the Dutch ministry. The question has already arisen whether the court judgment could have consequences for tourism in the area, and in general for all activities that take place near a protected area.

17 This declaration is one of the main results of the Earth Summit on Environment and Development held in Rio de Janeiro in 1992. For the whole text see www.unep.org (accessed August 4, 2011). The precautionary principle has a long history (see O'Riordan and Cameron 1994: 2-30) and was mentioned in Proclamation 6 of the Stockholm Declaration (1972).

18 Reid (1995: 109) uncovers the first interpretation; O'Riordan and Cameron (1994: 18) emphasize the second aspect of the precautionary principle: ". . . to act prudently when there is sufficient scientific evidence and where action can be justified on reasonable judgments of cost effectiveness and when inaction could lead to potential irreversibility or demonstrate harm to the defenders and future generations" (emphasis in original).

It is widely recognized that an appeal to the precautionary principle alone, even when enforced by law as in the example in Box 4.6, would not be enough to counterbalance the concern for growth and steer all economic actors toward a more sustainable approach to nature. Most authors think that at least two other measures should be taken.

The first is to assure that prices of goods and services reflect fully all costs made in the process of production and distribution so that no liabilities are passed to society and future generations. In Chapter 2 we touched on the fact that modern industry is not keen to assume costs that can be avoided (Chapter 2 Section 1). As Benjamin Friedman (2005: 378) forcefully says, "there is nothing in the ordinary market mechanism to induce a company to take these costs into account."

Environmental—and social—costs are in economic terms externalities: that is, social consequences of private actions where the private actor has a positive return on its action (e.g., lower costs of production) and society a negative one (e.g. pollution) (see, e.g., Schumacher 1973 and 1999: 28ff; Friedman 2005: 377). Forcing companies by law to internalize the costs of externalities is advocated as a remedy to further social and environmental degradation by many sides, including scientists such as the authors of *Limits to Growth* (1972: 144 Italian edn), environmental economists such as David Pearce (Pearce *et al.* 1989), scientists and politicians such as Ernst Ulrich von Weizsäcker (1994: ch. 10), economists such as Herman Daly (in his 1994 farewell speech to the World Bank) and even captains of industry such as Stephan Schmidheiny, chairman of Anova Holding AG (1992), and Charles Holliday, Chairman and CEO of DuPont (2002). Principle 16 of the above-mentioned Rio Declaration also endorses the necessity to internalize environmental and social costs.

The second measure in the hands of governments to support a more sustainable stance is offered by the "polluter pays principle." This principle supports internalization of costs in the specific case of pollution. The idea that the polluter should bear the costs of pollution has a long history. Its origin might be traced back to the Ancient Greek philosopher Plato who in his book *Laws* said:

> if any one intentionally pollutes the water of another . . . let him not only pay damages, but purify the stream or the cistern which contains the water, in such manner as the laws . . . order the purification to be made by the offender in each case (Plato 360 BCE: VIII 845d-e).

The polluter pays principle was reaffirmed in 1972 in the Stockholm Declaration as a call for laws on liability and compensation for the victims of pollution (Principle 22) and one year later formed one of the cornerstones of the First European Environmental Action Programme (1973–1976). In the Rio Declaration (1992) the polluter pays principle is phrased in principle 16 in very broad terms even though it is qualified with a reference to the public interest and free international trade. The idea behind these qualifications is that no country should be obliged to do more than it can bear and that countries should not use environmental issues to restrict trade, an issue that was very dear to the South as trade is seen as an important means to enhance growth and attempts to restrict it in ways that could be detrimental to the interests of developing countries as a form of neo-colonialism.[19] In the words of Agenda 21, another document developed during the Rio Conference, "Environmental concerns should not be used as an excuse for restraining trade" (Final Summary: 3).[20]

Though it is not easy to strike the balance between letting organizations internalize the costs of pollution and enhancing healthy growth through trade, some interesting steps in this direction have been taken. For example, the market in CO_2 emission permits that was launched in 2005 under the European Union Emissions Trading System can be seen as an attempt both at internalizing environmental costs and at letting the polluter pay.[21]

To conclude, environmental laws and regulations are surely one of the most promising avenues for governments to steer development toward a more sustainable position. Well-framed environmental regulations, as management scholar Michael Porter notes, have a double edge: they contribute to the competitiveness of a nation by enhancing the quality of the natural environment and encouraging innovation to manage natural resources more efficiently or devise new materials with a zero and even a positive impact on the environment (Porter and van der Linde 1995).

4.4 Growth and environment: major challenges

The difficulty in reconciling economic growth and environmental protection is clearly and painfully illustrated by the slow progress made in addressing the major environmental challenges we face: the loss of biodiversity; climate change; and, a third challenge directly linked to the first two, deforestation.

Biodiversity loss

In reviewing the ideas of Rachel Carson, James Lovelock, Herman Daly, John Cobb, and Barbara Ward, we have had occasion to notice that they all see humans as part of a wider web of living species: the Earth ecosystem (see Box 4.7). With different

19   On this principle, the so-called proportionality principle, see O'Riordan and Cameron 1994: 17ff.
20   See also Elliott 2001: 60. Even though the Rio Declaration positions itself in line with the Stockholm Declaration, many environmentalists saw it as less progressive (Dresner 2002: 40-41). The WTO has made the most use of this qualification of the polluter pays principle to protect trade in ways that have deeply worried environmentalists, activists, and even some politicians (Gillespie 2001: 63-96; Wallach and Woodall 2004).
21   For further information see the official EU website: ec.europa.eu/environment/climat/emission.htm (accessed August 4, 2011).

nuances they also believe that human life is supported by this web and that all living creatures help in maintaining it. That loss of species is a threat to the strength of the Earth's ecosystem was recognized by the late 1970s in a study for the American President Jimmy Carter, known as the Global 2000 Report. It became a worldwide issue in 1986 when Edward O. Wilson, one of America's most prominent biologists, organized a conference on biodiversity and was able to convey to politicians and the public at large the sense of apprehension that he and his colleagues felt on the topic. Human activity, Wilson warned, is causing species to disappear at a much faster rate than they are born. His message was heard both by NGOs such as the WWF, UN organizations such as the IUCN and the UNEP, and by pharmaceutical and chemical companies for which plants and animals constitute an important source for new products (von Weizsäcker 1994: 104 and 109). This consensus paved the way for the Convention on Biodiversity signed during the Earth Summit in Rio de Janeiro in 1992 and in force since 1993.

Box 4.7 **A web of life**

In the summer of 2007 one of the authors of this book spent her vacation in the Langhe, a region in northern Italy renowned for its food and wines.

When walking in the lower hills she passed vineyard after vineyard. Talking with the locals she understood that, after the 1970s, grapes become a monoculture in the region and that, as a consequence, the use of fertilizer and pesticides increased. As she was not able to spot any insects and only very few birds, she felt all the force of Rachel Carson's warnings against a *Silent Spring*.

Uphill hazelnut trees replace the ranks of grapes. These trees are strong and there is less need for pesticides. There was plenty of life alongside the path: ants, beetles, birds, and butterflies. The contrast with the vineyards downhill could not have been more striking.

Comments on this international agreement vary from appreciation, because it sets species conservation in a broader context than past agreements (Munson quoted in Elliott 2001: 71; von Weizsäcker 1994: 109), to the observation that it seems more concerned with assuring the rights of countries with biotechnological industries (in the North) to access reservoirs of biodiversity (in the South) than with protecting endangered species. More problematic is that some countries, such as the U.S., refused to sign the convention on biodiversity, thus materially restricting its reach and significance (Reid 1995: 200; Dresner 2002: 40). This episode illustrates clearly how politics and the political color of major world leaders influence the international environmental agenda. The 2007 UNEP report on biodiversity is clear on this point: "Biodiversity loss continues because the values of biodiversity are insufficiently recognized by political and market systems" (UNEP 2007: 185).

Climate change

Differently than biodiversity loss, climate change has been able to attract attention, at least in the last few years, both from politicians and from the public at large. The first official warning of an abrupt change in the Earth's climate dates back to 1990 when the Intergovernmental Panel on Climate Change (IPCC), a group of scientists advising the UN, published their first report: *Climate Change*. It contained a serious warning about global warming due to increasing levels of CO_2 in the atmosphere. Since then the evidence that our climate is changing and that human activities are responsible for this change has mounted and, even though there are still some skeptics, it might be fairly said that after the 2007 IPCC report the question seems settled: our way of living is the major cause of global warming.[22] In this respect climate change is the last of a series of events warning us that the Earth's capacity to absorb the output of our activities is limited and that this limit has been trespassed.

Public attention to climate change was commanded by the film by Al Gore, *An Inconvenient Truth* (released in May 2006), and the Nobel Prize he and the IPCC were awarded with in 2007. Notwithstanding this mounting interest, the records of international political actions against climate change are (at best) mixed. As early as the 1992 Earth Summit in Rio the Janeiro, the U.S.A. opposed any concrete target on reduction of CO_2 emissions. As a consequence, the Convention on Climate Change contained only a broad call to industrialized countries to stabilize their CO_2 emissions at 1990 levels in 2000. Both concerned scientists and environmentalists underlined that this measure was absolutely insufficient to combat climate change. On the positive side it should be mentioned that the Convention included arrangements for future negotiations. These led to the Kyoto Protocol in 1997. Even though the U.S.A. of the George W. Bush administration and other industrialized countries fiercely opposed the Protocol and were successful in seriously limiting its scope, it came into force in 2005 following ratification by Russia in November 2004 (see Dresner 2002: 39 and 50ff. for more information). The Kyoto Protocol is due to expire in 2012. The efforts by the UN to start talks on a new agreement encountered the same resistance from the U.S.A. backed up this time by the worries of other countries that the efforts made to reduce CO_2 in developed countries will be counteracted by the mounting emissions of nations such as China and India that, owing to their situation as developing countries, enjoy a special position.[23]

On this issue the environmental agenda meets the social agenda: "luxury emissions" to support the affluent consumption of the North are contrasted with "survival emissions"—those required to bring about a better standard of living in the

---

22 "Most of the observed increase in global average temperatures since the mid-20th century is very likely due to the observed increase in anthropogenic Greenhouse Gasses concentrations" (IPCC 2007: 17).

23 See the conclusion of the UNFCCC Bali Conference on Climate Change (2007) where all concrete agreements on greenhouse gases reduction were confined in a footnote to the final document, the Bali Roadmap.

South (Sutton 2007: 156; Box 4.8). The same intertwining of social and environmental issues is present in the third major environmental challenge that will be discussed here: forest protection.

Box 4.8 **Climate change and the social agenda**

The 2007 Human Development Report of the UNDP is wholly dedicated to the consequences of climate change for the fight against poverty. The report insists that "it is the poorest who did not and still are not contributing significantly to green house gas emissions that are the most vulnerable" (UNDP 2007: vii).

Poor people do not have the means to defend themselves, by, for example, building dams against floods, and are more directly affected by harsh climate conditions. For a farmer in the South drought means no harvest and thus no food.

Moreover, the risk of being exposed to major disasters is skewed toward developing countries: "For the period 2000–2004, on an average annual basis one in 19 people living in the developing world was affected by a climate disaster. The comparable figure for OECD countries was one in 1,500 affected—a risk differential of 79" (UNDP 2007: 76).

Deforestation

In addressing the U.S. Senate with an appeal for saving what remains of American forests, the biologist Edward Osborne Wilson said (1998: 2):

> ... when you cut a forest, an Ancient Forest in particular, you are not just removing a lot of big trees and a few birds fluttering around in the canopy. You are removing or drastically imperiling a vast array of species even within a few square miles of you. The number of these species may go to tens of thousands. Many of them, the very smallest of them, are still unknown to science, and science has not yet discovered the key role undoubtedly played in the maintenance of that ecosystem, as in the case of fungi, microorganisms, and many of the insects.

His words are echoed by entrepreneur and environmentalist Paul Hawken (1993, 2005: 38): "Rot, rust, ants, worms, skunks, toads, pikas, voles, bats, moles, mites, alder, gentian, lichens and several thousand other plants, invertebrates, birds, reptiles, and mammals make up a forest."

Forests are a key link in the Earth's ecosystem, not only because they offer a home to innumerable species. They also help regulate our climate mainly by affecting the amount of CO_2 in the atmosphere. When forests grow, carbon is removed from the atmosphere and absorbed in wood, leaves, and soil. Because forests can absorb and store carbon over an extended period of time, they are considered "carbon sinks."

Overall, the world's forests are estimated to store more carbon than the entire atmosphere. When forests are cut and the wood burned, the carbon is released into the atmosphere.

The annual net loss of forest area between 2000 and 2005 was 7.3 million hectares per year—an area about the size of Sierra Leone or Panama—down from an estimated 8.9 million hectares per year between 1990 and 2000. This is equivalent to a net loss of 0.18% of the world's forests annually. The greatest loss of forests is in developing countries where timber is exported as a commodity, forests are cut to expand crop land, or the wood is used for heating and cooking. This process has already taken place in most developed countries, as would be clear to anyone who flew above one of them: the expansion of cities and crop land has pushed trees to the top of hills and to remote areas. When asked to protect their woods, developing countries often point to this fact and to their right to foster economic growth using their resources as developed countries already did. Hypocrisy is not the only fault developed countries are accused of when they call for protection of virgin forests. Recently, a Brazilian economist spoke of neo-colonial paternalism and summarized the request of the North to the South as follows: the South is required not to exploit their forest to compensate for the North's pollution.

The concept of sustainable forestry was developed at least 200 years ago. Its basic principles are straightforward: to replant trees that are cut and to harvest trees respecting their rate of growth. Sustainable forestry offers a venue for protecting the role of forests as carbon sinks and—at least partially—of biodiversity sanctuary. However, unrelenting demand from the North and the rapidly developing economies of China, India, Brazil, and Russia, the pressure on producing food for an expanding market, and the absence of other means for the poor to warm their homes and cook, make the fate of forests uncertain (FAO 2005: 30-36).

4.5 **Growth, environment and social justice**

At the core, the social dimension of sustainability requires that human basic needs, both material and spiritual, are met now and in the future so that people are free and capable of living the life of their choice. Development is about people, not things, as the Nobel laureate Amartya Sen keeps reminding us. As we have already noticed, in a world with clear ecological limits and where people are separated by a vast gulf in wealth and possibilities, sharing is unavoidable.

By most measures the gap between rich and poor, globally and within countries, has been growing. The difference in per capita income between the world's wealthiest 20% and the poorest 20% was 30 to 1 in 1960; this ratio jumped to 78 to 1 in 1994, and decreased slightly to 74 to 1 in 1999 (Wade 2001; UNFPA 2002: ch. 2). The graph that the UNDP published in its 1992 report has thus not changed its champagne-glass shape (see Fig. 4.2).

First published in 1992, the figure reproduced in Figure 4.2 was then printed unchanged in the UNDP 2005 Human Development Report (p. 37). In the 2005 report the figure is explained as follows:

> Global income distribution resembles a champagne glass . . . At the top, where the glass is widest, the richest 20% of the population hold three-quarters of world income. At the bottom of the stem, where the glass is narrowest, the poorest 40% hold 5% of world income and the poorest 20% hold just 1.5%. The poorest 40% roughly corresponds to the 2 billion people living on less than $2 a day (UNDP 2005: 36, Box 1.5).

To put it more bluntly: "On the (conservative) assumption that the world's 500 richest people listed by *Forbes* magazine have an income equivalent to no more than 5% of their assets, their income exceeds that of the poorest 416 million people" (UNDP 2005: 37).

Figure 4.2 **Income distribution**

Source: UNDP 1992. Design and copyright by CCIDD 2001

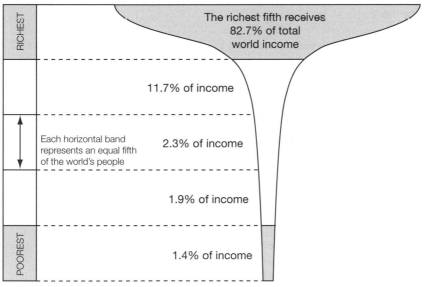

The richest fifth receives
82.7% of total
world income

RICHEST

11.7% of income

Each horizontal band
represents an equal fifth
of the world's people

2.3% of income

1.9% of income

POOREST

1.4% of income

The poorest fifth receives
1.4% of total world income

With this information in mind, it has to be concluded that the appeal for a fairer distribution of resources made by the Brundtland Commission is still unmet. There are different, very complex reasons why the situation has not yet changed. Here we will focus on three: a lack of attention to the social dimension of sustainability in the debate following the publication of the Brundtland Report; the limits of economic growth as the most viable way to combat poverty; and inequality in trade relations.

Social vs. environmental sustainability: anew

As mentioned above (Section 4.1), the Brundtland Report called for attention to the social aspects of sustainable development and the need to strive for a just and equitable society. After its publication, though, the spotlight was taken quickly back by environmental issues. As also recalled above, two of the documents signed at the Earth Summit in Rio de Janeiro—the Convention on Climate Change and the Convention on Biodiversity—focus on the environment. Agenda 21, a third major result

Box 4.9 **Agenda 21**

Agenda 21 is an impressive, complex document of over 800 pages intended as a detailed framework for action to achieve sustainable development. "It covers all conceivable topics from overcoming poverty to solving all kinds of pollution problems" (von Weizsäcker 1994: 100).

A unique feature of Agenda 21 is that it lists actions to be taken *and* the costs connected. The estimated costs for implementing all Agenda 21 recommendations were $600 billion a year for the period 1993–2000. Though impressive, this amount could be compared with 0.7% of the GDP of developed countries, a sum that these countries had by then already promised as aid to developing countries (von Weizsäcker *et al.* 1998: 219). Sadly, however, this amount never materialized (at least not in full) (Dresner 2002: 42; Carley and Christie 2002: 109).

Agenda 21 defines sustainable development as enhancement of human quality of life inside the limits posed by the ecosystem. The focus is on environmental issues even if related social issues are not forgotten. The steps needed to combat poverty, for example, are presented in Section 1, Chapter 3. Here Agenda 21 also raises the issue of a more equitable income distribution.

Agenda 21 touches in Section 1 only briefly on some social and socio-economic issues, such as population growth (Chapter 5) and international debt (mentioned briefly in Chapter 2). Other issues (such as health in Chapter 6 and the need for a decent dwelling in Chapter 7 on human settlement) are seen through an environmental lens.

The environmental bias of Agenda 21 is evident in Section 2, a section totally dedicated to environmental problems, such as: the ozone hole; climate change; energy (Chapter 9); deforestation (Chapter 11); desertification (Chapter12); water (Chapter18); hazardous and solid waste (Chapters 20 and 21); and so on. In line with the Rio Declaration, Agenda 21 strongly connects the protection of the environment to the need to secure our survival as a species.

Section 3 of Agenda 21 is briefly considered in Box 4.11.

of the Rio Conference, covers for the most part environmental issues, even though it also calls for a more equitable distribution of resources and points to the need for democratic participation to achieve sustainability (Box 4.9).

After Rio the institutional agenda remained entangled with the environmental challenge. Even when themes dear to the South such as unfair trade relations, debt, and extreme poverty were on the agenda, as during the UN Conference on Social Development held in Copenhagen in 1995, they were not able to get the same level of attention commanded by the discussion on climate change and biodiversity loss. Most recommendations of the social agenda remained unmet even after the UN took the initiative again with the launch of the Millennium Development Goals in 2000 (Reid 1995: 202; Elliott 2001: 47; Box 4.11). It is not surprising that, as a consequence, the divide between North and South, which the Brundtland Commission had tried to bridge, widened again. The call for growth to combat poverty resonated anew in the face of concern for the environment.

Box 4.10 **The Millennium Development Goals**

The Millennium Development Goals (2000) are a UN initiative aimed at government, although in the implementation phase NGOs took a leading role in several countries. They consist of eight major goals to be achieved worldwide by the year 2015. The eight goals are: halve extreme poverty and hunger; achieve universal primary education; empower women and promote equality between women and men; reduce under-five mortality by two-thirds; reduce maternal mortality by three-quarters; reverse the spread of diseases, especially AIDS/HIV and malaria; ensure environmental sustainability; and create a global partnership for development, with targets for aid, trade, and debt relief.

A special agency of the UN was created to monitor progress and to help ensure that continuous efforts are taken to meet the goals. The results to date are mixed: some goals are almost on target (e.g. education) some are improving in some countries and worsening in others (e.g. poverty reduction).

Since 2000, the UNDP Human Development Report has aimed to measure progress toward the achievement of the Millennium Development Goals.

Limits of economic growth in the fight against poverty

Economic growth is often invoked as the only recipe to eradicate poverty. Though, as we have seen, this claim is questioned by many authors on different grounds. The UNDP 2005 report, for example, notes that "were high-income countries to stop growing today and Latin America and Sub-Saharan Africa to continue on their current growth trajectories, it would take Latin America until 2177 and Africa until

2236 to catch up" (UNDP 2005: 37). Environmental economists point to the physical impossibility for our limited world to support further economic growth, thus bringing back the linkage between environmental limits and the need for reducing consumption and using the world's resources to cope with basic human needs first (see Chapter 1 Section 5 on limits to growth).

Probably, the most striking illustration of this linkage is offered by the ecological footprint.[24] The ecological footprint measures how much land and water area a human population requires to produce the resources it consumes and to absorb its wastes. For example, to compensate for CO_2 emissions a certain area has to be planted with trees; to feed the community a certain area is needed for crops, and so on. Calculations of the ecological footprint show a great difference in the land area required by developed and developing countries to sustain their way of living: a U.S. inhabitant, for example, needs on average more than nine hectares in a year to sustain his or her standard of living; for an African citizen this is less than one (see also Chapter 2 Section 5). In the words of one of the conceivers of the ecological footprint, William Rees (1992: 121), "Wealthy nations appropriate more than their fair share of the planet carrying capacity."

The gap is terrific. It becomes terrifying if we consider that the so-called fair share of the Earth (the red line in the graph shown in Fig. 4.3), obtained by dividing the Earth's land area by the Earth's inhabitants, is approximately 1.8 hectare per person per year and that this amount decreases when the population increases because the Earth's dimensions are (of course) fixed (see Fig. 4.3).[25] The point here is that the total exceeds what is available. To provide the resources used and to dispose of the waste humanity presently produces needs not one, but one and a half planets. If all people on Earth shared the same lifestyle as an average U.S. citizen, then we will need five planets. Yet, of course, there is only one Earth.[26]

24 The ecological footprint was devised in 1990 by Mathis Wackernagel and William Rees. It is now in wide use by governments, communities, and businesses to monitor natural resource use. See Rees 1992; Wackernagel 1994; Venetoulis and Talberth 2007.
25 In this calculation no provision is made for any species other than the human race. The recurring issue of population growth was addressed at the UN International Conference on Population and Development (Cairo, 1994). The preparation and work of this conference were impaired by the stance taken by the Vatican and some Arabic countries against any form of birth control except refraining from sexual intercourse. Still a plan was agreed where the issue of population growth was connected with the need to increase women's education and empowerment; contraception was recognized as a human right also thanks to the supportive stance taken by the Clinton administration. Funding will again prove to be a major issue (Reid 1995: 201; Dresner 2002: 50).
26 For more information on the ecological footprint see Ewing 2010.

Figure 4.3 **Ecological footprint by region**

Source: Global Footprint Network. Adapted from www.footprintnetwork.org/gfn_sub.php?content=global_footprint (accessed March 28, 2008)

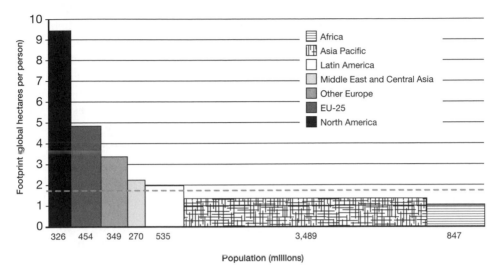

Appropriation by developed countries of more than their fair share is a direct consequence of the high standard of living and consumption patterns of these countries, with the associated flow of energy and raw materials needed to sustain it. Reduction of the energy and materials used per produced unit through better technology is of course necessary.[27] It is, however, hardly sufficient to curb the skewed relation between North and South (see Figs. 4.2 and 4.3). More fundamental questions will have to be asked in line with Nicholas Georgescu-Roegen (quoted in Chapter 4 Section 5) and Ernst Schumacher (1973: ch. 4): does this product or service contribute to a good life, for all people? In the words of Johan Galtung (1980: 24): "Before producing anything, however, the question only asked in a penetrating manner during times of crisis should *always* be asked: do we really need this product?"

Summarizing: economic growth alone is not a viable answer to the issue of poverty because we have already reached and passed the ecological limits of our planet. Greater use of natural resources and sinks—both needed for further growth—will only hasten the collapse of the natural system on which we all rely for our survival. While poverty cannot be tolerated, humanity has to live within the limits of Earth's ecological system. We all need to switch to a less resource-intensive economy; Northern countries will have to learn to reduce their demands and share resources

---

27 At the Earth Summit in Rio de Janeiro the North was called upon to transfer this technology freely to South to allow their economies to grow without a major impact on the environment. For the role of technology see the discussion of the formula I=P*A*T proposed by Ehrlich and Holdren in Chapter 2 Section 5.

more equitably. It would be naïve to deny that this is a very difficult task: who would vote for a political party whose major program point is to reduce national consumption in favor of reduction of poverty somewhere else on the globe? On the whole, only a minority of citizens has objections against redistribution of income inside a nation to take care of the poor and support facilities such as health care and access to education for all. The moral law on which democratic, modern nation states were born rules that "there should exist among the citizens neither extreme poverty nor again excessive wealth, for both are productive of great evil" (Plato, *Laws*, V 744d). In the seventeenth and eighteenth centuries, with the rise of the nation state, we were able to extend this rule beyond the boundaries of a small community. To broaden the validity of this moral imperative beyond the border of a nation and yet within the ecological capacity of our planet is probably the major challenge of our age.

Trade inequalities

The last of the three reasons for the growing wealth divide between North and South that will be considered here is trade inequality. The point that scholars make is that the trade between North and South has retained the pattern inherited from the colonial era: raw materials flow from the South to the North and finished goods, complex services, and new technologies from the North to the South (see Chapter 3 Section 1). Authors such as Samir Amin (1973) and Johan Galtung (1980) have clearly described this pattern where the North forms an economic center that benefits from the peripheral economies in developing countries. The insistence by organizations such as the World Bank on the idea of competitive advantage at national level has reinforced the pattern of dependency: developing countries were encouraged to specialize in those products or services that were required on a world market dominated by the spending power of developed nations. Production of cheap goods in China for the American and European market is a contemporary example of the same pattern.

For this international division of labor to be effective, from a strict economic perspective, free trade is needed. Subsidies and trade barriers that protect goods produced in one country against goods produced in a foreign country impede competition and thus ultimately an efficient allocation of resources. However, both subsidies and trade barriers are still in place and mostly to the detriment of developing countries. Efforts during the so-called Doha negotiations to lower trade barriers around the world have at the time of writing (summer 2011) not produced the desired effect.

The idea that free trade could constitute the solution to the dependency situation of most developing countries' economies encounters similar criticism to the idea that economic growth would do the trick. Critics called and call for curbing the economic effort to cope first with the most pressing need of the nation or community. People and their basic needs should again be put at the center of the development agenda.

4.6 **Growth, environment, and social justice: new challenges**

In the last few years new challenges have developed for the reconciliation of the environmental and social dimensions of sustainability. Two major ones, both connected with the concern for global warming, are the use of land for fuel and the negative consequences of transport.

The U.S. and the European Union have lately encouraged the use of bio-ethanol as fuel. Bio-ethanol is mainly produced from crops that are grown specifically for energy use and include corn and wheat crops. One of the advantages of bio-ethanol over oil is that it is CO_2-neutral: during the growth process the fuel crops absorb the CO_2 they emit. However, the production of fuel crops conflicts with the use of land to produce food. This has resulted in deforestation on one side and an increase in prices of basic foodstuff such as flour on the other side. The satisfaction of basic human needs is impaired by the unforeseen consequence of what seemed a good technological answer to the problems caused by the heavy use of oil for transport. Robert Malthus seems vindicated.[28]

Transport is responsible worldwide for 24% of CO_2 emissions and—even though there are wide differences among countries—on average the relative share by freight transport is increasing (ECMT 2007: 6-9; van Essen 2010). The advocates of a localized economy use this data to support their idea that to enhance sustainability a community should consume what is locally produced. The concept of food miles—the miles traveled by food before it reaches our table—has been introduced and used at this scope. However, leaving aside the fact that food produced through manual labor in a foreign country could result in lower CO_2 emissions than food produced by highly mechanized means domestically, eating only local food can have very harsh social consequences in a world where (as we have seen) countries have specialized in the production of some specific crops for export.

These two examples highlight the complexity of the path toward sustainability and the need to assess all three dimensions of sustainable development holistically when taking a step on this path. This task is far from easy. The need for specialized knowledge to cope with so many complex issues has resulted in fragmented attention to specific aspects of the three sustainability dimensions. Different UN agencies are responsible for single themes and as a consequence dedicated international conferences were called for population issues (Cairo); trade issues (Doha negotiations); climate change (Kyoto Protocol) and so on.

As Norichika Kanie puts it (2007: 69):

> The concept of Sustainable Development calls for simultaneous and concerted efforts to deal with pollution, economic development, unequal distribution of economic resources, and poverty reduction. It contends

28 For the warning by the FAO on world food shortages see Chapter 1 Section 5; for Malthus, Chapter 1 Section 1.

that most social ills are non-decomposable, and that environmental degradation cannot be addressed without confronting those human activities
that give rise to it. Sustainable Development dramatically expanded the
international agenda by stressing that these issues need to be simultaneously addressed and that policies should seek to focus on the interactive
effects between them.

Summarizing: specialization and fragmentation are understandable due to the
sheer number of complex issues to be considered in the path toward a more sustainable form of development. They are, though, not helpful in achieving sustainability
because issues that may appear different or separate, are in reality connected and
intertwined as the dilemma "land for fuel/land for food" shows. What is needed
is cooperation and institutions and organizations able and willing to look further
than their own specialization.

In this context it is positive that in 1997, during the review of the implementation
of Agenda 21, it was clearly stated that "the achievement of sustainable development requires the integration of its economic, environmental and social components" (Earth Summit II 1997: chs. 1, 3). The need to integrate the three dimensions
of sustainable development was reaffirmed during the World Summit on Sustainable Development (Johannesburg, 2002). That the UNDP 2007 report connects the
eradication of poverty with the fight against climate change is also a step in the
right direction. The same may be said of the new course of the World Bank in which
development is approached from an economic, a social, and an environmental
perspective. However, a better integration of the economic, social, and environmental dimensions of sustainability at the level of society is still needed.

4.7 Change agents

Sustainable development as understood here aims at a better quality of life for people, notwithstanding when or where they live. To paraphrase Amartya Sen: the aim
of sustainability is to increase the capability of people to live the life of their choice.
This aim is not met by pushing economic growth at the expense of the environment
and people. Global prosperity is lessened when environmental health decreases
and social needs are not met. Sustainable development implies positive impact on
all three dimensions: economic, social, and environmental.

The main issues that the world faces in achieving sustainability were discussed
in the previous pages. They range from fighting and adapting to climate change,
strengthening biodiversity, and stopping deforestation (environmental value) to
equal distribution of resources to eradicate poverty and hunger, providing education and health care affordable to all, and reducing (child) premature mortality (social value). Most of these issues are global in nature; all have regional and
national impacts.

In the previous pages we have also seen that a large number of initiatives have been deployed to better understand the challenges in front of us, to look for solutions and promote consensus and commitment. Progress toward sustainability, though, has been slow. The question may then be raised whether real change is possible and where are the change agents to be found. In the words of Simon Dresner (2002: 59): "why is it that sustainability and sustainable development have been such easy idea to talk about, but so difficult to bring closer to reality?"

Different scholars have given different answers to the question.

One of the most compelling answers was given by the authors of *Limits to Growth* back in 1972, far before the term sustainable development was coined. In the introduction to their work, Meadows and the MIT team draw a matrix representing human interests plotted against space and time (see Fig. 4.4). What they conclude is that most of us are caught in a very small quadrant: our sense of responsibility is mostly limited to our family, maybe to our community and region; our thoughts are mostly focused on the next few days, months, or in the best case years. This is understandable and even good as human beings cannot psychologically afford to be concerned for others every moment of their lives. The other side of the coin is that a focus on the "here and now" prevents individual human beings from being deeply aware of problems of a global nature and that seem far away in time. And being aware is a precondition for action. From this perspective, then, it would be naïve to rely on individuals to foster the change needed to achieve sustainability.

Shifting the burden of action to governments does not solve the problem. On the one side it is true that governments such as all collective institutions "have larger cognitive powers than the individual, and may be able to carry out decision-making processes of a higher rational degree than the individual" (Tacconi 2000: 58). On the other side, though, politicians do not differ substantially from the majority of people: their time horizon is mostly limited till the next election (in most Western countries four years); their focus is primarily on their constituency—local or national; and therefore they will not take any action that their constituency cannot understand or will not support (Robèrt *et al.* 1997). Global problems such as population growth, resource depletion, pollution, and so on are long-term problems that usually take place far away from our home. Therefore they command sustained public interest with difficulty. In the words of the WCED report (1987: 27): "The Earth is one but the world is not."

As a solution to this dilemma, some scholars have proposed to reinforce UN institutions at the expense of state sovereignty to create a kind of global government.[29] Nobody denies that major difficulties would have to be overcome before a global government could be installed. And even if these difficulties might be eventually worked out, it is hard to think of this global government other than as a democratically elected body. And this means that its time horizon (if not its space horizon) will be limited. If we keep in mind the matrix from *Limits to Growth*, then

---

29 This suggestion was already worked out by Barbara Ward in 1966. For the most recent history of the idea, see Gillespie 2001: 136ff.

Figure 4.4 **Time, space, and interest matrix**

Source: Adapted from Figure 1: Human Perspectives, in *The Limits to Growth*, Meadows, D.H. *et al.*, Universe Books, New York, 1972, page 19.

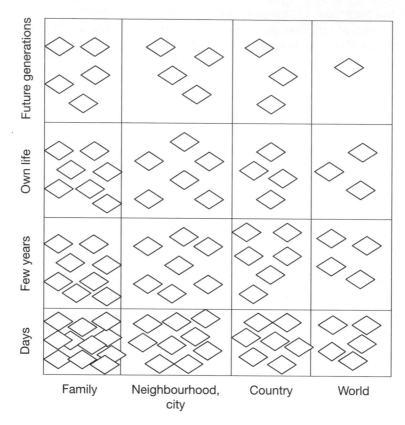

we may doubt that a global government will actually be able to answer those global challenges that require a long-term perspective.[30] Observing this is not the same as pleading for a non-democratic global government. As Sir Winston Churchill is reported to have said: democracy is the worst system of government, except for all the rest (quoted in von Weizsäcker *et al.* 1998: 143).

Notwithstanding the difficulties, an integrated approach involving people both as individuals and as citizens is the only viable path. Focusing on the level of societies and communities, the success of Local Agenda 21 (see Box 4.11) and other local or regional networks proves that it is possible to involve people in the process toward sustainability by distinguishing and integrating global, national, and local policies.[31]

30 See Carley and Christie 2002: ch. 7 for an analysis of other constraints to effective action by government and other organizations.
31 See for a discussion and examples Carley and Christie 2002.

Box 4.11 **Sustainability and democratic participation in Agenda 21**

The third section of Agenda 21 is dedicated to the involvement of all social groups in the transition toward sustainable development with special attention to women, youth, indigenous people, and NGOs. Clearly, the choice is here for a bottom-up, participative approach instead of central planning or costly aid-sponsored projects.

In this respect Agenda 21 marks a difference between how future development toward sustainability should take place and the way growth strategies are usually implemented (Reid 1995: 87). Some commentators consider this approach as naïve because, for example, it does not take into account that communities are often split by conflicts between social groups (Holmberg *et al.* 1993 in Reid 1995: 189; for a realistic answer to this criticism see Tacconi 2000: 85ff.). Notwithstanding possible negative aspects of participation, people's role in sustainable development was recognized by Agenda 21 and, as we will see, stakeholders' dialogue and NGOs were to gain a firm place in sustainability from the 1990s on.

Without doubt one of the major and most impressive results of this participative stakeholder-led dialog is the development of national and regional Agenda 21.

Several authors also note that national and international institutions will never be able to complete the job alone, without the involvement of those organizations—both profit and not for profit—that actually constitute a society. How business got involved in the sustainability agenda is the theme of the next part of the book.

4.8 **Concluding remarks**

Most of the authors quoted in this chapter point out that what is most acutely needed to achieve lasting change is a change in "the way in which our societies look at themselves" (Stiglitz *et al.* 2009: 9). The focus should shift from the here and now to there and later. It is indeed a profound change touching on the prevalent world view shaped by economic thinking. The point here is that change will not come from the outside. Circumstances may help. A crisis or disaster may help to wake people up. Yet, in the end, it is each individual who has to choose to change and push for change at the level of society and organization. To quote one author for all: in concluding *Small is Beautiful* Schumacher (1973, 1999: 252) insists that in the face of mounting difficulties there is something each individual can do:

> work to put our own inner house in order. The guidance we need for this work cannot be found in science and technology, the value of which utterly depends on the ends they serve; but it can still be found in the traditional wisdom of mankind.

In line with Stiglitz and Schumacher, the authors' message is that change is an inside–out process. To achieve sustainability, change is needed not only at the level of society and the institutions governing it, whether supranational, regional, or national government. Change is also needed in the organizations that make up society and at the level of the individual citizen.

The aim of sustainability is a better quality of life for all people, now and in the future. It starts and ends with people, with individual human beings and what they consider valuable to pursue and strive for. In the end it is a question of values, of choosing the type of society we all wish to live in.

Part II
Sustainable organization

Introduction to Part II

Nobel laureate Paul Crutzen and his colleague Eugene Stoermer call the most recent period in human history the Anthropocene (from the Greek *anthropos*, human, and *kainos*, new) to indicate that the influence of human behavior on the Earth has become so significant as to mark the beginning of a new geological era.[1] From the nineteenth century on an exponentially growing world population has caused and still causes increasing stress on scarce environmental resources and services, while the development of technologies aimed at lessening these impacts has not yet achieved the hoped-for results (see Chapters 1 and 2).

But there is more. Alongside daunting environmental problems, humankind faces serious social distress, partly as a heritage of past history and partly as a consequence of more recent developments (see Chapter 3). Several steps have been taken to design a form of development respectful of the needs of people living now, of people living in the future, and of the natural environment. Yet to date results are mixed and, when confronted with the task at hand, largely unsatisfactory (Chapter 4). The conclusion that Paul Crutzen and Eugene Stoermer drew in 2000 is therefore still true: "To develop a world-wide accepted strategy leading to sustainability . . . will be one of the great future tasks of mankind" (Crutzen and Stoermer 2000: 18).

As Part I has shown, the aim of sustainability at the level of society is a better quality of life for people now and in the future. This aim can be achieved only if the economic, social, and environmental dimensions of sustainable development are equally and simultaneously addressed. It has also been maintained that the transition toward a more sustainable form of development can be properly guided only by multilateral institutions that act from an understanding of sustainability as a three-dimensional concept.

---

1 P. Crutzen received the Nobel Prize in 1995 together with F.S. Rowland and M. Molina for their studies of ozone depletion.

Though necessary, achieving sustainable development at the level of society is not a sufficient condition for sustainability. This is due to a second characteristic of the Anthropocene uncovered by authors such as Peter Drucker and Lynn Sharp Paine: modern life is organized life. This is a result of the industrialization process briefly described in Chapter 3: the basic unit of economic production ceased to be the family and become the factory. Compared with our ancestors, we spend most of our life inside organizations and—what is even more important—we derive our economic security and social status from the role we play in organizations. In other words, our well-being, as Howard Bowen noted in 1953, depends greatly on what we earn through our work; on what we can buy with our salary; and on the working conditions we meet inside the organization we work for. Organizations, moreover, have a major impact on the environment: a third of all materials extracted from the Earth, just to give one example, are used in the construction industry. The involvement of organizations in the process toward sustainability is therefore mandatory.

Yet, as Peter Drucker (1993: 53) observed, in modern society "organizations are special-purpose institutions" and their effectiveness is directly linked to their focus on one special goal. Modern corporations, for example, were born to produce a profit on the invested capital: they see themselves (and are more often than not seen by others) as merely responsible for this specific goal and not for the well-being of the community as a whole. The well-being of all people is considered to be the goal of another institution: the government. The focus of organizations on specific and limited goals seems to be at odds with the necessity to involve them in the quest toward a more sustainable form of development, because, as has been skillfully explained by John Elkington in his landmark book *Cannibals with Forks* (1997), sustainability at the level of organizations requires us to meet not one, but a triple bottom line involving people and planet alongside profit (see Fig. II.1).

Part II of this book explores the tension between the idea of organizations as special-goals institutions and the requirements of sustainability at the level of organizations. Similarly to the first part, it is composed of four chapters. Chapter 5 offers a brief overview of the historical development of (for-profit) organizations where the worth of profit and its pitfalls are outlined following a similar line to that taken in Chapter 1. Chapter 6 shows how society has come to question the paramount focus of business organizations on profit and to require that they take into account responsibilities toward people and planet, too. This chapter also briefly highlights and explains the diverse schools of thought that have evolved to understand and clarify the range of responsibilities of organizations and to support their transition toward a more socially responsible and sustainable position. Building on Chapter 6, Chapter 7 highlights the path to be followed by organizations to set sustainability principles at the core of their vision, mission, strategy, and operations. Chapter 8 briefly reviews the main instruments that are at the disposal of organizations to manage and measure their efforts toward sustainability. Chapters 7 and 8 are devoted to the change path toward sustainable organizations. The main point that is made in these chapters is that, although change has become an endemic aspect of contemporary life, the change toward sustainability has its peculiarities and has to be approached differently than "change as usual."

A final note before the discussion begins: although for-profit organizations are the most studied in the context of sustainability, the authors are convinced that their analysis applies also to not-for-profit organizations such as unions, nongovernmental organizations, and in some cases hospitals and universities. This issue will return throughout Part II.

Figure II.1 **Two levels of sustainability: society and organization**

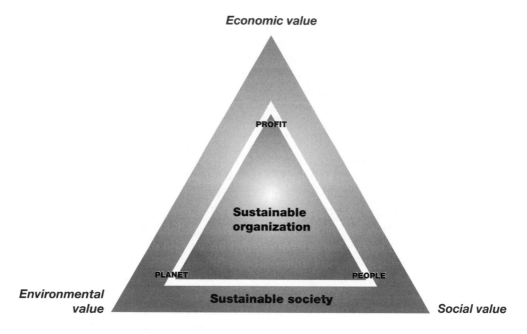

5
The concern for profit

> Our ability to properly serve our customers, to finance research and development, to offer rewarding employment opportunities, and to make contributions to the communities in which we operate all depend directly on our ability to generate an adequate profit (David Packard 1995: 83).

According to Greek mythology, Achilles' spear could wound and heal. Something similar can be said of business. It would be impossible to explain the wealth of modern societies without reference to modern corporations while on the other side it is difficult to deny that they are also the cause of several drawbacks plaguing our societies.

Paradoxically, both the healing and the wounding power of business seem to lie in their focus on profit. Thanks to this focus business is successful in providing society with much-needed products and services, as Peter Drucker, the well-known management theorist, observed. Yet, because of the same focus, business tends to deny responsibility for any negative impact that its operations have on the natural environment and even on people. At the time when modern business originated, this position could have been defended: natural and human resources were abundant and business's operations were small and local. The situation changed dramatically after World War II, making a reconsideration of the role of business in society not only necessary but also urgent.

By looking back at the origin of modern, for-profit organizations and briefly touching on their further development, this chapter explores the tension between the focus of modern corporations on their economic responsibility and the mounting demand from society that business should take responsibility for its impact on people and planet.

The spotlight is set here on for-profit organizations, because it is with a focus on them that the concepts of corporate social responsibility and (later on) sustainable organizations were proposed. When appropriate, reference will be made to not-for-profit organizations.

To clarify the unique features of modern business organizations, this chapter begins by telling the story of one of the first examples of corporations: the Dutch East India Company (Section 5.1). The fate of the Dutch East India Company shows how a focus on profitable growth can be both a blessing and a curse—could both wound and heal like Achilles' spear. The worth and limitation of profit will be further probed in Sections 5.2 and 5.3 following a similar line to the analysis of growth in Chapter 1. Section 5.4 illustrates how corporations evolved to become the most pervading and powerful institutions in contemporary society. Finally Section 5.5 presents the forces that push businesses to reconsider the boundaries of their responsibility. This section offers, thus, a bridge to Chapter 6, where the concepts of corporate social responsibility and sustainable organizations will be discussed in more depth.

5.1 **The birth of corporations**

As we have seen in Part I, economic growth is a recent phenomenon. The same may be said of the quest for profit by organizations specially devised for this aim and considered to be separate legal entities with rights, privileges, and liabilities distinct from those of their members.

Although we can point to instances of organizations doing business in Ancient Rome, the Maurya Empire in Ancient India, and the late Middle Age in Europe, it is widely recognized that the Dutch East India Company, founded in 1602, is one of the first examples of a modern corporation (Sharp Paine 2003). The story of the Dutch East India Company is interesting for three reasons: because it offers an illustration of how modern corporations were born; because it foreshadows the fate of other corporations, including contemporary ones; and because it can function as a bridge to a critical examination of the role of organizations in our society.

At the dawn of the seventeenth century the United Netherlands were fighting for their independence from the Spanish monarchy. Notwithstanding and even thanks to the war, the Dutch merchants took control of maritime commerce in the northern region.[1] With a population of one and a half million and their well-developed cities of Amsterdam and Rotterdam, the United Netherlands were ready to become the leading world economy (Kossmann 1986; Maddison 2001) and unrivaled world power (Chua 2007). An essential role in this process was played by the Dutch East India Company.

---

1 During the war the harbor of Antwerp—major competitor of Rotterdam and Amsterdam—was closed for international trade. Moreover, the Protestant elite left the Catholic provinces (roughly contemporary Belgium and the southern Netherlands) and joined the newly born Dutch state bringing with them their knowledge, skills, and wealth. Pluralism and tolerance have been seen as the key to Dutch world dominance in the seventeenth and early eighteenth centuries by historian Chua (2007).

The Dutch East India Company (or VOC from the abbreviation for Vereenigde Oostindische Compagnie) was created on March 20, 1602 by the State Generals of the United Netherlands, the Dutch Government by that time. The Charter instituting the East India Company (from now on VOC) states that its intention was to institute: "a fixed, secure and orderly entity" so that previous trade activities in South and Southeastern Asia "will be bonded together, managed and expanded for the good of all the residents of the united provinces who would like to participate in it" (Reynders and Gerritsen 2009).

The provisions in the Charter were very innovative for their time. Not only did they constitute the VOC as a joint venture incorporating previous existing sea trade activities, but—as the quote above shows—they also made the VOC responsible only for the people participating (i.e., investing) in it and stated that the VOC should seek to comply with this responsibility by expansion or, in modern terms, profitable growth. The VOC exclusive focus on profit is nicely caught in the reported story of a West African tribesman who, in the early seventeenth century, said to the Dutch merchants that gold was their only god (Chua 2007: 155).

With its focus on the interests of a special group the VOC is a "special-purpose institution" (Drucker 1993: 53) exactly like its contemporary counterparts.[2] This is an important point, signing the divide between public-interest organizations (such as governments) and corporations. As Peter Drucker skillfully pointed out, the focus on the interests of a specific group is one of the ingredients that make modern corporations successful. Special-purpose entities do not need to take into account the interests of several, often conflicting groups and can, therefore, act quickly and efficiently. Organizations that have to carefully weight and trade off different needs because their aim is to benefit all parties (or as many parties as is reasonably possible) need more time before taking a decision. In this respect, thus, special-purpose organizations have an advantage. The other side of the coin is that the focus on the interests of a limited group can become so exclusive as to ignore and even damage the interests of other parties. In fact, a growing concern for corporations' disregard of parties whose well-being is affected by their operations was and still is the major driver toward corporate social responsibility (CSR). As the next chapter will show, the main message of CSR is that corporations need to take more interests than just those of the investors into consideration and that they, therefore, have to broaden the boundaries of their responsibilities. In the VOC case the focus on profitable growth to benefit its investors brought the exploitation of the sailors, of employees in the trade posts, of local people in the Indies, and even of the investors themselves.

---

2 There are, of course, also differences. Most noticeably, the VOC was set up as a monopoly and was armed with sovereign powers: it could raise and keep an army, sign treaties, form alliances, install viceroys, and declare war. The VOC made large use of these rights and became one of the few examples in history in which a private entity assumed the role of a government.

This last point has a familiar ring. Long before Enron, Parmalat, and Bernard Madoff, the VOC set the sad example of a company disregarding the interests of its investors. This could happen because of another innovative feature of the VOC: the opportunity for everybody, both citizens of the United Netherlands and foreigners, to participate in it.[3] Let us focus for a moment on this point.

To pool the huge sum needed to arm the VOC fleet, every contribution—large or small—was deemed necessary. Therefore, the Charter fixed no minimum amount and opened up the possibility to pay the investment in small installments. To further encourage the general public to invest, the Charter limited the liabilities of the members participating in the newly instituted company to the loss of the invested capital, making it the "first great limited-liability joint stock company in the world" (de Jong and Röell 2004: 2).[4]

A capital of 6,424,588 guilders—corresponding to almost $110 million these days and amounting to ten times that of the competing English East India Company—was, thus, raised not only by rich and powerful citizens but also by common people. The highest share in the Amsterdam chamber of the VOC was 85,000 guilders; the lowest 20 (Neal 2005). With over a thousand initial investors, the ownership of the VOC was very diffuse (Chua 2007).[5]

The VOC should have paid dividends to all its owners and, after ten years, completely repaid the capital, following one of the Charter's provisions. Yet the VOC did not do this, but fully reinvested the revenues from the first successful voyages in the company itself and in the end declared the invested capital to be non-refundable (Neal 2005). In this way the VOC was able to assure its survival for almost two centuries. Yet it is at the very least surprising that a company set up with the clear goal to benefit its investors considered it right not to do it.

Investors' needs could be disregarded first of all because, as we have seen, ownership was very diffuse. The almost complete absence of means of communication at the investors' disposal made it quite impossible for investors to join forces and speak with one voice. Besides, investors were not represented in the management of the VOC. And, last but not least, the VOC knew it was backed up by the State Generals.

3 It is interesting to note that 38% of the capital was brought in by immigrants (Kossmann 1986; Chua 2007).
4 Limited liability was a huge innovation: until then people were absolutely liable for their debts. This meant that on the death of an indebted person descendants inherited the debt and, when not able to repay the debts of their forefathers, ended up in prison (Hawken 1993: 106).
5 Looking from another angle it may be said that the VOC proved to be a very convenient device for pooling capital and set it at work to exploit the richness of the newly discovered lands (Sharp Paine 2003: 4). The VOC's success did not go unnoticed: in the seventeenth century a Danish and French East India Company were established and later on a Swedish one, while the Dutch themselves founded in 1621 a West India Company to replicate the success of the VOC on the Caribbean and American markets.

Discontented investors were appeased by paying dividends in kind and, from mid-1620 on, finally, in cash. Truly disappointed investors were able to sell their share to someone else. This led to the creation of the first Stock Exchange ever in Amsterdam. The financial innovation of permanent, but transferable, share capital was a fact.

The interest in East India Company's shares increased with the growing success of the company and in the second half of the seventeenth century they were traded (on average) at 400% above their original value. Monopolistic, intelligent, and prudent operations in the seventeenth century made continued success possible. During the eighteenth century the external situation altered dramatically: political changes in Asian countries restricted access to several markets; the competition by the English and French East India Companies increased; and demand on the European market changed, forcing the VOC to go for higher volume goods and lower profits. The operating costs (fortifications, army, bureaucracy, corruption, and so on) stayed nevertheless the same and this caused a weakening of the VOC's financial situation.

In spite of all this, the VOC kept paying high dividends even when the consequences of the fourth trade war with England (1780–1784) had actually completely drained its capital. This was likely done to keep up the VOC's image of solidity and not shake the trust of the market because—after the first share issue in 1602—a substantial part of the financial resources needed by the VOC was raised by debt notes. Surely, the fact that the board ruling the VOC was no longer composed of merchants but of "regents" (high bureaucrats) also played a role, alongside the fact that by that time most shares were in the hands of a few regents' families. In modern terms: it seems that the VOC management at that stage had no direct knowledge of the trade business and was more interested in gaining as much as possible in the short term than in the long-term survival of the company (Kossmann 1986).

After vain attempts to revitalize the VOC by pouring capital into it (a rescue strategy that started a long tradition), the Dutch Government was forced to nationalize the VOC on March 1, 1796. All assets and liabilities came into the hands of the New Batavian Republic (the name of the Netherlands by then) making the Dutch East India Company one of the first examples of socialization of private sector debts.[6]

5.2 **The value of profit**

The rather sad end of the VOC story may let people forget that the seventeenth century, the century in which the VOC most successfully operated, is known as the

6   For examples of socialization of private sector debts in developing countries see Buckley 2008: ch. 10; recent examples include the bailout of so-called system banks and major companies, such as General Motors, by the U.S. and several European governments during the 2008 financial crisis.

"Golden Age" of the Netherlands. Around 1670 the average income per person in the Netherlands lay at a level that France and England were able to reach only at the end of the nineteenth century, two hundred years later (van Duijn 2007: 150). Arts and sciences flourished through names such as Rembrandt van Rijn, Johannes Vermeer, Antonie van Leeuwenhoek, and Christiaan Huygens. Moreover, attracted by its tolerant and wealthy society, some of the most brilliant philosophers of the time wrote or lived in the Netherlands. Among them René Descartes (born in France, he lived twenty years in the Netherlands), Baruch Spinoza (son of Portuguese Jewish immigrants), and John Locke (expelled from England by James II). Alongside their works and paintings, the monumental houses on the inner canals in Amsterdam still testify to the immense wealth gathered during the Dutch Golden Century.

The focus of the VOC on profitable growth bore fruit and the VOC was, for a long time, up to its task: to contribute to "the greater benefit of these United Provinces" (Reynders and Gerritsen 2009). Yet, and this is the material point, the VOC created wealth at the expense of many people, both at home and in the Asian countries with which it traded and part of which it ruled. In this sense profit does not differ from economic growth. It has its worth for society, in general and from the point of view of sustainability in particular. Yet it also has its limitations. To better understand this point, it is necessary to explore the nature of profit a bit further, first focusing on its worth and then on its limitations.

Put simply, profit is generated when the revenues (or turnover) from a certain activity are higher than the costs. Profit (or a healthy financial situation) is vital to an organization's survival and a country's welfare. A financially fit company is able to meet its obligations and keep its commitments. It is, moreover, able to survive a period of downturn and to expand. As a result valuable products and services are brought to and kept on the market;[7] jobs are maintained and created; investments (e.g., in research) are made; tax is paid; and so on. Healthy companies create wealth for the society they are part of: in this respect the VOC and the Dutch Golden Age are a sparkling example.

As stated above, profit is generated when revenues exceed costs. Economizing on costs is, therefore, one of the two strategies that a company can follow to increase its profit. The other is, obviously, to increase revenues or, in other words, to chase market growth.[8]

Economizing on costs can be seen as a worthy activity from several points of view. For the sake of argument, let us take the example of economizing on the use of natural resources. Economizing in this case means producing as much as possible with as few natural resources as possible. Let us think of water, raw materials, and energy. Economizing on these resources makes sense first of all from a pure

---

7 The presupposition is here that companies produce goods and services that societies need and not only "trash-goods" people have to be convinced they need by mass publicity—see on this point, e.g., Naomi Klein's *No Logo* (1999).

8 A combination of both is of course possible. Yet for the sake of simplicity we stay in the following with these two possibilities.

economic viewpoint: one does not need to pay for resources that one does not use. Provided that demand, quality, and price stay the same, economizing on the use of natural resources immediately translates into higher profits or, if the decreased costs are used to lower prices, into competitive advantage. This is also the reason why most businesses approaching sustainability have started from environmental issues; that is, the planet dimension in the model illustrated in the introduction to Part II (see Schmidheiny 1992; Anderson 1998, 2009; WBCSD 2000; Dyllick and Hockerts 2002). Using fewer natural resources is like picking up money lying on the ground.

Yet there is more. In a limited world with scarce resources and (at least following the economic reasoning) unlimited needs, economizing on resources makes it possible to satisfy more needs from the same resource base.[9] It is evident that satisfying as many needs as possible with the same amount of resources is better for a society's stability than satisfying fewer needs. In other words, economizing on resources is socially more sustainable than not economizing because it helps to enhance the quality of life of as many people as possible.

It is also intuitive that, where natural resources are concerned, economizing is also a good choice from the viewpoint of environmental sustainability. Reducing the use of natural resources is intrinsically better than reusing or recycling them: what you do not use, you do not need to dispose of or recycle. Finally, economizing on resources to benefit as many people as possible seems also a good choice from an ethical point of view. Utilitarianism, an ethical theory that dates back to the eighteenth century, teaches us that it is good to benefit as many people concerned as possible.

Summarizing the discussion so far, profits are good for society for several reasons. First, they are a signal that a company has successfully economized on scarce resources and is, thus, able to cope with more needs with the same amount of resources. Second, they are good for society because thanks to profit a company can survive and keep producing goods and services needed and wanted by society. Third, profits are good for society because a healthy company means jobs and jobs in turn mean personal income for the employees and their family and a possibility of (meaningful) development. Lastly, they are good for society because profitable companies and people with an income pay taxes and thus contribute to the financing of social care, education, and other valuable societal goals.

If profit is looked at in this way, the conclusion seems unavoidable that profit and economizing on costs—one of the two strategies to achieve (higher) profits—are a good thing from society's point of view and not only from the point of view of the organization (see also Box 5.1).

---

9 For a critical discussion of the economic assumption of unlimited needs, see Part I. See also Part I for the idea that natural resources are limited.

Box 5.1 **The invisible hand**

The proposition that it is exactly by focusing on making a profit that a company makes its best contribution to society, is very often defended by calling on Adam Smith (1723–1790), the moral philosopher who is considered the father of political economics. In a very well-known passage from *The Wealth of Nations* Adam Smith warns that "it is not from the benevolence of the butcher the brewer, or the baker that we expect our dinner, but from their regard to their own interest" (Smith 1776: Book I, Chapter 2).

Adam Smith's point is that, if everyone in a society follows his or her best interests, this will, by definition, result in the highest possible degree of wealth for that society. It is, he says, as if an invisible hand (the market itself) leads the people who are looking only for their own gain to promote an end (the common good) which was not part of their intention (Smith 1776: Book IV, Chapter 2). If this is true, it is paramount for society's health that business follows only one goal, the promotion of its own interests, and nothing else.

Mostly this passage is quoted without any reference to another book by the same Adam Smith: *The Theory of Moral Sentiments* (1759). In this study Adam Smith draws the moral framework inside which an economy geared toward the satisfaction of personal interests will result in welfare for society. In this work he insists that "self-interest has to be pursued by people of conscience, informed by their capacity for moral awareness" (Porritt 2005: 34).

Only morally aware people will be able to recognize when in pursuing their own interest, they are going too far and encroaching on the rights of other individuals or the society as a whole. Markets are in this respect blind because, to use Paul Hawken's words (1993, 2005), "markets, so extremely effective as setting prices, are not . . . equipped to recognize the true costs of producing goods" (Hawken 1993: 13).

Though this last work is less quoted and thus less known, its message that pursuit of self-interest should be regulated by moral values, has not been forgotten and has become one of the underpinnings of corporate social responsibility.

5.3 **The limitations of profit**

The conclusion reached in the previous section that profit and economizing on costs are good for both society and business, needs to be qualified. The tangle is that economizing on costs can go too far and bring to society liabilities instead of benefits.[10]

In this respect, too, the VOC offers a striking example. It was noted above that in its drive to expand, the VOC disregarded the needs of its sailors, its employees in foreign posts, and even the interests of its investors. Modern corporations are not free from similar faults: the names of Enron, Parmalat, and Madoff were mentioned above as examples of businesses that, in the quest for higher and higher profits, have broken legal and moral laws and, in the end, have destroyed and not created value for society. Very recently, the BP Deepwater Horizon disaster has been attributed to an internal culture of cost-cutting to enhance short-term profitability, resulting in serious damage to people and planet notwithstanding public disclosure of attention to safety and environmental issues (Lewis 2010).

Though the limitations of the profit motive are quite well illustrated in these and similar examples, in the following the focus will not be on any particular company, but on two general instances in which economizing on costs goes too far from the point of view of society: externalization of costs, i.e. a case of a wrong saving or a saving that backfires on society; and saving on the wrong resource.

Externalization of costs happens when—in the value chain from extraction via production and consumption to disposal—costs are born by those other than the people enjoying the benefits.[11] To better understand this mechanism it is essential to remember that, with some notable exceptions such as the VOC and similar enterprises, until the late nineteenth century, firms were quite small and locally owned and operated. Moreover, modern corporations developed in a time when world population was a tenth of what it is now and natural resources and services seemed unlimited. In this "empty-world economy," as economist Herman Daly called it (1992, 2005), newly born firms had to struggle to survive and were surely prone to avoid all activities that they experienced as an unnecessary cost.

Under these circumstances, it is not surprising that, for example, discharging effluents in rivers, air, or land was considered a normal business procedure. As long as firms are few and their operations limited this strategy may be considered safe, both from a business and a society point of view. This stays true until, with growing population and expanding business activity, a point is reached when the waste produced exceeds the natural capacity to absorb it. Then, as Rachel Carson proved (1962), even small quantities of pollutants disgorged in rivers, land, and air start

---

10 "Going too far" is a moral judgment. For a further exploration of the ethical foundation of sustainability see Cavagnaro 2009.
11 In the context of sustainability the benefits and costs concerned are not only those enjoyed or borne by human beings but also those enjoyed or borne by living animals, nature, and the Earth as a whole.

accumulating and, in the long run, will reach a level threatening life. The smog that affected London in December 1952 and caused approximately 12,000 deaths was, in this sense, an early warning (Bell *et al.* 2004).

Though our world is no longer "empty" and the impact of contemporary business operations is quite incomparable to the impact of seventeenth- and eighteenth-century organizations, it is unfortunately still true that, when there is no legislation in place or no enforcement of existing legislation, the majority of companies consider disposing properly of waste or effluents an unnecessary cost. Pollution is the result and, in cases where decontamination is needed, much too often it is not the company that pays the costs but the government. In other words, all citizens pay including those who were not benefited by the company's activities. In this case we speak of externalization of costs.

Economizing on the wrong resource happens when a company economizes on a resource that is actually at hand and does not economize on resources that seem unlimited but are not. Here again it is important to consider that in the early business era both natural and human resources were abundant. It was, therefore, deemed unnecessary to economize on the use of both. Quite soon, though, machines started to replace people and this process took off when, at the end of the nineteenth and beginning of the twentieth century, the cost of labor increased.[12] Reducing labor costs per unit of product is still one of the major strategies applied by business to enhance profits.

Let us now imagine (which in our time is not so difficult) a situation in which there are people who are unemployed against their will while corporations keep developing technologies that save on labor (thus, on people) and not for example on (finite) natural resources. This behavior is clearly not beneficial for society as a whole: unemployment is not lessened while scarce natural resources are squandered.

What does this mean for the discussion on the worth and limitations of profit? The message is that in both the cases described above profit might still be constructed as a good thing for the organization but it is not good or only partially good for society, because in the end it is society that bears the disadvantages of externalized costs and economies on the wrong resources. Or, to paraphrase Milton Friedman again (1970), in these cases profit cannot be constructed as a social responsibility because in the end it does not create wealth for society.

Contemporary organizations and societies are still suffering from both wrong forms of economizing. Real, vivid examples were and unfortunately still are easy to find: they range from child labor via illegal dumping of chemical waste to the seemingly unstoppable cutting of pristine forests. Throughout the development of modern organizations and corporations several people have denounced these and other wrong forms of economizing. They have done this from different perspectives, some with the aim of unmasking capitalistic corporations as evil forces

12 The focus is here on the North, by then the only industrialized region in the world. Some of the reasons why labor costs increased were analyzed in Chapter 3.

sucking wealth from society (such as Karl Marx in the nineteenth century, referred to in Chapter 3 Section 2, and in recent times Naomi Klein). Others, such as Frank Abrams (Chairman of the Board of Directors of Standard Oil) and Howard Bowen in the twentieth century, exposed weaknesses in corporations with the intention of strengthening them (see further Chapter 6 Section 1). The proponents of corporate social responsibility (CSR) fall into this second group (see on this point also Frederick 2006: 19-21).

Before discussing CSR at greater length, however, it is important to pause a moment and ask the question why firms are seemingly irresistibly drawn toward a wrong form of economizing even now when it is quite evident that this strategy cannot be sustained. Without any pretence to be exhaustive, we would like to point here to three main causes: the focus on profit on the short term; management mandate; and negative feedback loops between organizations and society. Here, too, the story of the VOC can provide us with an example.

As we have seen above, halfway through the seventeenth century the focus of the VOC shifted from long-term growth to short-term survival. Increased competition, shifting market demands, changes in the composition of the board, and the need to attract and retain capital have been identified above as drivers of this transformation. All these factors play a role in modern times, too, and drive corporations to take a similar, short-term stance as the VOC did three centuries ago.[13]

Nearsightedness seems to be quite natural in humans. The matrix drawn in 1972 by Donella Meadows and her MIT colleagues and reproduced in Chapter 4 illustrates this point: the horizon of the majority of people ranges from days to a few years (Fig. 4.4). The tendency to focus on short-term profits is reinforced in listed corporations by the pressure of quarterly or even weekly reports, and daily ups and downs of stock prices. As William Frederick, one of the early proponents of CSR, states (2006: 19):

> A social role defines for an individual a pattern of behavior to which he is expected to conform in order to carry out his socially approved functions within the society. The businessman's role is defined largely, though not exclusively, in terms of private gains and private profit.

When management is hired with the mandate to boost quarterly revenues and when their benefit packages are linked only to this measure of success, then the inducement of enhancing profit at the cost of society or even at the cost of the company's long-term survival may become irresistible (Handy 2002). The fall of Enron, Parmalat, and major financial institutions such as Lehman Brothers testify to the destructiveness of this urge.

As David Packard puts it (1995: 90):

---

13 Globalization of money, i.e., the ease of shifting money rapidly around the world in search of the highest interest, makes firms compete not only with each other but also with financial markets; see Hawken 1993: 93-95 for further explanation.

It is always possible to improve profit for a time by reducing the level of our investment in new-product design and engineering, in customer service, or in new buildings and equipment. But in the long run we will pay a severe price for overlooking any of these areas. One of our most important management tasks is maintaining the proper balance between short-term profit performance and investment for future strength and growth.

From the above it is clear that the role and mandate of the people who run a company is crucial to the way it is operated. People in charge of a company can be the owners or—as is often the case in large organizations—a management layer that operates in the name of but separately from the owners or investors. Knowledgeable management is advantageous for a company because it fosters its expansion by a more effective allocation of a company's resources (Wren 2005: 3). The separation of control from ownership, though, may have its drawbacks. This was already evident in the VOC case: little by little management started to be sought no longer from people who knew the trade but from a group of powerful families, the so-called regents, an "old boys' network" *avant la lettre*. In a situation where ownership was very diffuse and had no means to be heard, these new VOC board members lost sight of whose interests they served. To use an expression created to describe managers in the 1930s, they became "economic autocrats" and formed a "controlling group [that] may hold the power to divert profit into their pockets" (Berle and Means 1932: 124 and 333, in Wren 2005: 359). This is quite a sobering view on management's destiny. Even more so if we consider that it will not be checked by the tendency of modern managers to stay in one function for a very short time.

The processes described above can be also explained as a series of negative feedback loops reinforcing each other in a way that is similar to many feedback loops found in nature. The natural human tendency to focus on the short term is reinforced in managers by the mandate to enhance profit on a quarterly, monthly or even weekly basis; by the direct link between their bonus and their success in this respect; by the separation between control (management) and ownership (investors); and by managers' short tenure. Diffuse ownership (as in many listed corporations today and in the VOC case in the past) offers no countervailing power to this shortsightedness, surely not when the investors themselves see their share in a company as a way to make their own fortune as soon as a possible.[14] As Charles Handy (2002) suggests, contemporary shareholders more often than not lack the mentality of an owner or trustee, and are better described as investors or even gamblers.

National and regional governments may offer counterweight through legislation. Yet, as we have seen in Part I, a society that sees as its main goal economic growth is as shortsighted as a company focusing on short-term profit. It is therefore unlikely

---

14 In 1952 John Kenneth Galbraith proposed the theory of countervailing powers (business, union, and active government) as a guideline for restructuring American society where, in his opinion, big businesses could avoid competition by their sheer mass and were thus left free to exercise their full power.

that the cure will come from these governments or other international institutions that see stimulating year by year economic growth as their goal (Willis 2010).[15] Moreover, through the interaction of several societal forces, legislation was enacted in the past that unintentionally also reinforced the wrong forms of economizing. Let us think for example of social legislation. On one side, legislation on minimum working hours and wages has improved the condition of workers in the North and has helped promote peaceful social development and economic growth thanks to the increased spending of the middle and working class. On the other, though, it has also driven the costs of labor so high that companies seem to have no other choice than to economize on labor costs by layoffs or by relocating in countries where cheap labor can still be found (Barry 2000). Finally, it cannot be ignored that many governments are too weak to oppose the will of major contemporary businesses.

These negative feedback loops have created a catch-22 situation: governments and businesses hold each other in a tantalizing and increasingly strangling grasp. Notwithstanding different voices pointing at possible ways out, for a long time both governments and businesses seemed unable to envision a way to keep the good things that profit and economic growth have brought to humanity while leaving the negative things behind. Corporate social responsibility wishes to cut this Gordian knot. In short, CSR reminds business that with power comes responsibility, and that this responsibility is not enhancing short-term profit to benefit only shareholders and owners. Profit is a necessary condition to enable companies to do something more or better, in ways that no single individual could (Packard 1995; Handy 2002). "Better" implies for CSR to have a positive impact on the quality of life of people. Seriously taking responsibility means thus abandoning all forms of economizing, or market expansion strategies, that negatively impact on society, both on its people and the natural environment.

The origin of the idea that business has broad responsibility toward society reaches deep into the nineteenth century, while its slow development can be followed throughout the first half of the twentieth century. Yet its message really got to corporations only in the late 1990s. To understand both CSR development and the business response to it, it is worthwhile analyzing how corporations evolved in the years after WWII.[16]

---

15 Lobbying by corporation to impede the development of laws seen as detrimental has, of course, not to be underestimated. On the negative effects of business lobbyism on environmental and social legislation in the U.S. see, e.g., Hawken 1993: ch. 7.

16 Of course, attention should not only be given to the "cost" side of the equation—profit = revenues – costs—but also to the growth side. Proper growth is as important as proper economizing, as the consequences of selling mortgages to people that cannot afford them have painfully shown in recent years. Yet, as in both cases the reasoning is similar, the growth side of the equation will not be discussed here.

5.4 **Evolving corporations**

Peter Drucker, the well-known management scholar often quoted in these pages, noticed that our time is the era of organizations. With this statement he did not mean to say that organized life is an invention of our time. The VOC, as we have seen, showed many features of modern corporations back in the seventeenth century, while religious institutions seem coeval with humanity itself. Ancient civilizations on all continents, such as the Indian, Mayan, and Babylonian ones, are unthinkable without central governments and, as a final example, banks were already well developed by the Middle Ages.

Organizations, though, were in the past neither so pervasive nor so powerful as today. During most of human history it was the extended family that formed the cornerstone of society, not organizations. And when organizations did rise they were more often than not "family owned and did not need more than the most elementary administrative structures" (Daft and Steers 1986: 223). Now that the family has lost its central function, our economic security, our social status, our physical security, and our well-being depend on the proper functioning of complex organizations such as the company we are working for, the school educating our kids, the police protecting us and our properties, the local store providing our food, and so on.

Organizations are not only everywhere in our time, they are also different than organizations of the past in another essential way: usually they are no longer a creature of the state with limited powers conferred—and controlled—by the state. They are more often than not a creature of private agreement. While organizations such as the VOC needed a Charter by the government to be able to operate, in the U.S. (the world's leading economy from the late nineteenth century till today) by 1875 a special charter by the state was no longer needed to found a corporation. All that was needed was filling in a form and paying a fee, as is the case now when an organization enrolls in a chamber of commerce (Sharp Paine 2003).

Another essential difference is that companies before the Industrial Revolution "were powerfully regulated by natural energy flows—mainly the solar energy captured by food, wood, and wind" (Hawken 1993, 2005: 130). With the Industrial Revolution the solar power stored in coal first and then oil was released, seemingly lifting any physical limit to company expansion and growth. Contemporary globalized trade is unthinkable without plants, planes, ships, and trucks powered by coal or oil.

Checks and balances for the freedom that organizations thus received were and are offered by competition (in well-functioning market economies), by (inter)national laws and regulations, and by unions and other pressure groups (where they are allowed). As we have already noted, though, this may not be enough to counteract the negative effects of a too exclusive focus by corporations on profit and growth.

Both the relative freedom in which corporations operate and their strengths as "special-purpose" organizations, have contributed to their success. This in turn has given to them power and influence, sometimes to an extraordinary and even frightening extent. Already by 1888 U.S. President Rutherford Hayes wrote in his diary: "This is a government of the people, by the people and for the people no longer. It is a government of corporations, by corporations, and for corporations" (Hayes 1922: Vol. 4, Ch. 45, March 11, 1888). A little more than a hundred years later Naomi Klein was to contend that corporations have not only enslaved Western governments to their own goals but that they have filled in all free space robbing individuals of their basic freedoms (Klein 1999).

A way to grasp the width and depth of contemporary corporations' power is comparing the financial resources that big, multinational corporations can command with those at the disposal of governments. In an often-quoted article written for the Global Policy Forum in 2000, Sarah Anderson and John Cavanagh (2000) reported that of the 100 largest economies in the world, 51 were global corporations and only 49 were countries (see also Prahalad and Hart 2002). Notwithstanding the dot.com crisis in 2000 and the recent financial meltdown, the resources at the disposal of multinational corporations surpass those of many governments. Table 5.1 illustrates this point clearly.

Table 5.1 **Multinational corporations' financial power**

Source: Adapted from The Global 2000 Rank (www.Forbes.com, accessed April 21, 2010)

Rank	Company	Country	Industry	Sales ($ billions)	Profits ($ billions)	Assets ($ billions)	Market value ($ billions)
1	JPMorgan Chase	United States	Banking	115.63	11.65	2,031.99	166.19
2	General Electric	United States	Conglomerates	156.78	11.03	781.82	169.65
3	Bank of America	United States	Banking	150.45	6.28	2,223.30	167.63
4	ExxonMobil	United States	Oil & gas operations	275.56	19.28	233.32	308.77
5	ICBC	China	Banking	71.86	16.27	1,428.46	242.23

These are staggering numbers and even more so when compared with governments' GDP and tax income. To refer as an example to the country where the authors met each other, the Netherlands, the estimate GDP in 2009 was $794.7 billion and the estimate tax income in 2009 $171.9 billion.[17] Despite being a small country, the Netherlands is considered the sixteenth largest economy in the world (IMF 2009;

17 Estimates are from the Dutch Statistical Bureau (CBS). Conversion into U.S. dollars was made by the authors on the basis of the November 2010 value of the U.S. dollar against the euro.

World Bank 2009). Thanks to their size and command of resources some even see corporations as the nations of the future (Hawken 1993, 2005: 92).

Major corporations do not only have a huge influence because of their financial resources. They also have it because they touch directly or indirectly the life of millions of people. Let's think, for example, of the argument that U.S. President Barack Obama used in the spring of 2009 to defend his decision to support the American automotive industry. It was not because of the technological know-how represented by these companies or their strategic importance for the U.S. international position, but because letting them go bankrupt could signify the loss of 300,000 jobs directly and probably 3 million indirectly (Cole *et al.* 2008). Modern corporations' power to destroy people's lives is even more frightening, as Paul Hawken noted in the 1990s. He reminds us of the tens of thousands of people killed or injured by dangerous or defective products, by exposure to toxins and other hazards in the workplace and by the consequences of industrial accidents such as the Bhopal Disaster (2003: 118; see also Box 2.6). In his own words:

> It is granted that a well-run business is one of the most efficient forms of human endeavor. But we must also acknowledge that a poorly run corporation has the power to be one of the most dangerous forms of human activity ever invented (Hawken 1993, 2005: 119).

The influence that corporations exercise thanks to their increasing power over our lives is also recognized inside the corporate world. In 1995 in an effort to come to terms with mounting discontent inside and outside the company, Royal Dutch Shell (the well-known oil and gas company) evaluated the difference between the 1950s and the 1990s in terms of four major social forces: politics, church, people (e.g., NGOs), and business (see Box 5.2). Shell's conclusion was that, while in the 1950s politics was considered to be the most powerful and strong institution, in the 1990s this was business. Not only is business financially powerful, it also offers to people the best opportunity to deploy their capacities and creativity. Thus, Shell reasoned, business is able to lure the best minds away from other institutions, such as governments or the church. This, of course, reinforces its power and strength. In Shell's eyes the leading role of business in present society is also evident in the fact that businesses' values have become the main reference point toward which the majority of citizens in the North and a growing number in the South direct their lives (SER 2000). Looking at U.S. society, sociologist Robert Bellah and his colleagues observed back in 1985 that the archetypal "American character" was no longer the religious or civic leader, but the businessman (quoted in Freeman and Liedtka 1991).

However, Shell's analysis also indicated that change was under way. People, who directly after WWII were mostly concerned with their immediate necessities and the process of reconstruction, became more and more interested in the way businesses were conducting their operations throughout the 1980s and 1990s. Recognizing business power and influence, people started questioning the boundaries of businesses' responsibilities (Frederick 2006: 57). In the process, new institutions representing people's interests, such as NGOs, gained power and became a force that business has to reckon with.

Box 5.2 **1995: Shell's *annus horribilis***

In 1994 after several studies and consultations with local environmental organizations and the British Government, Shell decided to dispose of a buoy called the Brent Spar, situated in the Atlantic Ocean, by sinking it in a deep water reef. Other options, including bringing the Brent Spar to land, cleaning it, and recycling the materials, had also been considered by Shell. They were all discarded because they were more expensive, technically more complicated and less safe for the personnel involved in dismantling the buoy.

After getting permission from the British Government for the proposed procedure, Shell announced the sinking of the Brent Spar to the wider public in the first days of May, 1995. Greenpeace, the renowned environmental NGO, reacted furiously. It contended that the Brent Spar was heavily polluted and that sinking it would have lethal consequences for the marine environment. A far better option, Greenpeace stated, was bringing the buoy to land, cleaning it, and recycling its materials. To prevent Shell from moving it, some Greenpeace activists reached the Brent Spar and occupied it. It was a dangerous and spectacular action which received full coverage from newspapers.

On May 23, Shell obtained legal permission to evict the Greenpeace protesters from the Brent Spar and, on June 11, a ship began bringing the Brent Spar into the open ocean. At this point the situation escalated. Shell gas stations were boycotted throughout Germany and the Netherlands. In Germany, fifty service stations were damaged, two were fire-bombed and one was raked with bullets. One person died. Politicians from several European countries, opinion makers and even Shell's employees sided more and more openly with Greenpeace in those heated days.

On June 20, Shell UK announced it would stop the transport of the Brent Spar and consider a different solution for its disposal. Though for different reasons, environmentalists, politicians, journalists, and business people were startled: Greenpeace had brought Shell to its knees!

While Shell UK was struggling with the Brent Spar, Shell Nigeria was confronted with a series of even more dramatic events.

Shell has been operational in Nigeria since the mid-1950s in a joint-venture with the Nigerian Government. One of the most oil-rich regions in Nigeria is Ogoniland. The Ogoni are an ethnic minority in Nigeria with very limited political power. This meant that the Ogoni people have been watching their land being polluted by oil operations for years without getting anything in return: no schools, no hospitals, no roads, no compensation for the land they have lost to companies such as Shell. Then, in the early 1970s, Ken Saro-Wiwa, a politician, novelist, and businessman of Ogoni origin, started campaigning for the rights of his people.

From 1990 onwards, Saro-Wiwa led a nonviolent campaign against environmental damage associated with the operations of multinational oil companies, Shell in particular. His campaign gained international attention in 1993, and in that same year Shell ceased operations in Ogoniland, while the Nigerian Government put the region under military occupation. In May 1994, Saro-Wiwa was arrested along with eight others and taken to jail. He was accused of provoking the deaths of four Ogoni elders. Saro-Wiwa denied the charges but was found guilty by a special court in May 1995, almost one year after his imprisonment.

During the trial, human rights organizations started pressing Shell HQ to lobby the Nigerian Government in favor of Ken Saro-Wiwa. Shell's first reaction was disbelief; it felt it was not involved with the issue and considered that, even if it had been involved, it had no right to interfere in the decision process of a court of justice in a sovereign state.

Justice had to follow its own course, Shell thought. And so it did: Ken Saro-Wiwa was condemned to death by hanging. Despite international protests and a personal letter from Cor Herkströter, Shell's managing director at that time, to the Nigerian prime minister pleading for clemency and calling for the execution sentence to be commuted, Ken Saro-Wiwa and his followers were put to death on November 10, 1995.

Both events prompted Shell to rethink its position in society. While the Brent Spar affair taught Shell to consider the value of consultations with environmental groups before taking decisions that could negatively impact the environment, the tragic story of Ken Saro-Wiwa clearly illustrated the depth of its social responsibility.[18]

Shell's *annus horribilis* not only offers an illustration of how organizations representing wide social interests (such as Greenpeace and Human Rights Watch) started questioning the boundaries of a corporation's responsibility, but it also offers a perfect illustration of Keith Davis's "iron law of responsibility." Keith Davis, one of the forerunners of CSR, expressed in this law its conviction that "social responsibilities of businessmen need to be commensurate with their social power" (1960: 71 quoted in Carroll 1999: 271). This means that with growing power, responsibility also grows. If business executives are not up to the challenge, Keith Davis continues, their social power will wear away. Looking back at Shell's *annus horribilis* it is evident how misjudging the depth of its responsibilities caused Shell to lose the support of society, or, as is often said, its social "license to operate." In Paul Hawken's words (1993, 2005: 121): "the ultimate penalty a society can give to a corporation is to demand that it cease to exist."

18 A more detailed discussion can be found in Cavagnaro and Bosker 2007: 63-70.

5.5 **Drivers of change: push and pull factors**

The increasing power of business on one side and people's concern over their rather exclusive focus on profit on the other, are two important drivers leading to a reconsideration of the role of business in society. They are, though, not the only ones. A host of other factors—both external and internal to companies—have played and still play a role. This section touches on some major drivers of change.

Among external factors, major environmental disasters, such as the Seveso dioxin release, Bhopal and the *Exxon Valdez* oil spill, take a particular place.[19] The reaction by the public to these and similar events, and the fear that their image could thus be damaged, pushed companies toward a reconsideration of the risks they could incur in their operations. Staying in touch with the public, understanding its moods, and communicating swiftly in case of incidents became an essential feature of risk or issue management.

Other external or push factors leading business to reconsider the extent of their responsibilities are considered to be: the shrinking role of governments; a growing call for transparency; globalization; upcoming economies; vanishing resources; and, finally and maybe surprisingly, scholarly reflection. Internal or pull factors are considered to be: personal values of owners, executives and employees on one side and special characteristics of an organization on the other. Our discussion starts from the external or push factors.

Shrinking role of governments and transparency

That governments should have a minimum role in society and leave the allocation of resources to the market is a view that is mostly ascribed to liberal or right-wing thinkers. Yet, from the 1980s on, this view has become more and more widespread, and is nowadays defended by people from both the right and the left of the political spectrum. Prompted by this shift in beliefs on the role of the government and by diminishing government resources due to the economic recession at the end of the 1980s, a wave of privatizations took place from the late 1980s.[20] While government's role shrank, the corporations' role grew in sectors that were considered till then to be public services such as transport and health care.

Diminishing government resources have also led to the exploration of voluntary and non-regulatory initiatives (covenants) to convey social and environmental objectives to the business sector. Self-regulation is less costly than law enforcement, and in this sense a good choice for governments with shrinking resources. Self-regulation has also many advantages for business, in terms of both costs and flexibility. The introduction of covenants, though, has shifted the burden of proof to businesses and has at the same time alerted the general public to the need for

---

19 See for more information Chapter 2 and Box 2.6.
20 On the role of social beliefs on what governments and organizations should do in prompting institutional evolution and change see Hoffman 1999.

checking business's complacency with these voluntary agreements. This has led to a second push factor toward CSR: the growing call for transparent operations and disclosure of data by businesses on their operations.

Globalization

One of the consequences of globalization is that the vast majority of companies operates in or receives supplies from countries with very different legal systems and cultures than the ones in the country of origin of the firm. Thus, more and more companies have to face the question whether all that is legal in a country (including subsistence wages and even child labor) could also be morally admissible and defendable. Clearly, answering this question means to reconsider the boundaries of a firm's responsibilities and in this sense globalization of a firm's operations reinforces the call by CSR to focus on more than profit alone.

Upcoming economies and vanishing resources

Globalization has also brought the development of new economies: in the 1960s–1990s the Asian Tigers (Hong Kong, South Korea, Singapore, Taiwan); and in the new millennium the so-called BRIC countries: Brazil, Russia, India, and China.

The economic growth of countries such as China and India, where almost half of the world's population is living, has reinforced the question mark on the "growth and business as usual" model that was posed from the late 1960s in Western Europe and North America (Daly 1992, 2005). If the calculations of the world's ecological footprint (presented in Chapter 4 Section 5) are correct, the aspiration of Chinese and Indian citizens to reach the level of material wealth enjoyed by U.S. or West European citizens, however legitimate, may result in an environmental catastrophe.

Even before the environmental pressure of 1.6 billion Chinese consumers is felt, the economic pressure of China's hunger for natural resources has alarmed both economists and political scientists in the West. Consider, for example, that the average consumption of a Chinese person is 2 barrels of oil a year, while the average consumption of an American citizen is 23. Oil production at this moment is around 30 billion barrels a year. A simple calculation shows that if China follows the same path of development as America, oil production will have to grow considerably. Yet most analysts agree that oil production is already over its peak: that is, the point where the maximum production is reached. The increase in oil prices in 2007 and 2008, before the last world economic recession set in, are a clear sign. And it is not only oil's scarcity that is begun to be felt, but also the possible shortage of many other strategic resources: from coal to steel; from timber to rare Earth metals; from corn to cocoa (Box 5.3).

Box 5.3 **Vanishing resources: cocoa**

In May 2009 Howard-Hana Shapiro, global director of plant science and external research for Mars (the global company best known for its chocolate bar), announced that Mars will source all its cocoa beans from sustainable farms by 2020. Sustainability means to Mars not only less negative impact on the natural environment but also better wages and training for the farmers. One of the reasons given for this huge leap is that the quality and quantity of cocoa beans is decreasing. Poor farmers cannot invest in good cocoa plants and manure. Unskilled farmers and cocoa workers may damage both plants and beans. The result is lower productivity and lower income for the farmers and workers, stopping them from escaping the poverty trap. In the end Mars suffers, too. Mars realized thus that it makes perfect business sense to support the switch toward more environmentally friendly and socially beneficial practices (van der Lugt 2009).

Interestingly, while on one side the Chinese government pursues an aggressive policy to assure its economy of vital resources, on the other it stimulates and promotes a less material- and energy-intensive form of economy. Though here, too, an increase in consumption may outweigh the efficiency gains in the end (Dyllick and Hockerts 2002: 137), it cannot be denied that the growth of the BRIC countries is a powerful push factor for businesses and governments alike to achieve a less resource-intensive and more sustainable form of development.

Scholarly reflection

Though rarely listed as one of the push factors that have led to a reconsideration of the "business as usual" model, scholarly reflection has actually had an important role. This is not only true for studies that directly addressed the role of business in society. It is also true for general managerial literature, such as the works of Peter Drucker to which we have often referred in these pages.

Interesting insights on the boundaries of business's responsibility can also be found in the literature on how businesses measure their success, and in particular in the book *Balanced Scorecard* by Robert Kaplan and David Norton (1992, 1996a, b).

In the introduction to this seminal work Robert Kaplan and David Norton criticize the managerial habit of relying on financial indicators alone to get information on the present state of a company and its future development. Their point is that financial indicators offer only a picture of the past and therefore are unable to offer any clue on how a company will perform in the future. Past performance is no guarantee of future results: this investment disclaimer should be printed at the bottom of all companies' financial reports.

In other words, Robert Kaplan's and David Norton's message is that, though businesses are special-purpose organizations aiming at profit, they need to consider indicators other than financial ones to get a more balanced and truthful view of their condition. Robert Kaplan and David Norton suggest that a company should also define and measure its capacity to innovate and learn, its internal processes, and clients' satisfaction. Proposed measures include how profit is achieved and how business operations affect the employees and clients, and not only the shareholders.[21]

It is interesting that Kaplan and Norton set at the center of their Balanced Scorecard a company's vision and strategy. Vision and strategy are by definition activities internal to a firm. For our discussion this means that an organization may not only reconsider the width of its responsibility as a result of external pressures; it may also integrate sustainability principles in its business model on the basis of the vision and mission on which it bases its strategy. In other words, alongside push factors such as NGOs' demands, retreating governments, clients' pressure, vanishing resources, and so on, internal pull factors can also account for the decision by a company to consider more than profit alone in the setting of its goals.

Just to quote one example: in its first report on social and environmental impact, The Body Shop, the well-known cosmetic chain founded by Anita Roddick in the late 1970s, stated that its mission was to change the world by changing the way the cosmetic industry was operating. Anita Roddick envisioned a cosmetic industry using only natural ingredients, paying producers a decent wage, and not testing its products on animals. Though reality proved harsher than expected (Entine 1994), The Body Shop was successful in rousing interest in alternatives to animal testing and opening up the market for "natural cosmetics."

Internal factors

Studying organizations that have integrated sustainability principles in their vision and mission, scholars have concluded that personal characteristics of owners, founders, or senior management play an essential role.

Sanjay Sharma, for example, has observed that environmental issues may be seen as a threat to an organization's survival owing to the accompanying regulation and compliance costs. Yet they may also be considered as an opportunity, prompting innovation and creativity, leading to savings and improved customer loyalty and thus supporting competitive advantage. Owners, founders, and executives who consider sustainability as an opportunity and not as a threat, are in a better position to reap its fruits (Sharma 2000).

A step further, business people may consider that "conservation of the environment and successful business development" are "opposite side of the same coin— the coin being the measure of the progress of human civilization" (Schmidheiny 1992: xxiii). In this sense, they may understand that society and organizations

21 For a further discussion on the Balanced Scorecard see Chapter 8.

actually depend for their functioning on a healthy ecosystem. They may, as a consequence, design their organizations not only as environmentally friendly but as restorative, not only as doing less harm but as doing good to the environment and the surrounding community (Anderson 1998, 2009; Hawken 1993, 2005). As Paul Hawken puts it, "the restorative economy . . . does require that people accept that business is an ethical act and attempt to extend to commerce the interwoven, complex, and efficient models of natural systems" (Hawken 1993, 2005: 11).[22] In the end, thus, it is a question of moral values.

Alongside people's values, a second major factor supporting sustainable organizations is their design and structure. It has been found that characteristics such as discretionary slack, coordination mechanisms among different departments, and performance evaluation based on more indicators than financial ones are conducive to a more sustainable stance. Discretionary slack makes it possible to free time for creative problem solving and, as a consequence, makes it easier to develop voluntary environmental and social programs. Responsive management and easy access to information from other departments are also mechanisms that improve and support innovation and experimentation, and thus the transition from a traditional to a sustainable business model. Performance evaluation based on a mix of indicators, and thus not only financial indicators, reinforces the idea that the business and its workforce have broad responsibility toward society. In this sense it supports the change process toward organizational sustainability (Sharma 2000).

There have always been business organizations that measure their success on more indicators than solely profit, organizations that reject the idea that to be successful on the market they should focus only on one purpose. To quote the famous words directed by David Packard, co-founder with Bill Hewlett of Hewlett-Packard, to HP management in March 1960:

> I think many people assume, wrongly, that a company exists simply to make money. While this is an important result of a company's existence, we have to go deeper and find the real reasons for our being. As we investigate this, we inevitably come to the conclusion that a group of people get together and exist as an institution that we call a company so they are able to accomplish something collectively which they could not accomplish separately. They are able to do something worthwhile—they make a contribution to society (a phrase which sounds trite but is fundamental). In the last few years more and more business people have begun to recognize this, have stated it and finally realized this is their true objective . . . You can look around and still see people who are interested in money and nothing else, but the underlying drives come largely from a desire to do something else—to make a product—to give a service—generally to

22 Stephan Schmidheiny was at the time president of the Swiss Eternit Group, co-founder of Swatch and several companies in Latin America, and chairman of the World Business Council for Sustainable Development; Ray Anderson was founder and CEO of Interface, a billion-dollar company in carpet tiles; Paul Hawken had by then already co-founded several companies including some of the first natural food companies in the U.S.

do something which is of value (David Packard as quoted by Collins and Porras 1998: 30).

Paul Hawken agrees with David Packard when he notes that "the question arises as to how long a company can prevail if its employees, consciously or unconsciously, perceive their products, processes or corporate goals as harmful to humankind" (1993, 2005: 127). If Paul Hawken, David Packard, and many others with them, are right that leaving a positive legacy is a primary necessity of human beings, a company that harms humankind will not prevail for long.

Paul Hawken and David Packard believe that a company should leave a legacy that goes beyond a contribution to society's financial stability on the short term. In this, they foreshadow the central message of corporate social responsibility.

6

More than profit

No corporation can prosper for any length of time today if its sole purpose is to make as much money as possible, as quickly as possible, and without concern for other values (Frank Abrams 1951: 31).

Bill Hewlett and I . . . did not believe that growth was important for its own sake (David Packard 1995: 141).

Taking another example from Greek mythology, the goddess of wisdom, Athena, was born as an armored maiden from the head of her father, Zeus. Yet new ideas seldom appear at once and fully developed. In the previous chapter we saw how the changing role of organizations in society has caused a slow but steady shift in the demands and expectations of the general public toward them. Alongside financially sound operations, the production of valuable goods and services, the creation of jobs and a contribution to a country's wealth, organizations came to be held responsible for the impact that their operations have on the natural environment and on people: in short for their "corporate social responsibility" (CSR). This chapter revisits the main schools of thought that have evolved to understand and clarify the range of an organization's responsibilities and to support the transition toward sustainability.[1]

To better understand these theories it is important to remember that in the first, fragile phase of their forming in the late eighteenth century, modern organizations tended to avoid everything that they considered as an unnecessary cost. In a world where natural resources and services seemed unlimited and where apparently

---

1　As will become clear later on, sustainability (and thus a better quality of life for the present and future generations) is in the authors' opinion the goal of CSR. CSR is used here broadly to refer to all theories supporting the idea that organizations have more responsibilities than just the economic one. In the discussion hereafter it will become clearer that there are indeed different approaches toward CSR.

there was an even infinite supply of cheap labor, companies did not easily take responsibility for the consequences of their actions on planet and people when this meant incurring extra costs (see also Chapter 5 on this issue).

That this stance may translate into exploitation of the workforce was noticed rather rapidly and vindicated Marx's economic theory and political movements inspired by his criticism of the capitalistic society, such as socialism (see Chapter 3 Section 2). That alongside employees other people may also be negatively affected is evident in the VOC case, while the debate around externalities shows that the impact of organizations on nature and the environment is more often than not a negative one (see Chapter 5).

Let us take a look at this point a little longer. Though mainstream economic theory holds that the parties involved in a voluntary exchange always benefit from the transaction, it also recognizes that economic transactions may have both positive and negative impacts on parties that are not directly involved in the transaction itself. Water pollution and health damages caused by air pollution are examples of negative impacts on parties not involved in a transaction. In the 1920s welfare economics came to the conclusion that the existence of externalities may result in outcomes that are socially undesirable. As a consequence, negative externalities eventually became central to the debate on companies' responsibilities (see also Chapters 1 and 5). In other words, in order to reconsider the boundaries of an organization's responsibilities we need to take into account both those parties that are directly involved in an economic transaction (e.g., employees and clients) and those parties that are not directly involved in it but are affected positively or negatively by the transaction (e.g., the community and the natural environment). The term "stakeholder" is increasingly used to refer to those entities whose well-being is directly or indirectly affected by a company's operation. Stakeholder theory, first developed in the 1960s in Finland and rekindled in the 1970s in the U.S., is now considered an essential tool in determining the nature and extent of a company's responsibility. This chapter will therefore not only take into account the dawn of the idea that organizations have broad social responsibilities (Section 6.1), its opponents (Section 6.2) and its main successive developments (Sections 6.3 and 6.4) but also—though briefly—consider the role and function of stakeholder analysis (Section 6.3 and Box 6.5).

6.1 The dawn of CSR: enlightened capitalism, philanthropy, Abrams, and Bowen

In previous chapters several examples have been given of negative impacts by business operations on the natural environment and people. It has also been restated that in the first phase of their evolution organizations tend to avoid what they consider unnecessary costs—for example, wages above subsistence level and environmental protection. This may give the false impression that organizations in general and corporations in particular are by nature antagonistic to the idea that they have obligations beyond being profitable. As a consequence, we may be persuaded to think that the concept of CSR was entirely developed outside (business) organizations and that these had to be pressured and even forced to comply with it. This is not true, at least not completely.

Looking back to the high days of the Industrial Revolution in the nineteenth century and in the beginning of the twentieth century, it is not difficult to find examples of captains of industry who saw it as their duty to use their influence and wealth to positively impact on the lives of the people nearest to them: their employees. These enlightened entrepreneurs built houses for their workforce, offered health care plans at the expense of the firm, and scholarships for employees' children. Box 6.1 looks more closely at two of them, Jean-Baptiste André Godin (France) and Anton Philips (the Netherlands). They both supported the creation of quarters for their employees with modern and at that time unique facilities. Many similar examples may be found on both sides of the Atlantic: from Lever's Port Sunlight in Merseyside (England) dating back to 1888[2] to McDonald town, developed by the Carnegie Steel Company (Ohio, U.S.) in 1909.[3] Henry Ford's ideas on welfare capitalism may be seen as part of this story of concern for employees' well-being, a concern in which philanthropic motives met the entrepreneur's aim to build an economically successful company.

From a twenty-first-century perspective enlightened capitalism and its motto "doing good to do well" may be considered paternalistic and self-serving; especially when one realizes that the employees would lose all the facilities when dismissed. Yet it may not be denied that these captains of industry were inspired by a deep sense of concern for their employees and their employees' families. Their concern allowed them to look further than their firm's immediate economic goal and far beyond the then existing laws and regulations. In this sense, enlightened entrepreneurs uncovered two aspects of CSR that are still considered valid today by both practitioners and scholars: that CSR requires organizations to look further than their short-term financial gain; and to go further than the law.

"Doing good to do well" was counterpointed in the high days of industrialization by another motto that referred to philanthropy: "doing well to do good."[4] The aim of philanthropy is to give back to society by financially supporting good causes and common purpose institutions such as theaters, schools, and hospitals. Probably one of the most well-known examples is Carnegie Hall, built thanks to a more than

---

2 On Lever's Port Sunlight village, see www.portsunlight.org.uk (accessed August 5, 2011). After the death of the founder, William Hesketh Lever, all the companies he had created were united in Unilever. Though Lever was a philanthropist at home, he was not immune from the faults of his own age in his dealings abroad: see, for example, on Lever's involvement with forced labor in Congo, Marchal 2001.

3 On McDonald's company town, see www.ysu.edu/mahoning_river/mcdonald.htm (accessed August 5, 2011).

4 Philanthropy means, literally, friend (*philia* in Ancient Greek) of men (*anthropos*).

Box 6.1 **Jean-Baptiste André Godin and Anton Philips**

One of the first examples of enlightened capitalism is offered by the *Familistère*, created by the French industrialist Jean-Baptiste André Godin in 1859 in Guise (France). Inspired by the utopian socialist Charles Fourier, Godin built an impressive complex to host his employees with houses, schools, shops, and several recreational facilities including a park, a swimming pool, and a theater near his factory. All 500 apartments were equipped with running water and toilets, a luxury reserved to the high bourgeoisie in those times. Later on Godin made employees co-owners of his factory, offering thus one of the first examples of employee participation in a firm. Godin believed that creating decent living conditions for his workforce would have a positive impact on their morale and productivity. "To do good in order to do well" will become one of the mottoes marking the dawn of the CSR concept. In his time Godin was proved right: his factory blossomed and his business thrived.

Jean-Baptiste André Godin was not the only businessman who looked on his employees not just as "tools with a soul,"[a] but as human beings with dignity and rights. He shared this view with many other industrialists of his age, such as the well-known Robert Owen.[b] Less well known, but operating along the same lines, was the Dutchman Anton Philips (of Philips light bulbs) who, from 1910 onward, financed the building of a completely new neighborhood for his employees in Eindhoven, the town in the Netherlands where his factory was located. The buildings were designed and realized by well-known architects following a modern view on healthy housing and, when compared with the existing accommodation for the workforce, were very comfortable. All houses featured running water and gas and were connected to a closed sewage system: a novelty in Eindhoven. Each house had a back yard to allow the newly hired blue-collar employees—who mostly came from the countryside—to tend their own vegetable gardens. The Philips company town was complete with parks, shops, schools, and sports facilities. The soccer stadium in Eindhoven, built on the site of the old sports facility, still bears the name of Philips although the firm left the city several years ago (Otten and Klijn 1991).

a With these words the Greek philosopher Aristotle (V–IV century BC) referred to slaves.

b On Robert Owen (1771–1858) see Royle 1998.

generous donation by Andrew Carnegie to the city of New York. Opened in 1891, the Hall quickly became a sought-after stage for leading artists in both classical and modern music. By hosting artists such as Gustav Mahler, Leopold Stokowski, Vladimir Horowitz, Liza Minnelli, Paul Robeson, and Bob Dylan, Carnegie Hall has set the standard for excellence in music for over a century.

Though it is a voluntary activity, captains of industry in the Anglo-Saxon world have long considered philanthropy as a duty. Actually, when visiting the U.S. it is impossible not to notice that almost every public building bears the name of one or more benefactors. We might then better understand Naomi Klein's sigh that there seems to be no space that is not branded (Klein 1999).

Philanthropy, of course, is not limited to the Anglo-Saxon world. The idea that people in general and the wealthy in particular should support the community or less fortunate people has deep religious roots both in Western and Eastern societies. This should be underlined in the face of the fact that philanthropic activities are often used to show off and are sometimes considered a necessary component of a marketing campaign promoting a business name. Be that as it may, alongside looking further than a short-term financial gain and going further than the law requires, philanthropy is considered a third building block of what would become corporate social responsibility.

A fourth, crucial building block was provided by Frank Abrams, chairman of the Board of Directors of Standard Oil (now Exxon). With a background of a strong liberal business tradition and though being part of it, Frank Abrams stated in 1951 in an article for the *Harvard Business Review* that managers "have responsibilities not just to one group but to many" (Abrams 1951: 29) and that management's task is "to conduct the affairs of the enterprise . . . in such a way as to maintain an equitable and workable balance among the claims of the various directly interested groups . . . a harmonious balance among . . . the stockholders, employees, customers, and the public at large" (1951: 29-30).

The words that have to be emphasized in the quote above are: "conduct the affairs of the enterprise." With these words Frank Abrams points to the inner machine of an organization. Activities such as building dwellings for employees or donating to good causes, find a place outside an organization. Without downplaying the impact that these activities can have on an organization's environment, Abrams helps us to see that it is inside an organization that the biggest gains may be achieved.

A way to understand this point is to make a comparison with the difference a single household can make when buying sustainable goods and services (e.g., organic food and solar energy) compared with only donating to a good cause. Using the Netherlands as an example, while each Dutch family donated on average €310 to a good cause in 2007, household average spending for consumption items in the same year was €31,400: bigger by a factor of 100.[5] It would make a material difference if this spending was on sustainable goods and services.

---

5 Data are from the Dutch Central Bureau for Statistics (CBS) see: www.cbs.nl/nl-NL/menu/informatie/deelnemers-enquetes/personen-huishoudens/budgetonderzoek/doel/default.htm (accessed August 5, 2011).

The same is true for several forms of investment that go beyond the requirements of the law and, even stronger, for business philanthropy. Compared with business operations their impact on stakeholders is lower. This is the rationale behind the idea that all business operations should be geared toward the achievement of a "harmonious balance" among the interests of various groups. Think, for example, of employees' welfare and security. Decent housing is, of course, an essential issue. Yet, as Frank Abrams clearly states (Abrams 1951: 31), the quality of life of the workforce depends strongly on the working conditions, on opportunities for promotion and on the recognition of the work done to support the company's growth. Consider that in the 1950s the vast majority of the labor force consisted of blue-collar workers spending around fifty hours a week in noisy, dirty, and often dangerous environments.[6] Social responsibility, thus, should be the principle around which "the affairs of the enterprise" are organized and not only the principle leading philanthropic activities.

Another crucial message from Frank Abrams' article is that managers should take care that the needs of different parties are met. Against the background of the idea that management's legitimacy is derived from the owners and stockholders of a company and that thus managers should focus all their efforts toward increasing wealth for owners and stockholders, this statement is quite revolutionary (see Box 6.2). In the *Social Responsibility of the Businessman*, published in 1953, Howard Bowen followed the line set by Frank Abrams and insisted that the task of management is to balance the requests of different parties whose well-being depends on the organization: employees, clients, suppliers, the surrounding community, and the state.[7] Though the name was not yet there, the idea that businesses should serve their stakeholders' needs (i.e., the needs of those groups who are affected by a company's operations) was already present in the 1950s.

We may ask on the basis of which arguments did Frank Abrams, Howard Bowen, and other early defenders of the social responsibility of business contest the, by then, basic assumption that management has a unique responsibility toward the owners of a company. Analyzing their writings, it is possible to distinguish two sets of arguments.

A first set sees CSR as instrumental to sustained business performance in the long term. The view that CSR brings long-term economic benefits to an organization became widely accepted in the 1970s and 1980s (Carroll 1999: 271-74).[8]

As Abrams intended it, focusing on long-term benefits means serving the interests of society as a whole, as society is benefitted by peaceful relationships among

---

6 Working conditions were a major issue also for Bowen (1953).
7 Bowen's book is considered to "mark the beginnings of the modern period of literature" on CSR (Carroll 1999: 269).
8 Though it has been recognized by several studies that there is no definitive evidence that embracing CSR has in all cases a positive influence on the economic performance of an organization, the argument is still strong in the contemporary debate (see, e.g., Wood and Jones 1995; Griffin and Mahon 1997; Rowley and Berman 2000; Margolis and Walsh 2003).

Box 6.2 **Managers as trustees**

The lawsuit launched against Henry Ford by two shareholders of his company in 1916 may serve to illustrate the strength of the idea that managers should act as trustees of the owners, with the exclusive duty to enhance the owners' interests. The brothers John F. and Horace Dodge sued Henry Ford for having disregarded dividend payments and having invested the company money in employees' compensation and the construction of a new plant. They alleged that Ford had broken his fiduciary responsibility toward his stockholders, though thanks to these investments Ford's profit skyrocketed in these years. They won (Gross 1996: 84-85).

The new paradigm of which CSR is an expression sees managers as trustees not of the owners alone but of all these individuals and groups that are affected by an organization's operations: its stakeholders (see also Box 6.5). As has been stated several times in these pages, in this new paradigm organizations are no longer single-purpose organizations.

its different components. This position prefigures what will be called the "social license argument": that is, the notion that "public approval is no less essential to the continued existence of today's kind of business than adequate capital or efficient management" (Abrams 1951: 30). The loss of public approval may bring an organization into serious difficulties, as the case of Shell in 1995 testifies (see Box 5.2).

A similar, yet more hard-nosed, line of reasoning points to the efficiency gains that result from good relationships between an organization and the groups on which the organization depends. To exemplify: well-paid employees do not strike; satisfied customers will return; a favorable local government and community will lessen bureaucratic barriers to business expansion; and so on. In this sense, long-run profit maximization is often offered today as an argument underpinning CSR activities. This argument is further supported by reference to image building, to risk management, and to the credits that an organization that operates in a socially responsible manner builds and that could then be "spent" when a sensitive issue arises. In a different though related way, S. Prakash Sethi (Distinguished Professor of Management at Zicklin School of Business in New York and one of the pioneers in CSR) described CSR in 1975 as "a step ahead of time—before the new social expectations are codified into legal requirements" (Sethi 1975: 62). The idea that underscores much of this approach is that by acting "proactively" a company can stay ahead of governmental regulations and thus achieve a competitive advantage and better financial results than its direct competitors. To put it bluntly, the first set of arguments in defense of the social responsibility of organizations sees CSR as a kind of prophylactic protecting the company from present or future society's requests.

The second set of arguments has a different, more normative nature and springs from a reconsideration of the tasks of a business executive and the goals pursued by the organization he or she leads. In the words of Howard Bowen, "the obligations of businessmen" are "to pursue those policies, to make those decisions, or to follow those lines of action which are desirable in terms of the objectives and values of our society" (Bowen 1953: 6). From a single-purpose organization, business is transformed to an organization that is co-responsible for the pursuit of social objectives and the reinforcement of social values. To clarify: this is not the same as believing that an "invisible hand" will take care that the pursuit of narrow business interests will bring general social welfare. For Frank Abrams, Howard Bowen, and all CSR scholars who follow this line, on the contrary, businesses have to make a conscious effort at benefiting the interests of different groups in order to sustain a peaceful, prosperous society. To paraphrase William C. Frederick, business's aim is to enhance total socioeconomic welfare (2006: 20).[9] Business and society are in this view intertwined: the one cannot pursue its goals without the other.

More specifically, the interaction between government, business, and society for the early CSR defenders is evident from the insistence by Frank Abrams and Howard Bowen that a better quality of life is the result of the wage level and the working conditions on one side and what people can buy with their salary on the other side. Companies and the government have different, though related, responsibilities when it comes to protecting and enhancing people's purchasing power. Companies' responsibility is to produce efficiently and let normal people enjoy the efficiency gains by offering cheaper products, as Ford did; governments' responsibility is fighting inflation by controlling money supply. This is a message that has not lost its force through age.

The analysis above has shown several main features of CSR. CSR implies that an organization looks further than short-term profit and takes on more responsibilities than those strictly required by law. Moreover, CSR is based on the insight that organizations have multiple responsibilities toward several groups and that to truly serve CSR, organizations should imbed it in their principles, strategy, and operations. In other words, CSR is not the same as philanthropy. A final component of CSR is its voluntary nature, a component that was put at the forefront especially by Howard Bowen and that has characterized CSR till today. Sustained by the idea that the financial bottom line of a company will be enhanced by its social behavior and living in the U.S., where there is deeply rooted skepticism on state intervention, Howard Bowen saw at that time no need for a set of rules compelling businesses to take responsibilities beyond profitability. Reflecting back on this point in the 1970s,

---

9 Bowen and Abrams reflected on the role of the businessman against the background of the cold war. Bowen's effort to defend capitalism against the allure of a socialist society is particularly evident throughout his book. While he attacks liberalism for not having lived up to the promise of creating a better quality of life for everyone, he claims that capitalism is the best way to achieve this goal provided that businessmen take their responsibility toward society seriously.

Howard Bowen seemed less sure about the possibility that a voluntary appeal to social responsibility could control the overwhelming power of corporations (in Frederick 2006: 10).[10]

Harmonizing different and often conflicting needs is not an easy task. In the 1950s, 1960s, and 1970s most attention was given to defending the statement that this should be done and why, and to the identification of CSR activities, while less attention was given to a systematic approach to CSR and an explanation of how harmony among the different groups affected by business's operations could be achieved. One of the first scholars, who was able to effectively and systematically distinguish the responsibility of business toward society and to offer an embryonic plan of procedure, was Archie B. Carroll in his seminal 1979 article and in later works. To better appreciate Carroll's views, though, it is important to look first at the criticisms directed at CSR by its major opponents.

6.2 **Opposing CSR**

As with all new concepts, CSR had its supporters and its opponents. Here the focus will be on two great critics of the idea that businesses have other responsibilities than the economic one: John Maynard Keynes (1930) and Milton Friedman (1970).[11]

Writing in the aftermath of the 1929 crisis, John Maynard Keynes insisted that the primary goal for society at that moment was to solve the "economic problem": that is, to assure an income to all people and, thus, liberate them from the struggle for subsistence. All other goals, however noble, had to be put aside unless, of course, they supported the overreaching goal of solving the economic problem. John Maynard Keynes firmly believed that it was possible to solve the economic problem in about a hundred years and most of his essay is dedicated to the contemplation of a society of leisure, where the highest concern to people is not how to satisfy their needs but how to spend their free time wisely and virtuously. Yet Keynes (1930: 373) warns us:

> The time for all this is not yet. For at least another hundred years we must pretend to ourselves and to everyone that fair is foul and foul is fair; for foul is useful and fair is not. Avarice and usury and precaution must be our

10 The debate on this point is still open, as we will see in the following pages.
11 The British economist John Maynard Keynes (1883–1946) is still today referred to as the father of macroeconomics and is considered one of the most influential economists of the twentieth century. Reflecting on the 1930 economic crisis he argued that governments should fight recessions and depressions through counter-cyclical spending by the government. During the recent economic crisis governments have embraced Keynes's views. U.S. economist and Nobel laureate Milton Friedman (1912–2006) was one of the major critics of Keynesian state intervention and defenders of free markets.

goals for a little longer still. For only they can lead us out of the tunnel of economic necessity into daylight.

The point that John Maynard Keynes makes here is that solving the economic problem requires us to follow impulses and passions that are not noble, such as avarice and the love of money. Yet, as solving the economic problem is society's priority, people will have to "applaud and encourage" (as Keynes puts it himself) these vices as virtues. Thus, business people and entrepreneurs should be encouraged to follow a path leading to more profit, disregarding, at least for the time being, other responsibilities. More strongly put: solving the economic problem comes first and for as long as it takes to solve it we cannot afford to behave morally. "Erst kommt das Fressen, dan kommt die Moral" (first we need to eat, then we can think about morality) as Macheath and Jenny state in the ballad "Denn wovon lebt der Mensch?" in the *Threepenny Opera* by Bertolt Brecht.[12]

Critics of sustainability and CSR recur often and in different forms to the theme that "a man needs first to eat." The form that the argument usually takes is that economic growth (as measured by the GDP) and profit come first, and that only when a satisfactory level of both has been achieved will humankind be able to address other problems such as pollution or a more equitable distribution of resources. The issue here is that a "satisfactory level" never seems to be reached while environmental and social problems are compounding and reaching a point at which the achieved economic security of many a country and the quality of life of all world citizens are threatened.[13]

Another argument that will become popular in the debate around CSR is the one put forward by Milton Friedman in his 1970 article "The Social Responsibility of Business is to Increase its Profits." Also owing to this catchy title, Milton Friedman's point is often roughly summarized with the saying, "the business of business is business." His argument, though, is much more sophisticated and less all-inclusive than most people suppose.

First, Milton Friedman's only concerns are corporate executives and their supposed social responsibility. In his opinion, "business," being an abstract term, cannot bear such a responsibility and owners are free to dispose of their earnings as they like. As trustees and agents of their employer, managers have the duty to "conduct the business in accordance with their [employers'] desires." The only responsibility of managers is, thus, toward the owners of the firm they are working for, and if the owners' wish is that profits are maximized, so it should be. This would seem to entail that if owners wish managers to engage in CSR activities, managers should. That owners of a firm may disagree on this point, and how a manager should then act, is a possibility not openly considered by Milton Friedman. Interestingly, Fried-

---

12 Performed for the first time in 1928 in Berlin, this opera breathes the same air of economic turmoil as John Maynard Keynes's article.

13 See on needs Chapters 1, 3, and 4 with Box 4.1; on quality of life and GDP see Chapter 4.

man even condemns those shareholders who do wish to use their power to steer organizations toward a more sustainable stance.[14]

Second, Milton Friedman insists that, if managers are using the firm's resources to meet broad social objectives, what they are actually doing is using the money of someone else for their own purposes, or, to put it bluntly, stealing from owners (who could get higher dividends), clients (who could get lower prices), and employees (who could get higher wages). This is a strong point. We could counteract that it is weakened by the assumption that meeting environmental and social goals should always cost or should always come at the expense of someone or something else. Though it is true that some interventions do not cost and may even result in a saving, either in the short or the long term, it is also true that other interventions do cost, at least in the short term. Even then, as Thomas M. Jones pointed out, "social responsibility need not be thought of as theft; the corporation which acts in a responsible manner may simply be paying society back for the social costs of doing business, costs for which the firm rarely receives an invoice" (1980: 61). Moreover it has to be remembered that the case for sustainability and CSR rests on the conviction that if these costs are not carried now they will have to be carried in the future and by other people than the ones enjoying the benefits (see the discussion of externalities in Chapter 5). Not engaging in CSR activities is, thus, actually stealing, and in a sticky manner because the people from whom a company is stealing have—in most cases—no voice.

Third, Milton Friedman contends that business executives are not elected by the public and giving them the faculty to spend money for broad social issues will disrupt the principle that public money should not be spent without public control. The issue of public control on CSR expenditure is surely a crucial one. As we will briefly see below, when CSR started to be codified, one of its major principles became stakeholders' dialogue and transparency. The enormous development of NGOs in the 1990s and the Internet in the last few years, connected with a perceived weariness of traditional democratic mechanisms,[15] have surely given a new connotation to the words "public control" (see Box 6.3 for a discussion of this point).

14 Consider that the question of corporations' ownership is in 2011 more complex than in the 1970s. Pension funds and state funds are very powerful shareholders in many listed companies.

15 Look, for example, at the declining numbers of voters during democratic elections in Western countries. Turnout of the voting-age population in U.S. elections declined from slightly above 60% in the 1960s to around 55% in the 1970s, 1980s, and 1990s, with an all-time low in the 1996 presidential elections when less than the half of the voting-age population actually voted. During the 2008 election (Barack Obama vs. John McCain) this trend was reversed.

Box 6.3 **Public control and people control**

When in 1995 Shell was confronted by the two major issues of the Brent Spar affair and the trial of Ken Saro-Wiwa, its first reaction was a refusal to accept the responsibilities that several groups, including NGOs, were imposing on them. In line with Friedman's arguments, Shell argued that it was not an elected body and, therefore, could not be expected to take broad social responsibilities and, in the particular case of Ken Saro-Wiwa's trial, to intervene in Nigeria's internal affairs. Yet opposition mounted and Shell had to come to terms with NGOs' requests on both issues (see Box 5.2).

To understand why the hostility to what then seemed a sensible stance was so fierce, Shell decided to bring in a team of experts. The team's answer was that, differently than the years immediately after WWII, when people believed that institutions such as the government and the church should take the lead in achieving society's goals, now this primacy was given to business. In other words, by the 1990s people had realized that businesses' actions had in many cases more impact on people lives than governments' actions. As a consequence, people's expectations toward companies also changed: to match its increased power business had to take broader responsibility and to be accountable to the people for its actions. As Tim van Kooten, then issue manager at Shell, put it during a personal conversation with one of the authors, "people are now chasing on business and keeping an eye on it."

In concrete terms this means that people require from organizations transparency on their operations: people do not trust organizations by their words alone but ask organizations to show them what they do and to involve them in the decision-making process. This request has supported the development of CSR reporting initiatives, as will be discussed later on.

The move from public control to people control has of course its own issues, including the question posed by Friedman on legitimacy and how to track those companies (such as small and medium-sized enterprises and family companies) who are not under the spotlight. Moreover, some scholars argue that transparency may push accountability faster than taking responsibility. Finally, people control may result in too many conflicting interest groups with little common space: an excess of civil society, as Ann Florini (Professor and Director of the Centre on Asia and Globalization at the Lee Kuan Yew School of Public Policy at the National University of Singapore) poses it, that may make it harder to achieve a sustainable society (Florini 2000: 24). People's control is nonetheless a reality that business can no longer ignore.

Another strong argument brought into play by Milton Friedman against CSR is that, even admitted that organizations should engage in CSR activities, it is not possible for corporate executives to meet this responsibility as long as there are no guidelines on how to select social goals and measure the impact of an intervention. Back in the 1970s this criticism was correct and even today it is still forceful. To quote Michael Jensen's words (2002: 242): "with no criteria for [social] performance, managers cannot be evaluated in any principled way." Yet, as we will see in Chapters 7 and 8, it has to be at least admitted that many successful efforts have been made to close this gap.

Milton Friedman's criticism of CSR has been and still is a forceful reminder of the need to craft arguments supporting CSR properly. Yet, in concluding this discussion on early CSR critics, it is good to remember that, in making his point that managers should steer their company in accordance with the owners' desires, Milton Friedman states clearly that business executives should conform "to the basic rules of the society, both those embodied in law and those embodied in ethical custom" (1970: 1). As Thomas M. Jones (1980: 61) notes, this means that also in Milton Friedman's eyes "corporations are social institutions and as such must live up to society's standards." Of course, this implies that, when the ethical standards evolve, corporations have to follow suit (see also Box 6.4).

By recognizing that business executives have to follow not only the law but also a society's ethical standards, Milton Friedman comes intriguingly near to the idea of CSR as propagated by scholars such as Thomas M. Jones and Archie B. Carroll. It is now time to consider their contribution.

Box 6.4 **Is CSR greenwashing or an idealistic activity?**

CSR has also been criticized for quite different reasons than those put forward by Friedman. It has been criticized not for going too far and being a form of socialism, but for being too idealistic and in fact not going far enough.

Levy and Kaplan (2008: 19), for example, argue that "the CSR movement has avoided challenging the core economic structures and managerial prerogatives of contemporary market societies, which retain a high degree of legitimacy." As a consequence CSR deflects and marginalizes demands for profound change in corporation land. Undoubtedly some organizations use CSR as a smokescreen or as a shallow marketing and PR instrument, a practice known as "greenwashing." Yet in opposition to Levy and Kaplan it may be argued that these organizations completely misunderstand the revolutionary message of CSR. As Interface CEO Ray Anderson also claims, CSR requires a new industrial revolution where organizations stop economizing on people and start economizing on what is really scarce, i.e. natural resources, while focusing on addressing real human needs (Anderson 1998; Anderson and White 2009).

The accusation of idealism leveled at CSR and sustainable development is also interesting. In his 2009 study on the relationship between business and society, Nikolay Dentchev (2009) argues that asking companies to accept responsibility other than the financial one is heavily idealistic. Idealism is "the advocacy of perfect but unrealistic business standards"

(Dentchev 2009: 13). CSR is unrealistic because it is based on a moral appeal that downplays the role of self-serving interest in achieving socially relevant outcomes, such as an increase in standard of living. Similarly, sustainable development is highly unrealistic because it supposes "collaboration at all possible levels, that is, individual, organizational, national, and supernational" and "requires the kind of action where one is ready to sacrifice (at least partially) one's own wealth and use one's own power for the common good, which is unfortunately not a common practice" (Dentchev 2009: 26). Dentchev considers other approaches to business and society relationships, such as stakeholder management, corporate social performance, and issue management, as less unreasonable because they focus on what is salient to management, or on clearly cut environmental issues (such as reducing a company's environmental footprint) and are "strategic" in nature (i.e., supportive of the financial bottom line). In the following we will come back to some of these approaches to CSR. Here we would like to observe only that while Dentchev correctly sees the ethical appeal and values on which CSR and sustainable development are based, his criticism is flawed by the fact that he considers "reality" Friedman's interpretation of the goal of business: self-interested pursuit of profit. What if this is not the case and authorities such as Paul Hawken, Stephan Schmidheiny, and Ray Anderson, for example, are right in seeing business as a restorative force aiming at a better quality of life and not exclusively at an increase in standard of living? Let us remember that all three are not romantic environmentalists but hard-nosed businessmen. More fundamentally, consider the following. To a person living before the Industrial Revolution and imbibing the economic views of mercantilism, the concept of expanding markets and a growing pie would have seemed as idealistic as the concept of a triple bottom line to Friedman and Dentchev.

6.3 Archie B. Carroll: connecting CSR with business ethics and stakeholder theory

Notwithstanding criticisms, by the late 1970s the idea that organizations have more responsibilities than an economic and legal one and that they should consider the interests of more people than their shareholders was quite well established. Yet CSR was still a rather vague notion. It was Archie B. Carroll who was able to explain in a comprehensive way what CSR entails, which specific responsibilities business executives should consider, and to which extent.[16] As Archie Carroll himself put it (1979: 504) to clarify the meaning of the term CSR "(1) a firm's social responsibilities

---

16 In discussing Archie B. Carroll's position, both his 1979 article and his later contributions to the CSR debate will be considered.

[should] be assessed, (2) the social issues it must address [should] be identified, and (3) a response philosophy [should] be chosen."

Archie Carroll's answer to the first point is that CSR includes four responsibilities: economic; legal; ethical; and discretionary or philanthropic.

The economic component of CSR requires that a company is profitable so that it can fulfill the task for which it was instituted: to produce goods and services for society. By including the economic responsibility in his CSR definition, Archie Carroll clearly conceives profit as a positive force. In open discussion with those scholars who set the economic responsibility aside from the other three CSR components as something that businesses do for themselves and not for others, Archie Carroll (1999: 284) insists that "economic viability is something business does for society as well, although we seldom look at it in this way." It will not come as a surprise that the authors agree with Archie Carroll on this point: as an indicator of proper economizing and as the foundation of an organization's continuity, profit or financial health is a positive component of CSR.[17]

The second component in Archie Carroll's CSR concept sets boundaries to the freedom of action of an organization: it specifies what an organization may and may not do in its pursuit of profit. More specifically, the legal responsibility gives voice to a further requirement by society of organizations: that is, to operate not only profitably but also fairly and justly. As was seen above, "fair" and "just" are ethical categories and posing limits is an ethical prerogative. Archie Carroll sees this point clearly by stating that law is codified ethics.[18] Though codification constitutes the strength of law and regulations and makes it possible to enforce them, it is, at the same time, a weakness. As Prakash Sethi already observed in 1975, while laws and regulations are rather fixed, societal norms are in a state of constant flux. Moreover, it may be the case, as Ray Anderson, founder of Interface, discovered to his dismay, that compliance with the law when it comes to social and environmental issues may mean "as bad as the law allows" and that, thus, while observing the law people and the planet may get hurt (Anderson 1998: 39, 51).

Therefore, the economic and legal criteria alone do not offer a solid foundation for an organization's legitimacy toward society. Ethical norms (i.e., new standards emerging in society and hence not yet codified) need also to be taken into account. The third component of Archie Carroll's pyramid of CSR covers society's expectation that organizations behave ethically. Society expects that organizations respect the customs of a community; recognize and respect emerging ethical standards; and prevent ethical norms from being compromised to achieve organizations' goals.

---

17 Provided of course that the goods and services produced by the organization are truly beneficial for society: see the discussion in Chapter 5.

18 For the sake of the argument we assume that laws and regulations are not unethical: that this is not always the case is evident in dictatorial regimes such as in Nazi Germany and, less evident, though still the case, in modern democracies. Let us consider for example the debate in Italy in 2009 and 2010 on laws seemingly designed to protect the private interests of the Prime Minister Silvio Berlusconi.

In short, society expects that organizations behave as good citizens by reinforcing and not weakening the ethical standards on which a community depends for its survival. Acting in accordance with this principle means going further than the law demands and treading in the steps of the enlightened entrepreneurs recalled above.

The last component in the CSR definition as provided by Archie Carroll is constituted by discretionary activities, such as philanthropy. With this last component Archie Carroll pays homage to the tradition of philanthropists briefly described above. The idea of "doing well to do good" has been present in American capitalism since its beginnings and finds here a proper place: discretionary activities are like the "icing on the cake" (Carroll 1991: 42). It is important to insist on this point: CSR in Archie Carroll's eyes requires more than only philanthropy because it is the sum of activities deployed on all four levels of his pyramid: the economic; the legal; the ethical; and the philanthropic. If discretionary and philanthropic activities constitute the topping of a CSR policy and not its full contents, then companies that consider themselves socially responsible only because they donate money to a good cause are deceiving both themselves and the public.[19]

Concluding the discussion so far, it is essential to understand that, though Archie Carroll insists that all four components are integrated in his CSR concept, he is also adamant in giving priority to the economic and legal responsibility above the ethical and discretionary ones. The first two are required by society, the second expected, and the third desired (Carroll 1998: 143). Though the distinction between the first two and the second two responsibilities is slight, the fact that there is a distinction exposes Archie Carroll's theory to the criticism that CSR is an "add-on" to business as usual and not a new perspective on the role of business in society.[20]

Alongside the need for a clear definition of CSR, Archie Carroll points to the necessity of identifying the social issues that organizations are expected to address. It is a consequence of Archie Carroll's vision of CSR that these issues depend on society's (ethical) concern for problems that go beyond an organization's financial performance or legal obligation. As it was noted above and amply illustrated in Part I of this book, society's concerns are not static; they develop over time. Moreover, society's requirements for, say, an oil company differ from society's requirements for a primary school and may even differ for companies in the same sector according to their size, ownership structure, past actions, and so on. In short, societal issues change over time and differ for different industries and organizations. As a consequence, pinpointing the issues for which organizations may be held responsible, has always been problematic in CSR history. To cope with this difficulty some scholars resort to a process approach to CSR. Thomas M. Jones (1980: 65) for example affirms that an action is socially responsible when it is the outcome of a fair process; that is, a process in which the social consequences of a decision

---

19 This point will become clearer in John Elkington's approach to CSR.
20 We will come back to this theme in analyzing Carroll's discussion of response philosophies later on and John Elkington's approach in the next section.

are considered and negative impacts on society minimized. One of the possibilities envisaged by Thomas M. Jones to implement this process-oriented approach to CSR is to appoint special purpose directors who, for example, will give a voice inside an organization to the interests of minorities. Building on the concept of stakeholders—newly brought to public attention by Edward Freeman in 1984 (see Box 6.5)—Archie Carroll takes a further step in this direction by linking stakeholder management and CSR. To quote his words (1991: 43):

> There is a natural fit between the idea of corporate social responsibility and an organization's stakeholders. The word "social" in CSR has always been vague and lacking in specific direction as to whom the corporation is responsible. The concept of stakeholder personalizes social or societal responsibilities by delineating the specific groups or persons business should consider in its CSR orientation. Thus, the stakeholder nomenclature puts "names and faces" on the societal members who are most urgent to business, and to whom it must be responsive.

In short, Archie Carroll concludes that the issues to be considered in designing a CSR policy are those that affect stakeholders' interests and needs, from a financial, legal, and ethical perspective.

While pointing to stakeholders seemingly makes an organization's social responsibility much less vague and more vivid, it still leaves open questions such as how stakeholders and their needs could be individuated in a sustainability context. This is a much-debated issue, because sustainability requires that the interests of all stakeholders (including future generations) are taken into account and met, thus going much further than most proponents of stakeholder theory are ready to do. Box 6.5 discusses this issue briefly and offers some indications and suggestions for further reading. Here it is important to note that, notwithstanding the objective difficulty and effort involved, stakeholders' consultation and dialogue have gained a prominent place in CSR policies. A 2007 survey of the websites of 100 companies (randomly selected from the Fortune 500) found that 64 companies embraced a stakeholder orientation and stated that they strive to maximize the well-being of all stakeholders; 22 embraced Archie Carroll's position and voiced a legally and ethically bounded stockholder focus; while only 10 companies followed the stance proposed by Milton Friedman with its focus on value maximization for stockholders (Agle *et al.* 2008).[21]

It is the norm for organizations to have open communication channels with their financiers. A stakeholders' orientation implies that there are processes and procedures in place that enable an organization to keep track and communicate with all its stakeholders and not only with its shareholders. Thanks to the information received, stakeholders get the opportunity to monitor the activities of the organization (see e.g. Hill and Jones 1992). As Chapter 8 will illustrate, there are CSR

---

21 Two companies went still further and aimed at solving social problems while making a fair profit: this form of CSR, where a company sees as its mission to address a market failure, will be discussed below in Section 6.4 and Box 6.6.

certification initiatives that focus exclusively on these processes and procedures: if the right processes and procedures are in place, then an organization can call itself socially responsible.

Though the process approach to CSR has gained in popularity, it has its own drawbacks. As Thomas M. Jones observed, we may put the proper processes in place—say, stakeholder consultation—and be proud of the change but in the end ignore stakeholders' input or shift the real decision-making power to other entities inside the organization. Changing processes may be a form of window dressing and may have no real impact on corporate behavior (Jones 1980: 66).

Here is where the third aspect of CSR as described by Archie Carroll comes in: the choice of a response philosophy. "Social responsiveness can range on a continuum from no response (do nothing) to a proactive response (do much)" (Carroll 1979: 501). Using a different terminology, an organization can avoid engaging with stakeholders; can act defensively; try to accommodate different interests; or proactively and honestly engage with stakeholders. As Donna Wood correctly observed, organizations may choose a different response philosophy toward each CSR component identified by Archie Carroll. To quote Donna Wood (1991: 695):

> For example, within the economic domain, a business organization might act on a principle of self-interest, trying to maximize profits, or on a principle of mutual interest, trying to balance the firm's interests with those of stakeholders, or even on a principle of societal interest, seeking to maximize jobs, production, or some other state-determined goal.

Most existing (business) organizations were not set up with the intention to promote sustainability or to do business using a CSR approach: the response philosophies proposed by Archie Carroll and other scholars describe quite accurately stances that are actually taken by organizations. The distinction of different CSR stances may also be used by organizations to design their CSR policy and (ideally) to grow from a "do nothing" to a "do much" approach. From a normative standpoint, however, it is clear that only a "do much" stance or a "proactive and honest dialogue with all stakeholders" with the aim to find solutions that benefit all, may qualify as a true CSR position in the context of sustainability.[22]

Concluding our analysis of Archie Carroll's views, it is appropriate to summarize the main points of the CSR concept as developed so far. First, CSR includes and yet goes beyond economic and legal responsibilities because it encompasses ethical and discretionary responsibilities as well. The inclusion of an ethical component is a full answer to Milton Friedman's attack on CSR because Milton Friedman also recognized managers' duty to act according to a country's ethical standards. Specific issues within all four components of CSR may be best individuated through dialogue with an organization's stakeholders. While the way of responding and the degree of involvement of firms with CSR vary, an organization that truly sets

---

22 For a keen discussion of the descriptive, instrumental, and normative aspects in relation to stakeholder theory see Donaldson and Preston 1995.

sustainability as its guiding principle falls under the category of proactive and open dialogue with all its stakeholders with the aim to find solutions that benefit all.

Box 6.5 **Stakeholder theory**

Though the concept of stakeholders was first developed in the Scandinavian world in the 1960s, it gained broad academic and managerial attention only with the publication of Edward Freeman's *Strategic Management: A Stakeholder Approach* in 1984. As Peter Sandam said in an interview with Dwight Holing in 1996, "More and more companies are realizing that having good corporate ear is as important as having a good corporate mouth" (Holing 1996).

Edward Freeman's main tenet is that (2007: 9) "business can be understood as a set of relationships among groups which have a stake in the activities that make up the business." Shareholders are in this view a specific category of stakeholders: that is, those groups or individuals who have a financial interest in the organization in the form of stock. Yet many other groups or individuals have stakes in an organization: financial (alongside shareholders, banks, and suppliers), legal (e.g., employees), physical (e.g., health of surrounding community members), or moral (e.g., the environment and future generations), or a combination of these four. In Edward Freeman's words (2007: 1): "businesses, and the executives who manage them, actually do and should create value for customers, suppliers, employees, communities, and financiers (or shareholders)." Managers thus have a responsibility toward all (legitimate) stakeholders.

Alongside aspirational, utilitarian, and pragmatic reasons, there are also instrumental reasons why organizations embrace stakeholder management: to maximize shareholder value over an uncertain time frame, managers ought to pay attention to key stakeholder relationships (Freeman and Phillips 2002). To focus on the last point and returning to Shell for exemplification, by not considering Greenpeace as a stakeholder in 1995 Shell fomented the opposition to its plan to sink the Brent Spar in the Atlantic Ocean; increased the expenses that had to be taken, and thus indirectly damaged shareholders' interests. Attentive readers will have noticed the similarity of this argument in favor of stakeholder management and one of the arguments discussed above in favor of a socially responsible stance.

Though instrumental reasons may be strongly voiced (recently, in 2002, by Michael Jensen, Emeritus Professor of Business Administration at Harvard Business School), stakeholder management—like sustainability and CSR—has a fundamental normative or moral component. This means that a stakeholder approach to management recognizes intrinsic value to the interests of the (relevant or legitimate) stakeholders without consideration of the instrumental value they may eventually have in promoting the interests of other stakeholders. To exemplify: an organization should take care of the working conditions of its employees without reference to gains that may result thanks to less absenteeism, and that—by enhancing profit—may in the end serve shareholders' interest (Donaldson and Preston 1995).

Considering stakeholders' interests requires first of all an identification of the stakeholders of a company and then an assessment of their specific interests. We will not discuss this at length here.[a] In general it may be said that scholars recognize as primary stakeholders of an organization the ones already individuated by Howard Bowen and before him by Frank Abrams: financiers, employees, customers, suppliers, and the community. Special interest groups, the government, the media, consumers' advocate groups, and competitors are often seen as forming a second tier of stakeholders, who (instrumentally) have to be considered in so far as they impact on the first tier. Pragmatic reasons have often been advocated for excluding the environment and future generations from the list (Freeman 2007). Yet, if ultimately a CSR organization is an organization that sets its contribution to sustainable development at the core of its strategy, then such an organization will find little help in stakeholder theory unless an approach is chosen where future generations and the environment are seen as relevant and legitimate stakeholders (Clifton and Amran 2010). The resulting practical problems are surely daunting, yet the principle holds that sustainability implies looking for solutions that benefit all (Clifton and Amran 2010).

Though many CSR advocates, including Archie B. Carroll and John Elkington, see an important role for stakeholder management in CSR, Edward Freeman himself is more critical. In his view stakeholder management makes CSR pointless because it includes in business operations those constituencies that until then were considered as being "outside" an organization and for which a CSR approach was considered necessary (Freeman and Liedtka 1991; Freeman 2007). Surely, if CSR is seen as an "add-on" above the primarily economic responsibility of business, Edward Freeman has a point here. Yet, as Carroll already tried to clarify and Elkington forcefully states, CSR is not an add-on because it requires integrating sustainability in an organization's strategy and operations. The material point here is that a CSR company setting sustainability as its aim will embrace a very broad view on stakeholders, where all constituencies that may be affected (now and in the future) by a decision are considered with the intention of finding a solution that positively impacts on all.[b] On this very last issue the proponents of an integrated CSR approach such as Elkington and stakeholder theorists such as Freeman find each other again. Compare John Elkington's appeal to manage the people, planet, and profit dimensions of sustainability jointly (see below) with the following quote from Edward Freeman (2007: 14):

> if tradeoffs have to be made, as often happens in the real world, then the executive must figure out how to make the tradeoffs, and immediately begin improving the tradeoffs for all sides. **Managing for stakeholders is about creating as much value as possible for stakeholders, without resorting to tradeoffs** [bold in original text].

a Interested readers may start from the article by Ronald Mitchell *et al.* (1997) and its critique from a sustainability point of view by Clifton and Amran (2010).

b Several scholars have noticed that stakeholder management can be used, and is often used, very instrumentally, i.e., to look for and communicate only with those stakeholder groups that will support the company's strategy (Clifton and Amran 2010). In short: stakeholder analysis and management are tools that can be used differently by different persons serving different aims. For stakeholder management to be of use in a CSR context, it should recognize sustainability as its guiding principle. See Davidson (2009) for a similar argument on CSR and Base of the Pyramid (BoP).

6.4 **John Elkington: from the triple bottom line to the phoenix economy**

It is in the middle of the 1950s in Northern Ireland. A seven-year-old boy is going home after eating with the family of a friend and, while crossing a field in the middle of the night, he finds himself surrounded by baby eels. Though the moonless night was completely dark, the boy reached down with his hands to feel the small creatures twirling at his feet. Even if he did not know exactly where they were coming from or where they were heading to, he knew that there was a link with a place as far away as the Sargasso Sea and felt to be part of a much bigger web of life. That boy was John Elkington and the feeling of connection he experienced at the age of seven became the start of a life dedicated to the study of the environment and how humans relate to it.[23]

Almost forty years after that life-changing experience, Elkington was one of the experts flown in by Shell to help understand the, for them puzzling, reactions to the Brent Spar and Ken Saro-Wiwa affairs (Elkington 1997: 62). At that time John Elkington had already created the concept of a triple bottom line (TBL) in response to companies defining sustainability as eco-efficiency and thus equating sustainability with economizing on natural resources. Of course, as has been seen above, eco-efficiency is an important link in the chain toward sustainability and makes perfect business sense. However, as John Elkington noted, this focus leaves many relevant areas unaddressed. Examples of areas left unaddressed by a focus on economizing on natural resources are: the impact of multinational corporations (MNCs) on developing countries' economies (see Table 5.1 and the accompanying discussion); working conditions and working hours in "special economic zones" (see e.g. the section "No Jobs" in Naomi Klein's *No Logo*, 1999); shifting expectations on the role

---

23 John Elkington often comes back to this moment in his life to explain where he is coming from: see, e.g., his interview with J. Carl Ganter during the 2008 World Economic Forum in Davos (www.youtube.com/watch?v=x-0wzZs-15w, accessed June 14, 2010) or his speech for the first Alumni Meeting of Bradford University, May 15, 2010 (www.brad.ac.uk/management/alumni/events/alumniweekend, accessed June 14, 2010). Elkington founded and directed SustainAbility (founded in 1987) and Volans (founded in 2008).

of business in addressing broad social issues such as climate change; and so on. Neglecting areas beyond an economic use of natural resources is risky, as was painfully revealed to Shell during the *annus horribilis* of 1995 (see Box 5.2).

In the same year John Elkington labeled the areas organizations should address as people, planet, and profit (the 3Ps). To quote John Elkington's words in his seminal work *Cannibals with Forks* (1997: 70), achieving the triple bottom line requires the integration of three dimensions: "economic prosperity; environmental quality and—the element which business had preferred to overlook—social justice."

A bottom line is nothing more or less than a calculation of value. The triple bottom line concept expresses vividly that organizations are expected to generate and calculate value on three dimensions: people, planet, and profit. While discussing CSR measurement, Chapter 8 will also briefly address some of the specific indicators developed for the three dimensions proposed by John Elkington. Here it is important to note that profit or economic prosperity does not only cover the economic responsibility of an organization, as for example indicated by Carroll. The profit dimension in the triple bottom line is designed in line with Donna Wood's suggestions and goes therefore beyond financial indicators to include indicators on, to give an example, fighting corruption and investments in the local infrastructure. Usually, the association of the planet dimension with sustainability at the organizational level is quickly understood. One reason is that, as we have seen in Chapter 2, the environmental movement has been one of the main forces promoting sustainability from the 1970s on. A second reason, as we will also see, is because it makes perfect business sense to try to reduce the use of natural resources, or water and electricity. The people dimension, with its appeal to social justice, seems, as John Elkington himself noticed, less addressed and less understood. Though, as Charles Holliday and his co-authors observed (2002: 19):

> In the mid-1990s, this changed. It was not that companies suddenly noticed that they were ignoring the social side of the concept; it was more that many companies' problems were shifting from being environmental to social. There were charges of exploitation because of their use of child labor and because they were running sweat-shops, were union bashing, and were being particularly nasty neighbors "out in the bush" where a mining or oil company might be the most powerful institution around.

The triple bottom line or 3Ps concept is, as John Elkington states, interpreted by many as a balancing act: trading the one dimension against the other. Yet, the point that John Elkington was trying to make when introducing the 3Ps was that the three dimensions are equally important to organizations and should be integrated in its operations. Far more explicitly than in Archie Carroll's pyramid of CSR, the triple bottom line rests on the assumption that environmental and social responsibilities have the same importance and status as the economic ones and that consequentially what most organizations still consider as an externality (i.e., their impact on people and the environment) should be internalized by building fundamentally new business and organizational models. In other words John Elkington points to a shift in the way CSR had to be addressed: from "more than profit" to profit as a blended value with an economic, social, and environmental dimension.

This observation offers a direct link to the recent analysis conducted by John Elkington and his team at Volans on the development of what they call a "phoenix economy" (Volans 2009). The phoenix is a mythical bird with a long life (500 years) that in dying burns and is reborn from its own ashes. A symbol of regeneration in many countries, the phoenix is taken by John Elkington as the symbol of a new economy where entrepreneurs address areas of extreme market and governmental failure and in solving these failures are able to create profit (see Box 6.6 for examples). Clearly these companies set a further step in the CSR story: for them CSR is not an "add-on"; it is part and parcel of their mission, purpose, and objective. The phoenix-economy companies realize what many proponents of CSR and stakeholder analysis envisioned. To quote again Edward Freeman's words (2007: 14):

> The primary responsibility of the executive is to create as much value as possible for stakeholders. Where stakeholder interests conflict, the executive must find a way to rethink the problems so that these interests can go together, so that even more value can be created for each. If tradeoffs have to be made, as often happens in the real world, then the executive must figure out how to make the tradeoffs, and immediately begin improving the tradeoffs for all sides. **Managing for stakeholders is about creating as much value as possible for stakeholders, without resorting to tradeoffs** [bold in original text].

Box 6.6 **Phoenix-economy enterprises and Base-of-the-Pyramid thinking**

The main characteristic of phoenix economy enterprises, also called "social" or "environmental" enterprises, is that they see profit in unprofitable pursuits. A well-known example of a social entrepreneur is Nobel Prize laureate Muhammad Yunus, who in 1976 founded the first bank for micro-credit in Bangladesh, the Grameen Bank (Village Bank). The starting point for Muhammad Yunus was the insight that very small loans could make a disproportionate difference to a poor person and that, although existing banks considered it too risky a business to be in, making tiny loans to poor people could be (under certain conditions) a profitable business. The total amount of loans paid out by Grameen Bank since its beginnings is Tk537.51 billion ($9.31 billion). The loan recovery rate is 97.11% and, even more important, since Grameen Bank came into being it has made profit every year except in 1983, 1991, and 1992.[a] The Grameen Bank has been used by the Grameen Group as a platform to develop other services directed to the very poor, such as the Grameen Shakti for the provision of clean rural energy and the co-venture Grameen Danone Foods.[b] Micro-credit is by now not confined to developing countries: to give one example, in Italy, one of the members of the G8 and considered the seventh economy in the world, micro-credit is a growing phenomenon (C.borgomeo & Co 2008).

The work of Yunus and the Grameen Group is a vivid example of what in 2002 was termed by Coimbatore Krishnarao Prahalad and Stuart Hart as "Bottom of the Pyramid" or "Base of the Pyramid" (BoP) thinking. Consider again the UN graph on distribution of the world's resources presented in Figure 4.2 in Chapter 4. The graph's "champagne glass" form reflects the fact that 20% of the world's population enjoys 80% of the world's resources. This is the top of an imaginary pyramid of world consumers and is the usual target group of for-profit business. The other 80% of the world population, and surely the lowest 20% who survive on 1.4% of the world's resources, is the bottom of the pyramid, a group of consumers that is not addressed by normal business because the individuals who compose it have very limited spending power. BoP points to the combined purchasing power of this group, to the possibility to consider its members as a viable target group and thus develop products and services they can afford. Critics of BoP rightly point to the necessity to involve the poorest in the economic game not only by selling to them but also by buying from them. This is essential not only in order to eradicate poverty but also to properly assess which product to market, to whom, how to price it, and how to advertise it. The point is that we should sell what people at the bottom of the pyramid need to improve their condition. Thus, for example, devising a way to sell a skin-whitening cream to India's poorest girls would not qualify as a proper action. Indian girls would buy the product in the hope of a better marriage, because a white skin is seen as a sign of beauty. Spending on the cream diverts resources from other, pressing needs. Thus, even supposing that the cream's claim is correct, it is very doubtful whether such a product will help in eradicating poverty (Karnani 2007; Davidson 2009).

Opportunities for phoenix-economy entrepreneurs are not limited to developing countries. Better Place (founded in 2007 by Shai Agassi in the U.S.A.) is working toward building electric car networks in countries like Australia, Canada, Denmark, Israel, and the U.S. Its goal is sustainable transportation, global energy independence, and freedom from oil.[c] Arup (founded in the UK in 1946) is now bending its knowledge on engineering, urban design, and management to serve the sustainable design of built environments.[d] Considering, as was mentioned in Chapter 3, that the majority of people live in cities and often under very harsh conditions, this is not a trivial endeavor.

For more examples, see Volans 2009. Here it is important to insist that social and environmental entrepreneurs exploit the economic opportunities of environmental and social market failures to create goods and services with positive environmental and social consequences. It is the aim that marks the distinction between these entrepreneurs and, to use quite a strong word, profiteers.

a www.grameen-info.org/index.php?option=com_content&task=view&id=26&Itemid=175, accessed June 24, 2010.
b See for more information www.grameen-info.org (accessed August 22, 2011) and Yunus and Jolis 1999.
c www.betterplace.com, accessed August 22, 2011.
d www.arup.com, accessed August 22, 2011.

Phoenix-economy organizations seem to have listened carefully to what Peter Drucker said in 1984 (NB: three years before the Brundtland Commission published its report *Our Common Future*): social problems can only be solved if they are treated as opportunities, and profitable ones (Drucker 1984: 54 and 59).

6.5 Concluding remarks

This concluding section attempts to bring together the lines that were discussed above and present the vision of CSR and organizations' sustainability that underlies this book.

First, though the idea was much debated in the beginning, the authors propose that profit (or financial prosperity) should be seen as a positive force of modern organizations. The message CSR conveys is that a profit that is obtained by endangering people or negatively affecting the environment is no longer seen by society as a profit after all. Organizations in contemporary society that wish to be considered legitimate are required to use all their ingenuity to find solutions that benefit at the same time people, planet, and profit, or in the stakeholders' version of CSR, all stakeholders that are affected and could be affected by the organization's activities including future generations.

In the authors' opinion, from the above follows a second characteristic of CSR: that a CSR organization sets sustainable development as its final aim. A CSR organization is a sustaining organization in that it contributes to the achievement of a sustainable world where economic development, social justice, and a healthy environment are pursued. As Don Clifton and Azlan Amran put it (2010: 269): "in the sustainable world context, a corporation's social responsibilities are to progress sustainable world outcomes consistent with the wellbeing + justice criteria."

This brings us directly to a third point: that in the authors' opinion stakeholder theory can support CSR as it is here understood only if it is performed from a normative stance requiring that the interests of *all* stakeholders are considered for their own sake. More strongly: it is our opinion that stakeholder theory and management is not conductive of CSR results unless it starts from the recognition that "planet" and "people" (including future generations) are relevant and legitimate stakeholders in any decision by organizations. This goes a good step further than stakeholder management as it is usually conceived, and is only possible if we approach it from a perspective where sustainability is the overarching aim. Managing from a CSR perspective, on the other hand, requires accountability toward stakeholders and (taken to its ultimate consequences as, e.g., in phoenix-economy companies) direct stakeholder involvement. In this sense stakeholder theory may surely offer a positive contribution to CSR.

Understood in such terms CSR is not an activity superimposed on the mission and goals of an organization. On the contrary, CSR frames an organization's principles, mission, vision, and strategy and is strongly connected with a company's activity (Wood 1991). And this—which the authors consider a fourth feature of CSR—should be held true for the "environmental or social" entrepreneurs of the phoenix economy and for the multinational corporations that still dominate our world as well as for the myriads of small and medium-sized enterprises that create, in most world economies, the majority of jobs.

All this has consequences for one of the traditional aspects of CSR, i.e., that it is considered a voluntary activity. As observed above, CSR was framed as voluntary from the beginning mostly because CSR activities were conceived as those activities that go beyond the economic and legal responsibilities on the one hand and constitute a direct response to value shifts in society on the other. Yet the matter changes if CSR is conceptualized as a responsibility by organizations to create value on the people, planet, and profit dimension, or for all their stakeholders. By definition responsibilities have to be addressed: when someone is considered responsible for something, he or she has to take action. As Donna Wood correctly observed (in Agle *et al.* 2008: 161): " 'voluntary' fulfillment of responsibility is in an important sense a contradiction in terms—duties require enforcement mechanisms."

Enforcement mechanisms have indeed developed, starting from Europe where CSR seems to have taken hold from the 1990s on (see Carroll 1999: 269). These mechanisms have taken the shape of formats for (again, voluntary) disclosure on the processes set in place to support a CSR/3Ps approach as well as on the outcome and, increasingly, on the impact of CSR activities. Disclosure and the values it is grounded upon (honesty and transparency) are in turn intertwined with the development of tools (such as the Internet) that seem to make public control over business more effective and efficient. The role of governments should not be neglected. As has been observed by many early and later proponents of CSR, the magnitude of the challenges we face is such that we will need the efforts of both organizations and governments to cope with them.

Finally, anchoring sustainability in both organizations and governments will never be possible without a vision of the human being behind the business executive, the owner, the supplier, the employee, or the community member. Part III of this book is dedicated to developing and supporting the authors' vision on this point. However, it is worth saying already at this stage that, together with scholar such as John Elkington and Edward Freeman (recently in Agle and Agle 2007: 163-64), we believe that there is enough evidence to justify a more articulated view on people than the one proposed by traditional economic theories. Human beings are not exclusively self-interested machines. Human beings have feelings of empathy with fellow humans and even with animals, as anybody who has observed people loving pets can testify. It is time to design organizations and markets to take into account the full complexity of humans. In the end, organizations, even when they were meant as single-purpose enterprises, were intended to serve people's interests and not the other way round.

7
Toward sustainable organizations
Integrating sustainability principles into organizations

> A new type of thinking is essential if mankind is to survive and move toward higher levels (Albert Einstein 1946, May 25, *New York Times*: 13).

Stephan Schmidheiny, entrepreneur (Eternit AG, Swatch Group, GrupoNueva, Terranova), philanthropist, and founder of the World Business Council for Sustainable Development, argues in *Changing Course* (1992: 84) that:

> . . . for a new context to emerge, deeply ingrained assumptions must be brought forward, tested and modified . . .

> Clear and committed vision leads to the development of strategies and actions that change corporate processes and systems in ways that align them with the new vision. The proof that the vision is becoming reality lies in the measurement and reporting of its results or outcomes.

In this passage Stephan Schmidheiny makes two points. First, he states that becoming a sustainable organization involves questioning the values and assumptions on which the organization is currently based. The resulting change process reaches deeply into the nerves and sinews of an organization (Doppelt 2003a). In short, sustainability requires profound, radical change throughout the corporation (Holliday *et al.* 2002: 125; Senge *et al.* 2005).

Stephan Schmidheiny's second point is that measurement and reporting are essential to check whether the new vision is becoming reality. Both proponents and critics of CSR agree on the necessity to measure and report corporate progress toward sustainability. In his critique of CSR, for example, Milton Friedman rightly affirms that it is pointless and counterproductive to ask managers to consider other objectives than profit if there are neither guidelines on how they could pursue these objectives nor a way to measure their success in this endeavor (see Chapter 6 Section 2). Moreover, "enterprises tend to be enabled and constrained by their measurement systems. There is common wisdom among managers that once one begins to measure something, many other things (e.g., externalities) don't get captured" (Mitchell in Agle *et al.* 2008: 179). To get the sustained attention of management, sustainable indicators should become part and parcel of the management, measurement, and reporting system.

Integration into an organization's principles, values, and vision on one side and measurement and monitoring on the other are fundamental issues in CSR. They deserve to be discussed in two dedicated chapters. This chapter focuses on the first issue and traces the steps that have to be followed to (re)build a sustainable organization (Sections 7.1 to 7.7). Its conclusion reassesses the need to distinguish between becoming sustainable and greening an organization's operations. Chapter 8 is dedicated to management, measurement, and reporting tools. Here, more than in any other place in this work, the warning is given that this field is in its infancy: what is offered in these two chapters is only an attempt at shedding some light on a fascinating, yet far from resolved, set of issues.

Before going further, it is essential to remember that with the term sustainable organizations the authors refer to organizations that set a contribution to sustainable development as their ultimate aim. In order to positively impact on the economic, social, and ecologic value at the level of society, sustainable organizations consider positive financial results a profit only when people and planet are also benefited in the process. Generating value on a triple bottom line thus constitutes an integral part of the principles, values, vision, mission, strategy, and processes of sustainable organizations (as Grayson and Hodges [2004] also observe).

Let us insist on this point: sustainable organizations are not acrobats performing a balancing act. They do not strive for the less negative tradeoffs among the three dimensions of sustainability at organizational level, but actively pursue solutions that positively impact on all three Ps (people, planet, and profit). From a stakeholders' perspective, sustainable organizations recognize responsibility toward all stakeholders—positively or negatively; directly or indirectly; willingly or unwillingly—affected by their operations. They strive to maximize value in win–win situations and, when this cannot be achieved, to reduce negative consequences for the involved stakeholders.[1]

Concluding, the generation of value on the people and planet dimension is seen by a sustainable organization not as an add-on to its economic responsibility, but

---

1 As Michael Porter notes in his 1996 article, while some tradeoffs are unavoidable, many are not but are caused by a lack of operational effectiveness. The authors would like to add that many avoidable tradeoffs result from a lack of knowledge, innovation, and creativity.

as "built in" to it. Building the concern for people and planet into the profit dimension may result in the design or redesign of the organization from sustainability principles. In analogy with the other two options (build-on and build-in), this last alternative can be labeled "build from." It is this last option that is mainly explored in the following pages.[2]

7.1 **The first step: a new paradigm**

The first step in a process of change is to become aware that change is needed. This is never an easy step and it is even less so when the status quo is considered by the majority as good or, at least, as the best possible option. Looking at corporations, it cannot be denied that business executives more often than not truly believe that their exclusive task is to increase shareholders' value. Embracing sustainability means thus for them not only reconsidering the role of their own companies in society, but also their own personal assumptions on that role and on their own task. This is not a minor change. It is a major paradigm shift.

A paradigm shift occurs when individuals or groups realize that the way they look at the world is no longer adequate. Paradigms, in fact, are like spectacles through which people perceive a situation. The spectacles' lenses are formed by a person's principles, knowledge, and experiences, and by the values and the norms of the surrounding society. In Stephen Covey's example quoted in Box 7.1 the norm at stake is that children should behave in public and should be checked if they do not. The important point is that how a person perceives a situation deeply influences how he or she responds to it. Stephen Covey's attitude immediately changed when he understood that he was not witnessing the behavior of unruly children and a selfish father, but of children who had just lost their mother, the man's wife.

Paradigms influence our behavior so deeply that it may be said that in the end it is all a question of paradigms. Recognizing this essential point, however, is not the same as subscribing to the view that all paradigms are equal. In Stephen Covey's example it is clear that his first paradigm, in which he saw a father unable or unwilling to check his noisy children, was wrong. In the context of this book, enough evidence has been brought forward to support the conclusion that the traditional world view—in which nature is considered to be a subsystem of the economy—is sadly inadequate and seriously misleading as an explanation of the relationship between human activity and nature. Sustainability, the authors conclude, offers a more adequate account of the interdependent nature of the relationship among social, environmental, and economic values at community level; among people,

---

2 In the following, CSR, sustainable organizations, and 3Ps/TBL organizations will be used as synonyms. 3Ps stands, as already noted, for the three dimensions of sustainable organizations: people, planet, and profit. TBL (triple bottom line) refers to the fact that sustainable organizations add value on all three dimensions.

Box 7.1 **Paradigm shift**

Stephen Covey gives a good example of paradigm shift in his *Seven Habits of Highly Effective People*. Once, a man with his children stepped into the same subway compartment where he and other passengers were quietly traveling. The children were restless and very noisy, while their father just sat down and seemed not to notice. After a while, and seeing that the man did not take any action and that more travelers were clearly annoyed but did not dare to say anything, Stephen Covey stepped in and asked the man to check his children. The father looked up and answered softly that they were coming from the hospital where the children's mother had just passed away. Instantly Stephen Covey's irritation vanished and compassion filled his heart. The way he saw the situation changed, and thus his feelings and behavior (Covey 2003: 30-31).

Several authors insist on the need for a paradigm shift in the transition toward sustainability. Let us recall, for example, the discussion in Chapter 1 on two ways to look at the relationship between economy and nature. Recently, Andres Edwards titled his book *The Sustainability Revolution: Portrait of a Paradigm Shift* (2005).

planet, and profit at the organizational level; and of the linkages between these two levels.

The concept of paradigm has, thus, two main lessons to offer. First, that the way we see a situation influences our thoughts and behavior; second, that not all paradigms are an adequate description of reality and that, if they are not and if we notice, a shift in paradigm usually occurs.

This brings us back to the need for a paradigm shift to start the transition process from traditional to sustainable organizations. The question may arise whether it can seriously be expected that business executives and entrepreneurs, who were formed from and thrive thanks to an economic world view, would recognize the inadequacy of their paradigm and embrace a sustainable world view. As a first answer, let's quote the example of Ray C. Anderson.

Ray Anderson was the founder and CEO of Interface, a U.S.-based, multi-million, global producer of carpet tiles.[3] In *Mid-course Correction* (1998) and in *Confessions of a Radical Industrialist* (2009), Ray Anderson describes how he came to understand that Interface was operating from a wrong world view and should be redesigned to fit a new, "more accurate view of reality" (Anderson 1998: 94). Table 7.1 reports his own understanding of the two world views, which he calls "old industrial revolution paradigm" and "new industrial revolution paradigm."

---

3 Sadly, Ray Anderson passed away on August 8, 2011. The authors are grateful to Interface for the permission to quote from Ray Anderson's 1998 book.

Table 7.1 **Ray Anderson's two paradigms**

Source: Anderson 1998: 93-95; Anderson and White 2009: ch. 4

	Old industrial revolution paradigm	New industrial revolution paradigm	Compare with
Natural resources and sinks	Earth is an inexhaustible source of materials (natural resources). We'll never run out of them There will always be substitutes available Earth is a limitless sink, able to assimilate our waste, no matter how poisonous, no matter how much	Earth is finite (see it from space; that's all there is!), both as a source (what it can provide) and as a sink (what it can assimilate and endure) An end will come to the substitutes that are possible. You cannot substitute water for food, air for water, food for warmth, energy for air, air for food. Some things are complementary	Part I (Section 1.5) Brundtland Report 1987 Daly and Cobb 1989 Lovelock 2000 Meadows *et al.* 1972 Ward and Dubos 1972 Ward 1966
Time frame	Relevant times frame are, maximum, the life of a human being; more likely the *working* life of a human being; sometimes, especially in business, just the next quarter	Relevant time frames are geological in scale. We must, at least, think beyond ourselves and our brief, puny time on Earth and think of our species, not just ourselves, over geological time	Part I (Sections 4.3 and 4.7); Part III (Chapter 10) Lovelock 2000 Kroonenberg 2006 Meadows *et al.* 1972
Humans and nature	Earth was made for humans to conquer and rule; *homo sapiens sapiens* (self-named "wise-wise man") doesn't really need the other species, except for food, fiber, and fuel, and maybe shade	Man was made for Earth, not the other way around, and the diversity of nature is crucially important in keeping the whole web of life, including us, going sustainably over geological time	Part I (Section 2.1) Lovelock 1979 Meadows *et al.* 1972 Schumacher 1973 White 1967
Technology	Technology is omnipresent, especially when coupled with human intelligence, specifically, left-brained intelligence (practical, objective, realistic, numbers-driven, results-oriented, unemotional)	Technology must fundamentally change if it is to become part of the solution instead of continuing to be the major part of the problem. In the equation Impact = Population * Affluence * Technology, the T of Technology must move to the denominator The right side of the brain, the caring, nurturing, artistic, subjective, sensitive, emotional side, is at least as important as the left side, perhaps a good bit more important since it represents the human spirit	Part I (Sections 1.3, 2.2, 2.3, and 2.5); Part II (Sections 7.5 and 8.2) Szirmai 2005 von Weizsäcker *et al.* 1998 Ehrlich and Holdren 1971 Hawken *et al.* 1999

➔

	Old industrial revolution paradigm	New industrial revolution paradigm	Compare with
Market	Adam Smith's "invisible hand" of the market is a honest broker	The market is opportunistic, if not outright dishonest, in its willingness to externalize any cost that an unwary, uncaring public will allow it to externalize. It must constantly be redressed to keep it honest	Part I (Section 2.1) Part I (Sections 3.1 and 3.2) Part I (Sections 4.3 and 4.5) Part II (Sections 5.2 and 5.3) Friedman 2005 Smith 1776

That Ray Anderson is not the only entrepreneur who experienced this paradigm shift may be proved by reference to the Ceres *Roadmap for Sustainability*, a guideline for the integration of sustainability in business featuring best practices of more than 200 companies. In the *Roadmap* we read: "company practices must reflect an understanding that they are dependent upon goods and services provided by nature, and that nature's limits and finite resources must be fully valued and managed for long-term growth and prosperity" (Summary: 4).

Summarizing the discussion so far it may be said that the first step in the transition toward sustainability is changing the paradigm through which we look at the world and on the basis of which we have designed our society and the organizations that constitute it, including businesses. As Peter Senge and his fellow researchers put it, we need "the courage to see freshly" (Senge *et al.* 2005: 35).

Though taking this first step is extremely difficult, it is here that the most may be gained. As Stephen Covey puts it (2004: 19): "If you want to make *minor*, incremental changes and improvements, work on practice, behavior or attitude. But if you want to make significant, quantum improvement, work on *paradigms*" (italic in original). Because everything else follows from the way we look at reality, the moment we are able to embrace a new, sustainable world view our minds will open to new possibilities; we will be able to understand which other steps are needed and find ways to actually take them (Meadows 1997).[4]

---

4 The role of leadership in the process of change toward sustainability is discussed in Part III.

7.2 **The following steps explained through the organizational effectiveness cycle**

Let us suppose that the top managers of an organization, either following their own insights or yielding to stakeholder pressure, have come to realize that the world view from which their organization is operating is flawed and that a transition toward sustainability is needed. This first paradigm shift will set in motion a cascade of changes. As Bob Doppelt states: "real change toward sustainability produces altered values and norms that lead to choices affecting every aspect of the organization that are different from those generated by the status quo" (2003a: 75).

The organizational effectiveness cycle (OEC), a tool developed by FranklinCovey,[5] can help to explain which aspects of an organization are affected and how (see Fig. 7.1).

Figure 7.1 **The organizational effectiveness cycle**

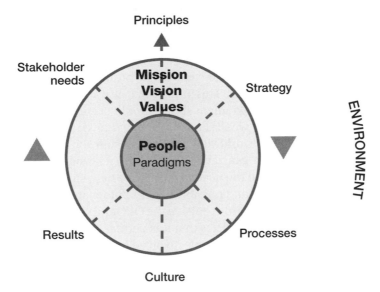

The OEC assumes that each organization is perfectly equipped to get the results it gets. If results are flawed, if they do not meet stakeholders' needs, then the whole organization should be analyzed and the necessary changes made, starting from its principles. Principles are indeed the foundation of an organization and dictate its values, mission, and vision. In Andres Edwards's words (2005: 52): "Companies

---

5 FranklinCovey (based in Utah, U.S.A.) was born in 1997 after a merger between Franklin Quest and the Covey Leadership Center founded by Stephen R. Covey. It offers leadership training, consultancy, and management. See www.franklincovey.com/tc, accessed September 15, 2011.

. . . are promoting their sustainability strategies with guiding principles . . . that support their mission statement." These in turn inform the strategy; strategy influences processes; processes shape the organizational culture; and culture brings forth results that would, hopefully, be in line with stakeholders' needs. Alignment among all aspects individuated by the OEC is essential to achieve results in line with the chosen principles.

At the center of the OEC are people's paradigms. These both influence and are influenced by all other steps in the cycle. The centrality of paradigms in the OEC reflects their influence on people's behavior. In the context of organizational change toward sustainability this means that a person who believes that economic growth is the cure for all problems; that firms are a vehicle for profit maximization; that competition is a zero-sum game; and human beings self-interested, utility-maximizing individuals will not help create nor feel comfortable in a sustainable organization. People who see the world as an interconnected web of life, firms as interdependent with society, and fellow human beings as complex creatures usually moved by a mixture of egoistic, altruistic, and bio-centric values will help create and feel comfortable in sustainable organizations.[6] As Charles Holliday and his co-authors notice (2002: 128), framing a sustainable organization "requires that we express our personal convictions."

It is highly probable that in a traditional organization most employees, suppliers, clients, and other stakeholders will consciously or unconsciously follow the first, economically oriented paradigm. This implies that also at this level a paradigm shift or, better, a whole series of paradigm shifts, should occur. Later on we will come back to this point. Here, we would like to insist that to start (re)building an organization from a sustainable world view a paradigm shift should have already taken place. Someone inside the organization should have realized the inadequacy of the old, economic paradigm and the need to embrace a new, sustainable one to create results that do not endanger and possibly benefit both planet and people. Imagine this first shift as a kick coming from outside the OEC and setting it in motion. A kick from which the organization realizes that it is getting bad results for stakeholders such as the planet or some of the people involved in its supply chain. The next step after this first paradigm shift has occurred will be reviewing the principles on which an organization is built. Then all other organizational aspects should be reconsidered and aligned with the reviewed principles. In the rest of this chapter all steps of the cycle will be briefly explained and examples of how to use them to (re)build a sustainable organization will be given.

6 Bio-centric stands for valuing nature and the Earth for their own sake. Part I has substantiated that the world is an interconnected web of life; Part II argues for interdependency between organizations and society; Part III will deploy a vision of humans as complex creatures able to take a bio-centric or "Care for all" perspective.

7.3 **Building sustainable organizations: from principles to values, vision, and mission**

Principles are seen by Stephen Covey as natural laws applying to the human dimension. They are natural laws in the sense that they operate whether we understand them or not, and thus independently from our will. They pertain to the human dimension in the sense that they apply to the interaction between people. One such principle is, for example, that mental creation precedes physical creation; that is, that we first need to envision a new reality before we start building it (Covey 2003). Sustainability proposes new standards for social and personal behavior on the basis of a new understanding of the natural environment and its relationship with human activity. As a consequence sustainability principles combine the physical with the human dimension. They are at once natural and social laws. That Earth's sinks have a limited capacity and that human activity should stay inside these limits, is such a principle. It contains a statement on the nature of the natural world and a statement on the behavior that adequately copes with it and is thus sustainable. This statement is a principle, in Covey's terms, because it uncovers a situation that has always been that way. Though it was Rachel Carson who first understood this principle and explained the consequences of acting as if it does not apply, it was, is and will be true that Earth's sinks are limited and that if they are systematically exceeded pollution will increase to levels threatening life (Carson 1962).

A list of sustainability principles that can reckon on a vast consensus was developed by Karl-Henrik Robèrt, the founder of The Natural Step (see Box 7.2).

Box 7.2 **The Natural Step**

Stimulated by the Brundtland Report and his experience as a cancer specialist, Swedish scientist Karl-Henrik Robèrt started looking for scientific consensus on the basic principles of sustainability. His aim was to put an end to unfruitful discussions on what sustainability exactly means and stimulate actions toward sustainability at individual, organizational, and community level.

To design the principles, Karl-Henrik Robèrt went back to the laws of thermodynamics. In short, these laws state that the Earth is a finite system where all matter that will exist is already present now, where quality is dissipated (or, in other words, disorder increases), and where the only source of new energy is the sun. It is worth noting that in finite systems the only activities that can continue indefinitely are cyclical, i.e. activities where the waste produced by one part of the system is food for another part. This excludes the cradle-to-grave activities that characterize modern economies.

On the basis of the laws of thermodynamics and after a discussion involving 50 scientists from different disciplines, Karl-Henrik Robèrt stated four basic conditions of a sustainable system and four sustainability principles to reach it (Holmberg *et al.* 1999; www.naturalstep.org [accessed

August 21, 2011]). Robèrt's system conditions are the same as what the authors have called the physical aspect of sustainability principles; his principles equal what has been called above the social or behavioral aspect of sustainability.

The four system conditions	The four principles of sustainability
In a sustainable society, nature is not subject to systematically increasing . . .	*To become a sustainable society we must . . .*
1. Concentrations of substances extracted from the Earth's crust	1. Eliminate our contribution to the progressive build-up of substances extracted from the Earth's crust (for example, heavy metals and fossil fuels)
2. Concentrations of substances produced by society	2. Eliminate our contribution to the progressive build-up of chemicals and compounds produced by society (for example, dioxins, PCBs, and DDT)
3. Degradation by physical means	3. Eliminate our contribution to the progressive physical degradation and destruction of nature and natural processes (for example, over-harvesting forests and paving over critical wildlife habitat)
4. And, in that society, people are not subject to conditions that systematically undermine their capacity to meet their needs	4. And eliminate our contribution to conditions that undermine people's capacity to meet their basic human needs (for example, unsafe working conditions and not enough pay to live on)

It may be noticed that the first three principles, on the use of natural resources and services, parallel those already alluded to by Daly and Cobb (1989). The fourth is formulated with a direct reference to the Brundtland Commission report *Our Common Future* (1987) and further defined by reference to Manfred Max-Neef's work (1989).

It is important to note that Robèrt's principles are based on system conditions that are in turn derived from the physical laws of thermodynamics. This means that his sustainability principles have to be conceived as universal, all-pervasive, and unchangeable. They are natural laws applying to the human dimension, in the same sense as Covey's. This is a crucial point and should be considered when analyzing other sustainability "principles" such as the one discussed in Edwards (2005).

Ray Anderson's Interface is one of the companies that have embraced the four principles proposed by Karl-Henrik Robèrt. On this basis it has reformulated its values, vision, and mission. The resulting vision is that of a firm with no pipes, and no chimneys (Anderson 1998; Anderson and White 2009). This vision was translated into Interface's Mission Zero, the pledge to eliminate any negative impact Interface has on the environment (Robèrt's Principle 1) and to reduce damaging emissions to zero (Robèrt's Principle 2) by the year 2020.

In the authors' view the basic principle of a sustainable organization will be as follows: organizations and society are mutually dependent and both dependent on a healthy natural environment; therefore this organization will contribute to a better quality of life for present and future generations and support the economic, social, and environmental development of the communities in which it operates by adding value on the people, planet, and profit dimensions of organizational sustainability.

Following the OEC principles informs the values on which organizations build their vision and mission. It seems almost unnecessary to say that a world view that sees organizations and societies as dependent on each other and both as dependent on the resources and services provided by nature, will translate into values supportive of a healthy natural environment, human development, and economic prosperity.

As Ben Cohen and Jerry Greenfield (the founders of Ben & Jerry's, the well-known ice cream brand now owned by Unilever) put it (1997: 30):

> Values-led business is based on the idea that business has a responsibility to the people and the society that makes its existence possible . . . Values-led business seeks to maximize its impact by integrating socially beneficial actions in as many of its day-to-day activities as possible. In order to do that, values must lead and be right up there in a company's mission statement, strategy and operating plan.

The values Ben & Jerry's stands for are summarized by Ben Cohen and Jerry Greenfield as "promoting social progress for the common good" (1997: 33). Indee, Ben & Jerry's mission reflects its values:

> Ben & Jerry's is founded on and dedicated to a sustainable corporate concept of linked prosperity. Our mission consists of 3 interrelated parts: social, product and economic.

> *Social mission*: To operate the Company in a way that actively recognizes the central role that business plays in society by initiating innovative ways to improve the quality of life locally, nationally and internationally.

> *Product mission*: To make, distribute and sell the finest quality all natural ice cream and euphoric concoctions with a continued commitment to incorporating wholesome, natural ingredients and promoting business practices that respect the Earth and the Environment.

> *Economic mission*: to operate the Company on a sustainable financial basis of profitable growth, increasing value for our stakeholders and expanding opportunities for development and career growth for our employees.[7]

---

7   www.benjerry.com/activism/mission-statement, accessed March 31, 2010.

Ben & Jerry's tripartite mission statement actually constitutes a blend of what John Elkington labeled the people, planet, and profit dimension of a sustainable organization, showing that, for Ben & Jerry's, one dimension cannot be conceived without the others. In the economic mission statement, for example, the reference to increasing value for its stakeholders (and not only for its shareholders) follows from and reinforces the commitment toward respect for the Earth stated in the product mission and Ben & Jerry's dedication to improve the quality of life stated in its social mission.

As is widely known, Ben & Jerry's was founded as a company with a social and environmental edge by Ben Cohen and Jerry Greenfield in 1978. In the beginning, the *P* with which Cohen and Greenfield had to struggle most was the *P* of profit, not the *P* of planet or people (Cohen *et al.* 1997). Yet, also, organizations established with an overarching economic goal have in recent years reviewed their vision and mission to align them with a changed world view and changed expectations on business's role in society. Interface's shift under the leadership of Ray Anderson has already been mentioned. In Box 7.3 some other examples are given of organizations that hold their values, vision, and mission against the light shed by a sustainable approach to business.

Box 7.3 **Aligning the mission with a changed world view**

Since the second half of the 1990s more and more companies have reviewed their values, vision, and mission to align them with a changed world view. Let's go back to a company that has been quoted repeatedly in this part of the book: Shell.

After the Brent Spar and Ken Saro-Wiwa affair, Shell reformulated its values, aim, and general business principles. Honesty, integrity, and respect for people were defined as Shell's core values while its "aim is to meet the energy needs of society, in ways that are economically, socially and environmentally viable, now and in the future."[a]

In this last sentence the reference to Brundtland's definition of sustainable development is quite clear. It is even clearer in Shell's General Business Principles where, after a reference to Shell's core values, is written: "As part of the Business Principles, we commit to contribute to sustainable development. This requires balancing short and long term interests, integrating economic, environmental and social considerations into business decision-making." Shell's concern for profit, people, and planet is evident throughout the General Business Principles booklet, where—alongside shareholders, employees, customers, and business partners—society as a whole is also identified as a stakeholder.

As was mentioned above, in 2000 Ben & Jerry's was bought by Unilever. Several observers thought that, despite assurances to the contrary, Ben & Jerry's environmental and social activism would come to a halt. The reality, a decade later, is quite the opposite: not only has Ben & Jerry's retained its triple-bottom-line focus, but Unilever has also been declared by the Dow

Jones Sustainability Index as the best company in the food and beverage sector.[b] Unilever states on its website that the transition toward sustainability has been fueled by the recognition that the world is changing and that organizations should engage with the social and environmental problems the world faces. As a consequence, Unilever reviewed its values and vision in the fall of 2009. Unilever's values are expressed in its purpose: to succeed requires "the highest standards of corporate behavior toward everyone we work with, the communities we touch, and the environment on which we have an impact."[c] The environmental and social dimensions of sustainability are here clearly linked with the economic dimension. Unilever's vision builds on its values by declaring in its first statement that Unilever aims at creating a better future every day. Other statements include a clear, more operational reference to sustainability: "We will inspire people to take small everyday actions that can add up to a big difference for the world" and "we will develop new ways of doing business with the aim of doubling the size of our company while reducing our environmental impact." It may be interesting to note that this last sentence seems to quote Ernst Ulrich von Weizsäcker's book title: *Factor Four: Doubling Wealth, Halving Resource Use.*

a www.shell.com/home/content/aboutshell/who_we_are, accessed March 31, 2010.

b www.sustainability-index.com/djsi_pdf/news/PressReleases/DJSI_PressRelease_090903_Review09.pdf, accessed March 30, 2010.

c www.unilever.com/aboutus/purposeandprinciples/?WT. GNAV=Purpose_&_principles (accessed March 30, 2010).

7.4 **Building sustainable organizations: strategy**

Values, vision, and mission inform strategy. Strategy is one of those concepts that are often talked of without being clearly defined. In the following our starting point is Michael Porter's definition where strategy refers to the choice of a distinctive set of complementary and mutually reinforcing activities that enable an organization to meet its objectives (Porter 1996).

Michael Porter's definition makes clear that a shift in objectives (in the case of sustainable organizations from value creation on a single, financial bottom line to sustainable value creation on a triple bottom line) should be reflected in the strategy of an organization and consequently in all its activities. Without alignment between strategy and activities, the chosen strategy will be watered down and die. To quote Stephan Schmidheiny (1992: 82): "For business, [sustainable development] means profound change: change in the goals and assumptions that drive corporate activities, and *changes in daily practices and tools*" (brackets and italic by authors).

The point here is that, to endure, new principles—and the values, vision, and mission based on them—should be institutionalized in the nerves and sinews of an organization. Sustainability constitutes no exception to this rule.

Michael Porter also insists that, to offer a competitive advantage, a strategy should consist of a *set* of complementary and mutually reinforcing activities. One activity can easily be imitated by a competitor. A whole set cannot. For our discussion this means that a strategy informed by sustainability principles and serving a sustainable vision and mission can never result in the deployment of a single or few activities detached from a business's main operations. Developing a new, eco-efficient product alongside the existing ones is not a suitable strategy in Porter's terms. Philanthropy, here understood as giving to charitable causes, also falls short of Michael Porter's requirements. Though it can have a positive impact on society and be used "strategically" to enhance a company's image, philanthropy does not require changes in the core activities of an organization. In other words, philanthropy alone does not constitute a *set* of complementary and mutually reinforcing activities ensuing from and supporting the sustainable stance taken by the organization.

Though some organizations unfortunately seem to forget (Epstein 2003), accepting Michael Porter's definition of strategy equates to abandoning the option of sustainability as an "add-on." To design a set of complementary and mutually reinforcing activities a sustainable organization should resort to a "build-in" or a "build-from" approach, or a combination of the two.

Michael Porter refers to strategy as a *choice* (Porter 1996). The strategic possibilities from which a sustainable organization may choose are in one sense the same as and in one sense different than the options open to a "traditional" organization. Choosing for cost leadership, product leadership or focusing on niche markets (Porter 1980) is open to both. What differs is the interpretation of these general strategies.

It is obvious that a sustainable company choosing for cost leadership will not chase reduction of costs to the consequence that the natural environment is endangered or employees deprived of fundamental rights.[8] Product leadership for a sustainable company will entail more than designing products that beat those of the competition. As a first step, it will mean designing products that, in comparison with similar ones, have a less harmful impact on the natural environment, as Toyota did with its hybrid motor and Interface did with its CoolCarpet™, a carpet tile manufactured with zero CO_2 emissions (Anderson and White 2009: 5). Going a step further, it will mean creating a product that has a positive impact on social and environmental values, as Michael Braungart and William McDonough propose through their cradle-to-cradle approach (see Box 7.5). Still a step further, it may

---

8 Park and Dickson (2008: 41) observe that a focus on price leadership negatively influences labor standards in the supply chain. "Firms with supply control, image differentiation, and product development strategic emphases were more engaged in partnership, whereas ones with a low-price emphasis were less engaged in partnership relationships."

mean setting at the core of the organization a social problem that still has to be solved, as Mohammad Yunus did with the Grameen Bank (see Box 6.6).

That sustainable organizations interpret the general strategic choices differently than "traditional" ones becomes particularly clear in the next stage of the cycle: processes. As Ben Cohen and Jerry Greenfield put it (1997: 33), a "values-led business recognizes that the greatest potential a business has for benefiting society is in its operations."

7.5 **Building sustainable organizations: processes**

Entrepreneur and environmentalist Paul Hawken notices that (1993, 2005: 148) "restorative businesses must rethink entire processes, from production and materials sourcing to employment, distribution, and marketing."

Indeed, the term "processes" covers a wide array of organizational activities. The OEC refers both to primary activities and to supporting processes. Typical primary activities of a business are inbound logistics, operations, outbound logistics, marketing and sales, and after-sales. Supporting processes are procurement, research and development, human resource management (HRM), information and communication technologies (ICT), and the firm's own infrastructure (Porter 1996). The point to be made here is that all these activities should be aligned with the strategy and thus with the principles, core values, mission, and vision of the organization.

The end in mind of a sustainable organization is to contribute to sustainable development by creating value on the triple bottom line of people, planet, and profit. Linking processes to this aim involves integrating economic, environmental, and social values into all primary activities and supporting processes mentioned above. To facilitate this task, the technique called "backcasting" may be helpful. While forecasting tries to picture the future on the basis of today's parameters, backcasting encourages organizations to redesign their processes starting from an envisioned sustainable future (see Box 7.4). Ray Anderson's vision of a plant without pipes and chimneys, for example, was translated back at Interface in their Zero Waste program starting with reduction of spillage, then progressing to recycling and redesign of products and services to achieve the height of ecological sustainability: a completely closed loop in the use of materials and energy (Anderson 1998; Anderson and White 2009).

In general, a sustainable organization will, on the basis of actual knowledge,[9] strive in all its processes for maximization of positive impacts on the triple bottom line. In case tradeoffs cannot be avoided, it will strive to minimize negative impacts while looking for innovative solutions to overcome such tradeoffs. Box 7.5

---

9   This is not a trivial addition but an important caveat: knowledge progresses. What today may seem the best choice on the basis of a sustainable world view may appear tomorrow as inadequate or even wrong. Remember the discussion on CFCs in Part I.

Box 7.4 **Backcasting**

A vision is often described as a compelling story highlighting where a company wishes to be in the future. The technique of "backcasting" can then been used to relate the future vision to today's operations by asking the question: what can be done today to reach that future outcome? In other words, backcasting compares the current situation with the desired future situation, designing steps that will gradually lead to it (Holmberg and Robèrt 2000).

Essential in the context of sustainability is to envision this future stage starting from widely accepted notions. For example, there is consensus on the need to phase out the use of fossil fuel to achieve sustainability. In envisioning a sustainable future, an organization may declare its wish to become independent from fossil fuels. An assessment of the current fossil fuel use and of opportunities for changes will lead to a list of steps needed to achieve this goal. Usually in energy matters, the first step is reduction: for example, a Belgian retailer devised a way to prevent trucks from leaving the distribution center unless they were totally full. A second step is substitution: for example, substituting fossil fuel with biofuel or electricity generated by wind and sun. And so on.

In the quest for sustainability, backcasting from a future vision has many advantages over forecasting from the present situation. For the scope of this work let us consider only two advantages. First, backcasting avoids extrapolating from the past, and thus designing possible solutions from the same framework that created the problem: for example, a profit-first mission statement. Second, it sidesteps several practical difficulties involved in discounting investments in sustainable products and services using current prices for natural resources or trying to predict future prices in a highly complex and insecure market.

---

describes some tools at the disposal of organizations that wish to minimize their environmental and social impacts. The following few pages give some practical examples, referring again to those organizations, like Ben & Jerry's and Interface, that have already successfully experimented with the integration of sustainability in their processes. Three examples will be given: the first is related to procurement, the second to accounting, and the third to HRM.[10]

In line with their product mission, Ben & Jerry's procurement is geared toward organic and fair trade ingredients (Cohen and Greenfield 1997: 55ff.). This is widely known and openly communicated to customers, not only on Ben & Jerry's website

10 For other, general examples of sustainable choices connected to business operations see Porter and Kramer 2006: 5 and Ceres 2010: 11. Ceres defines itself as a U.S.-based coalition of investors, environmental groups, and other public interest organizations working with companies to address sustainability challenges.

but also on the packages of their products. What is less generally known is that Ben & Jerry's chooses suppliers that help support their social and product mission. Greyston Bakery, for example, is a New York-based firm producing chocolate brownies for Ben & Jerry's and employing the unemployables: disabled, homeless, and disenfranchised people. Confronted with poor quality in the beginning, Ben & Jerry's did not pull out. On the contrary, after a process of open consultation it came to understand the challenges that Greyston Bakery was facing in meeting its demand and adjusted its own operations while helping improve those of its supplier (Cohen and Greenfield 1997: 60-65).[11]

Box 7.5 **Maximize positive impacts and minimize negative ones: from cradle-to-grave via LCA to cradle-to-cradle**

Different approaches have been proposed to curb the cradle-to-grave mentality of traditional production patterns to a more sustainable stance. Most products we sell and buy are designed for a one-trip to the landfill as several scholars and environmental activists have observed, but none as creatively as Anne Leonard in "The Story of Stuff" where she contends that 90% of materials used to produce goods are disgorged as waste while 99% of goods in the U.S. are used for only six months before being disposed of.[a] Similar numbers have also been calculated by Interface (Anderson 1998: 3-9 and 72-73). The cradle-to-grave approach is a typical outcome of a paradigm that sees the world as a supplier of unlimited resources and sinks.

LCA, or life cycle assessment, is used to evaluate or compare the environmental impact of products or processes in all phases of the life cycle: from the extraction of materials, via production, transportation, and consumption to disposal. The goal of LCA as commonly understood is to lessen the impact of a product on the planet by reducing, reusing, and recycling materials; reducing energy and water use and so on. In this sense the main goal of LCA is eco-efficiency over the complete life cycle. LCA can be interpreted as an answer to the view of our world as finite and thus of natural resources as limited. In this approach the people dimension of sustainability is less visible.

The aim of cradle-to-cradle is to break the linear model from extraction to disposal by closing the loop for every good or service entering the economy and providing that, after each useful life, a product constitutes either nourishment for nature or high-quality materials for new products (McDonough and Braungart 2002). To the well-known eco-efficiency triad "reduce, reuse, recycle," Braungart and McDonough added a fourth R: redesign. Cradle-to-cradle can be seen as the result of a realistic view on

11 Let us take this opportunity to state that most organizations face their main sustainability-related challenges in the supply chain. To start to understand the environmental challenges connected to chain management, refer to Cramer 1998. For an overview of salient issues, drivers, and barriers to social and environmental procurement see Adrien-Kirby and Hoejmose 2010.

limited natural resources connected with the optimistic insight that nature's web of life can be imitated by intelligent design to create products that flow back to the natural or technical cycle without losing quality. Cradle-to-cradle thus goes beyond recycling. During recycling, products' components are more often than not downgraded and, when used again as raw material, have not the same quality as newly extracted materials. To exemplify, in the same way as oxygen is waste for a tree but a nutrient for people, so everything people produce should in the end be food for someone or something else. A well known example of a cradle-to-cradle product is the compostable T-shirt: a T-shirt that after use can be disposed of in your own garden because it decomposes and in the process acts as a fertilizer for plants. Though sometimes reduced to its ecological component, McDonough and Braungart clearly devised the cradle-to-cradle concept to take into account the people dimension, too. Cradle-to-cradle is at the moment the outer frontier for solutions that maximize positive impact on people, planet, and profit.

a www.storyofstuff.com, accessed August 21, 2011.

The second example is taken from supporting operations and focuses, though briefly, on accounting. Stephan Schmidheiny notes that current accounting methods resemble GDP in so far as they fail "to account for, or at best undervalue, environmental costs and benefits in the long term" while "calculations of the internal rate of return in any given project are likely to prove more accurate over time if environmental costs are factored in at the project analysis stage rather than after unexpected cleanup bills have been paid" (Schmidheiny 1992: 61).

Life cycle assessment (LCA) and sustainability measurement and reporting have emerged in the last few years to address this challenge. LCA has briefly been addressed in Box 7.5; sustainability measurement and reporting will be addressed in the next chapter. Here we would like only to note that accounting for environmental and social issues in the decision-making process is one of the best ways to enhance creativity and innovation. Practically, it can be done by assessing a proposed project on the triple bottom line. Colruyt, a privately owned Belgian retail chain, has applied this technique successfully for many years and discards projects that do not bring a positive result on all three dimensions of profit, planet, and people. In deciding, for example, on the feasibility of an investment in a wind turbine at its distribution center, Colruyt looked not only at the usual financial measures such as return-on-investment and economic life, but also at the avoided emissions and social benefits that building a wind turbine could bring. Similarly, in its efforts to reduce packaging, environmental measures of non-used materials and avoided emissions, were put side by side with financial measures in investment for new machinery and social measures such as security and hygiene. Of course, this involves consulting with more people from inside the organization than only the experts from the financial department, and may even involve consultation with external stakeholders.[12] Ray Anderson (Anderson and White 2009: 99) calls this way of taking decisions "making decisions in the round."

The last example discussed here concerns HRM. After a few remarks on HRM as a managerial function, the focus will be on some specific policies. A sustainable organization, as has been said repeatedly in the previous pages, approaches business from a specific world view where the organization itself, society, and the natural environment are seen as deeply interconnected. Individual human beings are not considered as utility maximization machines only driven by selfish motives. People are seen as complex creatures and it is recognized that they may act from egocentric, altruistic, and bio-centric values. In this context, HRM is the most powerful instrument in the hands of an organization to reinforce and share its choice for a sustainable paradigm while supporting employees' behavior based on a less egocentric set of values.[13] This vision on the role of HRM affects all HRM-specific functions and policies from selection and recruitment via compensation and training to dismissal. This said, let us take some examples of specific policies in sustainable organizations.

At Ben & Jerry's HRM supports the achievement of its sustainability mission through a livable wage policy, both for its own employees and for its suppliers' employees; by favoring diversity on the work floor; by dedicated training programs; by giving employees the opportunity to do community work during working hours; and so on. Community work is seen not only as a way to give back to society, but also as a means to enhance team spirit through meaningful and rewarding activities (Cohen and Greenfield 1997: 161-95 and 269-71). Training programs are geared toward generating awareness—by explaining sustainability as a general world view—and toward enhancing support for the specific choices made at Ben & Jerry's. The choice of fair trade products is, obviously, linked to the livable wage policy. Fair trade implies paying a fixed price for the delivered products, a price that ensure that the producer can meet his or her own needs, even when the market price is below a "fair price" level. Alongside decent living conditions, fair trade gives security to farmers and other suppliers enabling them to invest in their farms or production facilities. For Ben & Jerry's, choosing fair trade products means living up to its livable wage policy not only when it comes to its direct employees but also when it comes to its suppliers and suppliers' employees. Sustainable organizations recognize that their responsibilities do not end at their firm's door.

Integrating sustainability in HRM has, of course, its own challenges. In line with its search for a just redistribution of income, Ben & Jerry's imposed a cap on salaries: the remuneration of higher-level employees was intended never to be more

---

12 Our thanks go to Koen Demaesschalck, Human Resource Manager at Colruyt Group, for this information.

13 Schoemaker *et al.* (2006) argue for human value management in CSR organizations that see themselves as an open system and recognize that their employees constitute an essential link with their stakeholders. This position will also require a reinforcement of the other-oriented values of individual employees.

than five times the wage of the lowest-level employees. After the takeover by Unilever this system was abandoned as it made it impossible to hire high-level employees from outside Ben & Jerry's itself. In other companies that are redirecting their strategy toward a more sustainable stance, for example Philips and DSM, employees' compensation is partially linked to environmental performance. Management bonuses in these companies depend for a significant percentage (up to 20%) on the environmental performance of the team. This implies that environmental and social targets are known and progress toward them calculated: the issue of measurement is forcefully brought back.[14]

7.6 Building sustainable organizations: culture, results, and stakeholders' needs

All activities deployed by organizations are intended to achieve results that meet stakeholders' needs. In terms of the OEC, activities are connected to results through culture.

Since Edgar Shein published his landmark book *Organizational Culture and Leadership* (1985), it has been widely recognized that culture has a profound influence on organizations. Edgar Shein defined culture as a pattern of shared basic assumptions that have proven successful in solving issues of internal integration and external adaptation faced by a specific organization. These patterns are then taught to newcomers as the correct way to perceive, think, and feel about these issues (Shein 1985: 17).

Culture is thus formed on the basis of past experiences. The point here is that the basic assumptions shared by employees may or may not be in line with the professed values of an organization and ultimately the principles on which it is grounded.[15] Most issues around culture are in fact the result of misalignment between individual and organizational assumptions (see Box 7.6). Touching far too briefly on this very complex concept, it can be noticed that in this sense culture is an issue both for companies that are considering a transition toward sustainability and for

---

14 The discussion is here mostly limited to remuneration for the sake of time and space. Yet all HRM tools, and not only remuneration, can be designed to serve sustainability: researchers are just beginning to understand and explore the possibilities. Ehnert (2006) summarizes the discussion so far and (2009) brings it a step further.

15 The organizational effectiveness cycle maintains that values shape a culture through processes. (Organizational) values are surely an orientation point for individuals and groups. Yet a distinction should be made between professed (or overt), covert (or underground), and actual (or revealed) values. Actual values may often reflect covert ones and these may be very different from and even opposed to the professed values. Day-to-day human actions expose the actual values of a company: on this tension see Schoemaker *et al.* 2006.

companies that have already taken a sustainable stance—though differently. In the first case, the organization will have to address and change an existing culture that (as may be assumed) is not informed by sustainable principles and values. In the second case, the concern will be nurturing the internal, sustainable culture in the face of an outside world that in the best case is skeptical toward and in the worst case openly opposes sustainability.[16] A second point arising from Edgar Shein's definition is that employees' basic assumptions may or may not be apt to solve the actual challenges faced by an organization in the environment in which it operates. All organizations, including sustainable ones, should take care that their culture does not petrify in defending solutions that are made obsolete by new research and development or by changes in the surrounding environment.[17]

Box 7.6 **Alignment: an example**

In his *Confessions of a Radical Industrialist* (2009: 170-71) Ray Anderson emphasizes the importance of alignment. He recollects the visit to Interface of a representative from a large American multinational food corporation. The representative was quite skeptical about the sustainability stance of Interface, so, during a break, she went out onto the factory floor to see for herself how employees lived up to the Mission Zero aim of the company. There she stopped a forklift driver and asked him what he was doing. The amazing answer was "Ma'am, I come to work every day to help save the earth." She probed him further and after a while the forklift driver interrupted her with "Ma'am, I don't want to be rude, but if I don't get this roll of carpet to the next process right now, our waste and emissions numbers are going to go way up. I've gotta go."

Ray Anderson recalls that the representative, when rejoining the meeting, "said that she had never before seen such a deep alignment of vision in an organization. From the top to the bottom. The only word she could think of to describe it was 'love' " (Anderson and White 2009: 170-71).

A last point: to achieve the desired results, alignment is needed among all steps in the OEC. Yet the fact that the OEC sets principles as the first step conveys the notion that choosing inadequate principles and then consistently following the rest of the cycle, will lead to results that are inadequate to meet the needs and expectations of our contemporary world.

A culture aligned with processes that in their turn are aligned with a strategy properly based on a sustainable mission, will be conducive to results that have the highest positive (or lowest negative) impact on the profit, people, and planet dimension of sustainability at organizational level. Here the need for appropriate

16 To further explore this point in general see Kotter 1996; in the context of sustainability see Doppelt 2003a and Senge *et al.* 2005.
17 This reflects the double nature of culture: stable, to a certain degree, and yet dynamic.

measures is felt again deeply. The last step in the OEC closes the loop: results meet the stakeholders' needs identified when designing the vision and mission.

The concept of stakeholder was introduced in Chapter 6. Here it is important to insist that, from the point of view of sustainability, meeting stakeholders' needs goes pretty far. It does not only include the obvious stakeholders, such as clients and financiers, but also the community and nature. As William McDonough and Michael Braungart state, sustainability requires, for example, that we meet the needs of a river when designing a new soap (2002: 146). "What kind of soap does the river want?" was one of the questions they asked themselves when developing a new shower gel for a major European company.

7.7 **Building sustainable organizations: environment and people's paradigms**

This section touches briefly on two elements in the OEC that have not yet been discussed: the environment in which an organization operates and people's paradigms.

Environment

In the OEC "environment" is similar to what Michael Porter calls an organization's competitive context (Porter 1980, 1996; Porter and Kramer 2006). In the environment forces are at work that fall outside the direct control of the organization and that can facilitate or impede its ability to pursue its goals.

Let's think, for example, of governmental rules and regulations. It has already been mentioned that many of the rules and regulations in force are not conducive to sustainable outcomes because, for example, they were set up from the paradigm that nature is an infinite source of raw materials and sinks. Coming from this paradigm, governments have designed their tax system to tax labor and not the amount of natural resources used. Similarly, sustained by their desire to improve workers' conditions, unions have pushed for higher salaries. Both actions, however natural at the time and well intended, have led to the development of technologies that economize on labor and not on natural resources.

Though rather fixed, rules and regulations are not unchangeable. In the last few years, for example, NGOs' pressure and a sharp increase in the price of some essential natural resources have resulted in more attention on the wastage of raw materials and fueled the eco-efficiency trend. Similarly, the realization that natural sinks are not unlimited and that overshot situations are a real danger, has resulted in new regulations, such as the cap-and-trade market for CO_2 emission permits in Europe. Organizations, including businesses, have thus a role to play in steering rules and regulations toward sustainability. One possibility open to sustainable organizations in this struggle is joining forces with other organizations that face similar dilemmas to bend those rules and regulations that hinder sustainability and draw up new ones that support it. Many multilateral and sector agreements are the result of such efforts.[18]

Within the limits of this work it is not possible to discuss the relationship between a sustainable organization and its competitive context further. The point that has to be made, though, is that a sustainable organization does not consider its environment as by definition hostile to and separate from the organization itself. On the contrary, a sustainable company is aware that through its stakeholders it is deeply connected with it and can influence it.

As a final illustration, and to connect back to the relation that a sustainable organization has not only with its competitive context but also with the natural environment and the community it is part of, we would like to refer again to the example set by Ray Anderson at Interface. Starting from his "new industrial revolution paradigm" (illustrated in Table 7.1 above) Ray Anderson envisions Interface as a dematerialized, zero-waste, no-emission company involved in meaningful ways with the communities it operates in. Dematerialization will be achieved by applying cradle-to-cradle principles so that nothing is extracted from the Earth's crust and all that is needed for Interface to produce its carpet tiles comes from already used materials. In the Interface model, zero-waste implies not only continuous reduction of solid waste disposed to landfills but also independence from oil as a source of energy. Involvement with the community means, for example, investments in education to sensitize people to the new industrial paradigm. Ray Anderson sees Interface also as an advocate for the redesign of commerce, including prices that reflect the true (social and environmental) costs of products and services, and a new tax system stimulating economizing on the use of natural resources and not on labor (1998: ch. 5).

People's paradigms

At the core of the organizational effectiveness cycle are people's paradigms. We have already seen that (re-)designing an organization to achieve sustainable results starts from a paradigm shift. Here the focus is on the paradigms of the people who constitute an organization.

In the terminology of the OEC, people's paradigms are influenced by the principles, mission, strategy, processes, and culture of that organization and in turn influence it. If this is true, it is then clear that to achieve sustainability it is vital that employees understand and share a sustainable world view.

To illustrate this last point, Karl-Henrik Robèrt, the developer of The Natural Step, refers to football players: "to merge the different skills of the goal-keeper, defenders and attackers into an effective whole, the players need to have exactly the same overall perception of what the game is about" (Robèrt *et al.* 1997: 79). If football

---

18 See Chapter 8 for an analysis of some major multilateral initiatives.

players do not share the same perception of the game and its rules, in other words if they do not share the same paradigm, they will not operate as an effective team but as a loose group of individuals each pursuing his or her own goal. Alignment of employees to the central paradigm is thus paramount, and can only be achieved by striving for coherence in all other steps of the OEC, and particularly in HRM processes.

Though the OEC focuses here on employees and though, of course, they are vital for an organization's success, employees are by no means the only people who depend on the organization and on whom the organization depends. Suppliers, clients, investors, and the surrounding community also fit this description. They, too, are an organization's stakeholders and therefore their views on reality influence the organization. To be succinct: their paradigms will influence their tendency to buy in and support the organization's sustainable stance, or not. Many organizations involved in the change process toward sustainability are aware of the need to involve all other stakeholders alongside their employees in the transition, to challenge their paradigms if needed and, in any case, to communicate to them and with them on their progress. This need fueled the measurement and reporting trend that will be the subject of the next chapter.

7.8 Conclusion: building sustainable organizations is not the same as greening organizations

Before discussing measurement and reporting it is important to insist that in the authors' opinion the integration of sustainability in an organization means ultimately to align all activities with principles based on a sustainable world view. This way of acting is far removed from the "greening" of an organization by setting up actions that are unrelated to and do not affect an organization's core activities, including donations to a good cause. As good as the intention behind these practices may be and notwithstanding the amount of money involved in them, they are no more than a drop in the ocean. We will never tire of insisting on this point: organizations' main impact on the social and environmental texture of their host communities is a consequence of their day-to-day operations.

It should also be obvious that the sustainable organization here envisioned is not to be reached by designing a marketing or communication campaign to suggest that it is sustainable while it is not—the so-called "greenwashing." Greenwashing is a major risk since it is not easy for stakeholders to control whether the claim that a good or service is sustainable, is actually true. With its three dimensions, its focus on the whole life cycle of a product, and its requirement to consider the (positive and negative; indirect and direct; willing or unwilling) impacts on all stakeholders, sustainability is an awfully complex concept to bring into life. Complexity causes knowledge gaps between the different stakeholders, and this asymmetry can be used by ill-intentioned companies to mystify people.

To illustrate the complexity of applying sustainability let's consider the question of whether it is more sustainable to drink tea from a ceramic mug and then wash it, or to use a disposable cup and then put it in the trash.[19] Most people will instinctively choose the first option: throwing a cup away seems by definition a very unsustainable thing to do. Yet reality is more complex: to answer this seemingly simple question, we need to find a reliable answer to a whole series of sub-questions touching on the entire life cycle of a cup (see Table 7.2). Focusing on materials and supposing all other parameters equal, if the throw-away teacup is produced using biodegradable material and can be used as mulch for our own garden, then it is a better choice than the ceramic one.

Table 7.2 **A sustainable cup**

Life cycle	Examples of specific issues
Extraction and production	• Intensity in use of natural resources, including raw materials, water, and electricity • Intensity in use of natural services, including waste and pollution management • Safety of working conditions • Fair remuneration • Chain management issues • Characteristics of materials
Distribution	• Transportation, including type of fuel used • Mileage per cup
Use	• How is the cup washed (e.g., under running water after each use; under running water after one day use; in a full washing machine; with or without organic detergent) • After how many days of use is the cup discharged • Water sewage treatment
Disposal	• Reuse as, e.g., a vase or penholder • Recycle, including transport and energy/water use • Trashed, including transport

Very few consumers will be willing to take the time and effort necessary to verify all answers to the relevant "sustainability" questions before buying a certain good or service. They will rely on information given by the organization offering the

---

19 In the Netherlands the first study on this question was conducted in 1991. In 2007 a second study appeared supporting the conclusion of the first: measured on a series of parameters a disposable, recyclable plastic cup scores better than a ceramic one (Ligthart and Ansems 2007). A cradle-to-cradle solution as described in the text was not considered by these studies.

product, or by other instances; information that, as we have seen, cannot be easily verified unless organizations are fully transparent on the way they substantiate their claims. The call for transparency has been one of the drivers behind the development of measurement and reporting instruments for sustainability. The need to join forces with other institutions to understand all dimensions and facets of sustainability is the main push factor behind multilateral initiatives. Multilateral initiatives, measuring, and reporting are the subjects of the next chapter.

8

Toward sustainable organizations
Managing, measuring, and reporting

> Virtuous but uncompetitive companies will not be part of our future. Socially or environmentally destructive companies must not be part of our future (Gonella *et al.* 1998: i).

> We should, as charitable organizations do, measure success in terms of outcomes for others as well as for ourselves (Charles Handy writing on the aim of business [2002: 55]).

To create profitable companies with a positive impact on people and planet, we need leaders and managers that not only see why such organizations are needed but also know how to create them and let them prosper. As was argued in Chapter 7, this implies aligning all activities in an organization with values based on sustainability principles in order to achieve results that meet stakeholders' expectations on the triple bottom line of people, planet, and profit. Yet, as Milton Friedman rightly says in his critique of CSR, it is pointless and counterproductive to ask managers to consider other objectives than profit if there are neither agreed upon guidelines on how they could pursue these objectives nor a way to measure their success in this endeavor.

The recognition that Milton Friedman is right in his criticism and the increasing unease on the social and environmental impact of corporate activities have spurred the development of guidelines to implement sustainability in management systems, to measure progress, and report on impacts (Epstein 2003). This chapter touches on these developments. It opens by analyzing tools and guidelines designed for or adapted to manage sustainable organizations (Section 8.1). It then outlines how progress toward sustainability can be measured and reported (Sections 8.2 and 8.3).

Owing to the complex and global nature of many sustainability issues, sustainable organizations will find themselves more often than not confronted with problems where unilateral action will not be incisive or could be highly detrimental to an organization's survival. A viable choice in these cases is to join forces with other organizations that are caught in the same dilemma and develop sector-wide principles. Section 8.4 is dedicated to multilateral initiatives and covers the major efforts undertaken by governments, businesses, NGOs, and other organizations to deal with some of the most challenging environmental and social problems facing humanity, from poverty to heavy pollution and from corruption to overexploitation of resources.

A concluding section reflects on the role of organizations as change agents toward sustainability (Section 8.5).

8.1 **Managing sustainability**

In his *History of Management Thought*, Daniel Wren (2005: 3) defines management as "an activity that performs certain functions to obtain the effective acquisition, allocation, and utilization of human efforts and physical resources to accomplish some goal."

The overarching goal that an organization sets itself leads the way it is managed. Managing an organization that strives for positive impacts on a triple bottom line requires a different way of acquiring, allocating, and utilizing resources than in an organization whose exclusive goal is to increase shareholder value. This is the reason why, to manage sustainable organizations, we need dedicated tools and guidelines.

Drawing the line between instruments developed to manage sustainability and instruments designed to measure and report on results is not an easy task. It may even be considered a useless endeavor based on an artificial distinction. Several instruments, such as the Balanced Scorecard, are intended both to manage and to measure. Though a question of shade, a distinction can be made among instruments that focus more on internal processes and tools that are more openly directed to measurement and reporting.

This section touches on three instruments with a management focus: the Balanced Scorecard, the EFQM Excellence Model and ISO 26000. Though different in their origin and relevance, all three offer leverage points to design, analyze, and improve internal processes in order to achieve other goals than profitability alone.

Balanced Scorecard

The developers of the Balanced Scorecard, Robert Kaplan and David Norton, are adamant in their judgment of organizations that focus exclusively on financial performance indicators to measure their success: they are heading for trouble. In their eyes managing an organization in this way is the same as pretending to fly an airplane relying only on an instrument measuring airspeed, or to safely drive a car looking at the road only through the rearview mirror. Financial goals and indicators are, of course, as essential as a rearview mirror in a car. Yet, exactly like the rearview mirror, they look only at what lies behind and offer no insight on the car's present functioning and on the condition of the road ahead (Kaplan and Norton 1996a: 1).

If this is true, managers are in need of indicators offering a more balanced view of their organization. Kaplan and Norton propose to integrate the financial viewpoint with three non-financial perspectives: learning and growth (including culture, communication, and employees' development); clients (including customer satisfaction metrics); and business processes. To be balanced an organization should formulate objectives and activities in all four perspectives on the basis of its vision (Kaplan and Norton 1992, 1996a, b).

The four perspectives in the Balanced Scorecard (BSC) are conceived as different and complementary: positive results on all four are needed for sustained success. This does not mean that activities in one quadrant do not influence activities in the other. On the contrary. To take only one example, business processes focuses on internal business perspective and includes processes with a heavy impact on customer satisfaction (client), such as those affecting product quality and employees' skills. Employees' skills, in turn, are also influenced by activities deployed in the development and growth quadrant. In this sense all perspectives are linked.

Though all perspectives are linked to each other, they do not influence each other equally. The asymmetry between the financial perspective—with its focus on the past—on one side and the non-financial perspectives—with their focus on the future—on the other, brought Robert Kaplan and David Norton to conclude that the three non-financial perspectives are leading and not the financial one. To better understand this point let's take an example. As already mentioned in Chapter 7, Ray Anderson, the founder of Interface, compares the next order for a company to the next heartbeat for a man. Loyal clients assure to a company, through their repeated orders, regular heartbeats. Out of metaphor, loyal clients are more profitable than disloyal or new ones. The tangle here is that clients' loyalty depends on clients' satisfaction, and clients' satisfaction is, in its turn, heavily dependent on product quality (business processes) and service delivery by competent employees (development and growth).[1] The conclusion that Kaplan and Norton draw from this and similar examples is that the three non-financial perspectives are leading because they not only inform managers on the direction taken by the firm but also determine the results achieved on the financial dimension.

In its original form the BSC is ultimately concerned with success from a shareholder perspective. Thanks to its focus on non-financial indicators and the

---

1   James L. Heskett, Earl W. Sasser, and Leonard A. Schlesinger forcefully argued for the linkages among employees' satisfaction, customers' satisfaction, and profit in *The Service Profit Chain* (1997).

medium–long term, though, it has been recommended to and applied by managers in sustainable organizations (Zingales *et al.* 2002; Emerson 2003; Murby and Gould 2005).

Both practitioners and scholars have attempted to adapt the BSC to the needs of sustainability. Some organizations, for example, renamed the financial perspective as stakeholder measures (Murby and Gould 2005). Scholars, on the other hand, have proposed to substitute stakeholders for clients, to add a fifth perspective on social and environmental goals or to integrate social and environmental goals in the four perspectives originally proposed by Robert Kaplan and David Norton (Zingales *et al.* 2002).

As often happens, some of these attempts have been more successful than others. One of the lessons learned is that the tough and lengthy process needed to devise relevant objectives and metrics on the four perspectives works against the addition of sustainability indicators in the BSC if they are not included in it from the beginning. Considering that the vast majority of organizations have not (yet) integrated sustainability principles in their values, vision, and mission, it is quite doubtful whether the wide adoption of the Balanced Scorecard will in the end support the development of sustainable organizations (Zingales and Hockerts 2003).

EFQM Excellence Model

Stephen Schmidheiny has observed that, to successfully address the sustainability challenge, companies should engage with the environmental and social impact of their products as if it concerned a quality issue (Schmidheiny 1992).

Quality management systems, in general, are meant to ensure continuous improvement by designing traceable procedures to identify (minimum) quality levels, to spot eventual non-compliance, and to take required (corrective) actions. To fulfill customers' requirements and specifications, quality assurance standards require the involvement of producers and suppliers all along the supply chain. Likewise, to guarantee total surveillance of product quality, quality assurance requires the inclusion in the system of all stakeholders: not only producers and suppliers but also distributors, retailers, and the final buyers (Powell 1995). A stakeholder approach is thus common both to quality assurance systems and sustainability. What is more, the link between the two may easily be made by specifying standards of quality that include environmental and social norms. From this perspective it may be less surprising that the second management tool presented here was proposed by the European Federation for Quality Management.

The European Federation for Quality Management (EFQM) was founded in 1988 by 14 CEOs who shared a concern on the poor performance of European businesses in comparison with their Japanese and North American colleagues. To strengthen the competitive capacity of European companies in the global arena, the EFQM developed the EFQM Excellence Model as a standard for quality in management and production processes.

The EFQM Excellence Model is based on nine criteria, five of which are considered to be enablers (leadership; people; strategy; partnership and resources; processes, products, and services) and four results (people results; customers' results; society results; key performance results). Enablers criteria, in short, cover what an organization does, while the results criteria cover what an organization achieves and how it does it. The main idea behind the model is that results are caused by enablers and enablers should be improved using feedback from results (EFQM 2010). The cause–effect relationship among enablers and results in EFQM is similar to the one identified by the Balanced Scorecard between the non-financial perspectives on one side and the financial perspective on the other.

In the late 1990s social and environmental issues were integrated in the EFQM result criterion labeled "Society." The EFQM Excellence Model defines society as the stakeholders impacted by an organization's activities. The presence in the EFQM Excellence Model of a criterion that can be directly connected with stakeholders is surely an improvement on the Balanced Scorecard. Yet it is confusing that some organizational stakeholders, such as employees, clients, and shareholders, have their own result criterion, respectively "People," "Customer," and "Key Performance." Moreover, though EFQM insists that working at Society's results starts from the enabler Strategy, the position of the quadrant Society on the result side of the model wrongly suggests that organizations may start measuring their impact on society right away. Besides, the EFQM Excellence Model weights the relative importance of the nine criteria to match their relevance for a company striving for better competitiveness through higher quality: the weight given to Society's results is the lowest of all. This is surely no recommendation to management attention. Finally, measures for results on the criterion Society are geared toward society's and customers' *perceptions* of organizational performance. The obvious risk here is a "bolted-on," PR approach to sustainability.

Concluding, though the EFQM Excellence Model is by now widely used all over the world, in the authors' opinion it falls short of being an effective management tool for sustainable organizations unless sustainability principles are explicitly named in all enablers criteria, from Leadership to Processes, and not only measured in the result criterion Society.

ISO 26000

The last management tool addressed here is ISO 26000, a guideline for sustainability in organizations released in September 2010. While the Balanced Scorecard was designed by a scholar (Robert Kaplan) and a consultant (David Norton) and has as a frame of reference U.S. organizations (Zingales *et al.* 2002), and while the EFQM Excellence Model was originally proposed by a European business network, ISO 26000 was developed via a multi-stakeholder dialogue involving businesses, not-for-profit organizations, governments, NGOs, unions, customers, and scholars from over 90 countries, including several developing countries.[2] This broad base is seen by proponents of ISO 26000 as one of its major strengths and as supporting a higher claim on legitimacy than competing tools (McKinley 2010). ISO 26000, moreover, integrates several already existing guidelines and frameworks such as ISO 14000 (a series covering standards on environmental management and measurement, issued in 1996 by the International Organization for Standardization), SA8000 (on workplace conditions, issued in 1997 by the Council of Economic Priorities), and AA1000 (developed by the Institute for Social and Ethical Accountability, covering disclosure and verification of social, ethical, and environmental information). In contrast to some of these instruments, ISO 26000 is intended as guidance toward social and environmental responsibility. Therefore, it does not include minimum requirements and is thus not a standard for certification. On the one hand this may be considered as a positive feature of the ISO 26000 guidelines. Not posing (minimum) requirements does justice to the dynamic intrinsic to sustainability issues and may support continuous development toward better results. On the other hand, certification is sought after by organizations because it is a public recognition of the efforts and time invested in working in line with sustainability criteria. The work required to implement the seven main clauses, seven core subjects, 36 issues and related actions identified by ISO 26000 is surely going to be substantial. The lack of a certification opportunity may thus negatively affect its reception.

It is impossible to analyze ISO 26000 at length here. Yet it is at least essential to comment that ISO 26000 insists on the need to understand and embrace basic sustainability principles first. Only when the commitment to sustainability is made at this level will an organization be able to identify sustainability issues that are relevant to its operations and to address them by aligning all processes and activities toward the sustainability principles (ISO 2009). Though the principles delineated by ISO 26000 are less specific than the ones proposed in Chapter 7 (Section 7.3 and Box 7.2), ISO 26000 offers at this moment the most comprehensive and state-of-the-art guide for integrating sustainability in the strategy, processes, and day-to-day activities of an organization through stakeholder engagement.

Summarizing the discussion so far, the authors conclude that managing for sustainability means to acquire, allocate, and utilize human efforts and physical resources so that the organization adds value on the profit, people, and planet dimensions. "Adopting the sustainability paradigm," Charles Holliday and his co-authors write (2002: 134), "may require a tweaking, or even a radical reorganization, of a corporation's management systems." Tools intended to support management in this endeavor work with objectives and indicators that complement the financial ones, and recognize that an organization impacts on people and planet both directly—through its core business—and indirectly—through its supply chain and

---

2 It is interesting to note that, at the ballot on the final draft of ISO 26000, 93% of the involved countries voted for approval, including China, Brazil, and Russia. The U.S. voted against, together with India, Cuba, Luxembourg, and Turkey. See isotc.iso.org/livelink/livelink?func=ll&objId=3935837&objAction=browse&sort=name (accessed August 22, 2011).

through engagement with its stakeholders. The influence of a sustainable organization on its environment is like the ripples caused by throwing a stone into a pond: it continuously expands. Managing for sustainability is not for the faint-hearted.

8.2 **Measuring and reporting on impacts**

The choice of measures and indicators has far-reaching consequences because, as noted in Chapter 7, "enterprises tend to be enabled and constrained by their measurement systems. There is common wisdom among managers that once one begins to measure something, many other things (e.g., externalities) don't get captured" (Mitchell, in Agle *et al.* 2008: 179).

In this respect sustainable and mainstream organizations do not differ: both need to choose measures accurately so that the achievement of their main goal is supported and not hindered. In the previous pages it has been repeatedly stated that the main aim of sustainable organizations is to contribute to sustainable development by causing a positive impact on people, planet, and profit. The point made here is that impact measures are a specific type of measure that should be distinguished from measures of resource intensity, results, and outcomes. Though this may seem quite a technical and abstract distinction, it is vital to understand it because, to quote Ronald Mitchell again, "once one begins to measure something, many other things . . . don't get captured" (in Agle *et al.* 2008: 179).

Resource intensity

Resource intensity sets *outputs* against *inputs*. It measures, for example, how much water, gas, and electricity is needed per product or service unit: for example, a chair or a hotel room. The end in mind in measuring resource intensity is reduction in inputs without loss of (perceived) quality in the outputs (Gray 1992).

Resource intensity was one of the first measures to be reported on by organizations, for two main reasons. First, because it was championed by the major force behind sustainability for decades: the environmental movement. The environmental movement's campaigns in the 1970s were crucial in raising people's awareness of the limited capacity of the Earth to absorb waste and provide resources and in shaping consensus on the need to reduce both pollution and over-usage of natural resources (see Chapter 2). As a result people started putting pressure on business. After some resistance, business yielded because—and this is the second reason— though some initial measures aimed at eco-efficiency and pollution control may cost, for an organization it makes perfect economic sense to produce more from less and, in view of tightening governmental regulations and alert public control, abate pollution.

Reducing the use of natural resources and sinks is often compared with picking low-hanging fruit. It is a first, important step toward sustainability. Yet more steps have to follow because the main aim of sustainable organizations is not doing "less bad," but "doing good": that is, devising products and services that add value on the economic, social, and environmental dimensions and not just subtract as little value as possible. As several scholars observe, focusing on reducing the use of a specific resource or on abating pollution—and thus on strict input–output measures—will not serve sustainability's main aim well. Even worse, it may impede progress toward it because mainstream companies are not geared toward sustainability: doing less bad will therefore not lead to "do good." For example, producing a chair with fewer raw materials will not make the chair sustainable if at the end of its life cycle it has to be disposed of in a landfill. What is needed is radical innovation and thus completely different processes (see, e.g., McDonough and Braungart 2002).

Processes

If the above is true, sustainability requires innovation. Innovation, in turn, requires a change in processes, so that the impact on the natural and human environment of the new product or service is taken into account throughout its life, from the designer's table to disposal. Changing processes is pivotal to achieve sustainability, as many scholars and practitioners have observed (Anderson 1998, 2009; Dormann and Holliday 2002).[3]

In terms of the discussion on measurement, this means that indicators of resource intensity should be matched with indicators of the integration of sustainability in all processes, including decision-making processes. Examples of such indicators are: the presence on the board of directors of representatives for those whose needs are often disregarded, such as minorities; stakeholder involvement in designing new products or services; and ethical codes for employees and suppliers (see Box 8.1).[4]

Though a change in processes is necessary to achieve sustainability, it is not sufficient if it remains an end in itself. As Michael John Jones and Donna Wood observed, a process's change has to result in visible policies and programs guiding operations (Jones 1980; Wood 1991). To come back to the example of a director on the board to represent minorities, this move will have no effect if the power to take final decisions is moved from the board to another body, where minorities are not represented (Jones 1980).

3 The ISO 14000 guideline series, now integrated in ISO 26000, is a tool to which managers who wish to integrate sustainable considerations in processes could revert (Maas 2009).
4 On the challenges of a process-oriented approach to sustainability see Chapter 6 Section 3; on processes see also Chapter 7 Section 5.

Box 8.1 **Ethical codes**

An ethical code can be described as "a chart of behaviours, duties and rights defining the environmental, ethical or social responsibility of the organization, its employees and/or other stakeholders (e.g. suppliers) in an organization" (Gonella *et al.* 1998: 87). Ethical codes are thus instruments that can be used to help create a culture aligned with ethical or sustainability principles. There is a common understanding that, to be successful, codes should be designed through a process of consultation with all constituencies, so that people recognize themselves in the code and the norms expressed in it.

Implementing codes with external stakeholders, such as suppliers, requires special care. In the past organizations have been criticized for imposing their codes on suppliers and then so strictly applying them that suppliers lost their order and were forced to close, with disruptive consequences for the local communities. This has been the case, for example, with provisions against child labor. Though of course these provisions were well intended, many small, developing-world producers could not comply with the restrictions and had to close or lay off children who then, not having other options, joined rebel armies or became prostitutes. This evil could have been avoided by a more careful consideration of local conditions, as is now the case with provisions on maximum working hours for children in developing country firms and the creation of factory schools, with support and supervision by NGO organizations.

Codes of ethics have been widely adopted, also because under certain countries' regulations having a code constitutes a mitigating circumstance when a company is sued for environmental or social damages. They have also been heavily criticized: in reviewing research on ethical codes, William Frederick, for example, concludes that many codes seem "designed to protect the company more than the public" and that therefore it "may be naïve to rely to corporate code of ethics to curb *antisocial* business practices. Rather, the codes tend to check *anti-company* behavior" (Frederick 2006: 108-109, italic in the original). For codes of ethics and for all other tools discussed here it remains true that they can be used instrumentally when they are not based on an honest choice for sustainability principles by the company using them.

Results or outputs

Policies and programs resulting from processes oriented toward sustainability are still a step in the chain leading to results or outputs. Outputs or results are the final product or service, together with the waste or pollution caused.[5] All types of output should stand the scrutiny of sustainability. To evaluate the sustainability of products that improve on existing ones, input–output measures and life cycle assessment are still the most appropriate tools. To assess innovative products, products that break with the past, these tools are less appropriate. Take, for example, the cradle-to-cradle products promoted by Michael Braungart and William McDonough. Cradle-to-cradle products are designed to be entirely reabsorbed either in the natural cycle or in the technical one, without loss of quality and without causing any negative impact on people and planet. In this sense they are quite incomparable to existing products. How to assess the sustainability of such innovative products is still an open question (Maas 2009).

Outcomes

While outputs are the direct result of an organization's activity and are, so to speak, still in its hands, outcomes are "the ultimate changes that one is trying to make in the world" (Clark *et al.* 2004: 6). Outcomes are defined as "specific changes in attitudes, behaviors, knowledge, skills, status, or level of functioning that result from enterprise activities, such as finding a job, avoiding getting sick, or reducing emissions by a certain amount" (Clark *et al.* 2004: 14). In other words, the question that outcomes measurement answers is whether the product or service delivered actually meets the stakeholders' needs that the organization wished to address. A regular, open, and honest dialogue with the involved stakeholders is essential to design indicators to assess outcomes.

To better understand the difference among processes, output/results, and outcomes, let us consider as an example a philanthropic activity: the building of a primary school in a poor area near a company's operations. The process may have been designed to account for stakeholders' input, from both inside and outside the company. Consultation may have been held with the local government and community representatives, as well with employees wishing to participate in the project. The actual building of the school may have been done on the basis of the most recent relevant insights to mitigate the negative impacts of construction works on the environment and to offer a healthy inner climate to children and school staff. Local contractors may have been involved in the project. In short: the result or output of all these processes and activities, the new school, is an outstanding example of the company's engagement with sustainability and is proudly presented as such in its Annual Sustainability Report. Of course, the end in mind in building this

---

5 As was mentioned above in discussing input–output measures, waste and pollution are measured with the intent to avoid and reduce them.

school was to provide education to the children in the community and thus offer them a better future. This outcome will not be reached if the school never opens its doors owing to, for example, a lack of staff and teaching materials.

Impacts

Until recently, measuring outcomes was the outer frontier in sustainability measuring and reporting. Yet sustainability in the end is not about inputs, processes, results, or even outcomes but about impacts on people's lives and the environment (Clark *et al.* 2004; Maas 2009).[6] Impacts are "*the portion of the total outcome that happened as a result of the activity of the venture, above and beyond what would have happened anyway*" (Clark *et al.* 2004: 7, italic in the original text).

To go back to the example above and supposing that the school opens its doors, the school will have a positive impact on the children's life only if it offers education that is useful to them and that they indeed could not get anywhere else. If not, it has no impact: children's education could have happened equally well without the school. The newly opened school could even have a negative impact if it disrupts traditional learning practices or does not take into account the families' need for their children's help in certain seasons for certain economic activities.[7]

Measuring impact defined in this way is not an easy task, surely when—following the requirement of the approach of sustainability that is defended in this book—the goal is to measure both social and environmental impacts directly or indirectly caused by an organization. It is not easy and it can be costly, also because in order to assure that the measurement is accurate, reliable, and credible companies often revert to third-party certification schemes. Costs have to be gained back. Some companies choose to increase prices, relying on the willingness of customers to pay a higher price for products that are certified as sustainable. Yet for many this strategy is not viable because it results in a loss of competitive advantage (Clark *et al.* 2004). To avoid increasing prices for the final customers some companies hand the measurements and certification costs over to external producers and suppliers. This solution has been rightly criticized in those cases where producers are small, local entrepreneurs in developing countries: the weakest link in the chain. Restructuring the chain to avoid unnecessary costs is seen as a more feasible and acceptable alternative.

---

6 The impact of CSR on the financial bottom line has been at the center of a vast scholarly debate. The point made here is that the question of whether an organization's sustainable stance actually has a positive impact on a community or the environment has until recently not got the attention it deserves (Margolis and Walsh 2003; Maas 2009).

7 The authors' thanks go to Dr. Karen Maas, Assistant Professor at the Department of Business Economics of the Erasmus School of Economics (ESE) at the Erasmus University Rotterdam (The Netherlands), for having provided us with this example in one of our discussions on impact measurement.

Notwithstanding all these difficulties several instruments have been developed to measure resource intensity and sustainability in processes, outputs, and impacts. In 1992 Rob Gray distinguished at least six major social and environmental accounting practices with several subsets, while a recent count yielded 30 different tools (Maas 2009). In the context of this book it is impossible to analyze all or even a few of these instruments. Just to get the flavor, Box 8.2 touches on two initiatives.

Box 8.2 **Millennium Development Goal Scan and Measuring Impact Framework**

The UN Millennium Development Goals (MDGs) were developed as a challenge to governments and business to substantially alleviate major social wrongs, such as poverty and malnutrition, by 2020. In 2005 and 2006 NCDO Business in Development, in conjunction with SustainAlytics, experimented on ways in which organizations who have operations in developing countries could measure their positive contribution to the achievement of the eight Millennium Development Goals.[a] The MDG Scan is a result of these experiments, and was made accessible on the Internet in 2009. It is based on the assumption that companies can contribute to economic growth and poverty reduction in developing countries and that their effect on a developing country's national economy cannot be directly measured by the amount of company investment in that economy, because the impact of such an investment is often more far-reaching in space and time. To calculate the effects of a company's activity on a developing country's economy the MDG Scan focuses on four factors: value added; employment creation; products and services; and community investments. These four factors are then linked to MDGs as poverty reduction, reduction of infant mortality, increase in primary education, and so on. See for further information: https://www.mdgscan.com (accessed August 22, 2011).

Almost at the same time the World Business Council for Sustainable Development (WBCSD) developed the Measuring Impact Framework (MIF) to cope with the requests by its member companies for a tool to better understand their contribution to society, to use this understanding to inform their investment decisions, and to better structure stakeholder dialogue. More than twenty companies were involved in the framework development and testing, alongside NGOs such as Oxfam Novib. The MIF is intended to measure the social impact of business activities, including corporate governance and environmental management, jobs and training, infrastructure and products, procurement, and tax payments. It is intended as a simple, flexible tool to be applied in different circumstances by companies in different industries. It consists of four steps. The start is in defining the boundaries; that is, clearly identifying the objectives of the assessment and the geographic and temporal scope. This first step is essential to make the assessment manageable, yet it can be criticized from the point of view of inclusiveness: the organization may "cherry-pick" the data. The second step is measurement of the business impact, followed by the identification of the actual impact of these activities on the development of the considered region or country. A point of criticism here is that stakeholders' involvement in this step is seen as optional. Though this enhances feasibility, it obviously affects the credibility of the measurement (see on this point also Clark *et al*. 2004). The final step is choosing a managerial response to grasp opportunities and avoid risks. For more information see www.wbcsd.org/web/measuringimpact.htm (accessed August 22, 2011).

For a description and critical assessment of these two (and other) measurement tools see Maas 2009, Edwards 2005 and Clark *et al*. 2004. Though geared toward social impacts only, this last work is particularly useful as it shows examples of application by organizations of the nine tools it describes.

a The NCDO is a Dutch expertise and advisory centre for citizenship and international cooperation. SustainAlytics is devoted to environmental, social, and governance research and analysis, sustainability benchmarks, and advisory services to investors around the world. See for more information ncdo.nl/aboutncdo/About_NCDO and sustainalytics.com/about-sustainalytics, accessed September 15, 2011.

The existence of several instruments to measure impacts is applauded by some because it offers to organizations in different phases of development the possibility of finding a tool adapted to their needs. On the other hand, the absence of generally accepted accounting principles and of an international legal infrastructure to guide the measurement and reporting on environmental and social results, has been denounced as a weakness of sustainability accounting compared with financial accounting where such a system exists (Clark *et al.* 2004).[8]

In this light, it is encouraging that there is a strong consensus building on the principles on which sustainability reporting should be based and its main components.

8.3 **Measuring and reporting: building consensus and challenges**

It is quite uncontested that progress toward sustainability should be measured. Reporting, in contrast, has been heavily attacked because it does not seem legitimate to require companies to report on initiatives that are considered to be voluntary by definition. Yet, as observed in Chapter 6 Section 5, although CSR and

---

8 Sustainability accounting is defined as "the systematic development, tracking and analysis of information about the social, environmental and economic affairs of an organization for the benefit of one of more of its stakeholders" (Gonella *et al.* 1998: 86). Because it includes both measurement and reporting it is used here as synonymous for the two.

organizational sustainability are framed as voluntary activities, accepting a responsibility means accepting accountability. This point was felt so deeply that by the late 1970s and early 1980s the concept of corporate social performance (CSP) emerged "as a way of organizing the inputs, throughputs, outputs, and outcomes" of corporate social activities (Wood in Agle *et al.* 2008: 161). The end in mind was to create the means to inform stakeholders on all activities developed by a company and not only on the economic ones.[9]

Truly, a stakeholders' approach to sustainability requires not only measurement on all dimensions of sustainability but also disclosure by reporting. Results of the measurement should be disclosed so that stakeholders are given the means to control whether or not their legitimate interests are met. Stakeholders have a right to know so that they are empowered to act. As Rob Gray stated in 1992: "accountability is concerned with the right to receive information and the duty to supply it" (1992: 413).

Yet there is more. In the context of sustainability, reporting is "not simply a matter of disclosure, but an integral element of the process of communication between the company and the key stakeholders" (Gonella *et al.* 1998: 20). Stakeholders are not only at the receiving end of the accounting process, but are involved in it because, as we have seen above, it is quite impossible to devise and measure outcome and impact indicators without involving stakeholders. Alongside the right to know and empower, accountability also serves the aim of instituting an open dialogue with stakeholders.

Stakeholder dialogue is also needed to assess whether their needs are actually met, and thus to understand whether improvement is needed. The last aim served by measurement and reporting is in fact to improve on the achieved results (Gonella *et al.* 1998: 19; Gupta 2010: 3).[10]

One of the earliest definitions of sustainability accounting summarizes all these points: sustainability accounting is "a regular, externally verified process to under-

---

9 In an effort to support the business case for CSR, the academic and management debate on CSP focuses mainly on the question whether CSP has a positive, neutral, or negative impact on corporate performance. Evidence to date is mixed, though a negative impact on the financial bottom line is excluded by the vast majority of researchers. How and why the 1970s effort on CSP failed is well analyzed by Epstein 2003.

10 In parallel to what has been observed in discussing management tools and to what will be seen when addressing multilateral agreements, also in measurement and reporting there are multiple initiative-takers. As Aarti Gupta noted they include "private actors promoting transparency as a means to further voluntary corporate sustainability goals and public actors seeking to correct perceived democratic and accountability deficits" (Gupta 2010: 2). Transparency may also be sought as a means to enhance market efficiency (Gupta 2010). That these different aims may sometimes contrast is evident. Yet the call for transparency is here to stay (GRI 2010).

stand, measure, report on and improve upon it social [and] environmental . . . performance through stakeholder dialogue" (Gonella *et al.* 1998: 89).[11]

In this early definition both the similarities and differences between sustainability and financial accounting are clear. Both are regular, say yearly, activities and are externally verified. Both are intended not only to measure the actual situation but also to assess it on the basis of set targets so that improvement is possible. Both are written to be disclosed. The difference lies in their focus (on profit alone or on people and planet) and in the process through which sustainability reports should be written: through stakeholder dialogue.

Starting from the definition proposed by Claudia Gonella and her colleagues and without wishing to dig into the tiny details of sustainability accounting, in the following we will touch on those issues on which there is consensus or consensus is rapidly building.

For a start, it has to be noted that measuring and reporting on sustainability targets is indeed becoming for many organizations a regular, externally verified activity. The Global Reporting Initiative (GRI) website counted over one thousand reports based on the GRI guidelines in 2008, an increase of 46% compared with 2007. GRI reports cover mostly environmental and social performance (see Box 8.3). Yet there is a clear tendency in connecting people and planet indicators with relevant financial measures.[12]

A challenge of sustainability accounting that has not yet completely been answered is inclusivity: that is, measurement of and reporting on *all* activities and *all* their relevant environmental and social aspects. Inclusivity is considered a basic principle of sustainability accounting because it opposes the temptation to gloss over sensitive areas and issues.[13] The downside of inclusivity is the time, effort, and costs involved in tracking down all social and environmental issues in all areas of operation; in devising indicators; in setting minimum requirements; and finally in measuring and reporting on them. The complexity intrinsic in sustainability issues

---

11 Gonella *et al.* (1998) refer here to The Body Shop. The reference in their text to animal testing has been left out to underline the general applicability of this approach to accounting for sustainability.

12 Social and environmental reports are seen usually as a second tier of reports alongside financial ones. Integration of the two in reports covering all three aspects of sustainability at once is the next frontier.

13 The importance of the inclusivity principle can be illustrated by referring to a study conducted by Craig Deegan and Michaela Rankin in 1996. The study focused on 20 Australian firms that were successfully prosecuted a total of 78 times by the New South Wales and Victorian Environmental Protection Authorities because of breaches of environmental laws during the period 1990–1993. Deegan and Rankin found that, though these firms had something negative to disclose, the information on environmental issues provided by 18 of them in their annual reports was positive. The two companies reporting on the negative news did it only very briefly. This contrasts with the attitude of firms when reporting on financial issues. Though the costs may be huge (e.g., a disproportionate fall in share price for listed companies), firms are still likely to disclose negative financial information.

and the fact that standards and requirements tend to shift as our knowledge of (un)sustainable practices increases, add to the difficult job of abiding by the principle of inclusivity.[14]

That reports should be comparable is also a principle of sustainability accounting on which there is broad consensus. Comparability is needed for benchmarking among companies and inside the same company but also to support improvement. Yet here too practice is thornier than theory. First of all because, as has been pointed out already, the environmental and social issues that companies face vary from sector to sector and even inside one sector. Second, because the same company often sets the spotlight on different indicators in different years.[15] Third, because, as was observed above when discussing inclusivity, flexibility is needed to take into account shifts in knowledge on what is sustainable and what is not. Fourth, and more fundamentally, because the focus of measurement, as has been seen above, is shifting: from measures of resource intensity, to outcomes and impacts. Though impact measures are what are needed to truly measure progress toward sustainability and though—or maybe because—there are several measurement instruments, companies have only recently started to explore this field.

Box 8.3 **Global Reporting Initiative**

In discussing what should be measured in the context of sustainability in Box 8.2 we have looked at two instruments: the UN Millennium Development Goal Scan and Measuring Impact Framework. Neither is intended for reporting, though disclosure of results is encouraged. The Global Reporting Initiative (GRI), in contrast, has developed a framework setting out the principles and indicators that organizations can use to measure and report on their economic, environmental, and social performance. The GRI framework is centered on reporting guidelines and supported by sector- and country-specific supplements and indicator protocols.

The GRI is a network organization, started by Ceres in 1996 and supported by UNEP since 1999. The GRI created its reporting framework through a multi-stakeholder, consensus-seeking process involving business, civil society, labor organizations, accounting, investors, academics, governments, and practitioners.

The first version of the GRI guidelines was issued in 2000, and 50 organizations then published reports based on it. In 2006 the third version was published. In the first half of 2010 more than 750 companies published GRI reports on the GRI site.

---

14 Remember the discussion in Chapter 2 on the use of CFCs in refrigerators: they are less toxic than ammonia and therefore were valued as a good substitute, yet after a few decades of use it was proved that when released in the atmosphere CFCs destroy the ozone layer.
15 The link to the issue of inclusivity is almost too obvious to be pointed out.

Economic indicators in the GRI supplement financial reporting by focusing on "organization's contribution to the sustainability of a larger economic system" such as the local community in which an organization operates (GRI 2000–2006: 25). For example, the sixth main economic indicator asks for reporting on "policy, practices, and proportion of spending on locally-based suppliers at significant locations of operation" (EC6, GRI 2000–2006: 26).

Environmental indicators focus on consumption efficiency or resource intensity (materials, energy, and water), influence on biodiversity, and impact minimization (emissions, wastes and effluents, products and services, transport). The main focus is on input and output measures. This has been criticized for falling short of a life cycle assessment approach (Moneva *et al.* 2006).

GRI focuses on four key categories of social indicators: labor practices, human rights, society, and product responsibility. In specifying indicators for these aspects, the GRI draws on existing multilateral declarations and conventions such as the UN Universal Declaration of Human Rights (UNUDHR) and the International Labour Organization (ILO) declaration on Fundamental Principles and Rights at Work.

Organizations joining the GRI have since 2006 the choice to present their report on three Application Levels indicating the extent to which the GRI Guidelines have been applied in sustainability reporting. Organizations can also choose to let an external party audit their report. In that case, if the result is positive, a plus sign (+) is added to the achieved Application Level.

It is important to note that the GRI framework is based on a set of principles that is similar to the one used in financial accounting and the one proposed by Gonella *et al.* in 1998. It includes materiality, stakeholder inclusiveness, sustainability context, completeness, balance, comparability, accuracy, timeliness, clarity, and reliability (see on this point also Moneva *et al.* 2006). Compared with financial accounting "sustainability context" is obviously a new and essential principle: it sets out the final aim of striving for sustainability at organizational level; that is, its contribution "to the improvement . . . of economic, environmental, and social conditions, developments, and trends at the local, regional, or global level" (GRI 2000–2006: 11). In other words the aim of organizational sustainability should be contributing to sustainable development at the level of society.

One of the major challenges for sustainability reporting is that to date all main initiatives, including the GRI, do not use integrated indicators assessing impact on all three dimensions of sustainability at once. Measuring and reporting on three sets of indicators separately may encourage the vision of sustainability as a balancing act among its three dimensions and not as enhancement of all three simultaneously.[16] The challenge, as Jed Emerson (2003: 38-39) puts it, is to "consistently advance a Blended Value Proposition that integrates and affirms the greatest maximization

16 Even worse when the focus is on one dimension only, for example the environmental one, as is unfortunately still the case even in very recent research (such as in Jones 2010).

of social, environmental, *and* economic value within a single firm (whether for-profit or nonprofit), investment opportunity, or community" (italic in original).

Another major challenge derives directly from the use of indicators notwithstanding their type: indicators are static while achieving sustainability implies a process of change and is thus dynamic by its very nature. The tension here is between comparability and flexibility. Though from a point of view of comparability it is important that organizations report on the same set of indicators year by year, it is on the other hand essential that methodological advances, more valuable indicators of impact and indicators on new social and environmental concerns are integrated in existing measuring and reporting initiatives (Dierkes and Antal 1986).

The choice of specific indicators is also subject to challenges. If it is the company that chooses the indicators on which to report, the danger is to gloss over sensitive areas. If the indicators are chosen through a process of stakeholder consultation, the risk is real that the final set of indicators reflects the concern of the most vociferous group (Dierkes and Antal 1986). Moreover, the sheer number of indicators on which to report, and the different and sometimes highly specialized instruments now at a company's disposal, may preclude the view of the big picture of sustainability with its painful issues of unfair wealth distribution and diffuse poverty while we are already living beyond the Earth's supporting capacity.

Fragmentation of initiatives, though they may be celebrated as giving the possibility to as many organizations as possible to measure and report on their sustainability efforts, may lead to confusion and low quality standards (see Boxes 8.1–8.4 for examples). The divide between financial reports on one side and social and environmental reports on the other has also to be bridged to achieve true sustainability reporting. It is very positive that both challenges have not only been recognized by individual institutions (such as the ISO and the GRI) but have also been taken up internationally with the formation of the International Integrated Reporting Committee in August 2010.[17]

Finally, measuring and reporting may become an (expensive) gimmick: a way to throw sand in stakeholders' eyes without any intention of evaluating whether the outcomes or impacts of the organization's activities met desired goals and of determining what can be done to improve operations (Lewis 2010). It cannot be emphasized enough that goal alignment is paramount for an honest and credible approach to sustainability measuring and reporting. It all starts with values informed by sound principles based on a paradigm of sustainability and consistently integrated in all organizational activities (see Wartick and Cochran 1985 and the discussion on the organizational effectiveness cycle in Chapter 7).

Concluding the discussion so far the authors would like to stress that, alongside an integrated approach to sustainability starting from the principles on which an organization bases its values and vision, a second condition for organizational sustainability is to have the means to measure, monitor, and report upon inputs, throughputs, outputs, results, and impacts according to the three dimensions of

17 www.theiirc.org (accessed August 22, 2011); Eccles and Krzus 2010.

people, planet, and profit. The rationale behind this need is twofold. On the one hand, given the public interest in sustainability and the call for stakeholders' involvement, sustainability is closely related to transparency and accountability. On the other hand, if contributing to sustainability has to be seen as the aim of all activities of an organization, it is difficult to see how the organization itself could refuse to monitor the impact of its activities and assess the value it adds (or destroys) across the ecological, social, and economic dimensions (see, e.g., Holliday *et al.* 2002: 22-26 and 77-79).

Box 8.4 **Dow Jones Sustainability Indexes**

In discussing measurement and reporting, the establishment of the Dow Jones Sustainability Group Indexes in 1999 cannot be passed over without comment. These indexes track the financial performance of sustainable companies worldwide and provide investors and companies with a way to compare performance.

The basis for inclusion or exclusion from the Dow Jones Sustainability Indexes is provided by the Corporate Sustainability Assessment by SAM Research. A specific set of criteria is used to assess the opportunities and risks deriving from economic, environmental, and social developments for the eligible companies. A major source of information is a questionnaire which is completed by companies participating in the annual review. Further sources include company and third-party documents as well as personal contacts between the SAM analysts and companies. Assurance on the assessment process is provided by Deloitte.

Companies are then ranked within their industry group and selected for the Dow Jones Sustainability Indexes when they are among the sustainability leaders within their field.

Inclusion in the Dow Jones Sustainability Indexes has become for several companies, such as the Dutch AkzoNobel and Shell, a matter of honor. In 2010 Shell announced that it would link its executives' bonus to the position of the company in the Index. A few months later, to its dismay, Shell was dropped from the 2010 Index. AkzoNobel was confirmed world leader in its sector, chemicals.

See for more information: www.sustainability-index.com (accessed August 22, 2011) and Holliday *et al.* 2002: 37-38.

8.4 **Multilateral initiatives**

Several forces have contributed to the development of multilateral initiatives to support the integration of sustainability into business operations. Two such forces have already been touched on: the complexity of applying sustainability and the ensuing need to share knowledge. The global scale of many sustainability issues is also a compelling reason to choose a multilateral approach. Besides global issues, quite a few local social and environmental problems are of interest for several organizations in the same industry. In this case, and taking into account that tackling sustainability issues can be costly and thus detrimental to a company's competitive position, cooperation offers an effective and feasible option. Looked at from this point of view, the attention given to organizational stakeholders in recent decades receives a new light.

A further factor that has enhanced cooperation among businesses, and between businesses and other institutions, is trust or, to be more accurate, the decreasing trust of society in business (Wren 2005). To quote the WBCSD (2005: 3): "The crisis of trust in business is impossible to ignore. Across 21,000 people surveyed by GlobeScan at the end of 2003, nongovernmental organizations (NGOs) were once again the most trusted, and global companies the least."

On their side, NGOs and not-for-profit organizations have come to see cooperation with for-profit organizations as a way to scale up solutions to pressing social and environmental problems. These forms of cooperation know their own challenges and problems. Yet, before discussing the less positive side, let's take some positive examples of agreements that are the results of multilateral initiatives.

A recent survey counted more than two hundred legally binding multilateral environmental agreements or MEAs (Brack and Grey 2003). Considering that MEAs are only a specific segment of multilateral initiatives and that existing instruments constantly evolve and new ones emerge, it is clear that making a complete and coherent list of all multilateral schemes is impossible. A choice among existing initiatives has thus to be made. Within the limits of this book, the authors will look at the most well-known multilateral schemes considering both the environmental and the social aspects of organizational sustainability.

Our discussion will start from broad, general initiatives and proceed to more specific ones.[18]

Earth Charter

Before going on, let us remember that Part I has already touched on several initiatives, such as the UN Universal Declaration of Human Rights (Chapter 3 Section 4); the Rio Declaration on Sustainable Development and Agenda 21, with the ensuing agreements on specific environmental issues such as deforestation and climate change (Chapter 4; Box 4.10 and Box 4.12); and the UN Millennium Development Goals (Box 4.11). Chapters 1 and 2 have also repeatedly cited the work of the UNEP and the ILO: for example, the Declaration on Child Labor.

It is interesting to note that the first step in the development of the agreements and declarations mentioned above was taken by the United Nations. Yet both the

18 For a broader overview see OECD 2009: part II, ch. 6; Edwards 2005.

Brundtland Report and the Rio Conference recognized the need to involve civil society and businesses by developing sustainability initiatives through democratic and multilateral processes. Both the Brundtland Report and the Rio Conference also advocated the need for new principles and a new charter to guide the transition toward a more sustainable future.

A direct answer to this call was the Earth Charter, officially published in 2000 after many years of development and a consultation process in which over 100,000 people in 47 countries were involved. The aim of the Earth Charter is to offer a set of fundamental, ethical principles for building a just, sustainable, and peaceful global society. Though ecological integrity is its major theme, the Earth Charter "recognizes that the goals of ecological protection, the eradication of poverty, equitable economic development, respect for human rights, democracy, and peace are interdependent and indivisible".[19]

Global Compact

The Earth Charter devises as its target group, alongside the UN, individuals and businesses. And indeed the involvement of for-profit organizations in the sustainability agenda has become deeper as time passed. To respond to and at the same time strengthen this trend, the UN launched in 2000 the Global Compact (UNGC), a policy initiative pointedly directed to businesses. The aim of the Global Compact is "to align business operations and strategies everywhere with ten universally accepted principles in the areas of human rights, labour, environment and anti-corruption" (UN Global Compact Office 2008: 1). The Global Compact builds on existing initiatives and quotes as its sources the Rio Declaration on Sustainable Development alongside the UN Universal Declaration of Human Rights, the International Labour Organization's declaration on Fundamental Principles and Rights at Work and the UN anti-corruption declaration. The Global Compact is a non-regulatory and voluntary initiative; yet, interestingly, it holds its participants accountable for their actions and uses a system of disclosure that enables organizations joining the Global Compact to report on the efforts taken and the results achieved. Since 2008 companies that do not abide by the "Communication of Progress" policy are delisted from the index. In the words of Georg Kell, Global Compact Executive Director:

> while the delisting of companies is regrettable, it is essential that the
> UNGC initiative stays true to its accountability policy. This helps protect
> the integrity of the initiative as a whole, while also protecting the engagement of seriously committed companies (UN Global Compact 2008).

Ten years after its launch, the Global Compact counted more than 8,000 participants, of which the vast majority is constituted by for-profit organizations. In 2010 the business participants of the UN Global Compact Leaders' Summit restated

19 www.earthcharterinaction.org, accessed August 27, 2011.

their commitment by signing the so-called New York Declaration by Business. In the preamble they state:

> Future advances in global integration, sustainable development, protec-
> tion of our planet and, ultimately, peace critically depend on the ability
> to collectively address challenges. The need for responsibility and leader-
> ship has never been greater.
>   We believe that embedding principles and responsibility into the mar-
> ketplace is an essential part of the solution. Sustainable and inclusive
> global markets can contribute significantly to a future world where all
> people live in societies that are prosperous and peaceful.[20]

The stance taken by the business leaders who developed and signed the New York Declaration is clearly one of complete integration of sustainability in a compa-ny's values, strategy, and operations. Also interesting in the New York Declaration is that cooperation between business and government is recognized as a crucial success factor in the creation of sustainable communities. Businesses and govern-ments have responsibilities in their own sphere. In the Declaration governments are called on to enable situations supporting (sustainable) innovations, to regulate markets, and encourage business to take voluntary initiatives to "promote univer-sal values."

General business codes: ILO, Ceres Principles, ICC Business Charter for Sustainable Development, and OECD Guidelines for MNEs

Promoting universal values: this is the goal of all the agreements and declarations outlined so far. In this sense they represent the more general boundaries set by societies for organizations.

General business codes form a second tier, somehow nearer to an organization's own code. Among these we find the already discussed ILO Declaration on Child Labor (see Chapter 3 Section 2). It has to be remembered here that all ILO con-ventions and declarations are considered the standard for labor-related issues. They support and guide organizations in the effort to spell out their responsibili-ties on the people dimension of sustainability. ILO's work is so fundamental that it not only constitutes the standard reference for general declarations when these address labor issues, but it is also used as a basis for the development of measure-ment indicators (see, e.g., Box 8.3).

While the ILO focuses on the people dimension, the Coalition for Environmen-tally Responsible Economies (Ceres) Principles focuses on planet. Developed in 1989 after the *Exxon Valdez* oil spill—the biggest marine oil spill ever before the BP Deepwater Horizon disaster in 2010—the Ceres Principles were meant to become

---

20 unglobalcompact.org/docs/news_events/9.1_news_archives/2010_06_25/
LeadersSummit_NY_Declaration.pdf, accessed August 27, 2011.

a code of conduct on the basis of which companies could monitor, evaluate, and report on their environmental management processes and results. It took four years before a major company subscribed to the principles. Then, testifying to the shift in the business paradigm that took place at the end of the 1990s, more and more companies joined in until a membership of 60 was reached in 2010. Though this is a considerable achievement, Ceres's biggest contribution to the involvement of organizations in the sustainability agenda is probably co-founding the Global Reporting Initiative, whose work was cited in discussing sustainability reporting.

Two years after Ceres, the International Chamber of Commerce (an NGO representing business interests worldwide) launched its Business Charter for Sustainable Development. It contains 16 principles directed toward the improvement of and reporting on environmental management processes and results. The Business Charter focuses on reducing the use of natural resources and on minimizing the impact of products and services on the environment. Though it is a voluntary agreement, the last principle of the Business Charter obliges company to report on their environmental performance.

The International Chamber of Commerce (ICC) reaffirmed its commitment to sustainable development both in 1997 at the Rio + 5 meeting in New York and in 2002 at the Johannesburg Earth Summit. The ICC recognizes that the Business Charter contains less stringent principles than those of Ceres. The threshold for companies to join in is relatively lower: more than 2,300 had signed it by 2010.

In discussing the Global Compact we have noticed that a distinction is made there between the role of governments and the role of organizations, while it is also recognized that to achieve sustainability the one depends on the other. This view constitutes also the starting point of the OECD Guidelines for Multinational Enterprises.[21] The Guidelines are intended as a recommendation by governments to multinational enterprises on standards of responsible business conduct. Notwithstanding this focus, they are also deemed applicable to domestic organizations. The Guidelines address both the people and the planet dimension of sustainability at organizational level alongside good governance issues and fairness in competition. The first guideline states the overall purpose by arguing that enterprises should "contribute to economic, environmental and social progress with a view to achieving sustainable development" (OECD 2011: 17). It does not need to be underlined that the view on sustainable organization defended by the authors is completely in line with this statement.

---

21 First published in 1976, the Guidelines are reviewed on a regular basis. We refer to the 2008 review. The OECD is a forum of 30 (Northern) countries to address the economic, social, and environmental challenges of globalization. It was created after WWII to support the Marshall Plan. For an in-depth analysis of the OECD Guidelines, the ILO declarations, and the Global Compact see OECD 2009.

General business codes developed by business: Sullivan Principles, WBCSD, and the IETA

Not only multilateral organizations or NGOs have issued codes and guidelines for businesses. Business itself has taken action by developing business-wide or sector-specific codes and agreements. One of the first business-wide initiatives to have a deep impact was the Sullivan Principles. These principles were developed in 1977 by Reverend Leon Sullivan in his role as a member of the board of directors at General Motors, the global giant in the automotive industry. At that time General Motors was the largest employer of black citizens in the U.S. and, with Leon Sullivan, General Motors was the first major American corporation to nominate a black representative to the board. General Motors had operations in South Africa, and there also happened to be the major employer of black people.

The Sullivan Principles called for equal pay and equal opportunities for employees without any regard for their race. The South African government was then following a strict policy of racial segregation: the Sullivan Principles were thus calling on corporations to behave in contravention of the laws of South Africa. Yet 12 U.S.-based corporations signed the Sullivan Principles from the start while others slowly followed in subsequent years. The resulting economic pressure helped to accelerate the fall of the apartheid system.

In 1999, 20 years after their publication, the Sullivan Principles were reviewed under the auspices of Leon Sullivan and Kofi Annan (UN Secretary-General from 1997 to 2006 and Nobel laureate in 2001) and were published under the name "Global Sullivan Principles of Corporate Social Responsibility." Still, in line with their roots in the anti-apartheid fight, the Global Sullivan Principles focus only on the people dimension: employees' rights and communities' quality of life. A positive point is that a company subscribing to the Global Sullivan Principles is requested to apply them in all processes and procedures, including reporting. In this sense the Principles support the call for transparency and an integrated approach to sustainability that was also defended above.

A final note: the support given by companies to the first version of the Sullivan Principles is the most intriguing proof that, notwithstanding Archie B. Carroll's definition (discussed in Chapter 6 Section 3), under certain circumstances being socially responsible requires going against the law of a (host) country.

Another widely supported set of initiatives was developed by the World Business Council for Sustainable Development (WBCSD).[22] The WBCSD stepped into the debate on the role of organizations in the transition toward sustainable development in 1992 when it presented a paper with the title *Changing Course: A Global Business Perspective on Development and the Environment* at the Rio de Janeiro

---

22 Founded in 1990 as the Business Council for Sustainable Development with the aim of providing a voice for the point of view of business at the Rio Conference, it changed its name after merging in 1995 with the World Industry Council on the Environment, an ICC organization.

Conference. The WBCSD was founded by Stephan Schmidheiny, the Swiss industrialist referred to throughout this book, with the aim of involving the private sector in sustainability issues. *Changing Course* sees poor environmental performance as inefficiency, exactly as total quality management sees poor quality. Inefficiencies have by definition to be eliminated in a business context and therefore *Changing Course* argues that it is in the interest of business to respect the environment and lower its operational impacts on nature. *Changing Course* has been instrumental in initiating and fuelling the eco-efficiency approach to environmental sustainability.

That the appeal came from business itself and not from an environmental NGO was a real novelty in 1992. Yet, as Stephan Schmidheiny recognized, there are limits to what eco-efficiency can do. As Michael Braungart and William McDonough say, eco-efficiency is doing less harm and not yet doing good: it lessens negative impacts but is not productive of positive or at least environmentally neutral impacts. Eco-efficiency is moreover focused toward the planet dimension of organizational sustainability and has only indirect positive consequences for people. Stephan Schmidheiny also points to areas, such as forest management and climate change, where business needs either government regulation to behave sustainably or the support of supra-national institutions. The WBCSD point of view is here that governments should develop laws and regulations that enable market mechanisms and trade to positively impact on planet and people. In this respect the WBCSD agrees with many other supporters of sustainability, from Herman Daly and John Cobb to Ray Anderson and the OECD.

Pointing to governments' role does not mean for the WBCSD waiting passively until something happens. On the contrary, the WBCSD has shown that business can take an active role in fighting global issues by co-founding with the UNCTAD the International Emissions Trading Association (IETA) in 1999. IETA aims to establish a functional international framework for trading in greenhouse gas emission reductions by business (see Box 8.5).[23] The IETA not only supports research but it is also an active participant in and organizer of meetings on climate change and the implementation of the Kyoto Protocol. In 2010 it counted 170 business members, from both developed and developing countries.

In preparing for the 2002 Johannesburg Conference, ten years after Rio, the WBCSD pointed more strongly to the impact business has on people and widened its approach to include the fight against poverty. Though the WBCSD has actively participated in the discussion, its perspective is not the creation of new guidelines but creating awareness for the business case for sustainable development while supporting and disseminating best practices on how to achieve this.

23 www.IETA.org, accessed August 27, 2011.

Box 8.5 **Emissions trading**

Emissions trading (or cap-and-trade) was considered earlier by Herman Daly and John Cobb (1989) as an effective mechanism to fight climate change. The basic assumption is that the Earth can cope with a finite amount of pollutants, such as greenhouse gas emissions. Once this amount is defined—and here of course lies a first area for disagreement—it should be considered as a maximum that should not be trespassed by the waste caused by any form of human activity. This maximum amount should then be allocated among users.

Users can be defined as people or communities or countries or organizations. Here, too, lies an area open to discussion on which is the most effective and fair alternate among these four.

Once the division has taken place, people (or communities or countries or businesses) that consume less than their allowed share may sell permissions to emit to other people (or communities or countries or businesses) that consume more than their allowed share.

Emissions permits become thus a scarce commodity and a market is created in which an economic incentive will lead to the reduction of emissions. Scarcity of emissions permits is assured by the lowering of the cap on a regular basis. The need for international cooperation and consistency in application is evident.[a]

a   The largest existing greenhouse gas market is the European Union Emissions Trading System (ec.europa.eu/environment/climat/emission/index_en.htm, accessed August 27, 2011). A good start for people wishing to know more is, alongside the EU website, Ellerman and Buchner's 2007 article reconstructing the origin and functioning of the scheme. For an analysis of the European experience in the light of the challenges faced by Asian countries and the U.S. see, respectively, Grubb and Sato 2009 and Grubb et al. 2009. Though the scheme is a laudable initiative, it should not be forgotten that greenhouse gases are only one of the noxious substances emitted into the atmosphere as a result of human activities.

Sector-related initiatives

Sector or industry-related initiatives form a layer directly above a company's own guidelines and codes. To date it would be difficult to find an economic sector where no initiatives have been taken. Examples of widely supported initiatives are the Equator Principles for the financial sector and the Extractive Industry Transparency Initiative. Both schemes were initiated in 2002, the first by nine international banks that agreed on the development of guidelines to address social and environmental risks in financial projects. The resulting Equator Principles were launched in 2003 and signed by ten international financial institutions. By May 2010, 68 financial institutions had joined this initiative.[24]

The Extractive Industry Transparency Initiative was started by the British Government to fight corruption, a widespread cancer in the sector, by disclosing all corporate payments to governments in the countries in which a firm operates (see Porter and Kramer 2006: 9; the website of the initiative: eiti.org [accessed August 28, 2011]; and Haufler 2010).

To these two sector initiatives, a third example is considered here. It is related to tourism. Representing 9.2% of world GNP and 235 million jobs in 2010 (almost 1 in 12!), tourism is a force to be reckoned with (World Travel and Tourism Council 2010). Involvement with sustainability has been an issue for tourism organizations for a few decades: the World Tourism Organization, for example, has reflected since 1980 on the role of tourism in social and environmental sustainability. The International Eco-tourism Society (founded in 1990), the World Heritage Alliance for Sustainable Tourism (created in 2005 by the UN Foundation and Expedia, the online travel company), and the Global Sustainable Tourism Council (created in 2009 when the Partnership for Global Sustainable Tourism Criteria merged with the Sustainable Tourism Stewardship Council), alongside international tour operators and several other players in the tourism industry, developed guidelines and codes to support a more sustainable stance to tourism from both businesses and tourists. This multiplicity of actors involved has resulted in dozens of different guidelines, with different scope and criteria.

The tourism industry seems, therefore, not to be immune from the fragmentation that haunts sustainability initiatives. Recently, though, the Global Sustainable Tourism Council launched a counteroffensive and developed the Global Sustainable Tourism Criteria after a two-year consultation process during which 100,000 stakeholders were involved and more than 4,500 criteria from 60 existing guidelines, principles, or other sets of standards analyzed.[25] In the end, four main criteria were established. They are summarized in Table 8.1. Indicators have also been developed to measure results and offer a possibility to benchmark against best practice.

24 www.equator-principles.com, accessed August 27, 2011.
25 gstcouncil.org, accessed August 28, 2011. The criteria are summarized here by courtesy of the Global Sustainable Tourism Council. The Council expects to issue a slightly revised set of criteria in autumn 2011.

Table 8.1 **Global Sustainable Tourism Criteria**

Source: new.gstcouncil.org/page/adopt-the-criteria, accessed August 28, 2011

Main criterion	Specific criteria/areas
1. Demonstrate effective sustainable management	• By implementing management systems • By complying with relevant international and local laws and regulations • By educating personnel on their role in management for sustainability • By measuring customers' satisfaction and taking corrective actions • By honest promotional material • By designing and constructing buildings in accordance with (local) rules, preserving heritage, and applying sustainability principles • By informing and educating the customers
2. Maximize social and economic benefits to the local community and minimize negative impacts	• By supporting initiatives for community development • By employing residents, including women and minorities, also in management positions • By buying locally at fair prices • By designing and implementing a code of conduct in cooperation with locals • By fighting commercial exploitation of children • By respecting international labor standards • By not jeopardizing the local community's access to water and other resources
3. Maximize benefits to cultural heritage and minimize negative impacts	• By minimizing visitors' impact on the visited site • By not selling, trading, or displaying historical and archeological artifacts, except as permitted by law • By contributing to the protection of local sites that are historically, archeologically, culturally, or spiritually important and by not impeding residents' access to these sites • By respecting the intellectual copyright of local artists and communities
4. Maximize benefits to the environment and minimize negative impacts	Fourteen criteria in three areas: • Conserving resources • Reducing pollution • Conserving biodiversity, ecosystems, and landscapes

Comparing this initiative with others also aimed at combining existing schemes and reducing dozens of indicators to a few manageable ones—such as ISO 26000—it may be argued that a new integration trend has replaced the trend toward fragmentation. This is a very promising development.

Business and NGOs

Before concluding this section on multilateral initiatives, it is worth remembering some instances of direct cooperation between businesses and NGOs. Out of the many forms this cooperation can take, the authors wish to point to the joint development of guidelines and eco-labels such as the Marine Stewardship Council (MSC).[26]

The MSC offers both guidelines and certification of sustainable fishing and was created in 1997 by Unilever in cooperation with the World Wildlife Fund (WWF). MSC guidelines are directed toward wild-capture fisheries and require compliance with a set of criteria around three major principles: the fishing activity must not over-exploit the fish population and endanger its reproductive capacity; environmental impact should be minimized, so that the ecosystem supporting the fishery is not damaged; and a management system should be in place to assure not only compliance with all relevant rules and regulations but also continuous improvement. Measurement and disclosure are mandatory for fisheries that wish to obtain the MSC logo.

In 2009 over 350 million items of MSC-labeled products were sold in 42 countries. Items sold grew by 67% compared with 2008, while the global market for MSC-labeled products grew by over 50% to reach a retail value of $1.5 billion. Impressive numbers, and yet in 2009 MSC covered only 7% of the world's total wild-captured fish (MSC 2009).

WWF has cooperated with other business organizations: for example, with the well-known Swedish furniture and home decoration giant IKEA, to support forest conservation.[27] Other NGOs also started partnerships with businesses: Greenpeace, for example, joined forces with iPhone on energy reduction schemes.[28]

Without wishing to disregard the importance of these initiatives or deny their impact, it has to be recognized that there are also drawbacks. As has been noted several times, one of the highest risks implied in them all is fragmentation. Take the Marine Stewardship Council (MSC) as an example: the MSC covers only wild-caught fish. Yet the market share of farmed fish is increasing sharply, also as a result of the declining stocks of wild fish. This means that the impact of farmed fish on the marine ecosystem is also increasing; yet the MSC does not take it into account. Moreover, as the focus of the MSC is mostly on the environment, social, and cultural aspects may be disregarded. Yet sustainability asks for an integrated approach to all its dimensions: profit, people, and planet.

A second consequence of fragmentation is the proliferation of different initiatives that often overlap, sometimes proposing different standards for sustainability, some more stringent than others, and in certain instances even conflicting ones.

---

26 Reference to earlier initiatives directed to a more sustainable management of commons is evident already in the name of the MSC: it refers to the Forest Stewardship Council established in 1993 (www.fsc.org, accessed August 28, 2011).

27 wwf.panda.org, accessed August 28, 2011.

28 www.greenpeace.org, accessed August 28, 2011.

Above we have quoted the Ceres versus the ICC principles: two initiatives with the same scope yet very different when it comes to the strictness of their guidelines for sustainable business. Similar considerations may apply to labeling schemes. Though they are good instruments to shape and support the link between the organizational and societal level of sustainability, here too focus and criteria vary on a continuum from very strict to quite loose (see Box 8.6).

Box 8.6 **Sustainable coffee labels**

On the coffee market at least four labeling initiatives may be found. Max Havelaar Fairtrade coffee focuses on the social aspects of sustainability and guarantees to the producer a premium price far higher than other initiatives such as UTZ CERTIFIED and Rainforest Alliance. UTZ CERTIFIED was co-founded as Utz Kapeh in 1997 by Ahold Coffee Company with the open aim of further developing the market for sustainable coffee by introducing a less strict standard than the one set by the fair trade organization Max Havelaar. Since 1999 UTZ CERTIFIED has become an independent organization and has reassessed its strategy, although its criteria are still considered looser than those applied by Max Havelaar/Fairtrade. The Rainforest Alliance (well known for its logo with a frog) concentrates, as the name indicates, on the protection of ecosystems. A fourth imitative, the 4C Association, was set up in 2002 by the German Government to offer small coffee farmers the opportunity to join the market for high-quality, sustainable coffee. Different than the above-mentioned schemes, the 4C Association does not guarantee a premium or fixed minimum price to producers and does not use a product label. Finally, we may remember the Coffee and Farmer Equity program initiated by Starbucks.

Though this diversity implies the possibility for more actors to participate, it makes it difficult for organizations (and individuals) to check the claims of the different initiatives and choose accordingly. This drawback has been felt keenly by several organizations and has led to initiatives to try to close gaps and enhance synergy among different schemes. As an example we may remember not only the effort to link new and old initiatives through cross-referencing, as the 4C Association did with UTZ CERTIFIED and Rainforest Alliance when setting up their standard for sustainable coffee, but also overt efforts at synergy such as that between the GRI, Global Compact Initiative, and the Earth Charter (Hohnen 2008), and finally efforts at compounding several initiatives in one as ISO did with ISO 26000 and the Global Sustainable Tourism Council with the Global Sustainable Tourism Criteria.[29] This is, as has been discussed above, a very promising trend.

---

29 In the U.S. the Houston Principles constitute an interesting example. They were designed in 1999 in a joint effort by environmental and labor organizations that together opposed the clearing of ancient redwood forests in northern California by the Pacific Lumber

There are also specific drawbacks to the closer relationship of NGOs with corporations. The risk for NGOs is to become too reliant on business for their financial security. This may lead the broad public to lose trust in their independent judgment. As an example, let's go back to the Marine Stewardship Council (MSC) initiative. In September 2010 *Nature* published a very critical study on the work of MSC certification organizations. MSC certification organizations work on a commercial basis. This guarantees their independence from MSC, but at the same time tempts them to compromise with clients in order not to lose them to a competitor. As a consequence, fisheries that are still overfishing and are thus unsustainable have become MSC-certified. This of course disrupts the whole system (Jacquet *et al.* 2010). Paradoxically, it was because of their independence that NGOs were sought after by business, as has been noted above, in an effort to convince the public of the authenticity of their concern for sustainability.[30]

Undoubtedly, engaging in sustainability and stakeholder dialogue enhances the complexity of managing an organization. The same is true for joining multilateral agreements, though agreed rules and standards are ultimately intended to ease the pursuit by organizations of a more sustainable stance. The slowness of the process to achieve multilateral and multi-stakeholder agreements also forms a challenge, especially for those for-profit organizations that are used to acting quickly on changing market conditions. When endorsed by the majority of players, multilateral agreements support the forming of a level playing field and discourage free-riding. The disadvantage for businesses here is that first movers will no longer be able to use their commitment to sustainability as a source of competitive advantage. A strategic approach through which sustainability is fully integrated into all activities of an organization remains the only viable way for long-lasting differentiation from competitors, as Michael Porter and Mark Kramer stated (2006).

8.5 The role of organizations as change agents toward sustainable development

Without any doubt the concept of *corporate* social responsibility was intended to target for-profit organizations alone. The call to business was, as we have seen, to accept responsibility for the impact of their operations on all stakeholders and not only for value creation for shareholders and owners. From here the triad of people,

---

Company. Though the interests of nature and human beings are often deemed to be in irresolvable conflict, the Houston Principles reaffirm their interdependence (see Edwards 2005: 64-67).

30 See O'Rourke 2003: 22-23 for a summary of literature on adverse effects of NGO involvement in regulating business practices.

planet, and *profit* was born with the consequent issue of clarifying how not-for-profit organizations could be hooked to the sustainability agenda.

Proposals have been made to substitute the profit dimension with prosperity at the risk of alienating corporations (Roorda 2006). Other scholars have observed that the effectiveness of not-for-profit organizations is actually determined by the extent to which their missions are being achieved and an actual impact on society is created. In this respect, these scholars continue, both for-profit and not-for-profit organizations have to take equal responsibility and accept accountability for their social impacts (Maas 2009). It has also been argued that the opposition of for-profit and not-for-profit in terms of the essential indicators to manage and assess their operations is the result of a misconception of the real world as constituted by two not-to-be-reconciled opposites: financial value vs. social and environmental value (Emerson 2003). The moment the economic responsibility of organizations is identified as a subset of their social responsibilities, the difference disappears (Wartick and Cochran 1985; Emerson 2003).

The insight that the social responsibility of for-profit and not-for-profit organizations is fundamentally equal is by now quite widespread. So much so, in fact, that it is one of the starting points for ISO 26000 that, as has been seen above, constitutes a quite broad consensus on what social responsibility is all about. The introduction to the final draft of ISO 26000 states (2009: 5):

> Attention to social responsibility has in the past focused primarily on business . . .
>
> The view that social responsibility is applicable to all organizations emerged as different types of organizations, not just those in the business world, recognized that they too had responsibilities for contributing to sustainable development.

And:

> **Social responsibility** has the organization as its focus and concerns the responsibilities of an organization to society and the environment. Social responsibility is closely linked to sustainable development. Because sustainable development is about the economic, social and environmental goals common to all people, it can be used as a way of summing up the broader expectations of society that need to be taken into account by organizations seeking to act responsibly. Therefore, an overarching goal of an organization's social responsibility should be to contribute to sustainable development (ISO 2009: 9; bold in original).

This is the material point: sustainable organizations see themselves as contributing to sustainable development. This is, as was observed above, a complete paradigm shift from the traditional, "old industrial revolution paradigm" in which corporations are seen as tools for economic value creation alone, while governments, NGOs, and not-for-profit organizations should take care of the social and environmental value.

On the question of who is the primary agent of change, scholars and practitioners give very different answers, varying from a firm faith in an organization's capability to drive change toward sustainability to complete disbelief in such capacity and in the honesty of firms' CSR endeavors. For example, Stuart Hart, Professor of Management and Organizations at Cornell University, seems to believe that only business organizations have the technologies, skills, and resources needed to successfully implement the sustainability agenda (Hart 2005). On the other hand, in his *The Market for Virtue* (2005) David Vogel, Professor in Business Ethics at Berkeley University in California, warns that business cannot be a substitute for government: CSR initiatives (either collective or unilateral) cannot bring us very far on the route toward sustainability without supporting governmental regulations and policies on one side, and customers' and consumers' support on the other. This is also the opinion of the business executives from the WBCSD, as we have seen above.

The point to be made here is that without any doubt the concept of social responsibility redesigns the relationship between organizations (including business) and society in general and between organizations and the government in particular. Yet these two levels should not be blurred "because there is a grave and crucial difference between a country and a corporation" (Hawken 1993: 92). Responsibilities such as the drawing and enforcement of laws and regulations, imposing taxes (including environmental or socially informed taxes in order to internalize social and environmental costs in the market price), taking care of citizens' security, supporting education for all citizens and the like are the prerogative of governments. Legitimacy for the deployment of these functions comes from democratically held elections. This is a legacy from our history that should not be disregarded.

Alongside the levels of societies and organizations, there is a third level at which responsibility can be assessed: the individual level. Confronted with the havoc of environmental pollution and social inequalities it is easy to point an accusing finger toward greedy corporations and weak governments. Yet, as Paul Hawken observes (1993: 212-13):

> If we want businesses to express a full range of social and environmental values in their daily commercial activities, then we, too, will have to express a full range of values and respond to the presence or absence of principles by how we act in the marketplaces.

Alongside governments and (business) organizations, individuals have a responsibility, too. Individuals might take this responsibility as consumers and investors (as Hawken suggests in the quote above) or as citizens, by looking critically at the stance taken by political parties. They can take this responsibility as individual human beings, too, by looking for and developing values that support the transition toward sustainability at the level of society and organizations. This point will be further explored in Part III of the book.

A last set of remarks concerns the type of change needed to develop organizations that add value on the triple bottom line of people, planet, and profit and thus contribute to sustainable development at society level. Change is the natural condition in which modern organizations find themselves, although the change needed to build a sustainable organization is of a different nature than this "change as usual." There are at least two main reasons for this difference.

First, sustainability requires a reconsideration of the principles guiding the organization. Sustainability, it has been argued, is grounded on the pursuit of justice and fairness for the present and future generations. Justice and fairness are ethical principles. Sustainability requires thus both for-profit and not-for-profit organizations to become aligned with fundamental ethical principles. This requires internalizing these principles and is thus quite different than grudgingly yielding to external pressure, doing as little as possible, or waiting until it passes over (Wartick and Cochran 1985).

Second, it has also been argued here that the change process toward sustainability for an organization starts by grounding its values, vision, and mission into sustainability principles and then aligning all activities toward these same principles. This again involves all aspects of an organization, including the deepest assumptions on which its culture is based and the paradigms of all people connected to the organization; from employees to clients; from suppliers to communities.

Concluding: profound change is needed. Setting change in motion and guiding processes of change is seen as the prerogative of leaders. Leadership and sustainability are the themes of the third and last part of this book.

Part III
Leadership for sustainability

Introduction to Part III

This closing part will expand on the third and most critical level in the **three levels of sustainability** framework (see Fig. III.1): namely the individual level or the leadership level. Societies consist of organizations and organizations consist of people. They are the movers of ideas and ideals and they are the end receivers of the fruits of all processes. As we have seen in Part I, the ultimate goal of sustainability is a better quality of life for all people. This implies that the process of sustainability has to be led by the people, with the people, and for the people. As such, the narrative of leadership for sustainability starts with the self and consequently with the person behind the leader. The most important question is: what values are needed to lead the self, organizations, and societies on the path of continuous change toward sustainability and higher quality of life for all? The three dimensions of the individual level represent the three stages of development that are critical in the journey of men and women who are willing to widen their circle of compassion, to embrace all living creatures and the whole of nature in their quest for a more sustainable world.

The leadership of self goes back to the early thinking about leadership. In Chinese history, for example, Confucius stressed the cultivation of character as the main concern in the life of a leader. This is the basis for gaining wisdom in order to improve and enrich one's leadership potential. Therefore, a leader should demand much of him- or herself, in order to bring harmony, respect, cooperation, and trust within the group. Only then can a leader expect the same from followers. Peter Senge *et al.* (2004: 186) refer to Confucius and observe, "if you want to be a leader, you have to be a real human being. You must recognize the true meaning of life before you can become a leader. You must understand yourself first." Despite the early understanding of this critical role of the individual and personal dimension of leadership, the focus in the sustainability debate has been very much on the process of change on the organizational and the societal level and not as much on the individual level. Though it is precisely this individual level that in the end will determine the success or failure of organizations and societies in their voyage toward sustainability.

Considering the many great books that have dealt with leadership in the past decades and the ongoing debate, this part of the book will only briefly touch on the concept of leadership in general.

The focus will be more on the crucial role of leadership of self. The variability in definitions and terms used will be touched on to indicate the fluidity of the leadership discussion (Chapter 9). The TLS framework is then used to introduce the three distinct dimensions of the individual level, analogous with the three dimensions of the organizational and the societal level (Chapter 10). Finally, we will zoom in on the importance of the leadership of self and the critical role of the third dimension (Care for all; see Fig. III.2). This most critical dimension has the essential qualities to support the path toward leadership for sustainability (Chapter 11).

Figure III.1 **Three levels of sustainability framework**

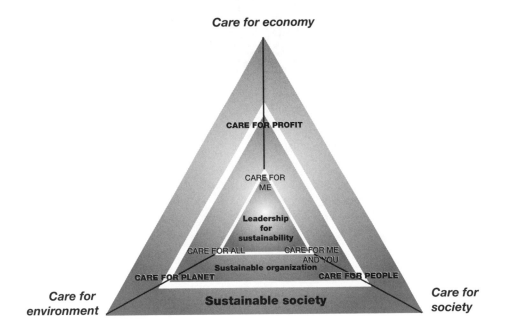

The TLS framework uses the term "Care" to indicate that each dimension of each level is an area of concern. This term became apparent for all levels, after the three Care dimensions of the individual level were established

Figure III.2 **Individual level**

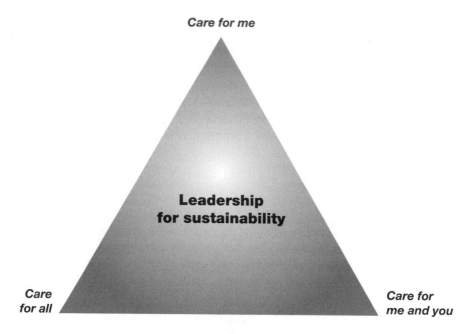

9

Many faces of leadership

This chapter will look briefly at some important aspects in the discussion on leadership to give an impression of the complexity and at some times confused nature of the debate. The chapter will indicate that the issue of leadership goes back to the early days of the famous philosophers and religious leaders, and that over the course of time many different theories evolved (Section 9.1). A wide and growing spread of definitions characterizes the discussion, fueled from many different disciplines, making it a widespread and unfinished discourse, difficult to grasp (Section 9.2). Inconsistent and overlapping use of terminology such as leaders, leadership, and management complicates the discussion even more (Section 9.3).

9.1 Glimpse back at the beginnings

In Bass and Stogdill's *Handbook of Leadership* (1990), also known as the indispensable "bible" for serious students of leadership, the authors take a quick look back at the beginnings of the leadership discussion. The subject of leadership, they admit, was not limited to the Western literature, but was as much of interest to Asoka[1] and Confucius as to Plato and Aristotle (Bass and Stogdill 1990: 3). Myths and legends about great leaders were in those days important in the development of societies

---

1 Asoka (*c*. 300–232 BCE) was born into the Mauryan royal family. After his father's death, he became in 270 BCE the ruler of an empire extending from Afghanistan to Bengal, and covering the Ganges Plain and the Deccan Plateau. He pushed out the boundaries of his empire during the next decade, conquering Kalinga in 262 BCE. In this way he unified nearly all of India under his rule. He converted to Buddhism in 260 BCE and thenceforth propagated ideals of tolerance, equality, and public service.

and it was recognized that the leader was the most important element of good government (and still is?). As such, the study of history has been at the same time a study of leaders, what they did and what they did not (Bass and Stogdill 1990: 3).

A review of the leadership literature reveals an evolving series of "schools of thought" from "great man" and "trait" theories to "transformational" leadership (see Table 9.1). While early theories tend to focus on the characteristics and behaviors of successful leaders, later theories begin to consider the role of followers and the contextual nature of leadership.

Table 9.1 **From "great man" to "transformational leadership"**

Source: Bolden *et al.* 2003: 6

Great men theories	Based on the belief that leaders are exceptional people, born with innate qualities, destined to lead. The use of the term "man" was intentional since, until the latter part of the twentieth century, leadership was thought of as a concept which is primarily male, military, and Western. This led to the next school of trait theories
Trait theories	The lists of traits or qualities associated with leadership exist in abundance and continue to be produced. They draw on virtually all the adjectives in the dictionary which describe some positive or virtuous human attribute, from ambition to zest for life
Behaviorist theories	These concentrate on what leaders actually do rather than on their qualities. Different patterns of behavior are observed and categorized as "styles of leadership." This area has probably attracted most attention from practicing managers
Situational leadership	This approach sees leadership as specific to the situation in which it is being exercised. For example, while some situations may require an autocratic style, others may need a more participative approach. It also proposes that there may be differences in required leadership styles at different levels in the same organization
Contingency theory	This is a refinement of the situational viewpoint and focuses on identifying the situational variables that best predict the most appropriate or effective leadership style to fit the particular circumstances
Transactional theory	This approach emphasizes the importance of the relationship between leader and followers, focusing on the mutual benefits derived from a form of "contract" through which the leader delivers such things as rewards or recognition in return for the commitment or loyalty of the followers
Transformational theory	The central concept here is change and the role of leadership in envisioning and implementing the transformation of organizational performance

John Antonakis *et al.* (2004: 4-6), in *Leadership: Past, Present, and Future*, next to the schools of thought mentioned above refer to the "information-processing school of leadership." In this theory the focus is on understanding why a leader is legitimized by virtue of the fact that his or her characteristics match the prototypical expectation that followers have of the leader. None of the schools mentioned above, however, has a clear focus on the role of the person behind the leader.

9.2 **Defining leadership, an unfinished project?**

According to Fleishman *et al.* (1991) in Northouse 2007: 2, in the last 60 years as many as 65 different classification systems have been developed to define the dimensions of leadership. One of the most complete schemes is that proposed by Bass and Stogdill (1990). Bass and Stogdill admit that there is no clear definition of leadership and state: "There are almost as many different definitions of leadership as there are persons who have attempted to define the concept" (1990: 11). Departing from this reality, Bass and Stogdill tried to construct a classification scheme based on the similarities found among the multitude of definitions. Table 9.2 gives a snapshot of the many definitions used in the scheme of Bass and Stogdill.

Table 9.2 **A few of the many definitions of leadership**

Source: Bass and Stogdill 1990: 11-20

Leadership as a focus on group processes	The leader is seen as the center or focal point of group change and embodies the will of the group. Leaders have to stay ahead of the group to avoid being run over
Leadership as personality and its effects	Leadership is a combination of traits or qualities that individuals possess and that enable them to induce others to accomplish tasks. Leadership is thus seen as a one-way track. Leaders possess qualities that differentiate them from followers
Leadership as the art of inducing compliance	Some scholars define leadership as "the ability to handle men so as to achieve the most with the least friction and the greatest cooperation . . . Leadership is the creative and directive force of morale" (Bass and Stogdill 1990: 12). The role of the followers is minimal while the leader tends to be authoritarian
Leadership as the exercise of Influence	The concept of influence recognizes the fact that individuals differ in the extent to which their behaviors affect the activities of a group. It implies a reciprocal relationship between the leader and the followers. In contrast to the previous characteristic, this one is not by dominance, control, or indication of compliance by the leader
Leadership as an act of behavior	Bass and Stogdill cite one of the advocates of the behaviorist school of thought, namely Hemphill (1949a), who defined leadership as "the behavior of an individual while he is involved in directing group activities." Fiedler (1967a), according to Bass and Stogdill, explains what is meant by leadership behavior: "By leadership behavior we generally mean the particular acts in which a leader engages in the course of directing and coordinating the work of his group members. This may involve such acts as structuring the work relations, praising or criticizing group members, and showing consideration for their welfare and feelings" (Bass and Stogdill 1990: 14)

➔

Leadership as a form of persuasion	As the title suggests, this form of leadership is based on the ability to convince followers to do what the leader has decided should be done. According to Bass and Stogdill, several scholars defined leadership as successful persuasion without coercion; followers are convinced by the merits of the argument, not by the coercive power of the arguer. Persuasion is said to be a powerful instrument for shaping expectations and beliefs, particularly in political, social, and religious affairs
Leadership as a power relation	Bass and Stogdill describe power as a form of influence relationship. Most political theorists from Machiavelli through Marx and political scientists of the twentieth century have seen power as the basis of political leadership. Some of these scholars defined leadership in terms of differential power relationships among members of a group
Leadership as an instrument of goal achievement	Some leadership definitions that have been used under this heading include: Cowely (1928), "a leader is a person who has a program and is moving toward an objective with his group in a definite manner" (Bass and Stogdill 1990: 15). Belows (1959) defined leadership as "the process of arranging a situation so that various members of a group, including the leader can achieve common goals with maximum economy and a minimum of time and work" (Bass and Stogdill 1990: 15). According to Bass and Stogdill, the classical organizational theorists defined leadership in terms of a group's objectives. Urwick (1951) stated that the leader is "the personal representation of the personification of common purpose not only to all work on the undertaking, but to everyone outside it" (Bass and Stogdill 1990: 16)
Leadership as an emerging effect of interaction	Some theorists have seen leadership as an effect of group action. Bogardus (1929), for example, described it as follows: "as a social process, leadership is that social interstimulation which causes a number of people to set out toward an old goal with new zest or a new goal with hopeful courage—with different persons keeping different places" (Bass and Stogdill 1990: 16)
Leadership as a differentiated role	Bass and Stogdill explain that, according to the role theory, each member of a society occupies a position in the community, as well as in various groups, organizations, and institutions. They describe leadership as a differentiated role or as a requirement to integrate the various other roles of the group and to maintain unity of action in the group's effort to achieve goals. Newcomb, Turner and converse (1965) are quoted by Bass and Stogdill (1990: 17), to clarify: "Members of a group make different contributions to the achievement of goals. Insofar as any member's contributions are particularly indispensable, they may be regarded as leaderlike; and insofar as any member is recognized by others as a dependable source of such contributions, he or she is leaderlike. To be so recognized is equivalent to having a role relationship to others members"
Leadership as the initiation of structure	Hemphill (1954), according to Bass and Stogdill (1990: 17), defines leadership as follows: "to lead is to engage in an act that initiates a structure in the interaction as part of the process of solving a mutual problem." Hemphill refers to Stogdill (1959), who defined leadership as "the initiation and maintenance of structure in expectation and interaction."

New interpretations of the nature of leadership have emerged since Bass and Stogdill completed their list. In recent years, for example, "servant leadership" and "authentic leadership" have been introduced. See Box 9.1 for a short description of these interpretations of leadership.

Box 9.1 Servant leadership and authentic leadership

The phrase "servant leadership" was coined by Robert K. Greenleaf. In his book *Servant Leadership: A Journey into the Nature of Legitimate Power and Greatness*, Greenleaf states (1977: 27):

> The servant-leader *is* servant first. It begins with the natural feeling that one wants to serve, to serve *first*. Then conscious choice brings one to aspire to lead. That person is sharply different from one who is *leader* first, perhaps because of the need to assuage an unusual power drive or to acquire material possessions . . . The leader-first and the servant-first are two extreme types. Between them there are shadings and blends that are part of the infinite variety of human nature.

From the practitioner's perspective, Bill George (2003: 11) has defined authentic leadership as "being yourself; being the person you were created to be" rather than "developing the image or persona of a leader." From a researcher's perspective, Luthans and Avolio (2003: 243) have defined authentic leadership as "a process that draws from both positive psychological capacities and a highly developed organizational context, which results in both greater self awareness and self-regulated positive behaviours on the part of leaders and associates, fostering positive self development."
On "authentic leadership" see, further, Sexton 2007.

Bass and Stogdill rightly conclude that the search for the one and only proper and true definition of leadership can be fruitless, since the appropriate choice of definition will depend on the methodological and substantive aspects of leadership in which one is interested.

For the purpose of the journey toward sustainability, however, it is the concept of "authentic leadership" which clearly recognizes the need for leadership of self. This fundamental prerequisite for leadership for sustainability has already been emphasized in the introduction to this part of the book and will become more apparent in the sections to come.

9.3 **Leaders, leadership, and management**

Sara Parkin, Founder and Director of the UK-based Forum for the Future, observes that the world of leadership development is extraordinarily loose in its use of language (Parkin 2010). Next to the almost infinite blend of definitions, there seems to be a blurred area between the use of the terms **leaders**, **leadership**, and **management**. This section touches on the discussion on who leaders are and then, more extensively, on the difference between leadership and management.

In *Leading Minds* Howard Gardner (1997: 8-9) defines *leaders* as, "persons who, by word and/or personal example influence the behavior, thoughts, and/or feelings of a significant number of their follow human beings. The leaders' voices affected their worlds, and ultimately our world." Gardner clearly departs from the premise that a leader can be any person. Parkin, however, defines the leader as a post-holder (see Table 9.3).

Table 9.3 **Parkin on leaders as post-holders**
Source: Sara Parkin 2010: 94

A leader is a post-holder and may be elected, chosen or appointed to lead something—an army, an organization, a government, a project team. The post-holder is viewed as the source of leadership. The holder may or may not be good at leadership	**Leadership may be exercised by anyone**, from anywhere in an organization or group. Even when an appointed leader exists, others may exercise leadership

In the context of the TLS and leadership for sustainability, the focus is first of all on the person behind the leader. This is why the view of Gardner as described above is most relevant. Another way to look at the leader from the perspective of the person comes from the theory of Lawrence (2010: 4), who argues that: "In fact, leadership has become our primary means of adapting to changing circumstances, which Darwin cited earlier as the key to survival. Since circumstances are always changing, we all have to lead ourselves."

The second issue raised above is the blurriness between the terms leadership and management.
According to Kotter (1996: 25):

> Management is a set of processes that keep a complicated system of people and technology running smoothly. The most important aspects of management include planning, budgeting, organizing, staffing, controlling, and problem solving. Leadership is a set of processes that creates organizations in the first place or adapts them to significantly changing circumstances. Leadership defines what the future should look like, aligns people with that vision, and inspires them to make it happen despite the obstacles.

One may wonder, however, if leadership can be exercised without having the basic skills of management. Hunt (in Antonakis *et al.* 2004) refers to W.L. Garner and J. Schermerhorn (1992), to describe a three-part conceptualization of the differentiation between leadership and management as they distinguish:

> leadership equals management;
>
> leadership does not equal management (they are entirely separate concepts); and
>
> leadership and management are complementary (Antonakis *et al.* 2004: 26).

Referring to Kotter (1996), Hunt envisions the specific function of leadership as producing adaptive or useful change, and management as being used essentially to make the organization operate smoothly. The authors recognize that leadership qualities and management skills are complementary and that the degree of input from each factor will vary from case to case. This complementary character is important both for the leadership of self and for the leadership of others. One may think, for example, of the person who has a great vision for life, but cannot manage his or her time.

To conclude, one may think of management as mainly about more tangible and measurable operational aspects such as systems, structures, and procedures and leadership as more about intangible and less measurable strategic aspects such as vision, values, and cultures. Departing from this differentiation, one may conclude that an over-managed and under-led culture has been created. Kotter (1996: 27) gives a possible explanation for this behavior when he writes:

> For most of this century, as we created thousands and thousands of large organizations for the first time in human history, we didn't have enough good managers to keep all those bureaucracies functioning. So many companies and universities developed management programs and hundreds of thousands of people were encouraged to learn management on the job. And they did. But people were taught little about leadership.

Meanwhile the discrepancies are still unresolved as one may conclude when reading the critical observations expressed in the *Handbook of Leadership Theory and Practice* (Nohria and Khurana 2010: 4) about business schools and leadership development (see Box 9.2).

A careful conclusion of the discussion about leadership may be found in the findings of James Kouzes and Barry Posner (2010). After more than 30 years of research based on empirical evidence, they arrived at ten enduring **truths** about leadership that prevail regardless of changing context and circumstances. These truths give insight and understanding about how exemplary leaders, all over the world, get extraordinary things done. Most of the qualities of leadership reflected in the definitions above can be recognized in these ten truths (see Box 9.3).

These truths once more indicate that leadership relies most strongly on less tangible and less measurable values such as trust, inspiration, attitude, decision-making, and personal character. These are not processes or skills or even necessarily

Box 9.2 **Leadership development in universities**

"Many universities, especially in their graduate programs of business administration, law, education, public health, and public policy, claim that their mission is to educate leaders who will advance the well-being of society in their respective fields. For example, Harvard Business School's formal mission statement is 'to educate leaders who make a difference in the world.' Dartmouth's Tuck School of Business defines its primary educational goal as preparing 'students for leadership positions in the world's foremost organizations.' Stanford Business School aims to 'develop innovative, principled, and insightful leaders who change the world,' and MIT's Sloan School of Management has developed a new framework built around four leadership capabilities, including sense-making, relating, visioning, and inventing . . . Yet, the reality is still that research on leadership is at best at the periphery rather than at the center of most schools that profess to educate the leaders of the future. There are many signs of this intellectual neglect: adjunct rather than tenure track faculty teach most leadership courses; there are few papers on leadership published in the most prominent academic journals; and there are virtually no doctoral courses on leadership" (Nitin Nohria and Rakesh Khurana 2010: 4).

the result of experience. They are facets of humanity, and are enabled mainly by the leader's character and especially his or her emotional reserves.

As mentioned in the beginning of this chapter, the discussion on leadership is still very open. Although difficult to conclude, we choose the combination of definitions as proposed by Lawrence (2010) to wrap up this chapter. To arrive at a general definition, he refers first to Jay Lorsch, a professor at Harvard Business School, who defined a leader as: "an individual who influences others to follow her lead" (Lawrence 2010: 81). This choice corresponds with the formulation used by Gardner at the beginning of this chapter. Then Lawrence refers to Chatman and Kennedy who defined leadership as: "a process of motivating people to work together collaboratively to accomplish great things" (Lawrence 2010: 81). There are, however, *multiple ways* to *motivate* people to follow a process to accomplish *great things*. Two indispensable variables make the discussion on leadership infinite and out of the ordinary: **multiple ways** and **great things**. In the end, it is the people who have to resolve to collaborate with the leader, and to follow the process to accomplish those things they also consider great things.

One of the great things to be strived for in the coming decennia is considered to be sustainability. Sustainability implies a process to achieve the highest quality of life for all people now and for generations to come. Individuals at all levels have to become aware that sustainability is a *great thing* to strive for. Consequently the process to achieve sustainability needs leaders at all levels, not only post-holders. The next chapter will elaborate on the qualities that are needed by the person behind the leader to accomplish this mission.

Box 9.3 **Kouzes and Posner's truths about leadership**

Source: Kouzes and Posner 2010: xxi-xxiv

- **You make a difference**. You have to believe in yourself. Leadership begins when you believe you can make a difference

- **Credibility is the foundation of leadership**. You have to believe in you, but others have to believe in you too!

- **Values drive commitment**. People want to know what you stand for and believe in.

- **Focusing on the future sets leaders apart**. The ability to imagine and articulate exciting possibilities is a defining competence of leaders

- **You cannot do it alone**. No leader ever got anything extraordinary done without the talent and support of others. Leadership is a team sport

- **Trust rules**. Trust is the social glue that holds individuals and groups together, and the level of trust others have in the leader determine the amount of influence he or she has

- **Challenge is the crucible for greatness**. Exemplary leaders—the kind of leader people want to follow—are always associated with changing the status quo. Great achievements don't happen when you keep things the same

- **You either lead by example or you don't lead**. Leaders keep their promises and become role models for the values and actions they espouse. You have to go first as a leader. You cannot ask others to do something you are not willing to do yourself

- **The best leaders are the best learners**. You have to believe that you (and others) can learn to lead, and that you can become a better leader tomorrow than you are today

- **Leadership is an affair of the heart**. It could also be the first truth. Leaders are in love with their constituents, their customers and clients, and the mission that they are serving. Leaders make others feel important and are gracious in showing appreciation

---

10
Leadership for sustainability
A three-dimensional approach

In previous chapters the three-dimensional framework of the sustainability process has been introduced and discussed for the societal and the organizational levels. As has been discussed earlier, sustainability is more than just a discourse on sustainable development or corporate social responsibility or parts of these. The three levels, three dimensions design has been developed to gain a better understanding of sustainability as an interrelated and integrated process. After all, societies consist of organizations which in turn are made up of individuals, and sustainability is about a better quality of life for all these individuals. The unfolding of the dimensions of the societal and organizational levels covered already explored territory, although not always related to the sustainability debate. To complete the construct, however, an intensive search for the equivalent of the three dimensions at the individual level was needed. The discovery voyage to arrive at these three dimensions has been largely through uncharted territory. The discussion on leadership for sustainability has merely started. As Petra Kuenkel puts it in *Mind and Heart* (2008: 68): "Leading for sustainability is not something we really know how to do yet."

Therefore the best introduction to this chapter is to share our journey to establish the three dimensions of leadership for sustainability.

The logical sequence mentioned above, where the interrelatedness of the societal, organizational, and individual levels are exposed, is not always the way the real world behaves.

One of the authors has been for years involved in development management of small islands in the Caribbean. In this position he has been confronted with many real-life consequences of the neglect of this commonsense understanding. First of all there was and still is a structural lack of shared interpretation of the meaning of both development and sustainable development. There is also a widespread lack of the logical interrelatedness and interaction between human beings, organizations/ institutions, and society as a whole. These missing factors can be found with political leaders, high-ranking local and foreign government officials, with captains of industries, and well-known consulting firms. For most of these groups, sustainable means "long-lasting" or "able to be maintained," while the majority of them are trapped in the conventional paradigm in which economic growth equals development. The challenge has been and still is to make sense of the relationship between development management (societal level), institutional development (organizational level), and leadership development (individual level). For one of the authors, the journey to define the interrelatedness between the different levels of sustainability took off after the leadership programs of the Covey Leadership Center were introduced on the island of Curaçao in the Dutch Caribbean. These leadership programs were mainly dealing with the individual and the organizational level. In this methodology there is no direct link with the societal level. The concept used nevertheless followed a comprehensive transformational program consisting of three distinct components: an island-wide visioning track; an institutional development track; and a leadership training track.

This experience was crucial in inspiring a critical discussion that started in early 2000 in the School of Graduate Study of Stenden University of Applied Sciences in the Netherlands, where the other author worked (and still works). As a lecturer in business ethics she was exploring ways to embed the basic message of the Western ethical tradition into a curriculum that was heavily management oriented. Sustainable development and corporate social responsibility seemed to her interesting venues to make ethics more palatable to business students. Both authors were, and are, proponents of the need to prepare future managers and leaders with a basic understanding of sustainability next to solid knowledge of the hardcore courses of management. In 2000, for most professionals not aware of the meaning of sustainability, these concepts were too "soft." The framework of the three levels of sustainability was designed and used to facilitate the discussion and create a better level of understanding of the interrelatedness of the three levels.

It took a while and some major business catastrophes (such as Enron, Parmalat, and others) for most of the "hardware" advocates to realize that leadership needs both the software and the hardware. The principle of sustainability makes this combination even more an obligation than an option. The meaning and interconnectedness of sustainable development dealing with the societal level and corporate social responsibility dealing with the organizational level, was not yet a point of discussion with many people involved. Leadership for sustainability and the individual level were not even an issue.

Consequently, the design of the third level of sustainability has been a long and sometimes fatiguing search that is still ongoing.

As mentioned above, the authors' journey took off by using the practical knowledge of the Covey Leadership training programs. The work of Stephen Covey, Roger Merrill, and Rebecca Merrill in their book *First Things First* (1994) gave a first critical direction. In Chapter 3 they describe the four human needs that are fundamental to human fulfillment. They argue that, if these needs aren't met, the individual feels empty and incomplete (Covey *et al.* 1994: 44). These needs are: to live, to love, to learn, and to leave a legacy. The first one, to live, relates to the physical requisites to survive, such as food, shelter, clothing, and health. The second, to love, refers to the social longing to relate to other people. The third, to learn, is the mental need to develop and to grow. The fourth need, to leave a legacy, relates to the spiritual aspirations of the human being.

The first version of the inner triangle representing the individual level, presented the three dimensions in perspective by using the four needs as discussed above (see Fig. 10.1).

Figure 10.1 **First version of the TLS inner level**

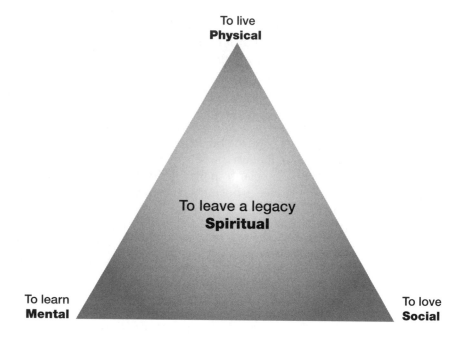

The crux of the discussion became the understanding that leadership starts with the self.

David Gergen, Professor at Harvard's John Kennedy School of Public Management, described it strikingly in his foreword in *True North* (George and Sims 2007):

> Growing up in the shadow of a great university, I always believed that the smartest person made the best leader. That was only natural in an academic family where my dad was a professor of mathematics and two of my older brothers became professors of medicine and psychology. Moving to Washington in my late twenties, began my education in the real world in earnest. Over a period of some three decades, I had the privilege of serving as an adviser to four presidents in the White House and working

alongside leaders in government, the press, business, and other fields. Yes, there is no substitute for ability: to lead others you must know what you are doing, have deep curiosity, and develop keen judgment. Competence counts. But what ultimately distinguishes the great leaders from the mediocre are the personal, **inner qualities that are hard to define** but are essential for success, qualities that each of us must develop for ourselves (George and Sims 2007: xii; bold added by the authors).

The next sections introduce the relationship between self-leadership and triple care (Section 10.1), explore supportive evidence for the three dimensions of the individual level (Section 10.2), and finally revisit the three dimensions from the vantage point reached following the discussion in the first two sections (Section 10.3).

10.1 **From self-leadership to triple care**

In *Heroic Leadership* (2003), Lowney explains that all leadership begins with self-leadership, and self-leadership begins with knowing oneself: "First comes the foundation: goals and values, an understanding of personal strength and obstacles, an outlook on the world. Then comes the invigorating daily habit of refreshing and deepening self-knowledge while immersing oneself in a constantly evolving world" (Lowney 2008: 98).

On the same line, Harvard Business School professor Joseph Badaracco (1998) emphasizes the importance of the habit of self-reflection for leaders when he states:

> They are able to dig below the busy surface of their daily lives and refocus on their core values and principles. By repeating this process again and again throughout their work lives, these executives are able to craft an authentic and strong identity based on their own, rather than someone else's understanding of what is right. And in this way, they begin to make the transition from being a manager to becoming a leader (Badaracco 1998:116).

As we have already observed in the introduction to this part of the book, the understanding that leadership starts from within is not new. Confucius recognized that "if you want to be a leader, you have to be a real human being. You must recognize the true meaning of life before you can become a leader." Cashman explains in *Leadership from the Inside Out* (2000), that the act of leadership cannot be separated from the person, as people lead by virtue of who they are. The authors agree with Lowney, Badaracco, Quinn, Cashman, and others on two important viewpoints. First, that leadership starts from within and that a leader is first of all a human being. Thus, to bring about change, the first change leaders have to realize is a change inside themselves. Second, that there is a relationship between leadership and authenticity. In *Authentic Leadership* Bill George (2003: 11) conveys his understanding of leaders as follows: "I believe that leadership begins and ends with authenticity. It's being yourself; being the person you were created to be."

Maser (1999: 146) explains that authenticity is the condition or quality of being trustworthy or genuine. Trustworthiness is defined as the foundation of trust at the personal level and is based on character (what a person is) and competence (what a person can). Authenticity, trustworthiness, character, and competence of an individual are also recognized by Stephen Covey as important capabilities for leadership. In *Principle-Centered Leadership*, Covey distinguishes four levels of leadership: personal, interpersonal, managerial, and organizational (Covey 1992: 31). He emphasizes the importance of the personal level. Here is where trustworthiness is born and the ground is laid for trust at the interpersonal level which will be the foundation for groups and organizations to work together to achieve common goals (social capital).

From the above the authors conclude that the foundation of the leader lies in the person behind the leader and that, as Cashman (2000: 18) remarks: "a person's ability to grow as a leader depends on his or her ability to grow as a person." If this is true, then the next question is how this process of personal growth and development evolves.

To explore processes of personal development one avenue is the field of human development. Here people's capability to be more open to concerns beyond individual needs is disclosed. Quinn (2000) refers to a sacred potential for transformation in living systems and asserts that: "Each human being can make a significant contribution to positive change in ourselves, our relationships, and in any organization or culture in which we take part" (Quinn 2000: 3).

In *A Theory of Everything* (2000: 17) Ken Wilber gives the most succinct description of how human development takes place: "development, in fact, can be defined as a successive decrease in egocentrism." According to this definition, development involves decreasing narcissism and increasing consciousness, or the ability to take other people, places, and things into account and thus increasingly extend care to each. Wilber refers to three general stages that have been identified by Carol Gilligan to illustrate moral development (see Box 10.1). Yet Wilber sees these stages as quite common for most forms of development and known by many names such as: ego-centric, socio-centric, and world-centric.

Box 10.1 **Carol Gilligan's three stages of human moral development**

Quite soon after she started teaching at Harvard, Carol Gilligan became an assistant to Lawrence Kohlberg, the well-known scholar in human moral development. Kohlberg's theory states that the capacity to take moral decisions develops through several stages: from pre-conventional (the isolated self is central) via conventional (family or societies' agreements and rules are central) to post-conventional (universal principles are central). In the last stage a theory of justice develops to balance different rights and guide us toward decisions based on an equal respect for all. Justice is in Kohlberg's analysis founded on a clear hierarchy of principles that are conceived as universal.

To test at which stage of development an individual is, Kohlberg used to present dilemmas to his respondents and ask them to make and motivate their choice. One of these is the Heinz dilemma, where people are asked their opinion about Heinz who steals a drug to save his wife because he cannot afford to pay for it and nobody is willing to give it to him for free or at a price he can afford. Gilligan noticed that women tend to answer the dilemma differently than men: they do not seem to take a clear-cut decision based (for example) on the principle of protecting human life at any cost. They have doubts and tend to look at the possibility of explaining the situation better to people who could intervene (e.g. the druggist who provides the drug) and so on. In Kohlberg's terms these women are stuck at a lower stage of moral development than the people who, driven by an inner sense of justice, approve of Heinz stealing because (for example) saving a human life is a higher value than respecting the property rights of another person.

Gilligan disagrees with Kohlberg on this point and proposes that there are two different but equally worthy paths toward moral maturity. The first path, mostly followed by men, is the one proposed by traditional theories such as Kohlberg's. It starts from the recognition that a human being is separated from other individuals; it then leads to individuation (e.g., id, ego, and superego) and a vision of responsibility as limitation of influence (the golden rule); and it finally conceives a theory of justice where different rights are balanced on the foundation of a clear hierarchy of universal principles. The second path, most clear in women's moral development, starts from connection and an image of self as part of a net of relations; it then leads to a view of responsibility as (active) response to needs and to the moral imperative of inclusion, communication, and non-violence (do not hurt); and finally flows in a theory of contextual morality (where circumstances are important) and care. From this analysis Gilligan concludes that the path of (women's) moral development goes through three main stages: selfish, care, and universal.

As stated above, both paths are equally worthy, and both present a challenge. In Gilligan's own words: the girl "assuming connection, begins to explore the parameters of separation, while he [one of the boys studied], assuming separation, begins to explore the parameters of connection" (Gilligan 1982: 38). There is thus the possibility that the exploration of each other's path leads to an integration of the two. Gilligan suggests that this is the major task of the adult years (Gilligan 1982: ch. 6). Giving attention to women's moral development brings Gilligan to see care, and not justice, "as the most adequate guide to the resolution of conflicts in human relationships" (Gilligan 1982: 105).

See further: Kohlberg 1981; Gilligan 1982; Crain 1985: especially Chapter 7.

On the basis of Gilligan 1982 and Wilber 2000, the following dimensions for the individual level in the three levels of sustainability framework were introduced: "Care for me," "Care for me and you," and "Care for all" (see Fig. 10.2). Care for me relates to the value of the individual human life. Care for me and you relates to the value of relationships. Care for all relates to the value of nature and the universe. Creating value on all three dimensions lays the foundation for leadership for sustainability.

These organizations will strive for societal values that are aligned with the principles of the leader and the values of the organization and of a sustainable society on nine dimensions of care (C^3).

Figure 10.2 **Leadership for sustainability**

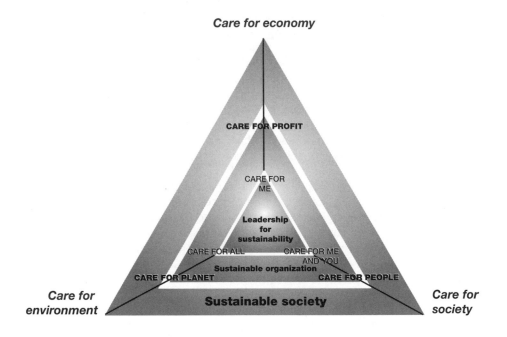

10.2 **Supporting evidence for the three dimensions of the individual level**

In *A Theory of Everything* (2000) Ken Wilber relates that developmental studies have shown a striking similarity in the way they tell a generally similar story about the growth and development of the mind. These theories all indicate that the process of development unfolds through three broad stages or, better, capabilities present in each individual.

It is indeed quite extraordinary that scholars from different disciplines and walks of life all seem to agree that there are three main facets in human development. To the authors it was even more extraordinary that the theories proposed by these scholars seem to offer supporting evidence for the three dimensions of the individual level of the TLS framework.[1] The authors hope that the discussion of some of these approaches will offer to the reader a stepping stone to better understand this crucial level.

The approaches discussed here have been chosen for their diversity. They vary from the spiral dynamics approach (introduced by clinical psychologist Clare Graves and refined by consultants Don Beck and Christopher Cowan, whose background was in communication and group dynamics studies) to the theory of needs (proposed by Abraham Maslow, clinical psychologist and developer of humanistic psychology as a new discipline, and refined by psychologist Clayton Alderfer). Other approaches used are leadership development theories (such as the one proposed by Stephen R. Covey, author of the best seller *The 7 Habits of Highly Effective People* and Professor of Leadership at Utah State University); studies on social, emotional, and ecological intelligence (as introduced by psychologist and science journalist Daniel Goleman); and insights from environmental psychology. The approach derived from the Renewed Darwinian Theory developed by Paul Lawrence, sociologist and Professor of Organizational Behavior at Harvard Business School, gave some critical new insights.

Spiral dynamics

The spiral dynamics approach of Clare Graves, as refined by Don Beck and Christopher Cowan, can be summarized by using Graves's own words (in Beck and Cowan 1996: 28): "Briefly, what I am proposing is that the psychology of the mature human being is an unfolding, emergent, oscillating spiraling process marked by progressive subordination of older, lower-order behavior systems to newer, higher-order systems as man's existential problems change."

Spiral dynamics sees human development as proceeding through eight general stages, which are also called memes (see Fig. 10.3). A meme is a basic stage of development that can be expressed in any activity. Each stage has a color and distinction is made between two tiers. The first tier moves from the first meme (beige) up to the sixth meme (green). Once at the green meme, the human consciousness is ready for a leap toward the second tier. In contrast to the move from one meme to the other in the first six waves, the move toward the seventh wave or entering the second tier, involves a much higher degree of integrality. At this stage, one can grasp the whole spectrum of interior development. None of the previous stages can do this, and none can appreciate the existence of other memes. Each of these stages

---

1 As stated earlier the authors developed their view on the inner level of the TLS on the basis of Stephen Covey, Ken Wilber, and Carol Gilligan. It was only in preparing this book that other theories were explored.

considers its world view to be the correct one. Consequently these stages have a continuous fight among themselves to defend their position. Second tier stages on the other hand can grasp the big picture and appreciate the necessary role of all the other memes/waves. What makes the theory of spiral dynamics particularly interesting for the TLS framework is the fact that it is applicable on all three levels (individual, organizational, and societal); even more so when it comes to the individual level, considering the three different stages (ego-centric, ethno-centric, and world-centric) which support the three dimensions of the individual level (care for me, care for me and you, care for all).

Figure 10.3 **Spiral dynamics**

Source: Beck and Cowan 1996: 8 and 197

World-centric	Holistic	TURQUOISE	**Turquoise** • Spiritual bonds pull people and organizations together • Work must be meaningful to the overall health of life
	Integrative	YELLOW	**Yellow** • People enjoy doing things that fit who they are naturally • Workers need free access to information and materials
Ethno-centric	Communitarian/ egalitarian	GREEN	**Green** • People want to get along and feel accepted by their peers • Sharing and participating are better than competing
	Achievist/ strategic	ORANGE	**Orange** • People are motivated by the achievement of material rewards • Competition improves productivity and fosters individual growth
	Purposeful/ authoritarian	BLUE	**Blue** • People work the best when they are told how to do things the right way • Doing duty and being punished when failing to do so gives meaning to life
Ego-centric	Impulsive/ egocentric	RED	**Red** • People need to be dominated by strong leadership that gives rewards • Workers will put up with a lot if their basic needs are met regularly
	Magical/ animistic	PURPLE	**Purple** • People are "married" to their group — nepotism is normal • Workers owe their lives and souls to the parent-like organization
	Instinctive/ survivalistic	BEIGE	**Beige** • People are centered on satisfaction of human biological needs • Minimal impact or control over environment

Maslow's pyramid of needs

Another approach to put the human needs in perspective is the model developed by the psychologist Abraham Maslow,[2] also known as Maslow's hierarchy of needs as discussed in Box 10.2 and illustrated in Figure 10.4 together with Clayton Alderfer's ERG theory.

Box 10.2 **Maslow's hierarchy of needs**

Physiological needs
These are required to sustain life, such as: air, water, food, and sleep. According to this theory, if these fundamental needs are not satisfied then one will surely be motivated to satisfy them. Higher needs such as social needs and esteem are not recognized until one satisfies the needs basic to existence.

Safety needs
Once physiological needs are met, one's attention turns to safety and security in order to be free from the threat of physical and emotional harm. Such needs might be fulfilled by: living in a safe area; medical insurance; job security; and financial reserves. According to the Maslow hierarchy, if a person feels threatened, needs further up the pyramid will not receive attention until that need has been met.

Social needs
Once a person has met the lower-level physiological and safety needs, higher-level motivators awaken. The first of the higher-level needs are social needs. Social needs are those related to interaction with others and may include: friendship, belonging to a group, giving and receiving love, and esteem needs. After a person feels that they "belong," the urge to attain a degree of importance emerges.

Esteem needs can be categorized as external motivators and internal motivators. Internally motivating esteem needs are those such as self-esteem, accomplishment, and self-respect. External esteem needs are those such as reputation and recognition. Some examples of esteem needs are: recognition (external motivator); attention (external motivator); social status (external motivator); accomplishment (internal motivator); and self-respect (internal motivator).

Maslow later improved his model to add a layer in between self-actualization and esteem needs: the need for aesthetics and knowledge.

Self-actualization
Self-actualization is the summit of Maslow's motivation theory. It is about the quest to reach one's full potential as a person. Unlike lower-level needs,

2   www.abraham-maslow.com/m_motivation/Hierarchy_of_Needs.asp, accessed August 29, 2011.

this need is never fully satisfied; as one grows psychologically there are always new opportunities to continue to grow.

Self-actualized people tend to have motivators such as: truth, justice, wisdom, and meaning.

Clayton Alderfer's interesting revision of Abraham Maslow's hierarchy of needs, the **ERG theory** (existence, relatedness, and growth), appeared in *Psychological Review* in 1969 in an article titled "An Empirical Test of a New Theory of Human Need." He addresses here the findings of studies that have shown that the middle levels of Maslow's hierarchy overlap. Alderfer dealt with this issue by reducing the number of levels to three. The letters ERG represent these three levels of need, which can be related to the three Care dimensions:

- Existence needs refer to physiological and safety needs (see first two levels of Maslow): **Care for me**

- Relatedness needs refer to social and external needs relationships (see third and fourth levels of Maslow): **Care for me and you**

- Growth needs refer to an intrinsic desire for personal development and self-actualization (see Maslow's fourth and fifth level): **Care for all**

Unlike Maslow's hierarchy, the ERG theory and the TLS three dimensions of care allow for different levels of need to be pursued simultaneously. In Figure 10.4, the three dimensions of care are presented together with the needs of Alderfer and Maslow.

Figure 10.4 **Three dimensions of care and Maslow's and Alderfer's needs**

Zohar and Marshal (2004: 16-17) have serious reservations on the hierarchical nature of Maslow's theory and propose to reverse the order. They state that Maslow's pyramid created a paradigm of the human condition that gave precedence to the need for survival, physical survival at all costs. Maslow's model considers higher needs, only if the more basic needs for survival and security are taken care of. According to Zohar and Marshal (2004: 17), "in a developed culture like ours Maslow's pyramid of needs is upside down. Most of us in the wealthy Western world have our basic needs for food and security met as a birthright."

This may sound a very arrogant statement for all those who do not belong to the so-called "Western world." Another argument they use may be more sensible and in line with the thinking behind the TLS framework. They observe:

> Since Maslow's work was done, nearly half a century ago, anthropologists, neuroscientists, and psychologists have reached a far deeper understanding of human nature and the origins of our humanity. We know today that human beings are by definition primarily creatures of meaning and value (that is, of self-actualization) (Zohar and Marshal 2004: 17).

Paul Lawrence: Renewed Darwinian theory

Professor Paul Lawrence of Harvard also argues that there is no hierarchical relationship in human development. Coming from a different angle, he uses the Renewed Darwinian theory (RD theory) to emphasize the crucial role of the human brain and the innate drives that are essential for survival and development of humans. According to Lawrence the brain is where the capacity for leadership is settled. Lawrence uses his four drives theory of human behavior to explain how leadership, like all human behavior, can be understood as a function of the balance, or lack of balance, of four human drives. He distinguishes "the drive to acquire" (also known in animals), "the drive to defend" (also known in animals), "the drive to bond" (not known in animals), and "the drive to comprehend" (also not known in the animal world). The first two of these drives, or criteria, are the obvious ones any species must have to survive as a species. The two other drives are unique to human beings. The first two drives, to acquire and to defend, are considered to correspond to Care for me; the drive to bond, to Care for me and you; and the drive to comprehend to Care for all.

Stephen Covey: leadership development

Covey, on the other hand (2004a), introduces in the *7 Habits of Highly Effective People* the maturity continuum to explain the development from a dependent to an interdependent stage going through an independent stage. The assumption here is that the seven habits promote a continuous move from one stage into the other (see Box 10.3).

Box 10.3 **Seven habits of highly effective people**
Source: Covey 2004a

The first three habits focus on self-mastery: that is, achieving the private victories required to move from dependence to independence. The first three habits are:

1. Be proactive
2. Begin with the end in mind
3. Put first things first

Habits 4, 5, and 6 then address interdependence:

4. Think win–win
5. Seek first to understand, then to be understood
6. Synergize

Finally,

7. Sharpen the saw, the habit of renewal and continual improvement

---

As one can observe in Box 10.3, Covey also distinguishes three distinct stages in personal development: a dependence stage, an independent stage, and an interdependent stage. These stages also involve a move from Care for me to Care for all.

Social psychology

In *Emotional Intelligence* and in *Social Intelligence*, Daniel Goleman explores, respectively, the crucial role of emotions in how human beings interact with themselves, with others, and how they deal with their social lives. In *Ecological Intelligence*, Goleman reflects on people's impact on the planet. The first two intelligences give insight in the Care for me and the Care for me and you dimensions of the individual level, while ecological intelligence relates to the third dimension. According to Goleman (2009) ecological intelligence refers to an all-encompassing sensibility that can bring together cognitive skills and empathy for life. "Just as social and emotional intelligence build on the abilities to take other people's perspective, feel with them, and show our concern, ecological intelligence extends this capacity to all natural systems" (Goleman 2009: 44).

Insights from environmental psychology

The field of environmental psychology studies the relationship between humans and the natural or built environment. One of the themes it considers is how to explain behavior that positively affects other human beings or the environment when no direct individual benefits are received by engaging in this behavior. Let's think, for example, of donating blood on a regular basis or taking public transport instead of our own car to go to work even though this may imply a loss of time, less freedom or, in general, an extra effort. Why do certain people engage in these and similar behaviors? The answer given by scholars in environmental psychology refers back to the values held by people. Values are seen as broad guiding principles in one's life. As such they are quite stable motivators of our behavior and help us to take a stance when confronted with new circumstances. Until recently scholars in the field of environmental psychology distinguished two main sets of values or value orientations: egocentric (benefiting oneself) and altruistic (benefiting others). Pro-social and pro-environmental behavior can be explained by both value orientations. For example, a person may choose organic food because he or she believes that this food is both more tasty and healthier. Considering costs and benefits of a certain behavior especially for oneself reveals an egoistic value orientation. Another individual may choose organic food because, being farmed without the use of chemicals, it is safer for the farmer. Including perceived costs and benefits for others discloses an altruistic value orientation.

Recently, a third value orientation has been proved to play a role in pro-environmental behavior: biospheric values. This value orientation holds that people have a moral obligation to protect all living creatures and the Earth due to their intrinsic value. The choice of organic food in this context may be motivated with reference to the deadly effects of pesticides on all forms of life, from invertebrates to mammals, and on the land itself.

These three value orientations are quite similar to the care dimensions proposed here. It is interesting to note that scholars in environmental psychology insist on three main characteristics of these three value orientations. First, the three value orientations are present in each human being. Second, egoistic (or hedonistic) values are the strongest because they are directly linked to personal survival. Third, notwithstanding the first two characteristics, individuals and societies can prioritize the importance of values and value orientations. This means that each individual has the potential to be motivated by altruistic and biospheric values. It also means, though, that altruistic and biospheric values have to be properly fed and stimulated so that they can overcome the strength of egocentric values (for further reading, see also Rokeach 1973; Bilsky and Schwartz 1994; Stern 2000; Lindenberg and Steg 2007; De Groot and Steg 2008; De Groot 2008).

The different approaches reviewed all arrive at some interesting similarities, indicating a consistent unfolding pattern of waves or stages. From "me" to "us" to "all of us"; from "pre-conventional" to "conventional" to "post-conventional"; from "selfish", "care" to "universal care"; from "egocentric" to "ethnocentric" to "world centric"; from "dependent" to "independent" to "interdependent"; from "egoistic" to "altruistic" to "biospheric"; or from "care for me" to "care for me and you" to "care for all"; all these follow a pattern of achieving higher degrees of consciousness (increase in the capacity to take deeper and wider perspectives into account) and declining degrees of egocentrism. As Kuenkel (2008) puts it in *Heart and Mind*, "As you become more whole, yourself becomes less important. As you develop inner serenity you become more concerned with others, with the world" (Kuenkel 2008: 148).

10.3 Care for me, Care for me and you, and Care for all revisited

On the basis of the insights acquired in the previous section, here the three dimensions of the inner level of the TLS framework are revisited and their contribution to the development of leadership for sustainability is clarified.

Care for me

Care for me relates to the basic condition of all species (see Fig. 10.5): the need to acquire and defend what one requires for one's survival and the conception and survival of one's offspring, as Professor Paul Lawrence observes (2010). On the same line is Covey's definition of the basic human need "to live" (1992) and Maslow's physiological needs. These authors refer to the basic necessities to sustain life: air, water, food, clothes, sleep, shelter, and so on. As we have seen, in his revision of Maslow's hierarchy of needs, Alderfer (1969) proposes to include in the first stage also basic psychological needs, such as the need for safety.

While one can contend that the need for survival has a positive or at least a neutral connotation, other authors have described the first stage of human development in more negative terms. Ken Wilber, for example, describes the first stage as selfishness. The selfish stage is also called pre-conventional and is characterized by egocentrism and narcissism.

Selfishness, egocentrism, and narcissism are mostly considered negative emotions. There are, though, other authors who approach the first stage more positively because it is here that self-awareness and self-knowledge are developed; self-mastery is acquired; a character is formed; competences are built—it is through leadership of the self at this stage that the personal foundation is laid to lead others (e.g. Covey 1992; Cashman 2000; Goleman 2009). Against this backdrop, the expression "Care for me" wishes to indicate that this human dimension is not by definition to be equated with selfishness or egocentrism. As a dimension of leadership for sustainability it is surely not because, as stated above, it is then intended to develop the personal capabilities on which leadership for sustainability is further built. Leadership for sustainability, though, implies that one also develops the other two dimensions (Care for me and you; Care for all). If this is not the case then a "Care for me" person becomes indeed selfish and egoistic.

Figure 10.5 **Linkages between Care for me and the theories discussed**

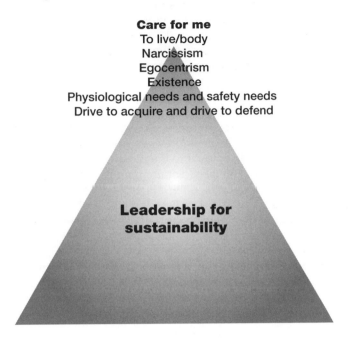

The actual situation of humankind, however, indicates that a vast majority of people are trapped in the Care for me stage. The idea that people are mainly driven by rational self-interest has conditioned the interaction of humans, mainly in the Western world. This may be partly due to the concept of humans as rational decision-makers, or *Homo economicus*, created by a (mis)interpretation of Adam Smith's economic theory (see Box 10.4).

Box 10.4 *Homo economicus*

In Part II we briefly recalled the neoliberal interpretation of Adam Smith's view on trade and economic exchange as based on egoistic and self-serving motives. The basic idea is then that, in taking decisions, an individual looks only at the costs and benefits of that decision for him or herself and chooses that course of action that maximizes the benefits. The *Homo economicus* is thus born.

With the development of economics as a science and as a reference point for decision-makers, the view of men as motivated only by egoistic values has taken a firm hold on people's minds and hearts. It was also strengthened by a popular, though wrong, interpretation of Charles Darwin's view on natural selection: that it is the strongest who survives. Charles Darwin's point, however, was that it is the fittest who survives; that is, the creature that can best adapt to the environment. Adaptation more often than not means cooperation, such as in the case of those birds that feed on parasites in alligators' teeth or trees that grow near each other because they produce a substance that kills the parasites of the other tree. As we have seen Adam Smith was also wrongly interpreted. In the society he envisioned, moral values have a paramount role and among these is the value of *sympathy*: the human capacity to relate to others and feel compassion for others.

Recent studies in game theory have also proven that people in complex societies (as in most countries by now) have a strong sense of fairness. If, for example, a person is asked to divide a certain amount of money, say 10 euros, between herself and another (previously unknown) individual, she will very often allocate a certain amount to the other even though this reduces the amount that she then can take (dictator game). If the other person has the power to refuse or accept the offer, it is proven that in the majority of cases she will refuse a "low" amount (less than 30% of the total), though even one euro is better than nothing and—if the person in question would reason as a *Homo economicus*—she should accept it (ultimatum game and impunity game).

These and other studies and experiments prove that human beings are far more complex than the *Homo economicus* will let us believe. See also the discussion in Section 10.2 on theories of human development (for further reading on game theory, see Camerer 2003).

Care for me and you

The essence of this dimension is perfectly caught in an observation by Benjamin Franklin: "A man who is wrapped up in himself makes a very small package" (*Poor Richard's Almanack*, Franklin 1732–1758: 173 in the 2007 edition).

In other words the Care for me and you dimension gives voice to the insight which Martin Buber described as the relational aspect of the "self," "Man becomes I through a You" (Buber 1970: 69 in Kuenkel 2008: 49). Buber reminds us that no identity, no self is thinkable without the innate longing for the "You" (Kuenkel 2008: 49).

This human need can also be illustrated with a non-Western belief that is renowned in African culture, known as *ubuntu* (see Box 10.5). Parkin (2010) uses this principle thought in conjunction with morality, values, and ethics when explaining the interdependence of people and the environment.

Parkin observes that "The culture of *ubunto*, or recognizing our interdependency one with another and with nature, has shriveled in many of the richer countries, with the consequent social and personal impoverishment chronicled by writers like Robert Putman and Robert Lane" (Parkin 2010: 173).

The following box elaborates on the principle of *ubuntu*.

Box 10.5 *Ubuntu*

That individuals are capable of feeling empathy toward others and harbor altruistic values is not a typical Western idea or discovery. Many cultures recognize that people are interdependent. Probably the strongest affirmation of this truth is offered by *ubuntu*, one of the most important aspects of African philosophy and culture. *Ubuntu* states that a person is a person through other persons. In short: I am because you are.

Ubuntu is based on values such as humaneness, compassion, care, understanding, and empathy. It does not prescribe what is good and how one should behave. It is not a commandment such as the Western "love thy neighbor." *Ubuntu* simply exists in everyone. "It is emotional and deep, and people simply act in a way they intuitively know to be right" (Boon 2007: 28).

Thus *Ubuntu* is in all of us but is only shown in acts of kindness unthinkingly done for each other and the community. *Ubuntu* and its philosophy of openness, sharing, and welcome are manifested, for instance, at weddings. Traditional African weddings do not have a limited number of guests as in the Western world. On the contrary, everyone who wants to join and celebrate is invited, and people usually bring not only a gift for the bridal couple but also food and drinks to share with the other guests. *Ubuntu* is also reflected in traditional ways to address people who have misbehaved. Here the culprit is set at the center of a circle formed by the members of the community. Then people start remembering the good deeds of the offender to heal the wound he or she has done not only to him or herself, but also to the community.

Nelson Mandela (the well-known civil rights activist, Nobel Prize laureate and the first President of South Africa to be elected through a fully representative and democratic vote) is considered to offer one of the highest examples of *ubuntu*. It is striking, for example, the way he related to his guards during his (18-year-long) imprisonment on Robben Island. Starting from the core principles that "I am because you are" he refused to feed any hatred he could feel toward the people who were keeping him prisoner. He refused to see them as enemies because otherwise, following the principles of *ubuntu*, he would become an "enemy," too. The point here is that a person can only be a true human being if he or she recognizes humanity in others and treats them with respect. As Archbishop of Cape Town and Nobel Prize laureate Desmond Tutu puts it: persons with *ubuntu* "know that they are diminished when others are humiliated, diminished when others are oppressed, diminished when others are treated as if they were less than who they are" (Tutu 2004: 25). It was this attitude that made it possible for Mandela, after his release, to become the first freely chosen president of South Africa, trusted and respected by white, black, and mixed race people.

The Nelson Mandela example shows that *ubuntu* does not mean that the individual is lost in the group. It takes a strong, independent individual to practice *ubuntu* and develop an interdependent community (for further reading, see Boon 2007; Desmond Tutu 2004).

In *Driven to Lead*, Lawrence (2010) arrives at the same human need when explaining the workings of the human brain. The third drive he describes is the drive to bond. This criterion refers to the need to form long-term, mutually caring and trusting relationships with other people.

He observes that this has nothing to do with an innate goodness of people, but one of the four survival criteria by which the brain evaluates what is going on and what should be done about it (Lawrence 2010: 20).

This second dimension of the third level of the TLS can also be related to Maslow's social needs and internal esteem needs. Alderfer here refers to related-ness, the motivation to have interpersonal relationships. Other theories, such as environmental sociology, refer to altruism as a value orientation present in each individual.

If one relates this dimension of the inner level Care for me and you, with the work of Daniel Goleman in *Emotional Intelligence* and in *Social Intelligence*, there seems to be some common ground. These two intelligences may be considered as complementary to each other and have the ability to see other people's perspectives, feel with them, and show concern.

Figure 10.6 **Linkages between Care for me and you and the theories discussed**

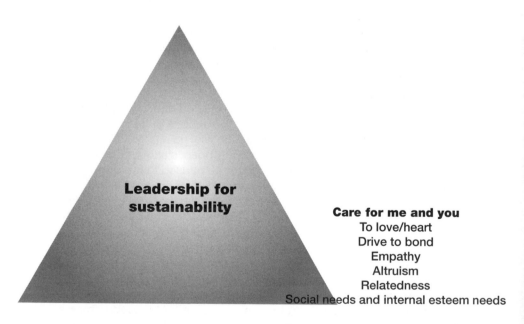

As in the first dimension of the individual level, the second dimension is also characterized by some concepts as discussed by Stephen Covey, Ken Wilber, Daniel Goleman, Howard Gardner, Paul Lawrence, and others, reflecting altruism, empathy, and a socio-centric behavior (see Fig. 10.6). Differently than for the Care for me dimension, the Care for me and you dimension is associated in most of the theories discussed with positive terms. However, this dimension also has its challenges. One main challenge is bonding by excluding others; a second is identification with the group in such a strong way as to lose one's critical capacity to assess what the group is doing (also known as group-thinking). Holding a group together by stressing the danger represented by the enemy may go so far as bringing the people to destroy the enemy. Sustainability is by definition inclusive: it is about a better quality of life for this *and* future generations all over the world.

Care for all

The Care for all dimension concludes the journey toward leadership for sustainability. This last and most critical dimension of the TLS framework has an exceptional breadth. As became apparent at the end of the introduction to this chapter, the process of human development entails a consistent pattern which follows a gradual increase of consciousness and a continuous decrease of egocentrism. An increase in consciousness implies an unfolding awareness of one's being in relation to others and in relation to the world, while egocentrism refers to the innate need to develop one's own identity. According to Petra Kuenkel (2008: 14) the underlying theme of the journey toward leadership is:

> uncovering a deep rooted concern for humanity through becoming aware of one's own humanity. This in turn creates authentic value and has a potentially positive impact on the world, for people, for humankind. It is the cornerstone for leadership for sustainability.

The previous two dimensions of the individual level defined the relationship of the individual with him or herself, and with others. The Care for all dimension brings together the relationship of the individual not only with him or herself and the other **but also with all of humanity and nature, now and in the future**. The way humanity has evolved, however, makes this stage difficult to understand and to achieve. In *The Positive Deviant*, Sara Parkin (2010: 60) markedly describes the actual state of humanity: "Perhaps most important of all, we've become so wrapped up in ourselves—so narcissistic—we've forgotten that not so very long ago we lived intimately with nature, very cognizant of our dependence on her for spiritual and physical nourishment." The Care for all dimension concentrates on the less tangible aspects of human needs, aspects to which several authors refer as spiritual intelligence and spiritual capital.

In *Spiritual Capital*, Danah Zohar and Ian Marshall (2004) describe the link between spiritual intelligence, spiritual capital, and sustainability and conclude that spiritual capital and sustainability are crucially linked. Spiritual intelligence, they state, is "the intelligence with which we access our deepest meanings, values, purposes, and highest motivations" (Zohar and Marshall 2004: 3).

They discuss three kinds of capital that are derived from three major human intelligences and illustrate these as shown in Table 10.1.

Table 10.1 **Three kinds of human capital with corresponding human intelligences**

Capital	Intelligence	Function
Material capital	IQ: Rational intelligence	What I think
Social capital	EQ: Emotional intelligence	What I feel
Spiritual capital	SQ: Spiritual intelligence	What I am

Further on, Zohar and Marshall (2004: 4) insistently accentuate the crucial quality of spiritual intelligence as the ultimate intelligence which allows the human being to comprehend and search for deeper meaning. In the Box 10.6 some of these explanations are highlighted.

Box 10.6 **Citations from Zohar and Marshall on Spiritual Intelligence (2004)**

"Toward the end of the 1990's neurological research suggested that the brain has a whole third 'Q' or kind of intelligence. This is the intelligence with which we have access to deep meaning, fundamental values, and a sense of abiding purpose in our lives, and the role that this meaning, values, and purpose play in our lives, strategies, and thinking process. This is the intelligence Mats Lederhausen was exhibiting in his concern to make his life serve some deep purpose. I called this third Q 'SQ,' or 'spiritual intelligence' " (p. 64). [. . .] "Spiritual intelligence is 'the soul intelligence.' It is the intelligence that makes us whole, that allows us to integrate the many fragments of our lives, activities, and being. It allows us to know what we and our organizations are about" (p. 65). [. . .] "SQ is a transformative intelligence that allows us to break old paradigms and to invent new ones" (p. 67).

If one relates the explanation given by Zohar and Marshall with the theory used by Lawrence (2010), it becomes evident that spiritual intelligence can be derived from the drive to comprehend, which Lawrence characterizes as a biological need. In explaining the drive to comprehend as one of the four human drives, he observes that:

> The need for dignity, mastery, self-esteem, or self-actualization is a manifestation of the drive to comprehend—we need to make sense of ourselves as well as make sense of the world . . . In fact the need for mastery or self-actualization is one form of an innate biological drive which, though

not as immediately urgent as the need for oxygen, is in the long run just as much a determinant of how people will act (Lawrence 2010: 25).

The two approaches discussed above radiate an exceptional meeting of spirit and mind. This brings us to a culminating point in the journey to discover the final dimension of the TLS framework. The Care for all dimension may be considered the spark that will gradually ignite and synchronize all dimensions of the TLS (see Fig. 10.7).

Figure 10.7 **The spark of Care for all affects all dimensions of the TLS**

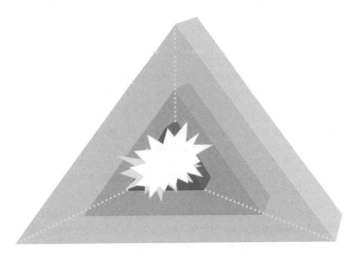

In an effort to rank the spiritual capital in countries around the world, the Research Method Institute in California developed a methodology to measure spiritual capital in organizations and countries with a spiritual capital index (SCI). Box 10.7 gives some selected information. According to this measurement, the spiritual capital index has more impacts on sustainability than other indices of material capital (point 4 in Box 10.7). The fact that CSR data have been used to calculate the final index may have skewed the outcome toward sustainability.

If one includes the theory of ecological intelligence in the discussion, it becomes clear that, although no specific reference is made by Goleman (2009) to spiritual intelligence, the following statement may indicate the connection.

> To tap into this intelligence, we need to get beyond the thinking that puts mankind outside nature; the fact that we live enmeshed in ecological systems and impact them for better or worse—and they us. We need to discover and share among ourselves all the ways this intimate interconnectedness operates, to see the hidden patterns that connect human activity to the larger flow of nature, to understand our true impact on it, and *to learn* how to do better (Goleman 2009: 44-45).

Box 10.7 **Spiritual capital index**

Source: www.researchmethods.org/sci/RM-SCI-Ranking.pdf (accessed March 15, 2011)

As this SCI is the first ever published spiritual capital measurement, we understand that there are a lot of areas for us to make improvements and we do welcome suggestions. We will continue to improve our datasets and work to produce a complete country list in 2009, while we plan to complete a SCI ranking of Global 500 corporations by May of 2009. We at the RM Institute believe it takes four capitals:

- material capital,
- intellectual capital,
- social capital, and
- spiritual capital

for a country to achieve optimal and sustainable development. Our preliminary empirical results are confirming this hypothesis. Our results show that spiritual capital index has more impacts on sustainability and democracy, than indices of material capital.

Our results also show that difference between the spiritual capital index value and the economic competitiveness value at country level has significant negative impacts on country's average satisfaction with life. This confirms our hypothesis that the imbalance between spiritual capital and material capital is the main source of personal unhappiness and national crisis.

Another notable observation in this regard is a statement made by Dr. Sfeir-Younis of the World Bank at the World Summit on Sustainable Development, held in Johannesburg in 2002 (see Box 10.8).

Goleman (2009: 44) refers to empathy that may result in the motivation to help solve the problems the planet is confronted with. Both Zohar and Marshall (2004) and Parkin (2010) make an exacting differentiation and refer to empathy with motivation to help as "compassion." Zohar and Marshall (2004: 92) explain the meaning of compassion as follows:

In the Latin, compassion literally means "feeling with." A quality of deep empathy, compassion is not just knowing the feelings of others but feeling their feelings . . . Hence it is an active feeling—with, a willingness—no, almost a compulsion—to get involved.

According to Parkin (2010: 178), compassionate people do not stand by while others suffer. "Compassion for other people near and far is what fuels sustainability."

The awareness that it is all about compassion, all about living creatures, and all about nature is not a discovery of our times.

Box 10.8 **Dr. Sfeir-Younis on spiritual capital**

Source: www.worldcivilsociety.org/REPORT/EN/06/17-jul-02/summ_17.33.html (accessed March 15, 2011)

Dr. Sfeir-Younis of the World Bank stated that it is important to bring spirituality into public policy in sustainable development. According to him, everybody knows what sustainability is, but nobody is doing enough to make it happen. He pointed out four fallacies:

- Environmental degradation is not due to economic industrialisation and exploitation;
- Human beings are adaptable and the situation is not so problematic;
- Technology is going to solve the problem;
- There is a clash of values.

Dr. Sfeir-Younis believes that a big debate needs to take place at the conceptual level, in order to define the real meaning of sustainable development. According to him, it means *"spiritual capital"* and whether it is possible to change the course of humanity with a *"spiritual view"* that is, through *sustainable being*, empowerment and the capacity of oneself to self-realisation. In order to reach a *sustainable development*, a 200% committed society is needed, otherwise positive environmental changes are not likely to happen.

As was acknowledged in the introduction to this book, Albert Einstein described this connection of mankind with themselves, with all living creatures, and with nature clearly and convincingly in 1950.

"Widening our circle of compassion, to embrace all living creatures and the whole of nature, now and in the future" is exactly what the dimension Care for all is all about. The different theories and approaches reviewed bring us to the conclusion that the Care for all dimension is strongly related to the capability of the human being to acquire and defend spiritual capital.

Consequently we consider leaders for sustainability to be those men and women who widen their circle of compassion, to embrace all living creatures and the whole of nature on their leadership journey for a more sustainable world. The three dimensions of leadership for sustainability, spearheaded by the Care for all dimension, are meant to support this journey (Fig. 10.8).

Figure 10.8 **Linkages between Care for all and the theories discussed**

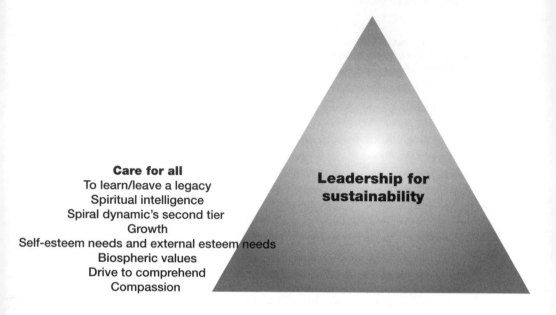

The next chapter elaborates on how the third dimension becomes the key to move toward leadership for sustainability, by considering the moral aspect used in the theory of human development on the one hand and the authentic leadership approach on the other hand. The journey of individual leadership is seen as a process of unfolding consciousness and increasing awareness of one's contribution to a better world.

11
The path to leadership for sustainability

> When deciding whether to become a sustainable thinker, it is therefore important to understand that, just as ecological systems constantly adapt to new conditions, humans have an innate capacity to change (Doppelt 2008: 69).

In this part of the book, the individual level of the TLS framework has been used as a guide to understand the intricacy of sustainability and self-leadership. Based on this approach, two aspects are important to bear in mind as one discusses the path to leadership for sustainability.

First, all change starts with oneself. The path to leadership for sustainability implies change and transformation of paradigms and behaviors, starting with the individual. Robert Quinn (2000: 19) explains that:

> To develop transformational capability, we cannot be normal people doing normal things. We must stand outside the norm. To do that we need to go inside ourselves and ask who we are, what we stand for, and what impact we really want to have. Within ourselves we find principle, purpose, and courage. There we find the capacity not only to withstand the pressures of the external system but also actually to transform the external system. We change the world by changing ourselves.

Second, change toward leadership for sustainability, as we saw in Chapter 10, is driven by three human qualities: Care for me, Care for me and you, and Care for all. Chapter 10 concluded that three key intelligences as referred to by Zohar and Marshall (2004)—rational intelligence (IQ), emotional intelligence (EQ), and spiritual intelligence (SQ), human endowments present in all human beings—are critical in the process. Emotional and social intelligence have been identified as two facilitating merits to move from a Care for me stage, to a Care for me and you stage of development. It has also been recognized that in the end spiritual intelligence can be instrumental in helping each individual to pursue a higher sense of meaning and values, leading to a Care for all stage of personal development.

The change path toward sustainability can be considered a transformational effort, requiring those qualities Quinn is talking about. To achieve this milestone, however, takes a complex voyage, which has to start with oneself.

The next sections will elaborate on the process of change of the self, the role of the three Care dimensions in the change path, and the importance of core beliefs (Section 11.1). Section 11.2 discusses how paradigm shifts may affect and change leading core assumptions.

11.1 The individual change path toward sustainability

It is a common understanding that, although human beings are changing both physically and mentally all the time, human change remains a much-debated phenomenon. Especially when it comes to significant changes in human minds, the process can be very complicated.

Howard Gardner identifies in *Changing Minds* (2004: 63), six different arenas in which mind changing ordinarily takes place. They are illustrated as an inverted pyramid:

Large-scale changes involving the diverse population of a region or an entire nation
Large-scale changes involving a more uniform or homogeneous group
Changes brought about through works of art or science
Changes within formal instructional settings
Intimate forms of mind changing
Changing one's own mind.

The bottom of Gardner's inverted pyramid is where the process begins. The last, but not least, important as stated earlier, is change of the self. According to Gardner (2004: 65):

> our own minds are changed—either because something happens in the real world or in our mental life that warrants a major change. The change can occur in any sphere: our political beliefs, our scientific beliefs, our personal credo, our views about ourselves.

Gardner (2004) identifies four important mental contents: concepts, stories, theories, and skills. He considers concepts to be the most elementary unit and describes it as "an umbrella term that refers to any set of closely related entities" (Gardner 2004: 19). In his book *The Power of Sustainable Thinking: How to Create a Positive Future for the Climate, the Planet, your Organization and your Life* (2008), Bob Doppelt refers to Gardner when explaining the mental process and the role of concepts in understanding what we see, sense, and experience in the world (Doppelt 2008: 59). Most of the important concepts are formed in early childhood. These concepts are gradually transformed in what Doppelt denominates as mental frames.

> Mental frames are the deeply felt beliefs, assumptions and stories we hold in our minds about the nature of other people, how the world works and our role in it all (Beck 1979). Mental frames have three interlinked elements: core beliefs, core assumptions and automatic thoughts. Core beliefs are the deepest level of cognition. They are unconditional views we hold about the world around us including the physical environment, other humans and ourselves (Doppelt 2008: 60-61).

Core beliefs can be considered to be absolute; they lead to basic assumptions (paradigms) which lead to rules that guide the thinking. These rules lead to automatic thoughts which form our day-to-day behavior. Core beliefs are deeply rooted and the roots are not easy to trace back (see Fig. 11.1).

Figure 11.1 **The hidden nature of core beliefs**

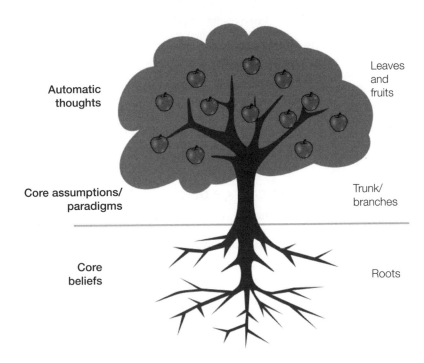

One of the collective core beliefs that get in the way of a sustainable future is the belief that only a technical way of thinking can solve the sustainability problems the world is facing. Senge and his colleagues at the Society for Organizational Learning see the task of shaping a sustainable, flourishing world for life beyond the industrial age as follows (2006: 10):

> A new era in human development is not going to arise because govern-
> ments decree it, or because a few companies change their strategies. It
> will happen because a diffuse and diverse critical mass of people and
> organizations decide to live and act differently—as parents, as profession-
> als and as leaders, as suppliers and as customers, as citizens and as entre-
> preneurs, as friends and as colleagues, as teachers and as students.

In an article published in the *Systems Thinker*, "Overcoming the Seven Sustainability Blunders," Doppelt (2003b) refers to the so-called "cradle-to-grave" production system. "This system focuses on producing products and delivering them to
the customer in the fastest and cheapest way possible." It became firmly embedded
in our psyches as the dominant paradigm. One may consider this to be one of the
critical core assumptions that stems from the core belief that natural resources are
infinite and that technology will solve all related problems. The path to sustainability implies a fundamental change in this core belief, which still is the credo of many
people, among others, political leaders, captains of industry, heads of multilateral
institutions, and leaders of nongovernmental organizations. Most of these leaders
are not easy to inspire to follow a path less traveled such as the path toward sustainability. Doppelt (2008) gives important advice when it comes to supporting these
and other people in the change process, as he remarks:

> Motivate don't advocate. Many people who want to help others become
> sustainable thinkers have a built-in desire to make the world a better
> place. That's important because it takes passion to bring about change.
> This drive, however, can also cause change agents to become overzealous
> with people who are not ready yet to make a shift (Doppelt 2008: 154).

As has been observed above, all change has to start with the self, and the advice of
Doppelt cited above is a clear hint in this direction.

Different people, different change paths

The previous section proposed that it is only by deep, personal change that people
become leaders for sustainability. The change path followed will differ from individual to individual because each starts from a situation that is specific for him or
her. The direction of change and its purpose, however, are the same: namely, to
gradually develop the three care dimensions of the individual level (Care for me,
Care for me and you, and Care for all).

There are two more conclusions that can be drawn from the theories presented in
Chapter 10 Section 2 regarding the change path to become a leader for sustainability. Though in different ways, all theories agree that there is a difference between
the human development stages that here are called the three care dimensions. The
discipline of environmental sociology offers an interesting venue to explain the
difference, from an evolutionary perspective. In this view, the Care for me dimension is considered to have a very strong hold on us because it stems from our urge
to survive. An urge, as Lawrence noted, human beings share with all animals or,

as the Greek philosopher Aristotle would have preferred, with all living creatures including plants. This explains why, when confronted with conflicts among the dimensions, people tend to fall back on Care for me values and attitudes. In the view of environmental sociologists, altruism, the human quality that the authors have associated with the Care for me and you dimension, has a less strong claim than Care for me, yet stronger than biospheric and normative values, here associated with the Care for all dimension. From its prehistory, humankind has learned that cooperation with others makes it possible to achieve results that one cannot achieve alone. Of course, cooperation cannot be sustained if one does not take into account the needs of the other people involved. Empathy and loyalty toward the in-group are thus strengthened.

The claim brought to our attention by biospheric values—the values connected with compassion for all living creatures and nature—is considered to be the most difficult to pursue and maintain of the three. Environmental sociologists point to the fact that, from the time human beings started developing till recently, the world was empty: nature, though a force to be respected and even feared, was therefore not an issue.

The conclusion that can be drawn is that each care dimension is like a muscle. If it is not used it will become weaker and weaker until it deteriorates. If these theories are correct in stating that the values that the authors have connected with the Care for all dimension are the most difficult to pursue and maintain, then this dimension should get the greatest attention of the person who wishes to become a leader for sustainability. It should be trained so that, when things become rough, it is not easily taken over by a Care for me or even Care for me and you attitude. Acting from the Care for me and you dimension and not exclusively from a Care for me stance may also require training. Here is also true: what is not used will become useless.

A second conclusion regards the role of the four human intelligences in this process. On the basis of the theories discussed in Chapter 10 Section 2 it may be stated that it is thanks to emotional and social intelligence that people are able to step from the Care for me to the Care for me and you dimension, while the step toward Care for all is made possible by spiritual intelligence. It may be maintained that it is physical intelligence that prevents people from forgetting themselves in universal care and supports Care for me. From the theories discussed, though, it seems that a double role has to be ascribed to spiritual intelligence. On one side, spiritual intelligence is the force that compels individuals to expand their circle of care and compassion beyond their in-groups. On the other, it is the force that keeps the process running, by which leaders for sustainability continuously and positively develop their three care dimensions. Figure 11.2 illustrates this double function of spiritual intelligence.

Figure 11.2 **Double function of spiritual intelligence**

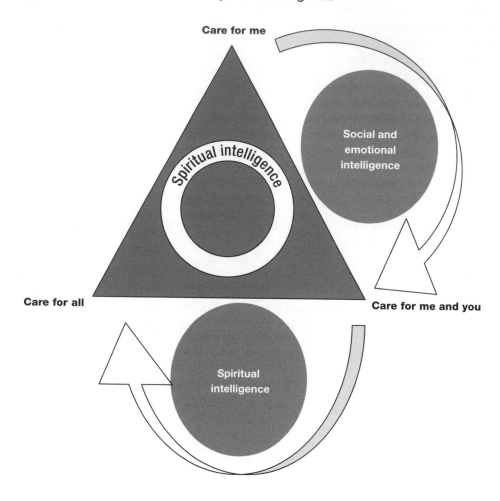

11.2 **Leaders for sustainability and paradigm shifts in the journey toward sustainability**

Authors such as Zohar, Parkin, and Kuenkel are in line with the thinking that the development of the three care dimensions at the individual level is essential to achieve sustainability at the level of organizations and society. Individuals who have been able to realize their innate capacity to care not only for themselves and their constituency but also for all, are in a better position to start and sustain the process of change toward sustainability. As such they can be called leaders for sustainability.

To substantiate this last statement, this section goes back to Parts I and II and the major paradigm shifts that were discussed there. Paradigms are deeply held assumptions about the world, about others, and about ourselves. Paradigms are thus interpretations of reality and not reality itself. As explained in Section 11.1, these paradigms or core assumptions are rooted in core beliefs.

A paradigm shift occurs when one realizes that one's core assumptions are not in line with reality and are no longer helpful to understand how things are. Paradigm shifts happen all the time. Some are major ones and completely change the way people look at our core beliefs.

"The mindset or paradigm out of which the system—its goal, power structure, rules, its culture—arises" (Meadows 1997: 2) is for Donella Meadows the most effective place to intervene to change a system, though in her opinion this is the most difficult to reach.[1]

A typical example from the sixteenth century is the breakthrough that the Earth does not stand still in the middle of the universe but moves around the Sun together with the other planets. Other paradigm shifts have a more limited impact such as the example quoted in Box 7.1. Yet both major and minor paradigm shifts start with individuals and their capacity to reflect on the existing paradigm and, if needed, break with it. Nicolaus Copernicus and Galileo Galilei were the two scientists *avant la lettre* who broke with the traditional view that the Earths stands still and the Sun moves. In analogy, it is the authors' view that paradigm shifts such us understanding the real nature of the relationship between the natural system and the economic system are quite impossible without leaders for sustainability. Let us insist on this point: leaders for sustainability have developed not only their Care for me and Care for me and you dimension, but also their Care for all capacity. To support this view the next pages come back to four major paradigms explored in Parts I and II: the relationship between economy and nature; the difference between growth and development; the discussion on a shareholders' or stakeholders' view of the firm; and the tension between each individual's frame of reference and the intergenerational and global nature of sustainability issues.

Relationship between economy and nature

Since World War II economic growth has been considered the cure for all problems (see Chapter 1). The message has been that eventual environmental or social limits will be overthrown by sustained economic growth supported by technological progress.

The assumption backing up this view is that indeed both the natural and the social system are part of the economic system (see Fig. 1.3).

Part I has shown that sustainability is embedded on the opposite core belief; more explicitly, it is nature that makes both human societies and economies possible (see Fig. 1.4). The Care for all dimension driven by spiritual intelligence may

---

1 sustainer.org/pubs/Leverage_Points.pdf, accessed August 31, 2011.

make this paradigm shift possible by recognizing that human beings are all part of a web of life.

Growth vs. development

Economic growth focuses on more of the same: it is an increase in the *quantity* of products and services. The implicit assumption and expectation is that through growth all people's needs will be satisfied. This fallacy has been exposed not only by the work of scholars such as Max-Neef and Ernst F. Schumacher (see, respectively, Chapter 3 Section 3 and Chapter 1 Section 5), but also by economists such as Amartya Sen and Herman Daly (see, respectively, Chapter 3 Section 3 and Chapter 4 Section 2). They all point to the fact that people have non-material needs that are not met by more products and services. Their message is that human beings are not utility maximizing machines but complex creatures with material, emotional, social, and spiritual needs.

On the basis of this vision of people as complex beings, development is called upon. Sustainable development focuses on a better *quality* of life for all people, and for all generations. This implies a certain degree of material wealth, but also the opportunity to exercise other, less material human capabilities in a healthy natural environment (Chapter 3 Section 5). This will be difficult to achieve if acting from a narrow "Care for me" and even a "Care for me and you" perspective.

Shareholders' and stakeholders' view on the firm

The shareholders' view holds a company responsible only toward its shareholders: the people who have a financial stake in it. The focus here is on satisfying a materialistic need (narrow Care for me needs) of a limited group (narrow Care for me and you). In its most radical form a shareholder view may lead to the sacrifice of others' needs (such as the safety of the employees; the health of the environment) to provide to its shareholders the highest return on capital possible.

The disaster with the Deepwater Horizon oil rig in the Gulf of Mexico is one of the most recent examples of the risks that companies seem willing to take to enhance short-term profit. As is widely known, on April 20, 2010 an explosion and fire on the Deepwater Horizon caused the death of 11 people, while 17 others were injured. For almost ninety days oil spilled from the well, causing major environmental damage in the Gulf of Mexico and on the fragile wetlands on the coast of Louisiana. Fishermen, tourism entrepreneurs, and many others lost their source of income. In the direct aftermath, the corporation responsible, BP, set up an investigation team. Its conclusions, published in September 2010, point to main weaknesses in quality assurance, maintenance, and testing (BP 2010).

Hearings held by several U.S. agencies to uncover the deep causes of the disaster have uncovered that BP people were willing to take risks to save time and money even against the advice of experts. In presenting the report of the White House Oil

Spill Commission, co-chair Bill Reilly summarized the point by saying, "There was not a culture of safety on that rig" (BBC 2010).

Of course, from this and other sad examples one cannot immediately conclude that companies who see themselves as responsible only toward their shareholders will by definition sacrifice values such as safety to short-term gain. Yet it is also true that, when taken in its strictest sense, a shareholders' view of the firm does not provide any intrinsic mechanism to stop the interests of a small group prevailing on the interests of other groups, such as the employees, the suppliers, and the broader community. Stakeholder theory, in contrast, reminds (for-profit) organizations that their success depends on more people than just the shareholders, and that the power they have to positively or negatively affect the well-being of large groups of people brings with it the moral responsibility to use this power wisely (Box 6.5 and Chapter 7 Section 6). In this sense stakeholder theory feeds itself from a more altruistic and broader Care for me and you perspective.

A stakeholders' view of the firm can be stretched to include animals and nature. As William McDonough and Michael Braungart (2002) observed, we can develop products that take into account not only the needs of people but also the needs of fish (Chapter 7 Section 6). This statement will sound preposterous and even offensive for people wrapped up in the Care for me and Care for me and you dimension. It becomes reasonable and logical for people who have reached the insight that humans and animals are all part of the web of life and that coping with human needs does not mean by definition jeopardizing the ability of other creatures to cope with their own needs.

The time–space and interest matrix by the MIT team

Limits to Growth, by a team from the MIT led by Donella Meadows, confronted people for the first time with the insights that unlimited economic growth supported by exploitative technology is impossible on a limited planet. The MIT team was aware that their message was shocking and that it would encounter resistance. They even explained why people will have difficulty in grasping the issues they were addressing in all their complexity by drawing a matrix with on one axis space and on the other time (Fig. 4.4). Their point is that to grasp the main forces driving the development of society one needs to think on the long term and globally. The same may be said of sustainability issues such as climate change, poverty reduction, resource depletion, equitable distribution of resources, and so on. People, though, live most of their life from a very narrow frame of reference. Individuals are mostly concerned with what may happen to us and to the persons dearest to us in a period of a few weeks or a few months. It is looking at life from a quite narrow Care for me and Care for me and you dimension.

The MIT team underlines that this nearsightedness is the major obstacle to understanding the nature of sustainability issues and to recognize that our life now is interconnected with the life of people in the past and in the future and, ultimately, with the health of the planet we all share. If one keeps acting from this narrow frame of reference, it is only by chance that a better quality of life for the present and future generation will be reached. This narrow-mindedness or near-sightedness, though, is a condition people can overcome through exercising the positive capacities linked with the three care dimensions, in general, and the care for all dimension in particular.

The message of the three care dimensions is that each of us has the ability to rise above the self limited in space and time, as Albert Einstein and many other scholars keep reminding us (see Chapter 10 Section 2).

11.3 **Concluding remarks**

The process of change toward sustainability depends strongly on the person behind the leader and on the individuals he or she wants to mobilize on the journey to create a better world; a journey which has to bring all involved back to the reality that we are all an integral part of an interdependent universe. The three-dimensional approach presented in this part of the book is meant to support this process, departing from the premise that sustainability has to lead to a better quality of life for all living now, and also for future generations. This individual level of the TLS has a most critical role considering its impact on the individual, on the organization, and on society. The change process to achieve this highest mission of humankind for the twenty-first century ultimately depends on the men and women who are willing to follow the advice of Einstein:

> A human being is a part of a whole, called by us "universe," a part limited in time and space. He experiences himself, his thoughts and feelings as something separated from the rest . . . a kind of optical delusion of his consciousness. This delusion is a kind of prison for us, restricting us to our personal desires and to affection for a few persons nearest to us. *Our task must be to free ourselves from this prison by widening our circle of compassion to embrace all living creatures and the whole of nature in its beauty.* Nobody is able to achieve this completely but the striving for such achievement is in itself a part of the liberation and a foundation for inner security.[2]

---

2 Quote from a letter of condolence Einstein sent to Norman Salit on March 4, 1950 (AEA 61-226). Used here by the kind courtesy of Mrs. Barbara Wolff, Einstein Information Officer, Albert Einstein Archives Hebrew University of Jerusalem, Jerusalem 91904, Israel (emphasis added by authors).

Epilogue

The driving force behind our endeavor to write a book about sustainability was a call for bringing together the many facets of a principle that can make a difference and create a new beginning for humankind. It seemed to us that in the existing literature sustainability is hardly ever discussed as a concept with an inherent, interrelated functioning between the levels of the society, the organization, and the individual. The discussion tends also to neglect the multidimensional nature of each level. Mostly the conversation focuses only on one level at a time and often on one of the dimensions. For example, literature on sustainable development accentuates environmental issues or economic growth issues, while the social dimension is rarely discussed. The link between sustainability and quality of life is rarely exposed and sustainability is mostly presented not as a process but as the end in itself. Moreover, sustainability on the organizational and societal level is described by many scholars; these two levels are, however, seldom presented in conjunction. And last, the role of the individual level and of personal leadership in the process of sustainability is hardly ever discussed.

The three levels of sustainability (TLS) framework was designed as a simple model to accentuate the interrelated nature of the individual, the organizational, and the societal levels. It then became the instrument to describe the content and the dynamics of the three domains related to the three levels: that is, sustainable development, corporate social responsibility, and leadership for sustainability. The TLS framework facilitates the thought process by emphasizing the following aspects:

- Sustainability plays a role at three levels: societies, organizations, and individuals

- At each level, each dimension corresponds with the dimension on the other two levels. Thus the need to survive and acquire present in the individual dimension 'Care for me' is matched at the level of organizations by the concern for profit and at the level of society by the concern for economic value

- The fundamental reason why the three levels are interrelated is that the level of society and the level of organization reflect the three basic human needs, 'Care for me,' 'Care for me and you,' and 'Care for all'. Moreover, all three levels depend on each other to thrive. That the three levels are interrelated is also the basis of our conviction that for sustainability to succeed, intervention is needed at all three levels

- Though interrelated, each level has specific responsibilities and possibilities for interventions. For example, setting laws, including environmental and socially inspired laws, is a responsibility of governments (level of society). Structuring processes so that no emissions and no wastes are produced is a responsibility that can be taken at the level of organizations. The architect of all these actions is the individual

- Each level has three dimensions. Scholars broadly agree on the dimensions at the level of society and organizations. Though the dimensions of the individual level have been drawn by the authors, scholars from very different fields support the authors' vision of human beings as complex creatures, not only with the need to survive, acquire, and defend, but also with the need to bond with others and to feel part of a greater whole

- Sustainability is an inside–out process: it starts and ends with the people. It ends with the people because its aim is a better quality of life for the people living now and in the future. It starts with the people for two reasons. First, because no one else but the people themselves can decide what quality of life means for them and how it can be achieved. Second, because it is the authors' conviction that it is through the development of our capacity to reach a 'Care for all' perspective by developing our spiritual intelligence that sustainability can be achieved at all levels

We started this journey almost ten years ago, in times of growing awareness about the implications of an unsustainable way of life. There have been many warnings from individuals, groups, scientists, multilateral institutions, and NGOs that the unbridled expansion and satisfaction of material wants, the widening gap between the haves and the have-nots, and the continuing neglect of nature cannot continue forever without serious consequences for all. At the end of the journey, the Western world lives in serious turmoil. It reaps the harvest of decades of unbalanced growth and unsustainable development.

Efforts to correct the failures of the system and culture that brought the world in danger are still very legalistic, are inspired by the same paradigm that caused the failures, and hardly touch the core of the problems humankind is facing. As the Indian business and thought leader Ravy Chaudhry puts it in his book (2011: 14): "In any government anywhere in the world today, the economic agenda virtually drives the entire gamut of policy making, and this agenda is invariably dominated by large corporations that prevail upon the state to do their bidding."

On the leadership level Chaudhry observes that leaders are blinded by power. He illustrates this statement as follows (2011: 40):

> It was less of a surprise that tyrants and kings used to display naked power, because they believed it was their unquestionable right. But what is most astonishing is that elected heads of democratic States and institutions and nominated heads of large enterprises (including corporations) have also set their sights on exercising the same level of absolute power. To do that, they are willing to ruthlessly thwart any attempts that could dilute their clout or control. They think they have an immutable entitlement to reshuffle reality and bend or twist anyone or anything that comes in their way.

We sincerely hope that our contribution will help inspire more and more people to become 'Care for all' leaders and join the pathway of sustainability, not as an ornament but as a principle. A path with many lanes, all leading in one direction: namely, *A Better Quality of Life for All, now and in the future.*

Bibliography

Abrams, F. (1951) "Management's Responsibilities in a Complex World," *Harvard Business Review* 29.3: 29-34.

Adrien-Kirby, A., and S. Hoejmose (2010) "Socially and Environmentally Responsible Procurement: A Literature Review and an Agenda for Future Research," working paper; cranfield.academia.edu/documents/0101/1470/
Contribution_to_IPSERA_2010_by_Adam_Adrien-Kirby_and_Stefan_Hoejmose.pdf, accessed October 14, 2010.

Agle, B., and L. Agle (2007) *The Stated Objectives of the Fortune 500: Examining the Philosophical Approaches that Drive America's Largest Firms* (Working Paper; Pittsburgh, PA: University of Pittsburgh).

——, T. Donaldson, E. Freeman, M. Jensen, R.K. Mitchell and D.J. Wood (2008) "Dialogue: Toward Superior Stakeholder Theory," *Business Ethics Quarterly* 18.2: 153-90.

Alderfer, C. (1969) "An Empirical Test of a New Theory of Human Needs," *Organizational Behavior and Human Performance* 4.2: 142-75.

Amin, S. (1973) *Le développement inégal. Essai sur les formations sociales du capitalisme périphérique* (Paris: Editions de Minuit).

Anderson, R.C. (1998) *Mid-course Correction. Towards a Sustainable Enterprise: The Interface Model* (Atlanta, GA: Peregrinzilla Press).

—— with R. White (2009) *Confessions of a Radical Industrialist, Profits, People, Purpose: Doing Business by Respecting the Earth* (New York: St Martin's Press).

Anderson, S., and J. Cavanagh (2000) "Top 200: The Rise of Global Corporate Power"; www.globalpolicy.org/component/content/article/221/47211.html accessed February 4, 2010.

Anger, C., and J. Schmidt (2008) "Gender Pay Gap: Gesamtwirtschaftliche Evidenz und regionale Unterschiede," *IW-Trends* 37.4: 3-16.

Antonakis, J., A.T. Cianciolo, and R.J. Sternberg (2004) "Leadership: Past, Present, and Future," in J. Antonakis, A.T. Cianciolo and R.J. Sternberg (eds.), *The Nature of Leadership* (Thousand Oaks, CA: Sage Publications).

Ashton, T.S. (1966) *The Industrial Revolution, 1760–1830* (Oxford, UK: Oxford University Press).

Badaracco, J.L. Jr. (1998) "The Discipline of Building Character," *Harvard Business Review*, March/April 1998: 116.

Bakken, P.W. (2000) "Freedom, Equality, and Community in the Eco-justice Literature"; www. meadville.edu/journal/2000_bakken_1_2.pdf, accessed March 15, 2007.

Bariloche Foundation (1974) *Limits to Poverty* (San Carlo de Bariloche, Argentina: Bariloche Foundation).

Barry, N.P. (2000) "Controversy: Do corporations have any responsibility beyond making a profit?" *Journal of Markets & Morality* 3.1 (Spring 2000): 100-107.

Bass, B.M., and R.M. Stogdill (1990) *Handbook of Leadership: Theory, Research and Managerial Applications* (New York: Free Press, 3rd edn).

BBC (2010) "Gulf Oil Spill: President's Panel Says Firms Complacent"; www.bbc.co.uk/news/world-us-canada-11720907, accessed March 24, 2011.

Beck, D.E., and C.C. Cowan (1996) *Spiral Dynamics: Mastering Values, Leadership and Change* (Oxford, UK: Blackwell Publishers).

Bell, M.L., D.L. Davis, and T. Fletcher (2004) "A Retrospective Assessment of Mortality from the London Smog Episode of 1952: The Role of Influenza and Pollution," *Environmental Health Perspectives* 112.1: 6-8.

Bell, S., and S. Morse (2003) *Measuring Sustainability: Learning by Doing* (London: Earthscan).

Berle, A.E., Jr., and G.C. Means (1932) *The Modern Corporation and Private Property* (New York: Macmillan).

Bilsky, W., and S.H. Schwartz, (1994) "Values and Personality," *European Journal of Personality* 8: 163-81.

Bolden, R., J. Gosling, A. Marturano, and P. Dennison (2003) *A Review of Leadership Theory and Competency Frameworks* (Exeter, UK: University of Exeter).

Boon, M. (2007) *The African Way: The Power of Interactive Leadership* (Cape Town: Zebra Press).

Boulding, K.E. (1966) "The Economics of the Coming Spaceship Earth," paper presented at the *Sixth Resources for the Future Forum on Environmental Quality in a Growing Economy*, Washington, DC, March 8, 1966; www.eoearth.org/article/The_Economics_of_the_Coming_Spaceship_Earth_(historical), accessed August 28, 2009.

Bowen, H. (1953) *Social Responsibilities of the Businessman* (New York: Harper & Row).

BP (2010) "Deepwater Horizon: Accident Investigation Report," report of the BP incident investigation team to BP; www.bp.com/liveassets/bp_internet/globalbp/globalbp_uk_english/incident_response/STAGING/local_assets/downloads_pdfs/Deepwater_Horizon_Accident_Investigation_Report.pdf, accessed March 24, 2011.

Brack, D., and K. Grey (2003) "Multilateral Environmental Agreements and the WTO," The Royal Institute for Environmental Affairs and International Institute for Sustainable Development; www.worldtradelaw.net/articles/graymeawto.pdf, accessed August 23, 2010.

Brown, L.R. (ed.) (1984) *State of the World 1984: A Worldwatch Institute Report on Progress Toward a Sustainable Society* (Washington, DC: Worldwatch Institute)

—— (1990) *State of the World 1990: A Worldwatch Institute Report on Progress toward a Sustainable Society* (New York: Norton).

Buber, M. (1970) *I and Thou* (trans. W. Kaufmann; New York: Simon & Schuster).

Buckley, R.P. (2008) *International Financial System, Policy and Regulation* (Alphen aan de Rijn, Netherlands: Kluwer Law International).

Camerer, C.F. (2003) *Behavioral Game Theory: Experiments in Strategic Interaction* (Princeton, NJ: Princeton University Press).

Canada Ministry of Environment (1997) "Sustainable Development Strategy, Summary Document"; www.ec.gc.ca/sd-dd_consult/final/ESDSSUMM.PDF, accessed March 12, 2008 [web page no longer exists].

Carley, M., and I. Christie (2002) *Managing Sustainable Development* (London: Earthscan).

Carroll, A.B. (1979) "A Three-dimensional Conceptual Model of Corporate Social Performance," *Academy of Management Review* 4.4: 497-505.

—— (1991) "The Pyramid of Corporate Social Responsibility: Toward the Moral Management of Organizational Stakeholders," *Business Horizons* 34.4: 39-48.

—— (1998) "Stakeholder Thinking in Three Models of Management Morality: A Perspective with Strategic Implications," in M.B.E. Clarkson (ed.), *The Corporation and its Stakeholders: Classic and Contemporary Readings* (Toronto: University of Toronto Press).

—— (1999) "Corporate Social Responsibility: Evolution of a Definition Construct," *Business and Society* 38.3: 268-95.

Carson, R. (1962) *Silent Spring* (Boston, MA: Mariner Books, 2002).

Cashman, K. (2000) *Leadership from the Inside Out: Becoming a Leader for Life* (Provo, UT: Executive Excellence Publishing).

Cavagnaro, E. (2009) "Difficile est deponere longum amorem: On Ethics and Sustainability," in S. Hertmans (ed.), *Grenzen aan de ethiek? Studium Generale 2008–2009* (Gent, Belgium: Academia Press).

—— and F. Bosker (eds.) (2007) *Services and Sustainability: A Travellers' Guide* (Leeuwarden, Netherlands: CHN).

C.borgomeo & Co (2008) *Quarto rapporto sul microcredito in Italia* (Soveria Mannelli, Italy: Rubettino).

Ceres (2010) *The 21st Century Corporation: The Ceres Roadmap for Sustainability, Summary* (San Francisco: Ceres; www.ceres.org/resources/reports/ceres-roadmap-to-sustainability-2010, accessed August 20, 2010).

Chaudhry, R. (2011) *Quest for Exceptional Leadership: Mirage to Reality* (New Delhi: Sage Response).

Chua, A. (2007) *Day of Empire: How Hyperpowers Rise to Global Dominance—and why they fall* (New York: Doubleday).

Clark, C., W. Rosenzweig, D. Long, and S. Olsen (2004) "Double Bottom Line Project Report: Assessing Social Impact in Double Bottom Line Ventures," methods catalog; www.impactalliance.org/ev_en.php?ID=22927_201&ID2=DO_TOPIC, accessed September 9, 2010.

Clark, L.L. (2008) *Women and Achievement in Nineteenth-century Europe* (Cambridge, UK: Cambridge University Press).

Clifton, D., and A. Amran (2010) "The Stakeholder Approach: A Sustainability Perspective"; *Journal of Business Ethics* 98: 121-36 (www.springerlink.com/content/k750050j034072xj/fulltext.pdf, accessed August 3, 2010).

Cobb, C., T. Halstead, and J. Rowe (1995) "If the GDP is Up, Why is America Down?" *The Atlantic Monthly* 276.4: 59-78.

Cobb, C.W. (2000) *Measurement Tools and the Quality of Life* (San Francisco: Redefining Progress; www.econ.tuwien.ac.at/hanappi/lehre/pee/measure_qol_Cobb.pdf, accessed September 18, 2011.

Cohen, B., J. Greenfield, and M. Maan (1997) *Ben & Jerry's Double-dip: How to Run a Values-Led Business and Make Money, Too* (New York: Simon & Schuster).

Cole, D., S. McAlinden, K. Dziczek, and D. Maranger Menk (2008) "CAR Research Memorandum: The Impact on the U.S. Economy of a Major Contraction of the Detroit Three Automakers"; www.cargroup.org/documents/FINALDetroitThreeContractionImpact_3__00 1.pdf, accessed February 8, 2009.

Collins, J.C., and J.I. Porras (1998) "Building your Company's Vision," *Harvard Business Review on Change* (Boston, MA: Harvard Business School Publishing): 21-54.

Covey, S.R. (1989, 2004a) *The 7 Habits of Highly Effective People: Restoring the Character Ethic* (New York: Free Press).

—— (1992) *Principle-Centered Leadership* (New York: Simon & Schuster).

—— (2005) *The 8th Habit: From Effectiveness to Greatness* (New York: Free Press, pbk edn).

——, A.R. Merrill, and R.R. Merrill (1994) *First Things First: To Live, to Love, to Learn, to Leave a Legacy* (New York: Simon & Schuster).

Crain, W.C. (1985) *Theories of Development: Concepts and Applications* (Upper Saddle River, NJ: Prentice-Hall, 2nd edn).

Cramer, J. (1998) "Experiences with Implementing Integrated Chain Management in Dutch Industry," *Business Strategy and the Environment* 5.1: 38-47.

Crutzen, P.J., and E.F. Stoermer (2000) "The Anthropocene," *Global Change Newsletter* 41: 17-18; www.mpch-mainz.mpg.de/~air/anthropocene, accessed January 4, 2010.

Daft, R.L., and R.M. Steers (1986) *Organizations: A Micro/Macro Approach* (New York: Harper-Collins Publishers).

Dag Hammarskjöld Foundation (1975) "What Now? Another Development: Report on Development and International Co-operation," *Development Dialogue* 1/2 (special issue).

Daly, H.E. (1977) *Steady-state Economics: The Economics of Biophysical Equilibrium and Moral Growth* (San Francisco: W.H. Freeman).

—— (1992) "From Empty-World Economics to Full-World Economics: Recognizing an Historical Turning Point in Economic Development," *Eco-Watch*, July 14, 1992 (www.fs.fed.us/eco/eco-watch/ew920714, accessed December 8, 2010).

—— (1999) *Ecological Economics and the Ecology of Economics: Essays in Criticism* (Cheltenham, UK: Edward Elgar).

—— (2005) "Economics in a Full World," *Scientific American* 293.3: 100-107.

—— and J.B. Cobb (1989) *For the Common Good, Redirecting the Economy towards Community, the Environment, and a Sustainable Future* (Boston, MA: Beacon Press).

Davidson, K. (2009) "Ethical Concerns at the Bottom of the Pyramid: Where CSR meets BOP," *Journal of International Business Ethics* 2.1: 22-32.

Davis, G. (2004) "A History of the Social Development Network in The World Bank, 1973–2002," *World Bank Social Development Papers* 56; www-wds.worldbank.org/external/default/WDSContentServer/WDSP/IB/2005/03/25/000011823_20050325122517/Rendered/INDEX/316180SDP0560H1of0SD0in0WB01public1.txt, accessed March 18, 2008.

De Groot, J.I.M. (2008) *Mean or Green? Value Orientations, Morality and Prosocial Behavior* (PhD thesis; RCG, Groningen: University of Groningen).

—— and L. Steg (2008) "Value Orientations to Explain Beliefs Related to Environmentally Significant Behavior: How to Measure Egoistic, Altruistic and Biospheric Value Orientations," *Environment and Behavior* 40.3: 330-54.

De Jong, A., and A. Röell (2004) "Financing and Control in The Netherlands: An Historical Perspective," paper prepared for *NBER History of Corporate Ownership Conference*, June 2004; www.bintproject.nl/textfiles/2005_dejong-roell.pdf, accessed January 11, 2010.

Deane, P.M. (1980) *The First Industrial Revolution* (Cambridge, UK: Cambridge University Press).

Deegan, C., and M. Rankin (1996) "Do Australian Companies Report Environmental News Objectively? An Analysis of Environmental Disclosures by Firms Prosecuted Successfully by the Environmental Protection Authority," *Accounting Auditing and Accountability Journal* 9.2: 52-69.

Dentchev, N.A. (2009) "To What Extent is Business and Society Literature Idealistic?" *Business and Society* 48.1: 10-38.

Diamond, J. (1997) *Guns, Germs and Steel: The Fates of Human Societies* (New York: W.W. Norton & Company, 2003).

—— (2005) *Collapse: How Societies Choose to Fail or Succeed* (New York: Penguin).

Dierkes, M., and A.B. Antal (1986) "Whither Corporate Social Reporting: Is It Time to Legislate?" *California Management Review* 28.3: 106-21.

Diouf, J. (2007) "Press Conference on Soaring Food Prices and Action Needed," Rome, December 17, 2007; www.fao.org/newsroom/common/ecg/1000733/en/facts99.pdf, accessed September 18, 2011.

Donaldson, T., and L.E. Preston (1995) "The Stakeholder Theory of the Corporation: Concepts, Evidence, and Implications," *Academy of Management Review* 20.1: 65-91.

Doppelt, B. (2003a) *Leading Change Toward Sustainability: A Change-Management Guide for Business, Government and Civil Society* (Sheffield, UK: Greenleaf Publishing).

—— (2003b) "Overcoming the Seven Sustainability Blunders," *The Systems Thinker* 14.5; www.pegasuscom.com, accessed April 4, 2011.

—— (2008) *The Power of Sustainable Thinking, How to Create a Positive Future for the Climate, the Planet, your Organization and your Life* (London: Earthscan).

Dormann, J., and C. Holliday (2002) *Innovation, Technology, Sustainability and Society: A WBCSD Project* (Stevenage, UK: Earthprint).

Douthwaite, R. (1999) *The Growth Illusion, How Economic Growth has Enriched the Few, Impoverished the Many and Endangered the Planet* (Gabriola Island, BC: New Society Publishers).

Dresner, S. (2002) *The Principles of Sustainability* (London: Earthscan).

Drucker, P.F. (1984) "The New Meaning of Corporate Social Responsibility," *California Management Review* 26.2: 53-63.

—— (1989) *The New Realities: In Government and Politics; in Economics and Business; in Society and World View* (New York: Harper Business).

—— (1993) *Post-Capitalist Society* (New York: Harper Business).

—— (2001) *The Essential Drucker: Selections from the Management Works of Peter F. Drucker* (New York: Harper Business).

Dyllick, T., and K. Hockerts (2002) "Beyond the Business Case for Corporate Sustainability," *Business Strategy and the Environment* 11.2: 130-41.

Earth Summit (1992) "Rio Declaration on Environment and Development," UN Conference on Environment and Development, Rio de Janeiro, June 3–14, 1992; www.unep.org/Documents.multilingual/Default.asp?DocumentID=78&ArticleID=1163, accessed March 3, 2011.

Earth Summit II (1997) *Programme for the Further Implementation of Agenda 21, Outcome of the General Assembly Special Session to Review Progress on Implementation of Agenda 21* (New York: UN; www.un.org/documents/ga/res/spec/aress19-2.htm, accessed September 18, 2011).

Easterly, W. (2001) *The Elusive Quest for Growth: Economists' Adventures and Misadventures in the Tropics* (Cambridge, MA: The MIT Press).

Eccles, R.G., and M.P. Krzus (2010) *One Report: Integrated Reporting for a Sustainable Strategy* (Hoboken, NJ: Wiley).

Edwards, A.R. (2005) *The Sustainability Revolution: Portrait of a Paradigm Shift* (Gabriola Island, BC: New Society Publishers).

EEC (1957) "Treaty Establishing the European Economic Community," Rome, March 25, 1957; ec.europa.eu/economy_finance/emu_history/documents/treaties/rometreaty2.pdf, accessed September 18, 2011.

EFQM (2010) *EFQM Excellence Model 2010* (Brussels: EFQM).

Ehnert, I. (2006) "Sustainability Issues in Human Resource Management: Linkages, Theoretical Approaches, and Outlines for an Emerging Field," paper prepared for *21st EIASM SHRM Workshop*, Birmingham, March 28–29, 2006; www.sfb637.uni-bremen.de/pubdb/repository/SFB637-A2-06-004-IC.pdf, accessed August 11, 2010.

—— (2009) *Sustainable Human Resource Management: A Conceptual and Exploratory Analysis from a Paradox Perspective* (Contributions to Management Science; Heidelberg, Germany: Physica-Verlag).

Ehrlich, P.R. (1968) *The Population Bomb* (New York: Ballantine Books).

—— and J.P. Holdren (1971) "Impact of Population Growth," *Science* 171.3977: 1,212-17.

Einstein, A. (1946) "Atomic Education Urged by Einstein," *New York Times,* May 25, 1946: 13.

—— (1950) *Letter of Condolence Einstein sent to Norman Salit,* March 4, 1950; AEA 61-226.

Elkington, J. (1997) *Cannibals with Forks: The Triple Bottom Line of the 21st Century Business* (Chichester, UK: Capstone).

Ellerman, A.D., and B.K. Buchner (2007) "The European Union Emissions Trading Scheme: Origins, Allocation, and Early Results," *Review of Environmental Economics and Policy* 1.1: 66-87.

Elliott, J.A. (1999) *An Introduction to Sustainable Development* (London: Routledge, 2nd edn).

Emerson, J. (2003) "The Blended Value Proposition: Integrating Social and Financial Returns," *California Management Review* 45.4: 35-51.

Emmerij, L., R. Jolly, and T.G. Weiss (2004) "UN Social Thinking in Historical Perspective," paper prepared for the *40th Anniversary Conference of UNRISD: Social Knowledge and International Policy Making—Exploring Linkages,* Geneva, April 20–21, 2004.

Entine, J. (1994) "Shattered Image: Is The Body Shop too good to be true?" *Business Ethics* 8.5: 23-28.

Epstein, M.J. (2003) "The Identification, Measurement, and Reporting of Corporate Social Impacts: Past, Present, and Future," in B. Jaggi and M. Freedman (eds.), *Advances in Environmental Accounting and Management* 2: 1-29.

Eurofound (2007) "Netherlands Industrial Relations Profile"; www.eurofound.europa.eu/eiro/country/netherlands_5.htm, accessed May 20, 2009.

European Conference of Ministers of Transport (ECMT) (2007) *Cutting Transport CO_2 Emissions: What Progress?* (Paris: OECD Publishing).

Ewing B., D. Moore, S. Goldfinger, A. Oursler, A. Reed, and M. Wackernagel (2010) *The Ecological Footprint Atlas 2010* (Oakland, CA: Global Footprint Network; www.footprintnetwork.org/images/uploads/Ecological_Footprint_Atlas_2010.pdf, accessed September 10, 2011.

FAO (2005) *Global Forest Resources Assessment 2005: Progress towards Sustainable Forest Management* (Rome: FAO).

Fischer, G. (1948) "Award Ceremony Speech," presentation speech for the *Nobel Prize in Physiology or Medicine 1948*; nobelprize.org/nobel_prizes/medicine/laureates/1948/press.html, accessed August 20, 2009.

Florini, A.M. (2000) "Who Does What? Collective Action and the Changing Nature of Authority," in R.A. Higgott, G.R.D. Underhill, and A. Bieler (eds.), *Non-state Actors and Authority in the Global System* (London: Routledge): 15-31.

Franklin, B. (1732–1758) *Poor Richard's Almanack* (Skyhorse Publishing: New York, 2007).

Frederick, W.C. (2006) *Corporations, Be Good! The Story of Corporate Social Responsibility* (Indianapolis, IN: Dog Ear Publishing).

Freeman, R.E. (1984) *Strategic Management: A Stakeholder Approach* (Boston, MA: Pitman).

—— (2007) *Managing for Stakeholders* (Working Papers Series; Charlottesville, VA: University of Virginia [UVA], Darden Graduate School of Business Administration; ssrn.com/abstract=1186402, accessed June 26, 2010); also published in T.L. Beauchamp, N. Bowie, and D. Arnold (eds.), *Ethical Theory and Business* (Upper Saddle River, NJ: Prentice Hall, 2008, 8th edn): 56-68.

—— and J. Liedtka (1991) "Corporate Social Responsibility: A Critical Approach," *Business Horizons* 34.4: 92-98.

—— and R. Phillips (2002) "Stakeholder Theory: A Libertarian Defense," *Business Ethics Quarterly* 12.3: 331-49.

Friedman, B.M. (2005) *The Moral Consequences of Economic Growth* (New York: Vintage Books).

Friedman, M. (1970) "The Social Responsibility of Business Is to Increase Its Profits," *New York Times Magazine*, September 1, 1970; reprinted in T.L. Beauchamp and N.E. Bowie (eds.), *Ethical Theory and Business* (Englewood Cliffs, NJ: Prentice-Hall, 8th edn, 2008): 51-55.

Galbraith, J.K. (1952) *American Capitalism: The Concept of Countervailing Power* (Boston, MA: Houghton Mifflin).

Galor, O. (2005) "From Stagnation to Growth: Unified Growth Theory," in P. Aghion and S.N. Durlauf (eds.), *The Handbook of Economic Growth* (North-Holland: Elsevier; www.brown.edu/Departments/Economics/Papers/2004/2004-15_paper.pdf, accessed March 31, 2008): 171-293.

—— (2011) *Unified Growth Theory* (Princeton, NJ: Princeton University Press).

—— and O. Moav (2002) "Natural Selection and the Origin of Economic Growth," Brown University Working Paper No. 2000-18; ssrn.com/abstract=246300 and 10.2139/ssrn.246300, accessed March 21, 2009.

Galtung, J. (1980) "Self-reliance: Concepts, Practice and Rationale," in J. Galtung, P. O'Brien, and R. Preiswerk (eds.), *Self-reliance: A Strategy for Development* (Geneva: IDS).

Gardner, H. (1997) *Leading Minds: An Anatomy of Leadership* (London: HarperCollins).

Gélinas, J. (2001) *Report of the Commissioner of the Environment and Sustainable Development to the House of Commons* (Ontario: Office of the Auditor General; www.oag-bvg.gc.ca/internet/English/parl_cesd_200110_e_1135.html, accessed August 21, 2009).

George, B. (2003) *Authentic Leadership: Rediscovering the Secrets to Creating Lasting Value* (San Francisco: Jossey-Bass).

—— with P. Sims (2007) *True North: Discover your Authentic Leadership* (San Francisco: Jossey-Bass).

Georgescu-Roegen, N. (1971) *The Entropy Law and the Economic Process* (Cambridge, MA: Harvard University Press).

Gillespie, A. (2001) *The Illusion of Progress: Unsustainable Development in International Law and Policy* (London: Earthscan).

Gilligan, C. (1982) *In a Different Voice: Psychological Theory and Women's Development* (Cambridge, MA: Harvard University Press).

Glendon, M.A. (2002) *A World Made New: Eleanor Roosevelt and the Universal Declaration of Human Rights* (New York: Random House Trade Paperbacks).

Global Compact Office (2008) *Corporate Sustainability in the World Economy: United Nations Global Compact* (New York: UN; www.unglobalcompact.org/docs/news_events/8.1/GC_brochure_FINAL.pdf, accessed August 20, 2010).

Goldsmith, E. (2001) "Development as Colonialism," in E. Goldsmith and J. Mander (eds.), *The Case Against the Global Economy* (London: Earthscan): 19-34.

——, R. Allen, M. Allaby, J. Davoll, and S. Lawrence (1972) "A Blueprint for Survival," *The Ecologist* 2.1 (Harmondsworth, UK: Penguin).

Goleman, D. (2009) *Ecological Intelligence: How Knowing the Hidden Impacts of What We Buy Can Change Everything* (New York: Broadway Books).

Gonella, C., A. Pilling and S. Zadek (1998) *Making Values Count, Contemporary Experience in Social and Ethical Accounting, Auditing and Reporting* (London: Certified Accountants Educational Trust).

Gray, R. (1992) "Accounting and Environmentalism: An Exploration of the Challenge of Gently Accounting for Accountability, Transparency and Sustainability," *Accounting, Organizations and Society* 17.5: 399-425.

Grayson, D., and A. Hodges (2004) *Corporate Social Opportunity! Seven Steps to Make Corporate Social Responsibility Work for Your Business* (Sheffield, UK: Greenleaf Publishing).

Greenleaf, R.K. (1970) *The Servant as Leader* (Indianapolis, IN: Robert K. Greenleaf Center for Servant-Leadership).

—— (1977) *Servant Leadership: A Journey into the Nature of Legitimate Power and Greatness* (New York: Paulist Press).

GRI (Global Reporting Initiative) (2010) *The Transparent Economy: Ten Tigers Stalk the Global Recovery—and how to tame them* (Amsterdam: GRI).

—— (2000–2006) *Sustainability Reporting Guidelines* (version 3.0; Amsterdam: GRI; www.globalreporting.org/ReportingFramework/ReportingFrameworkDownloads, accessed September 13, 2010.

Griffin, J.J., and J.F. Mahon (1997) "The Corporate Social Performance and Corporate Financial Performance Debate: Twenty-five Years of Incomparable Research," *Business and Society* 36.1: 5-31.

Gross, D. (1996) "Henry Ford and the Model T," in D. Gross (ed.), Forbes' Greatest Business Stories of All Time (New York: Wiley & Sons): 75-89.

Grubb, M., and M. Sato (2009) *Ten (plus one) Insights from the EU Emissions Trading Scheme: With Reference to Emerging Systems in Asia* (Cambridge, UK: Climate Strategies; www.climatestrategies.org/our-reports/category/17/204.html, accessed September 1, 2010 [web page no longer exists]).

——, Th.L. Brewer, M. Sato, R. Heilmayr, and D. Fazekas (2009) *Climate Policy and Industrial Competitiveness: Ten Insights from Europe on the EU Emissions Trading System* (Washington, DC: The German Marshall Fund of the United States; www.climatestrategies.org/our-reports/category/17/204.html, accessed September 1, 2010 [web page no longer exists]).

Guissé, E.-H. (2004) "Effects of Debt on Human Rights: Working Paper for the UN Sub Commission on Human Rights," E/CN.4/Sub.2/2004/27; www.cetim.ch/en/documents/dette-2004-27-eng.pdf, accessed March 18, 2008.

Gupta, A. (2010) "Transparency in Global Environmental Governance: A Coming of Age?" *Global Environmental Politics* 10.3: 1-9.

Handy, C. (2002) "What is Business For?" *Harvard Business Review* 80.12: 49-55.

Hannigan, J.A. (1995) *Environmental Sociology : A Social Constructionist Perspective* (New York: Routledge).

Hart, S.L. (2005) *Capitalism at the Crossroads: The Unlimited Business Opportunities in Solving the World's Most Difficult Problems* (Upper Saddle River, NJ: Wharton School Publishing).

—— (2007) *Capitalism at the Crossroads* (Upper Saddle River, NJ: Wharton School Publishing).

Haufler, V. (2010) "Disclosure as Governance: The Extractive Industries Transparency Initiative and Resource Management in the Developing World," *Global Environmental Politics* 10.3: 53-73.

Hausmann, R. (2006) "Economic Growth: Shared Beliefs, Shared Disappointments?" speech delivered at the *G-20 Seminar on Economic Growth*, Pretoria, South Africa, 4–5 August 2005 (CID Working paper no. 125; Harvard University; www.hks.harvard.edu/var/ezp_site/storage/fckeditor/file/pdfs/centers-programs/centers/cid/publications/faculty/wp/125.pdf, accessed February 23, 2011).

Hawken, P. (1993) *The Ecology of Commerce: A Declaration of Sustainability* (New York: Collins Business, 2005).

——, A. Lovins and L.H. Lovins (1999) *Natural Capitalism: Creating the Next Industrial Revolution* (New York: Little, Brown).

Hayes, R.B. (1922) *The Diary and Letters of Rutherford B. Hayes: Nineteenth President of the United States* (ed. Charles Richard Williams; Vol. 4, Chapter 45; Columbus, OH: Ohio State Archeological and Historical Society; www.ohiohistory.org/onlinedoc/hayes/Volume04/Chapter45/March11.txt, accessed February 11, 2010).

Heertje, A. (2006) *Echte economie, Een verhandeling over schaarste en welvaart en over het geloof in leermeesters en' lernen'* (Nijmegen, Netherlands: Valkhof Pers).

Heskett, J.L., W.E. Sasser, and L.A. Schlesinger (1997) *The Service Profit Chain: How Leading Companies Link Profit and Growth to Loyalty, Satisfaction and Value* (New York: The Free Press).

Hill, C.W.L., and T.M. Jones (1992) "Stakeholder–Agency Theory," *Journal of Management Studies* 29.2: 131-54.

Hoffman, A.J. (1999) "Institutional Evolution and Change: Environmentalism and the U.S. Chemical Industry," *The Academy of Management Journal* 42.4: 351-71.

Hohnen, P. (2008) *The Earth Charter, GRI, and the Global Compact: Guidance to Users on the Synergies in Application and Reporting* (Amsterdam: GRI; www.globalreporting.org/NR/rdonlyres/EC39A0A7-0947-4F6D-9AE3-AE73758C8756/0/TECGGReportweb.pdf, accessed September 9, 2010).

Holing, D. (1996) "It's the Outrage, Stupid," *Tomorrow Magazine* 2 (March/April 1996); www.psandman.com/articles/holing.htm accessed June 26, 2010.

Holliday, C.O., S. Schmidheiny, and P. Watts (2002) *Walking the Talk: The Business Case for Sustainable Development* (Sheffield, UK: Greenleaf Publishing).

Holmberg, J., and K.-H. Robèrt (2000) "Backcasting from Non-overlapping Sustainability Principles: A Framework for Strategic Planning," *International Journal of Sustainable Development and World Ecology* 7.4: 291-308.

——, U. Lundqvist, K.-H. Robèrt, and M. Wackernagel (1999) "The Ecological Footprint from a Systems Perspective of Sustainability," *International Journal of Sustainable Development and World Ecology* 6.1: 17-33.

Hunt, J.G. (2004) "What is Leadership?" in J. Antonakis, A.T. Cianciolo and R.J. Sternberg (eds.), *The Nature of Leadership* (Thousand Oaks, CA: Sage Publications): 27.

ICIDI (Independent Commission on International Development Issues) (1980) *North–South: A Program for Survival* (Cambridge, MA: The MIT Press).

ILO (International Labour Organization) (1944) "ILO Declaration of Philadelphia, Declaration Concerning the Aims and Purposes of the International Labour Organization"; www.ilocarib.org.tt/projects/cariblex/conventions_23.shtml, accessed August 21, 2009.

IMF (International Monetary Fund) (2009) "World Economic and Financial Surveys, World Economic Outlook Database"; www.imf.org/external/pubs/ft/weo/2008/01/weodata/download.aspx, accessed February 8, 2010.

Ioannes Paulus II (1991) "Centesimus annus, Encyclical Letter by His Holiness Pope John Paul II On the Hundredth Anniversary of Rerum Novarum"; www.vatican.va/holy_father/john_paul_ii/encyclicals/documents/hf_jp-ii_enc_01051991_centesimus-annus_en.html, accessed April 1, 2009.

IPCC (Intergovernmental Panel on Climate Change) (2007) "Fourth Assessment Report: Climate Change 2007 (AR4)"; www.ipcc.ch/publications_and_data/ar4/syr/en/contents. html, accessed September 10, 2011.

ISO (2009) *Guidance on Social Responsibility: Lignes directrices relatives à la responsabilité societal* (Final Draft; Geneva: ISO; isotc.iso.org/livelink/livelink/fetch/-8929321 /8929339/8929348/3935837/3974907/ISO_DIS_26000_Guidance_on_Social_ Responsibility.pdf?nodeid=8385026&vernum=-2, accessed September 23, 2010).

IUCN (International Union for Conservation of Nature and Natural Resources) (1980) *World Conservation Strategy: Living Resource Conservation for Sustainable Development* (Gland, Switzerland: IUCN-UNEP-WWF; data.iucn.org/dbtw-wpd/edocs/WCS-004.pdf, accessed September 18, 2011).

Jackson, J. (1984) "1984 Democratic National Convention Address"; www.americanrhetoric. com/speeches/jessejackson1984dnc.htm, accessed February 20, 2008.

—— (2007) "(Regional) Index of Sustainable Economic Welfare (ISEW)," contribution to *Beyond GDP "Virtual Indicator Expo,"* Brussels, November 19–20, 2007; www.beyond-gdp.eu/download/bgdp-ve-isew.pdf accessed March 12, 2008.

Jacquet, J., D. Pauly, D. Ainley, S. Holt, P. Dayton, and J. Jackson (2010) "Seafood Stewardship in Crisis," *Nature* 467: 28-29.

Jensen, M.C. (2002) "Value Maximization, Stakeholder Theory, and the Corporate Objective Function," *Business Ethics Quarterly* 12.2: 235-47.

Jones, M.J. (2010) "Accounting for the Environment: Towards a Theoretical Perspective for Environmental Accounting and Reporting," *Accounting Forum* 34.2: 123-38.

—— (1980) "Corporate Social Responsibility Revisited, Redefined," *California Management Review* 32.3: 59-67.

Kanie, N. (2007) "Governance with Multilateral Environmental Agreements: A Healthy or Ill-equipped Fragmentation?" In L. Swart and E. Perry (eds.), *Global Environmental Governance: Perspectives on the Current Debate* (New York: Center for UN Reform Education; www.ieg.earthsystemgovernance.org/sites/default/files/files/publications/GEG_Kanie. pdf, accessed August 23, 2010): Part II, 67-86.

Kaplan, R.S., and D.P. Norton (1992) "The Balanced Scorecard: Measures that Drive Performance," *Harvard Business Review* 70.1: 71-79.

—— and D.P. Norton (1996a) *The Balanced Scorecard: Translating Strategy into Action* (Cambridge, MA: Harvard Business School Press).

—— and D.P. Norton (1996b) "Using the Balanced Scorecard as a Strategic Management System," *Harvard Business Review* 74.1: 75-86.

Karnani, A.G. (2007) "Fortune at the Bottom of the Pyramid: A Mirage," *Californian Management Review* 49.4: 90-111; ssrn.com/abstract=914518, accessed June 24, 2010.

Kennedy, R.F. (1968) "Remarks of Robert F. Kennedy at the University of Kansas, March, 18 1968"; www.jfklibrary.org/Historical+Resources/Archives/Reference+Desk/Speeches/ RFK/RFKSpeech68Mar18UKansas.htm, accessed August 27, 2009.

Keynes, J.M. (1930) "Economic Possibilities for our Grandchildren," *N&A and Saturday Evening Post*; www.econ.yale.edu/smith/econ116a/keynes1.pdf, accessed March 23, 2011.

Klein, N. (1999) *No Logo: Taking Aim at the Brand Bullies* (New York: Picador).

Kohlberg, L. (1981) *Essays on Moral Development. Vol. I: The Philosophy of Moral Development* (San Francisco, CA: Harper & Row).

Kossmann, E.H. (1986) *De Lage Landen 1780–1980* (Amsterdam: Agon).

Kotter, J.P. (1996) *Leading Change* (Boston, MA: Harvard Business School Press).

Kouzes, J.M., and B.Z. Posner (2010) *The Truth about Leadership: The No-fads, Heart-of-the-matter Facts You Need to Know* (San Francisco, CA: Jossey-Bass).

Kroonenberg, S. (2006) *De menselijk maat: De aarde over tienduizend jaar* (Amsterdam: Atlas).

Kuenkel, P. (2008) *Mind and Heart: Mapping your Personal Journey towards Leadership for Sustainability* (Cape Town: Collective Leadership Institute).

Kuznets, S. (1934) *National Income, 1929–1932* (73rd U.S. Congress, 2nd session, Senate document no. 124; Washington, DC: U.S. Government Printing Office).

—— (1962) "How to Judge Quality," *New Republic*, October 20, 1962: 29-32.

Landes, D.S. (1999) *The Wealth and Poverty of Nations: Why Some Are So Rich and Some So Poor* (New York: W.W. Norton).

Lawrence, P.R. (2010) *Driven to Lead: Good, Bad, and Misguided Leadership* (San Francisco: Jossey Bass).

Leo XIII (1891) "Rerum Novarum, Encyclical of Pope Leo XIII on Capital and Labor, Città del Vaticano"; www.vatican.va/holy_father/pius_xi/encyclicals/documents/hf_p-xi_enc_19310515_quadragesimo-anno_en.html, accessed June 2, 2008.

Levy, D.L., and R. Kaplan (2008) "Corporate Social Responsibility and Theories of Global Governance: Strategic Contestation in Global Issue Arenas," in A. Crane, A. McWilliams, D. Matten, J. Moon, and D. Siegel (eds.), *Oxford Handbook of Corporate Social Responsibility* (Oxford, UK: Oxford University Press; www.faculty.umb.edu/david_levy/CSR2007.pdf, accessed October 14, 2010).

Lewis, S. (2010) "Learning from BP's 'Sustainable' Self-Portraits: From 'Integrated Spin' to Integrated Reporting," in R.G. Eccles, B. Cheng, and D. Saltzman (eds.) *The Landscape of Integrated Reporting: Reflections and Next Steps* (Cambridge, MA: Harvard Business School; www.hbs.edu/environment/docs/The%20Landscape%20of%20Integrated%20Reporting.pdf, accessed January 13, 2011): Part II, 58-71.

Ligthart, T.N., and A.M.M. Ansems (2007) *Eenmalige bekers dan wel méérmalige (koffie) drinksystemen: Een milieuvergelijking* (TNO Rapport R0246/B; Delft: TNO; www.tno.nl/downloads/2006_a-r0246_b_samenvatting.pdf, accessed August 18, 2010).

Lindenberg, S., and L. Steg (2007) "Normative, Gain and Hedonic Goal Frames Guiding Environmental Behavior," *Journal of Social Issues* 65.1: 117-37.

Linnér, B.-O., and H. Selin (2003) "How It All Began: Global Efforts on Sustainable Development from Stockholm to Rio," paper presented at the *6th Nordic Conference on Environmental Social Sciences*, Åbo, Finland, June 12–14, 2003, as part of the panel "Johannesburg: A First Anniversary."

Lomborg, B. (2001) *The Sceptical Environmentalist: Measuring the Real State of the World* (Cambridge, UK: Cambridge University Press).

Lovelock, J.E. (1994) "Taking Care," in T. O'Riordan and J. Cameron (eds.), *Interpreting the Precautionary Principle* (London: Earthscan): 108-16.

—— (2000) *Gaia: A New Look at Life on Earth* (Oxford, UK: Oxford University Press, 4th edn).

—— (2001) *Homage to Gaia: The Life of an Independent Scientist* (Oxford, UK: Oxford University Press).

Lowney, C. (2003) *Heroic Leadership: Best Practices from a 450-Year-Old Company That Changed the World* (Chicago: Loyola Press).

Maas, K. (2009) *Corporate Social Performance: From Output Measurement to Impact Measurement* (PhD thesis; Rotterdam: Erasmus Universiteit Rotterdam).

Maddison, A. (2001) *The World Economy: A Millennial Perspective* (Paris: OECD).

—— (2003) *The World Economy: Historical Statistics* (Paris: OECD).

Malthus, R. (1798) *Essay on the Principle of Population* (London: Penguin Classics, 1983).

Mandel, S. (2006) *Debt Relief as if People Mattered: A Rights-Based Approach to Debt Sustainability* (London: New Economics Foundation; www.scribd.com/doc/20560274/Debt-Relief-as-if-People-Mattered-A-Rights-based-Approach-to-Debt-Sustainability, accessed April 15, 2009).

Marchal, J. (2001) *Travail forcé pour l'huile de palme de Lord Leverhulme L'Histoire du Congo 1910–1945, tome 3* (Borgloon, Belgium: Editions Paula Bellings).

Margolis, J.D., and J.P. Walsh (2003) "Misery Loves Companies: Rethinking Social Initiatives by Business," *Administrative Science Quarterly* 48.2: 268-305.

Marten, G.G. (2001) *Human Ecology: Basic Concepts for Sustainable Development* (London: Earthscan).

Maser, C. (1999) *Vision and Leadership in Sustainable Development* (Boca Raton, FL: Lewis Publishers).

Max-Neef, M., A. Elizalde, and M. Hopenhayn (1989) "Human Scale Development: An Option for the Future," *Development Dialogue* (Uppsala: Dag Hammarskjöld Foundation).

McCloskey, D.N. (1981) "The Industrial Revolution, 1780–1860: A Survey," in R. Floud and D. McCloskey (eds.), *The Economic History of Britain, 1700–Present* (Cambridge, UK: Cambridge University Press): 103-27.

McConnell, J. (2002) "Going for Growth: On the Executive's Economic Strategy," Speech to the Institute of Directors in Edinburgh on September 10, 2002; www.scotland.gov.uk/News/News-Extras/102, accessed March 1, 2007 [web page no longer exists].

McDonough, W., and M. Braungart (2002) *Cradle to Cradle: Remaking the Way We Make Things* (New York: North Point Press).

McKinley, K. (2010) "ISO Standards for Business and their Linkage to Integrated Reporting," in R.G. Eccles, B. Cheng, and D. Saltzman (eds.), *The Landscape of Integrated Reporting: Reflections and Next Steps* (Cambridge, MA: Harvard Business School; www.hbs.edu/environment/docs/The%20Landscape%20of%20Integrated%20Reporting.pdf, accessed January 13, 2011): 40-44.

Meadows, D.H. (1997) "Places to Intervene in a System," *Whole Earth*, Winter 1997; www.wholeearth.com/issue/2091/article/27/places.to.intervene.in.a.system, accessed December 16, 2010.

——, D.L. Meadows, J. Randers, and W.W. Behrens III (1972) *The Limits to Growth* (London: Pan Books).

——, D.L. Meadows, J. Randers, and W.W. Behrens III (1972). *I limiti dello sviluppo*, Rapporto del System Dynamics Group Massachusetts Institute of Technology (MIT) per il progetto del Club di Roma sui dilemmi dell'umanità, Milano: Mondadori (original title: *The Limits to Growth*; London: Pan Books).

——, D.L. Meadows, and J. Randers (1992) *Beyond the Limits: Confronting Global Collapse, Envisioning a Sustainable Future* (Post Mills, VT: Chelsea Green Publishing Company).

——, J. Randers, and D.L. Meadows (2005) *Limits to Growth: The 30-Year Update* (London: Earthscan).

Mitchell, R.K. (2008) "The Joint-Stake Company and Accountability for Opportunity: What if?" in B.R. Agle, T. Donaldson, R.E. Freeman, M.C. Jensen, R.K. Mitchell, and D.J. Wood (eds.), "Dialogue: Toward Superior Stakeholder Theory," *Business Ethics Quarterly* 18.2: 176-81.

——, B.R. Agle, and D.J. Wood (1997) "Toward a Theory of Stakeholder Identification and Salience: Defining the Principle of Who or What Really Counts," *Academy of Management Review* 22.4: 853-86.

Molina, M.J., and F.S. Rowland (1974) "Stratospheric Sink for Chlorofluoromethanes: Chlorine Atomic Catalysed Destruction of Ozone," *Nature* 249: 810-12.

Moneva, J.M., P. Archel, and C. Correa (2006) "GRI and the Camouflaging of Corporate Unsustainability," *Accounting Forum* 30.2: 121-37.

Morse, S. (2004) *Indices and Indicators in Development: An Unhealthy Obsession with Numbers* (London: Earthscan).

MSC (Marine Stewardship Council) (2009) *Annual Report 2008/2009* (London: MSC; www.msc.org/documents/msc-brochures/annual-report-archive/MSC-annual-report-2008-09.pdf, accessed September 29, 2010).

Murby, L., and S. Gould (2005) *Effective Performance Management with the Balanced Scorecard: Technical Report* (London: Chartered Institute of Management Accountants; www.cimaglobal.com/Documents/ImportedDocuments/Tech_rept_Effective_Performance_Mgt_with_Balanced_Scd_July_2005.pdf, accessed September 22, 2010).

National Geographic (1981) *A Special Report in the Public Interest: Energy, Facing Up the Problem, Getting Down the Solutions* (Washington, DC: National Geographic Society).

Neal, L. (2005) "Venture Shares of the Dutch East India Company," in W.N. Goetzman and K.G. Rouwenhorst (eds.), *The Origins of Value: The Financial Innovations that Created Modern Capital Markets* (New York: Oxford University Press): 165-76.

Newman, P.A., E.R. Nash, S.R. Kawa, S.A. Montzka, and S.M. Schauffler (2006) "When Will the Antarctic Ozone Hole Recover?" *Geophysical Research Letters* 33.12 (30 June 2006; www.agu.org/pubs/back/gl/2006/index.php?month=June, accessed February 29, 2008).

Nohria, N., and R. Khurana (eds.) (2010) *Handbook of Leadership Theory and Practice: A Harvard Business School Centennial Colloquium* (Cambridge, MA: Harvard Business School).

Nordhaus, W.D., and J. Tobin (1972) "Is Growth Obsolete?" in M. Moss (ed.), *The Measurement of Economic and Social Performance* (New York: National Bureau of Economic Research; www.nber.org/chapters/c3621.pdf, accessed August 29, 2009): 509-64.

Nyerere, J.K. (1967) "Arusha Declaration," in R.O. Collins (ed.), *Eastern African History* (Princeton, NJ: Markus Wiener Publishers, 1997): 222-33.

O'Brien, D.J., and Th.A. Shannon (eds.) (2006) *Catholic Social Thought: The Documentary Heritage* (New York: Orbis Books, 7th edn).

O'Riordan, T., and J. Cameron (eds.) (1994) *Interpreting the Precautionary Principle* (London: Earthscan).

O'Rourke, D. (2003) "Outsourcing Regulation: Analyzing Nongovernmental Systems of Labor Standards and Monitoring," *The Policy Studies Journal* 31.1: 1-29.

OECD (Organization for Economic Co-operation and Development) (2006) *Decoupling the Environmental Impacts of Transport from Economic Growth* (Paris: OECD)

—— (2009) "Overview of Selected Initiatives and Instruments Relevant to Corporate Social Responsibility," in *Annual Report on the OECD Guidelines for Multinational Enterprises 2008* (Paris: OECD; www.oecd.org/dataoecd/18/56/40889288.pdf, accessed August 23, 2010): 235-60.

—— (2010) *OECD Guidelines for Multinational Enterprises* (Paris: OECD; www.oecd.org/dataoecd/56/36/1922428.pdf, accessed August 20, 2010).

—— (2011) *OECD Guidelines for Multinational Enterprises: Recommendations for Responsible Business Conduct in a Global Context* (Paris: OECD; www.oecd.org/dataoecd/43/29/48004323.pdf, accessed September 10, 2011).

Official Journal of the European Union (2004) "Judgment of the Court of 7 September 2004," *Official Journal of the European Union*, October 23, 2004; eur-lex.europa.eu/LexUriServ/LexUriServ.do?uri=OJ:C:2004:262:0002:0002:EN:PDF, accessed March 17, 2007.

Otten, A., and E. Klijn (1991) *Philips' woningbouw 1900–1990: fundament van woningstichting Hertog Hendrik van Lotharingen* (Zaltbommel, Netherlands: Europese Bibliotheek).

Packard, D. (1995) *The HP Way: How Bill Hewlett and I Built Our Company* (New York: Harper Business).

Park, H., and M.A. Dickson (2008) "Engaging in Buyer–Seller Partnership for Fair Labor Management: The Role of a Buyer Firm's Strategic Emphasis," *Clothing and Textiles Research Journal* 26.1: 41-56.

Parkin, S. (2010) *The Positive Deviant: Sustainability Leadership in a Perverse World* (London: Earthscan).

Pearce, D., and E.B. Barbier (2000) *Blueprint for a Sustainable Economy* (London: Earthscan).

——, A. Markandya, and E.B. Barbier (1989) *Blueprint for a Green Economy* (London: Earthscan).

Pepper, D. (1996) *Modern Environmentalism: An Introduction* (London: Routledge).

Plato (360 BCE) "Laws"; classics.mit.edu/Plato/laws.8.viiii.html, accessed March 14, 2008.

Pontifical Council for Justice and Peace (2000) "The Social Agenda: A Collection of Magisterial Texts, Libreria Editrice Vaticana: Città del Vaticano"; www.thesocialagenda.org/article1.htm#3, accessed June 2, 2008.

Porritt, J. (2005) *Capitalism as if the World Matters* (London: Earthscan).

Porter, M.E., and C. van der Linde (1995) "Towards a New Conception of the Environment–Competitiveness Relationship," *Journal of Economic Perspectives* 9.4: 119-32.

—— (1980) *Competitive Strategy: Techniques for Analyzing Industries and Competitors* (New York: Free Press).

—— (1996) "What is Strategy?" *Harvard Business Review* 74.6: 61-78.

—— and M.R. Kramer (2006) "Strategy and Society: The Link between Competitive Advantage and Corporate Social Responsibility," *Harvard Business Review*, Reprint R0612D; www.salesforcefoundation.org/files/HBR-CompetiveAdvAndCSR.pdf, accessed August 6, 2010.

Powell, T.C. (1995) "Total Quality Management as Competitive Advantage: A Review and Empirical Study," *Strategic Management Journal* 16.1: 15-37.

Prahalad, C.K., and S.L. Hart (2002) "The Fortune at the Bottom of the Pyramid," *Strategy + Business* 26 (First Quarter): 54-67.

Proops, J., and D. Wilkinson (2000) "Sustainability, Knowledge, Ethics and the Law," in M. Redclift (ed.), *Sustainability, Life Chances and Livelihoods* (London: Routledge).

Pulselli, F.M., F. Ciampalini, E. Tiezzi, and C. Zappia (2005) "The Index of Sustainable Economic Welfare (ISEW) for a Local Authority: A Case Study in Italy," *Quaderni dell'Università degli studi di Siena* 449.

Quinn, R. (2000) *Change the World: How Ordinary People Can Accomplish Extraordinary Results* (San Francisco: Jossey-Bass).

Rauschenbush, P.B. (ed.) (2007) *Christianity and the Social Crisis in the 21st Century: The Classic that Woke up the Church* (New York: HarperCollins).

Ray, D. (1998) *Development Economics* (Princeton, NJ: Princeton University Press).

Rees, W.E. (1992) "Ecological Footprints and Appropriated Carrying Capacity: What Urban Economics Leaves Out," *Environment and Urbanisation* 4.2: 121-30.

Reid, D. (1995) *Sustainable Development: An Introductory Guide* (London: Earthscan).

Reynders, P. (trans.), and R. Gerritsen (ed.) (2009) *A Translation of the Charter of the Dutch East India Company (Verenigde Oostindische Compagnie or Voc)* (Canberra: Australia on the Map Division of the Australasian Hydrographic Society; www.eurostudium.uniroma1.it/ricerche/didattica/strumenti_didattici/fonti/600/VOCengvers.pdf, accessed January 6, 2010).

Robèrt, K.-H., H. Daly, P. Hawken, and J. Holmberg (1997) "A Compass for Sustainable Development," *International Journal of Sustainable Development and World Ecology* 4: 79-92.

Roberts, B., and M. Cohen (2002) "Enhancing Sustainable Development by Triple Value Adding to the Core Business of Government," *Economic Development Quarterly* 16.2: 127-37.

Rokeach, M. (1973) *The Nature of Human Values* (New York: The Free Press).

Romer, P.M. (2007) "Economic Growth," in D.R. Henderson (ed.), *The Concise Encyclopedia of Economics* (Indianapolis, IN: Liberty Fund; www.stanford.edu/~promer/EconomicGrowth.pdf, accessed March 21, 2011).

Roorda, N. (2006) *Basisboek duurzame ontwikkeling* (Groningen, Netherlands: Noordhoff Uitgewers).

Roosevelt, F.D. (1945) "13th Message to Congress on the Bretton Woods Agreements," February 12, 1945; www.presidency.ucsb.edu/ws/index.php?pid=16588, accessed January 14, 2008.

Rowley, T., and S. Berman (2000) "A Brand New Brand of Corporate Social Performance," *Business and Society* 39.4: 397-418.

Royle, E. (1998) *Robert Owen and the Commencement of the Millennium: A Study of the Harmony Community* (Manchester, UK: Manchester University Press).

Sachs, J., and S.M. Collins (eds.) (1989) *Developing Country Debt and Economic Performance: Country Studies—Indonesia, Korea, Philippines, Turkey* (Chicago: University of Chicago Press).

Schein, E.H. (1985) *Organizational Culture and Leadership* (San Francisco: Jossey-Bass, 2004).

Schmidheiny, S. (1992) *Changing Course* (Cambridge, MA: MIT Press).

Schoemaker, M.J.R., A.H.J. Nijhof, and J. Jonker (2006) "Human Value Management: The Influence of the Contemporary Developments of Corporate Social Responsibility and Social Capital on HRM," *Management Revue* 17.4: 448-65.

Schumacher, E.F. (1973, 1999) *Small is Beautiful: Economics as if People Mattered* (New York: Harper & Row; Point Roberts, WA/Vancouver, BC: Hartley & Marks Publishers).

Scott, W.R. (1912) *The Constitution and Finance of English, Scottish and Irish Joint-stock Companies to 1720. Vol. 1: The General Development of the Joint Stock System to 1720* (Cambridge, UK: Cambridge University Press; socserv.mcmaster.ca/econ/ugcm/3ll3/scott/JointStockv1.pdf, accessed March 31, 2008).

Sen, A. (1987) *On Ethics and Economics* (Oxford, UK: Blackwell).

—— (1998) "Autobiography"; nobelprize.org/nobel_prizes/economics/laureates/1998/sen-autobio.html, accessed April 22, 2009.

Senge, P., C.O. Scharmer, J. Jaworski, and B.S. Flowers (2004) *Presence: Human Purpose and the Field of the Future* (Cambridge, MA: Society for Organizational Learning).

——, C.O. Scharmer, J. Jaworski, and B.S. Flowers (2005) *Presence: Exploring Profound Change in People, Organizations and Society* (London: Nicholas Brealey Publishing).

SER (Sociaal Economisch Raad) (2000) *De winst van waarden* (Den Haag: SER).

Sethi, S.P. (1975) "Dimensions of Corporate Social Performance: An Analytic Framework," *California Management Review* 7.3: 58-64.

Sexton, T. (2007) "Review of Research Literature on Authentic Leadership," Creative Edge Consulting; www.creative-edge-consulting.com/wp-content/uploads/2011/03/research-literature-authentic-leadership.pdf, accessed March 15, 2011.

Sharma, S. (2000) "Managerial Interpretations and Organizational Context as Predictors of Corporate Choice of Environmental Strategy," *The Academy of Management Journal* 43.4: 681-97.

Sharp Paine, L. (2003) *Value Shift: Why companies must merge social and financial imperatives to achieve superior performance* (New-York: McGraw-Hill).

Smith, A. (1776) "The Wealth of Nations"; www.online-literature.com/adam_smith/wealth_nations/2, accessed December 9, 2010.

Stern, P.C. (2000) "Toward a Coherent Theory of Environmentally Significant Behavior," *Journal of Social Issues* 56.3: 407-24.

Stevens, C. (2005) *Measuring Sustainable Development* (Statistics Brief No. 10; Paris: OECD, September 2005).

Stiglitz, J.E., A. Sen and J.-P. Fitoussi (2009) "Report by the Commission on the Measurement of Economic Performance and Social Progress"; www.stiglitz-sen-fitoussi.fr/documents/rapport_anglais.pdf, accessed April 30, 2011.

Stockhammer, E., H. Hochreiter, B. Obermayr, and K. Steiner (1997) "The Index of Sustainable Economic Welfare (ISEW) as an Alternative to GDP in Measuring Economic Welfare: The Results of the Austrian (Revised) ISEW Calculation 1955–1992," *Ecological Economics* 21.1: 19-34.

Sutton, P.W. (2007) *The Environment: A Sociological Introduction* (Cambridge, UK: Polity Press).

Szirmai, A. (2005) *The Dynamics of Socio-Economic Development* (Cambridge, UK: Cambridge University Press).

Tacconi, L. (2000) *Biodiversity and Ecological Economics: Participation, Values and Resource Management* (London: Earthscan).

TEEB (The Economics of Ecosystems and Biodiversity) (2010) *Mainstreaming the Economics of Nature: A Synthesis of the Approach, Conclusions and Recommendations of TEEB* (Malta: Progress Press; www.teebweb.org/Portals/25/TEEB%20Synthesis/TEEB_SynthReport_09_2010_online.pdf, accessed February 15, 2011).

Todaro, M.P. (1977) *Economic Development in the Third World: An Introduction to Problems and Policies in a Global Perspective* (London: Longman).

Tutu, D. (2004) *God Has a Dream: A Vision of Hope for Our Time* (New York: Doubleday).

UN (United Nations) (1948) *The Universal Declaration of Human Rights* (New York: UN Publications; www.un.org/en/documents/udhr, accessed May 14, 2008).

—— (1962) *The Development Decade: Proposals for Action* (Sale No. 62.II B.2; New York: UN Publications).

—— (1971) "The Founex Report on Development and the Environment"; www.earthsummit2012.org/fileadmin/files/Earth_Summit_2012/founex_report_1972.pdf, accessed August 29, 2009.

—— (1972) "Declaration of the United Nations Conference on the Human Environment, Stockholm 5–16 June"; www.unep.org/Documents.Multilingual/Default.asp?documentid=97&articleid=1503, accessed March 23, 2011.

UN Global Compact (2008) "630 Companies Delisted as Part of Integrity Measures"; www.unglobalcompact.org/newsandevents/news_archives/2008_06_25.html, accessed January 13, 2011.

UNDP (United Nations Development Programme) (2007) *Human Development Report 2007/2008, Fighting Climate Change: Human Solidarity in a Divided World* (New York: UNDP; hdr.undp.org/en/media/HDR_20072008_EN_Overview.pdf, accessed March 26, 2008.

—— (1990) *Human Development Report 1990: Concept and Measurement of Human Development* (New York: Oxford University Press; hdr.undp.org/en/reports/global/hdr1990/chapters, accessed September 8, 2011.

—— (1992) *Human Development Report 1992: Global Dimensions of Human Development* (New York: Oxford University Press; hdr.undp.org/en/reports/global/hdr1992/chapters, accessed September, 10 2011).

—— (2005) *Human Development Report 2005: International Cooperation at a Crossroads: Aid, Trade and Security in an Unequal World* (New York: UNDP; hdr.undp.org/en/media/HDR05_complete.pdf, accessed September 10, 2011).

UNEP (United Nations Environment Programme) (2007) *Global Environment Report, GEO-4: Environment for Development* (Valletta, Malta: Progress Press).

——/UNCTAD (1974) "The Cocoyoc Declaration"; www.juerg-buergi.ch/Archiv/Entwick-lungspolitikA/EntwicklungspolitikA/assets/COCOYOC_%20DECLARATION_1974.pdf, accessed August 29, 2009.

UNFCCC (United Nations Framework Convention on Climate Change) (2007) "Report of the Conference of the Parties on its thirteenth session, held in Bali from 3 to 15 December 2007"; unfccc.int/resource/docs/2007/cop13/eng/06a01.pdf#page=3, accessed September 10, 2011.

UNFPA (United Nations Population Fund) (2002) *State of World Population 2002, People, Poverty and Possibilities* (ed. A. Marshall; New York: UNFPA; www.unfpa.org/swp/2002/english/notes/page2.htm#1, accessed March 17, 2008).

UNHCHR (United Nations Universal Declaration of Human Rights) (1986) "Declaration on the Right to Development"; www.un.org/documents/ga/res/41/a41r128.htm, accessed August 21, 2009.

Van der Lugt, H. (2009) "Alleen korte termijn denken gaat een keer fout, interview with How-ard-Yana Shapiro," *NRC Handelsblad*, November 2, 2009.

Van Duijn, J. (2007) *De groei voorbij, Over de economishce toekomst van Nederland na de booming nineties* (Amsterdam: De Bezige Bij).

Van Essen, H. (2010) "International Road and Rail Freight Transport: Environmental Impacts of Increased Activity Levels," in *Globalisation, Transport and the Environment* (Paris: OECD): 197-223.

Venetoulis, J., and J. Talberth (2007) "Refining the Ecological Footprint," *Environment, Development and Sustainability* 10.4: 441-69.

Ventura, J. (2005) "A Global View of Economic Growth," in P. Aghion and S. Durlauf (eds.), *Handbook of Economic Growth* (Amsterdam: Elsevier): 1419-97.

Vogel, D. (2005) *The Market for Virtue: The Potential and Limits of Corporate Social Responsibility* (Washington, DC: The Brookings Institution).

Volans (2009) *The Phoenix Economy: 50 Pioneers in the Business of Social Innovation* (London: Volans Ventures; www.volans.com/wp-content/uploads/2010/04/The-Phoenix-Economy.pdf, accessed June 24, 2010).

Von Weizsäcker, E.U. (1994) *Earth Politics* (London: Zed Books).

——, A.B. Lovins, and L.H. Lovins (1998) *Factor Four: Doubling Wealth, Halving Resource Use* (London: Earthscan).

Wackernagel, M. (1994) *Ecological Footprint and Appropriated Carrying Capacity: A Tool for Planning toward Sustainability* (PhD thesis; Vancouver: School of Community and Regional Planning, The University of British Columbia).

Wade, R.H. (2001) "The Rising Inequality of World Income Distribution," *Finance and Development* 38.4; www.imf.org/external/pubs/ft/fandd/2001/12/wade.htm, accessed March 3, 2011.

Wallach, L., and P. Woodall (2004) *Whose Trade Organization? A Comprehensive Guide to the WTO* (New York: The New Press).

Ward, B. (1966) *Spaceship Earth* (New York: Columbia University Press).

—— (1973) "Justice in a Human Environment," *IDOC–North America* 53: 25-36.

—— and R. Dubos (1972) *Only One Earth: The Care and Maintenance of a Small Planet* (an unofficial report commissioned by the Secretary-General of the United Nations Conference on the Human Environment, prepared with the assistance of a 152-member Committee of Corresponding Consultants in 58 countries; Harmondsworth, UK: Pelican).

Wartick, S.L., and P.L. Cochran (1985) "The Evolution of the Corporate Social Performance Model," *Academy of Management Review* 10.4: 758-69.

WBCSD (World Business Council for Sustainable Development) (2000) *Eco-efficiency: Creating More Value with Less Impact* (Geneva: WBCSD).

—— (2005) *Beyond Reporting: Creating Business Value and Accountability* (WBCSD Accountability and Reporting Project co-chaired by T. Engen and S. DiPiazza; Geneva: WBCSD).

WCED (World Commission on Environment and Development) (1987) *Our Common Future* (Oxford, UK: Oxford University Press).

Weber, M. (1905) *The Protestant Ethic and the Spirit of Capitalism* (trans. P. Baehr and G.C. Wells; London: Penguin Books, 2002).

White, L. (1967) "The Historical Roots of Our Ecological Crisis," *Science* 155.3767: 1,203-207.

Wilber, K. (2000) *A Theory of Everything: An Integral Vision for Business, Politics Science and Spirituality* (Boston, MA: Shambhala).

Willis, A. (2010) "Integrated Reporting in a Disconnected World? The Macro Measurement Challenge!" in R.G. Eccles, B. Cheng and D. Saltzman (eds.), *The Landscape of Integrated Reporting: Reflections and Next Steps* (Cambridge, MA: Harvard Business School; www.hbs.edu/environment/docs/The%20Landscape%20of%20Integrated%20Reporting.pdf, accessed January 13, 2011): 22-24.

Wilson, E.O. (1998) "Address to the U.S. Senate," April 28, 1998; www.saveamericasforests.org/wilson/intro.htm, accessed March 13, 2008.

Wise, T.A. (2001) "Economics of Sustainability: The Social Dimension, Overview Essay," in J.M. Harris, T.A. Wise, K.P. Gallagher and N.R. Goodwin (eds.), *A Survey of Sustainable Development: Social and Economic Dimensions* (Washington, DC: Island Press): 47-57.

Wood, D.J. (1991) "Corporate Social Performance Revisited," *Academy of Management Review* 16.4: 691-718.

—— and R.E. Jones (1995) "Stakeholder Mismatching: A Theoretical Problem in Empirical Research on Corporate Social Performance," *The International Journal of Organizational Analysis* 3.3: 229-67.

World Bank (2009) "World Development Indicators Database: Gross Domestic Product 2008," siteresources.worldbank.org/DATASTATISTICS/Resources/GDP.pdf, accessed February 8, 2010.

World Council of Churches (1974) *Science and Technology for Human Development: The Ambiguous Future and the Christian Hope, Report of the 1974 World Conference in Bucharest (Romania)* (Geneva: Church and Society, World Council of Churches).

World Travel and Tourism Council (2010) *Travel and Tourism Economic Impact: Executive Summary* (London: WTTC; www.wttc.org/bin/pdf/original_pdf_file/2010_exec_summary_final.pdf, accessed September 29, 2010).

World Watch Institute (2004) "The State of Consumption Today"; www.worldwatch.org/node/810#1, accessed January 21, 2008.

Wren, D.A. (2005) *The History of Management Thought* (New York: John Wiley, 5th edn).

Yunus, M., and A. Jolis (1999) *Banker to the Poor: Micro-lending and the Battle against World Poverty* (New York: PublicAffairs).

Zingales, F.G.G., A. O'Rourke, and R.J. Orssatto (2002) *Environment and Socio-Related Balanced Scorecards: Exploration of Critical Issues* (INSEAD R&D Working paper 2002/47/CMER; Fontainebleau: INSEAD; www.insead.edu/facultyresearch/research/doc.cfm?did=1235, accessed September 22, 2010).

Zingales, F.G.G., and K. Hockerts (2003) *Balanced Scorecard and Sustainability: Examples from Literature and Practice* (INSEAD R&D Working paper 2003/30/CMER; Fontainebleau: INSEAD).

Zohar, D., and I. Marshall (2004) *Spiritual Capital: Wealth That We Can Live By* (San Francisco: Berrett-Koehler).

Zolotas, X. (1981) *Economic Growth and Declining Social Welfare* (Athens: Bank of Greece).

Index

Note: Page numbers in *italic figures* refer to illustrations

About the authors

Photo credit: Dikken & Hulsinga, Leeuwarden (NL)

Elena Cavagnaro was born in 1963 in Rome (Italy). In Rome she completed her undergraduate studies in ancient philosophy. Thanks to a scholarship she was able to continue her studies at the Croce Institute in Naples and at the Vrije Universiteit in Amsterdam where she completed her PhD in 1996. In 1997 she joined Stenden, a University of Applied Sciences in the north of the Netherlands, as a lecturer in business ethics. She renovated the BA curriculum of Stenden Retail Business School, focusing on business and society issues. In 2002 she was appointed senior lecturer in corporate social responsibility, sustainable development, and leadership for sustainability for Stenden Master's programs. In 2004 she became Stenden Professor in Service Studies. Following her understanding of sustainability as a multi-dimensional and multi-layered concept, her research focuses on issues where the organizational level meets the society level or the individual the organizational.

Stenden University of Applied Sciences, Rengerslaan 8, 8917 DD, Leeuwarden, The Netherlands

Elena.cavagnaro@stenden.com

George H. Curiel is a native of the island of Curaçao. He has served as Director of the Department of Development Cooperation for the government of the Netherlands Antilles and National Authorizing Officer for the European Development Fund. He has been involved as advisor in areas related to economic and social development, tourism development, development cooperation, and constitutional affairs, and has chaired or participated in numerous boards, working groups, and committees. After retiring in Curaçao in 2000, he lived in the Netherlands and worked as a part-time lecturer and advisor at the Stenden School of Graduate Studies. He earned a Master's in economics at Yale University, and his BSc in business administration at the University of the Netherlands Antilles in Curaçao. As a freelance advisor, he continues to consult with governments and organizations in search of new horizons and strategies for a more sustainable development path.

Jongbloedweg 6, Curaçao, Caribbean

ghctls@gmail.com